It's the BUSINESS

Business for Leaving Certificate

Joe Stafford
Seamus McGowan

Contents

unit 1

unit 2

unit 3

unit 4

unit 5

About the Authors

Joe Stafford works as a Business teacher in Skerries Community College, Co Dublin. He has 18 years' teaching experience and has corrected State exams.

In recent years he has contributed online revision material to the Examsupport website (now on Eircom Studyhub) and also conducts Leaving Certificate revision seminars throughout the country. Joe was also a contributing teacher for EOY.tv, an innovative website which offers teaching resources related to enterprise education.

Joe is also the author of the Edco publication *Get the points! Leaving Certificate Business.*

Seamus McGowan is a Business, Accounting and Economics teacher in Skerries Community College. He has 11 years' teaching experience. Seamus also teaches in the Independent Academy, Dublin.

We wish to express our sincere thanks to all those who helped us to complete this project. We are grateful to all at Edco, but in particular to Lucy, Simon and Niamh for the countless hours spent editing and (re)designing. Thank you for keeping us on our toes!

We also acknowledge the help and inspiration provided by our students and colleagues who reviewed and road-tested the material for us.

Special thanks to our families who were exceptionally patient and understanding. We look forward to spending some time with you again!

Foreword

We are teachers with almost thirty years of practical classroom experience between us, as well as several years of marking Leaving Certificate exams. We'd like to think we understand the needs of both teachers and students, and have a good idea of the requirements of Leaving Certificate examiners.

We have tried to meet the challenge of writing a textbook which serves the needs of both Higher Level and Ordinary Level business students, who are more often than not being taught in the same class.

We think this is one of the most comprehensive textbooks available and we have tried to make the material as accessible and relevant as possible for all students by using a variety of **case studies, examples, newspaper articles** and **illustrations** from the real world of business.

Bullet points and **bold font** are used throughout the text in order to highlight key issues.

Most sections of the book are written in a manner that is consistent with the recommended format **(State – Explain – Example)** required for Leaving Certificate exam answers. We believe that this will greatly assist students when revising or making notes as part of their exam preparations.

We have generally preferred a broad interpretation of the syllabus and think that this will not only make the material more relevant to the realities of modern business, but it will help ensure that students are adequately prepared for a diverse range of examination topics and questions.

Many sections of the syllabus have recently been updated or expanded and we have placed particular emphasis on the enormous impact of both the **economic environment** and **ICT** on business development. Where necessary we have also added material to cover **new legislation** (Consumer Protection Act) as well as **new marketing techniques**.

An innovative new feature of this publication is the inclusion of News Flash case studies at the beginning of each chapter. Each is a genuine newspaper article which relates the topic under discussion to the real world of business. These news items can be used as 'ice-breakers' or discussion documents when beginning a new section of the syllabus, or alternatively they can be used as a revision tool once the chapter is completed.

We have also chosen to provide **Applied Business Questions** at the end of each unit rather than on a chapter-by-chapter basis. Our decision is based on the belief that teachers and students will make greater use of these ABQs, which are close in style and standard to the Leaving Certificate exam. In the past we have often been frustrated by ABQs which are very limited in their content. The approach we've chosen has allowed us to produce applied questions which cover several aspects of the syllabus and therefore reflect the pattern of Leaving Certificate exams. Additional ABQs are available as part of our **online resources at EDCODigital**.

The textbook also provides students with a detailed guide to the Leaving Certificate business exam and offers helpful advice on preparation and exam technique. Many of the suggestions reflect the views expressed in the most recent Chief Examiner's Report (2010).

As teachers, and now as authors, we face the constant challenge of providing students with material that is relevant, interesting and up to date. For that reason, teachers using this textbook will have access to **regularly updated new material to support the book** on *edcodigital.ie*. This will include **case studies, weblinks, news items, ABQs** and **podcasts**.

We are ambitious teachers who have chosen an ambitious title for our book. We have done our best to fulfil, not only our ambitions, but also your expectations. Delivering this type of customer service will be a challenging departure in educational publishing, so we welcome your comments, feedback and suggestions.

Contact us at itsthebusiness1@gmail.com

Unit One
People in Business

Chapter 1
People in Business

Syllabus Outcomes

On completion, the student should be able to:
» 1.3.1 List the main parties and people involved in business;
» 1.3.2 Describe the relationships between people as workers, as trade union members, as managers, as entrepreneurs, as investors, and as customers;
» 1.3.3 Outline non-legislative ways of solving conflict;
» 1.3.4 Outline how a major piece of legislation and the elements of contract law help deal with conflict;
» 1.3.5 Analyse the relationships between people in business (HL).

News Flash

BP faces wave of protest at AGM

Press Association

Oil giant BP is facing a wave of protests as it holds its annual general meeting in London days before the first anniversary of the Gulf of Mexico disaster.

Fishermen and women from the US Gulf Coast who were hit by the massive oil spill that followed the explosion of BP's Deepwater Horizon rig last April will be at the AGM tomorrow as shareholders.

... activists will be holding protests outside the AGM and around London in the coming week against the oil giant.

Scores of workers involved in a dispute at a BP-owned biofuels plant near Hull will also stage a demonstration outside the meeting, some dressed as an oil slick, linking their row with the firm's "irresponsible" behaviour in the Gulf. Hundreds of workers say they have been "locked out" of the contract to build the new plant at Saltend, near Hull, after the project fell behind schedule.

Diane Wilson, a fourth-generation fisherwoman from Texas, says she is going to the meeting to "call BP to account for its actions in the Gulf".

"I am coming to articulate the anger of thousands of Gulf Coast residents whose lives and livelihoods have been destroyed while the BP board continues to prosper."

The group of Gulf Coast residents will be in the AGM with representatives of Canadian indigenous communities who are protesting over BP's involvement in extracting "tar sands", a heavily polluting form of oil, in their territories.

BP is also expected to face further shareholder ire over boardroom bonuses and its handling of a potential £10bn share swap deal with Russian government-owned Rosneft, which is on the verge of collapse.

This is an edited extract from the Irish Independent, WEDNESDAY, 13 APRIL 2011.

For more up-to-date newspaper articles see www.edcodigital.ie

1 Read the newspaper extract opposite and discuss the issues raised.

2 Make a list of all those who are affected by the actions of BP.

3 Can you explain any of the highlighted terms?

Business

A business is any organisation set up to provide goods and services to its customers.

If we make a list of the motives for business, we could include the following:

> To make a profit
> To increase market share
> To provide employment

> To provide goods and services
> To satisfy consumer demand
> To export goods and services

While this is not a complete list, it helps us to see that businesses may have several objectives and that their primary motivating factor may change over time.

Profit is not always the most important of these factors, but it is often used to classify businesses.

Types of business

> **Commercial businesses** are those which have profit as their primary motive. This means that commercial businesses need to make a profit in order to provide a return for their owners, and ultimately to continue operating. A commercial business which cannot satisfy this need for profit will eventually close down. The vast majority of businesses, especially those in the private sector, fall into this category; examples include Dunnes Stores, Ulster Bank and Toyota.

> **Private sector businesses** are owned and controlled by private individuals who invest capital into them and hope to receive a share of the annual profits. This share of profits is called a **dividend**.

> Some **state-owned businesses**, such as the ESB, operate on a commercial basis and are highly profitable. These profits go to the state or are reinvested in the business.

> There also exists a smaller number of businesses which are not driven by such a strong profit motive and are often set up to provide an important service to society. A business which fits this 'not for profit' operating model is called a **non-commercial business**. Charities like Trocaire and Concern are examples in this category.

> The lack of profit makes it an unattractive business model for private investment, so many non-commercial businesses are funded by the state. The **'public sector'** refers to any businesses or organisations which are set up or funded by the state. Examples include the National Museum of Ireland and CIE, as well as public hospitals and schools.

unit 1

Stakeholders

All organisations, including businesses, have people involved in their operation as well as having other groups of people who are affected by those activities and operations. These individuals or groups of people are called **stakeholders**.

« *syllabus signpost* 1.3.1

Stakeholders are all those involved in or affected by a business's activities. The stakeholder group contains both internal and external stakeholders and is made up of the following:

> Entrepreneurs/shareholders
> Investors
> Suppliers/service providers
> Employees/managers

> Consumers
> Government
> Local community/society

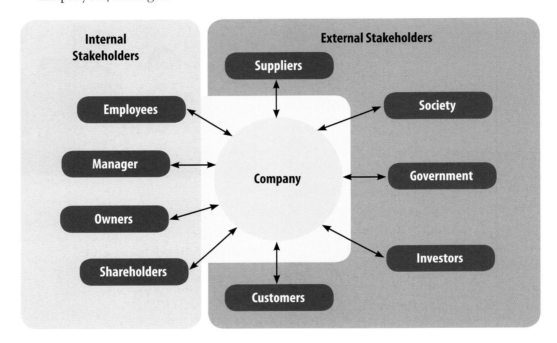

> **Entrepreneurs:** These are the individuals who think up new ideas and use their initiative to turn them into business realities. Profit is their reward for taking the risk involved in starting a business. Well-known entrepreneurs include Bill Cullen, James Dyson, Donald Trump and Oprah Winfrey. *Unit 2* contains a detailed analysis of the role of entrepreneurs.

> **Investors:** These are the people who also take a risk by investing money into a business. They provide assistance to entrepreneurs who lack the capital required for a business start-up or expansion. In return for their investment they expect to receive regular interest payments. Venture capitalists are particular types of investor, who take a shareholding in a new business and hope to see the value of that investment grow as the business grows. The investors on TV programmes like *Dragons' Den* are good examples of venture capitalists.

Dragons' Den features venture capitalists

> **Suppliers/service providers:** These are the providers of raw materials or other essential support services to businesses. Without the availability of raw materials, fuel, packaging, insurance and delivery services, many businesses would not be able to meet the needs and expectations of their customers. Other examples include accountants, transport companies and advertising agencies.

> **Employees/managers:** These are the workers who bring a range of skills and expertise to the business. In return for wages and salaries they are willing to work hard to help the business achieve its goals. Some businesses reward employees with bonuses and profit-sharing schemes.

   Managers are a specific group of employees who are given responsibility for planning, organising and controlling the operations of the business. They lead, motivate and communicate with all staff to ensure the future success of the business.

   Units 3 and 4 of this textbook will provide a detailed insight into the role of business managers, including the importance of human resource managers.

> **Consumers:** Customers have a crucial bearing on the success or failure of any business and companies which fail to meet the needs and expectations of consumers are unlikely to remain profitable for very long. Consumers want good quality at competitive prices and they would like to think that a competitive business environment will provide both choice and value for money.

   Businesses need to satisfy these consumer demands while also generating profits for their shareholders. For this reason the relationship between a business and its consumers is a fundamental one and goes to the very heart of commercial business. Satisfied customers will generate repeat business and revenue. Customers who are unhappy with the goods or services provided are unlikely to purchase additional goods in the future. They may also undermine a firm's reputation by spreading their dissatisfaction to other potential customers.

> **Government:** The government plays a role in creating a positive economic environment in which businesses can prosper. The state invests heavily in infrastructure such as roads, public transport, education and public utilities (water, gas and telecommunications networks). Governments also impose taxes on business and have the power to offer tax incentives which promote certain business activities. The government also regulates industry by enacting laws. These include the Consumer Protection Act, 2007, the Unfair Dismissals Act and the Data Protection Act.

Businesses are a source or revenue for the government and pay a whole range of taxes, including corporation (profits) tax and value added tax (VAT).

> **Local community/society:** Businesses have an impact on the lives of all those who live in close proximity to them, and the consequences of some business activities can be felt far beyond those local communities. Employment generation, sponsorship programmes, pollution and waste disposal are a number of areas in which businesses can have either a positive or a negative impact on those around them. Clearly a business which wishes to enjoy the support and goodwill of the wider public will need to act in a socially responsible manner.

Stakeholder	Brings to business	Wants from business
Entrepreneur/ shareholder	Ideas, initiative, capital	Profit, independence, control
Investor	Capital, expertise	Return on investment
Supplier/ service provider	Raw materials, services	Prompt payment for goods/ services, loyalty
Employee/manager	Labour, skills, expertise	Wages, job security, safety
Consumer	Sales revenue, loyalty	Good quality and prices
Government	Legislation, advice, infrastructure and stability	Taxes, compliance with legislation
Local community/ society	Customers, support	Social and environmental responsibility

Stakeholder relationships

While the chart on p. 4 summarises the stakeholder relationships with the business, it is equally important to understand the nature and scope of stakeholder relationships with each other.

Business Motives: The Shareholder view vs the Stakeholder view

While these terms appear to be the same, it is important to highlight the differences between the two.

> **Shareholders** are the owners of the business. They invest capital and expect a return in the form of dividends. In the short term they are concerned about profitability while in the longer term they hope to see the value of their capital investment rise. Businesses which adopt a shareholder view tend to focus on meeting the short-term goal of profitability.

> The term **stakeholder** has a much broader meaning and refers to a wider group of people who are affected by the business and who seek to influence its activities. Meeting the needs of some stakeholders (employees, customers, suppliers and government) will tend to add to business costs and reduce overall profitability. This is at odds with the shareholders' goal of profit maximisation and can lead to conflict.

A business which adopts a stakeholder view is less likely to experience conflict with stakeholders and will tend to pursue more social and ethically responsible policies (see also *Chapter 21: Business Ethics and Social Responsibility*).

Types of stakeholder relationship

The relationships that exist between stakeholders can be complex and dynamic. A **dynamic relationship** is one that is likely to change over time. A relationship that starts out being positive and co-operative may eventually become more negative, and this usually happens because stakeholders have different goals and aspirations for the business. Broadly speaking we categorise stakeholder relationships as being either competitive or co-operative.

« *syllabus signpost*
1.3.2 & 1.3.5

> A **competitive relationship** tends to pit one stakeholder against another. In this situation each tries to improve their own position or rewards at the expense of others. This is a win–lose scenario and can have a negative impact on the success of the entire organisation. A business may, for example, try to increase its profit by charging high prices to consumers for poor-quality goods.

Other examples of competitive relationships include:

> **Rival producers** competing for business in the same target market. Each will attempt to offer customers additional value for money in order to increase its market share at the expense of its rivals.
> **Shareholders/Employees:** The owners of a business may attempt to reduce operating costs by keeping staff wages at a minimum. This will result in higher profits and dividends for shareholders.
> **Entrepreneurs/Community:** Some business owners may seek to set up businesses which conflict with the needs or wishes of the local community. An obvious example is the recent controversy over the location of 'head shops' in towns and villages all over Ireland. Many communities viewed them as unwelcome and antisocial until successful lobbying of government eventually brought about a change in the law. Businesses which cause increased levels of pollution in the local environment also illustrate this competitive type of relationship.

> A **co-operative relationship** involves both parties working towards shared goals and for mutual benefit. Essentially a win–win situation, this approach tends to build strong positive relationships which bring rewards to all stakeholders. For example, a business that provides excellent pay and conditions for its staff may be rewarded by increased productivity and motivation. The employees benefit from the high levels of income and job security on offer while the company should see higher profits resulting from increased productivity and fewer industrial relations disputes.

Interest groups

Many stakeholders are represented by **interest groups.** These are essentially pressure groups which attempt to promote the interests of their members through lobbying, information campaigns or occasionally through protests.

Lobbying is a strategy which involves impressing the stakeholder's viewpoint on those who have power to make decisions. Very often this takes the form of meeting with politicians or running extensive media campaigns to gain public support. Whatever the tactic used, the aim of lobbying is to ensure that the best interests of the stakeholder are considered by the policy makers.

Examples of interest groups representing stakeholders in Ireland:

> Entrepreneurs (business owners) – Irish Business and Employers Confederation (IBEC); Irish Small and Medium Enterprises (ISME)
> Employees (trade unions) – Services Industrial Professional and Technical Union (SIPTU). The Irish Congress of Trade Unions (ICTU) is an umbrella organisation which represents the majority of trade unions in Ireland.
> Managers – Irish Management Institute (IMI)
> Consumers – Consumers Association of Ireland (CAI)

Some interest groups represent many businesses within the same type of industry, and are regarded as **trade associations**. Examples include:

> Irish Farmers Association (IFA)
> Licensed Vintners Association (LVA)
> Irish Travel Agents Association (ITAA)
> Society of the Irish Motor Industry (SIMI)

Conflict

It is important to understand that the roles and aims of stakeholders can be both **interdependent** and **independent**.

They are interdependent in the sense that the overall success of the business relies on a positive interaction between them. Each relies on the others to carry out their function reliably. This forms the basis for a co-operative relationship.

At the same time, however, there is an inevitable tension caused by conflicting needs and aims. When any stakeholder places the pursuit of its own independent goals above the pursuit of collective goals, a competitive relationship will develop. In these circumstances, it's almost inevitable that conflict will occur.

If and when this conflict arises, businesses need to implement strategies to resolve it. They can avail of both **legislative and non-legislative solutions**.

> **A legislative solution is one which has a clear legal basis.** Normally this involves applying the provisions of a relevant law, or involving an agency set up by law to resolve the issue.

 **Example**

> If a consumer conflict is resolved using the provisions of the Sale of Goods and Supply of Services Act, 1980, this is regarded as a legislative solution. The same can be said in situations where the National Consumer Agency intervenes to resolve a consumer complaint, since this agency was set up under the terms of the Consumer Protection Act, 2007.

> **A non-legislative solution does not rely on direct application of the law** and is generally achieved through negotiation and compromise. This negotiation may involve only the conflicting parties, or may be facilitated by an independent third party.

« *syllabus signpost 1.3.3*

 **Example**

> If a dissatisfied consumer returns to a shop with faulty goods and negotiates a resolution with the manager this represents a non-legislative approach. The intervention of the Consumers' Association of Ireland is also an example of a non-legislative resolution because this association is a voluntary body set up to promote the interests of consumers and therefore has no legal powers.

Mediation

Mediation can take the form of either **conciliation** or **arbitration**. Both conciliation and arbitration involve the intervention of an independent third party and both represent attempts to resolve a dispute between stakeholders. There is, however, a crucial difference between them and it relates to the role of the mediator and the manner in which the solution is reached.

It's important to understand that **conciliators** help the conflicting parties to reach a mutually agreeable position, but do **not** impose a solution. The conciliators will facilitate the process by encouraging both parties to sit down and discuss their differences. They may begin

by resolving minor issues which help to build trust and understanding between the parties before tackling the more serious conflicts. The role of the conciliator in all of this is simply to nudge the disputing parties in the direction of a solution. The **Labour Relations Commission (LRC)** offers a conciliation service to employers and employees when industrial relations disputes arise.

It is only in exceptional circumstances that the independent third party is empowered to investigate the conflict and make a binding recommendation as to its resolution. This type of approach where the mediator listens to both sides before making a judgement on the issue is called **arbitration**. In industrial relations disputes only the **Labour Court** engages in this type of binding arbitration.

Chapters 2 and 3 illustrate specific examples of both conciliation and arbitration being utilised in business situations.

Law of contract

A **contract** is a legally binding agreement between two or more parties. This means that a court of law may intervene to ensure the terms of a contract are carried out.

Contracts have **eight key elements** which are as follows:

> Offer
> Acceptance
> Consideration
> Consent

> Intention to contract
> Capacity to contract
> Legality of purpose
> Legality of form

« *syllabus signpost* 1.3.4

> **Offer:** An offer is a proposal which becomes legally binding if accepted. An offer may be written, oral or implied. An example of an implied offer occurs whenever consumers bring goods to the checkout in a shop. By placing the goods on the counter and producing payment, consumers are, by their actions, offering to purchase those goods.

This raises an important point about who exactly is making the offer.

When a shop places a price tag on goods, it is **not** offering these goods to consumers at the marked price. In fact the retailer is actually **inviting consumers to make an offer** to buy the goods. The legal term for this is **'invitation to treat'**. So producing the goods and payment at checkout is an implied offer by the customer to buy the goods. The retailer has a legal entitlement to accept or reject this offer. Obviously such an offer is almost always accepted, but it does allow a retailer to refuse to sell goods to a customer in circumstances where a pricing error has occurred.

Example

You proceed to the checkout of an electrical store with an MP3 player which has a price sticker of €14.99 on the box. When you go to pay for the item the retailer informs you that the item has been mispriced and should in fact cost €44.99. You are not happy and insist on being sold the MP3 player for the marked price. What will happen?

In terms of contract law, the marked price is an invitation to treat and does not constitute an offer from the retailer. When you offer to pay €14.99 for the MP3 player the retailer can either accept or reject that offer. If the retailer rejects your offer, no contract will exist and you cannot insist on being sold the item.

If you are wondering whether this retailer has a case to answer in relation to 'false or misleading indication of price' you would be correct and this will be outlined when dealing with the Consumer Protection Act, 2007, in Chapter 2.

> **Acceptance:** The original offer must be accepted unconditionally and unaltered. If changed it's regarded as a **counter-offer**. A combination of offer and acceptance results in agreement and is therefore the basis of an enforceable contract.

Example

A customer offers €15,000 to a car dealer for a used car. If the car dealer accepts the offer they now have agreement. If the car dealer is unhappy with the offer, he may suggest a price of €16,000. This higher price represents a counter-offer and it is now up to the customer to decide whether to accept or reject that counter-offer.

> **Consideration:** Something of value must be exchanged between parties to the contract. Note, however, that the value exchanged does not have to equate to the actual value of the goods/services. This means that very valuable items can sometimes be sold for minimal prices, provided an agreement is reached between buyer and seller.

In the used car example outlined above, the customer will hand over money in exchange for the vehicle and this fulfils the legal requirement for consideration.

> **Consent:** All parties entering into a contract must do so of their own free will. This means that a person who signs a contract after being subjected to undue pressure has not given legal consent to enter into the agreement.

Courts have also found in favour of those who signed contracts based on false or misleading information.

Example

A business misleads a customer into thinking that a used vehicle has never been involved in an accident, but it is later discovered that this is untrue. As a result the vehicle has many second-hand parts and has been substantially devalued. In these circumstances the court may decide that the consumer did not consent to the purchase of a crashed vehicle and may set aside the contract.

> **Intention to contract:** Making a contract must be deliberate or intentional. Social arrangements are not legally binding but all business agreements are legally enforceable. This means that courts take the view that when two or more businesses enter into an agreement, there is a contractual obligation involved.

Example

Once I get my new car I decide to travel to a music festival in England with two friends. There is a verbal agreement that fuel costs will be divided equally between the three of us. Upon returning from England one of my companions does not pay his share of the fuel bill. Unfortunately I cannot take legal action to recover the money as this was a social arrangement and was never intended to be legally binding.

> **Capacity to contract:** All parties to a contract must have the legal ability to enter freely into it. Individuals who are minors (under eighteen) or mentally incapacitated (drunk or insane) do not have the legal capacity to contract. Company directors who act outside of the powers given to them in the memorandum of association are said to be acting *ultra vires*. They too are acting without legal capacity and the company may not be held liable for such contracts.

Children under eighteen have the legal capacity to enter into contracts for goods or services which are normal for them to purchase. This allows young people to purchase everyday items like clothes, books, music and sweets. As we will discuss later, this ability to create contracts with retailers is important when it comes to consumer rights under the terms of the Sale of Goods and Supply of Services Act, 1980. People under eighteen years of age do not have the capacity to enter into a contract for the purchase of land or property.

> **Legality of purpose:** Contracts involving illegal actions or activities are not legally enforceable, for example, contracts to enter into a **cartel**, or to import stolen or illegal goods. A cartel is an illegal arrangement between a number of businesses to control and distort the market for a particular good or service.

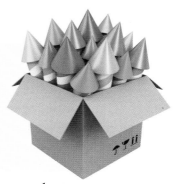

e.g. Example

If a business makes an arrangement to buy fireworks and import them into the Republic of Ireland from the UK, it would not be able to take court action to ensure the goods are delivered as the courts will not recognise the validity of the contract.

> **Legality of form:** In order to be legally valid some types of contract must be in writing. Examples include insurance policies and contracts for the sale of property. In an insurance contract, the insured person will complete a proposal form and pay their premium before receiving a receipt and a written policy document. This policy document sets out the terms and conditions of the insurance contract.

Conflicts

Most disputes over contracts arise from either the validity or the breach of a contract. When deciding whether a contract actually exists, a court may need to establish whether all of the above elements have been satisfied. For example, a business which is being sued for breach of contract may attempt to defend itself by showing that the contract in question is not valid and is therefore not legally binding. If this were the case they would not be in breach of such a contract.

Once its validity is recognised, a court may need to examine whether each party has fulfilled its obligations under the terms of the agreement.

Termination of Contracts

Contracts can be terminated in four ways:

> By agreement
> By performance
> By frustration
> By breach

> **By agreement:** Both parties agree to cancel the contract before it is carried out. If I have a contract with a builder to build my house, we might both agree to cancel the agreement prior to the work commencing. I don't get a house, and builder doesn't get paid. Both parties agree to be freed from our contractual obligations and so the contract is annulled.

e.g. Example

In the sporting world managers and coaches often agree to leave a club before their contract has expired. This is generally a negotiated departure resulting from sudden illness or changed circumstances at the club and is 'by mutual agreement'.

> **By performance:** In this instance the contract is carried out as agreed and to the satisfaction of both parties. If, for example, the house is built to my specifications and I pay the agreed price to the builder the contract will be at an end. This is clearly the ideal outcome for the contract.

> **Frustration:** Something unforeseen and beyond control of either party prevents a contract from being carried out. The death of either party would be an example. If my builder is fatally injured prior to completing my house, our contract will cease to be enforceable. I would need to enter into a contract with a new builder to complete the project.

Airport passengers stranded due to the Icelandic ash cloud

Example

The unprecedented disruption of flights following the 9/11 attack on the World Trade Centre in 2001 or the travel chaos caused by the eruption of the Icelandic volcano in 2010 also illustrate how legitimate contracts can sometimes be frustrated.

> **Breach:** One party does not carry out their part of the agreement. In this type of situation the other party to the contract is likely to feel aggrieved and may even suffer a financial loss. It is quite likely that they will take legal action to resolve the issue.

For example, if my house is built as per agreement and I refuse to pay the agreed price, the building contractor is likely to take me to court in order to ensure payment of the outstanding money.

Breach of contract is clearly the most contentious or acrimonious manner by which a contract can be terminated. If legal action is taken to resolve the dispute, it will be very important for the courts to establish just how serious the breach of contract was. Some breaches of contract are more fundamental or important than others and will result in more serious consequences for all parties involved.

Breach of condition vs Breach of warranty

> **A condition is an essential element which goes to the heart of the contract.** Breach of a condition is effectively breaking the agreement. A band failing to turn up for a concert would clearly be in breach of a condition and they cannot expect to be paid. They may also be sued for losses incurred by the concert promoter.

> **A warranty is a less important part of the agreement** and its breach may not actually invalidate the agreement. If the band did actually play the contracted show, but failed to turn up for pre-show sound check they would expect to be paid for the concert. The promoter may, however, withhold some payment to cover costs involved in the scheduled sound check.

Remedies for breach of contract

> **Sue for damages:** The aggrieved party can take court action to recover losses suffered. A concert promoter will sue the performer for all costs and losses which have arisen from their 'no show'.

> **Specific performance:** This involves asking the court to order that the contract must be carried out, as per agreement. Essentially the court enforces the contract. If my builder has failed to complete the construction of my house to the specifications set out in the contract, the court may issue an order compelling him to complete the necessary work within one month. Failure to comply with this court order is likely to result in further legal action and the builder being sued for damages.

> **Rescind the contract:** This means that the contract is cancelled and all parties are released from their contractual obligations. If, however, the breach of contract has caused damage or loss, the injured party may sue for damages. If my builder does not complete the necessary work within the one-month time frame, the contract may be rescinded. Setting aside the agreement in this way will release the builder from the contract and will also release me from my contractual obligation to pay. This will enable me to enter into a contract with another builder to complete the work. I may also seek to sue the original builder for any losses or costs incurred as a result of his failure to complete the work.

Chapter Review Diagram – People in Business

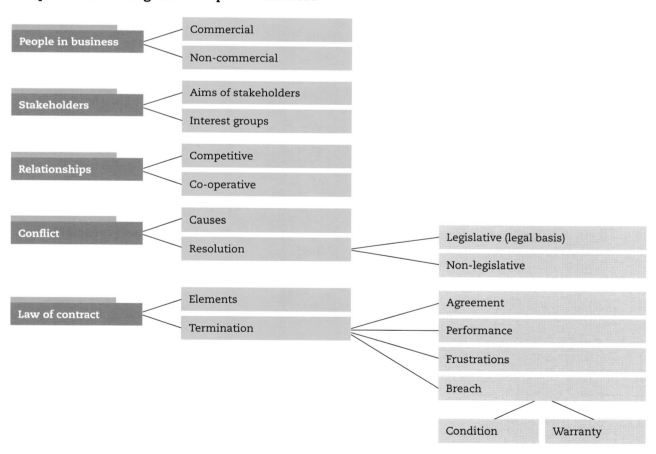

unit

1

Chapter Review Questions

1 Distinguish between commercial and non-commercial businesses. Support your answer with two examples of each.

2 Explain the term 'stakeholder' and give two examples of both internal and external stakeholders for a business.

3 Distinguish between 'entrepreneurs' and 'investors' in a business.

4 Outline the role and importance of business managers.

5 Explain what an 'interest group' is and outline its role. Name three interest groups.

6 Distinguish between a 'trade association' and a 'trade union'.

7 Distinguish between co-operative and competitive relationships in business. Use examples to illustrate your answer.

8 What do the following letters stand for?

(i) IBEC   (ii) ICTU   (iii) IFA   (iv) SIMI   (v) CAI

9 Outline the difference between a legislative and a non-legislative solution to conflict.

10 Explain both conciliation and arbitration.

11 What is a contract?

12 List the elements of a valid contract.

13 Explain the term 'invitation to treat'.

14 Illustrate your understanding of the term 'capacity' as it relates to contract law.

15 Distinguish between 'legality of purpose' and 'legality of form'.

16 List four ways in which a contract can be terminated.

17 Illustrate your understanding of 'frustration' as it relates to termination of contracts.

18 In relation to contract law, differentiate between breach of condition and breach of warranty.

19 Outline two remedies for breach of contract.

Questions · Ordinary Level

1 Outline the importance to a business of the following stakeholders:

> Entrepreneurs   > Investors

2 Distinguish between the terms 'employer' and 'employee'.

3 Describe the relationship between producers and consumers. Outline **two** possible sources of conflict that can arise between them.

4 Illustrate the role of interest groups in business.

5 Name **one** trade association and explain its role.

6 Explain the following: i) conciliation, and ii) arbitration. *LCOL 2000 (20 marks)*

7 Identify and explain any **two** elements of a valid contract. *LCOL 2008 (10 marks)*

8 Explain how a contract may be terminated (ended).

9 What is meant by 'capacity to contract'?

Q Questions · Higher Level

1 Outline, using examples, the relationship that can exist between 'investors' and 'entrepreneurs' in business. *LCHL 2011 (15 marks)*

2 Describe how conflict between an employer and an employee could be resolved in a non-legislative manner. *LCHL 2009 (15 marks)*

3 In relation to the Law of Contract, illustrate your understanding of capacity to contract. *LCHL 2009 (10 marks)*

4 Outline, using an example, the role of interest groups in the business world. *LCHL 2009 (10 marks)*

5 Discuss how consumers may benefit from the existence of a competitive relationship between producers. *LCHL 2009 (15 marks)*

6 'The relationship between an enterprise and its stakeholders may be competitive or co-operative.' Discuss this statement, with appropriate examples. *LCHL 2006 (15 marks)*

7 Demonstrate how the remedies for breach of contact can help solve conflicts between contractual parties. *LCHL 1999 (20 marks)*

8 Contrast the aims of producers and consumers.

9 Describe, using examples, **one** co-operative and **one** competitive relationship that may exist either between or within organisations. *LCHL 2002 (20 marks)*

10 Explain the relationship between producers and interest groups in business.

11 Illustrate the role of interest groups in business. *LCHL 2003 (10 marks)*

12 Describe, using examples, **three** legislative methods of solving business conflicts.

13 Explain, using examples where appropriate, the essential elements of a valid contract. *LCHL 2003 (30 marks)*

14 Define the term 'contract'. Outline why an invitation to treat is not a contract. *LCHL 2001 (20 marks)*

Chapter 2
Conflict Resolution: The Consumer

Syllabus Outcomes

On completion, the student should be able to:
- » 1.3.3 Outline non-legislative ways of solving conflict;
- » 1.3.4 Outline how a major piece of legislation and the elements of contract law help deal with conflict;
- » 1.3.6 Illustrate how legislation affects these business relationships (HL);
- » 1.3.7 Describe a possible business conflict and show how the law would be used to solve it (HL).

News Flash

Consumers advised over doorstep selling

By Conor Pope, Consumer Affairs Correspondent

New research from the National Consumer Agency (NCA) shows that 20 per cent of people who answer their doors to sales people feel pressurised into buying goods or services on the spot and run the risk of being ripped off as a result.

The research, carried out by Amárach Research, found that 41 per cent of consumers experienced a door-to-door sales pitch over the last 12 months. Some 80 per cent of those who had dealings with door-to-door salespeople said they represented energy suppliers...

The NCA has launched a nationwide public information campaign aimed at helping consumers make confident and better-informed purchasing decisions when buying goods or services on their doorstep.

"Many reputable companies use doorstep selling as a sales channel," said NCA chief executive Ann Fitzgerald, "However, some employ high-pressure sales tactics to sell their products or services. Consumers may feel obliged or pressured into signing up to contracts without having the time or information to decide if it is the best option for them."...

"Ask for clear information in writing on the offer. Also satisfy yourself about the cancellation policy and make sure that you get a cancellation form."

She warned that if a seller refused to give out this information "then you should not sign up until you get it and know for sure what you are getting into."...

"Our campaign aims to raise consumers' awareness of their rights when dealing with people selling on their doorstep and to encourage consumers to make an informed decision before signing up to or purchasing anything. If you are dealing with someone on your doorstep always ask for identification. Don't be hurried into a decision even if they offer you a discount or a one-day only offer," Ms Fitzgerald concluded.

This is an edited extract from **The Irish Times,** Tuesday, 30 August 2011.

For more up-to-date newspaper articles see www.edcodigital.ie

1 Read the newspaper extract opposite and discuss the issues raised. Have you any personal experience of this type of issue?

2 Can you explain any of the highlighted terms?

Introduction

A **consumer** is anyone who buys goods and services for their own use. The protection given to consumers does not apply to businesses when they purchase goods with the intention of reselling them.

Irish consumers are protected by two specific pieces of legislation:

> Sale of Goods and Supply of Services Act, 1980
> Consumer Protection Act, 2007

When the provisions of these laws are applied to resolve conflicts between consumers and retailers, this represents a legislative solution.

Sale of Goods and Supply of Services Act, 1980

When consumers buy goods from a retailer, both parties have entered into a contract. The following are the conditions of that contract, and they give consumers certain entitlements or rights.

« syllabus signpost 1.3.4 & 1.3.7

Goods

Goods must be:

> Of merchantable quality
> Fit for their intended purpose

> As described
> As per sample

> **Of merchantable quality:** This means all items for sale must be of good quality and in a fit condition to be sold. The definition of 'good' quality is related to the price paid.

  If a consumer buys a brand new car, they will pay full price and in return will expect the car to be pristine and perfect in every way. Consumers who purchase a used car will not have the same expectation of quality, but will not pay the same high price. Any decision on reasonable quality must be viewed in the context of the price paid.

> **Fit for intended purpose:** This can either mean the normal purpose for which those goods are used, or a particular purpose specified by the consumer. If a consumer buys a lawnmower, it goes without saying that it must be capable of cutting grass. If a consumer specifies a need for marine quality varnish, they would expect to be sold a product which is capable of being used to varnish a boat.

unit 1

> **As described:** Consumers often purchase goods based on verbal descriptions from sales people as well as written descriptions or illustrations in brochures. Retailers must ensure that the products delivered to consumers match those descriptions. For example, a TV which is described by the salesperson as being suitable for viewing programmes in high definition, must have the necessary technology to match that description.

> **As per sample:** If goods are purchased on the basis of a sample provided by the retailer, the customer has a reasonable expectation that all goods received will match the sample. While this would obviously apply in relation to products like fabric or paint, it should be remembered that demonstration models are also a type of sample.

Services

The Sale of Goods and Supply of Services Act states that services should be:

> Supplied by skilled and qualified service providers,
> Provided using proper care and attention, and
> Materials or parts used must be of merchantable quality.

> **Provided by qualified service provider:**
> If I leave my car into a garage for a service, I expect that the service will be carried out by a qualified mechanic. If it turns out that the job was done by a transition year student on work experience, I would have a clear cause for complaint, especially if I have to pay for the work.

> In addition to being qualified, the service provider must use **proper care and attention** when carrying out the work. A qualified surgeon may be careless when operating, or a qualified auditor may overlook some important details when reviewing company accounts. If these oversights result in loss or injury to clients, there will be legal and financial consequences for the service provider.

> Finally, where materials or parts are used to provide a service, those **materials must be of merchantable quality**. When I get the bill for my car service, I notice I'm charged for a new battery. On closer inspection, I discover the replacement battery given to me is not in fact new, but has been removed from another customer's car. As I've paid full price for a new battery, that's what I should receive. A builder using inferior quality materials would also be in breach of this provision.

It is very important to reiterate that all of the provisions outlined above are **conditions** of every contract between consumers and retailers. If the goods or services fail to meet any of these criteria, the retailer is guilty of breach of contract. In such circumstances, consumers are entitled to seek appropriate redress.

Other provisions of the Act

> **Rental, hire purchase or leasing agreements** are also covered by the Act. If a rented DVD does not work properly you are entitled to return it and complain to the retailer.

› **Second-hand goods** sold by retailers are also covered by the terms of the Act and must be fit for the purpose for which they are sold. It is not, however, reasonable to expect that second-hand goods will be of the same standard as new products and for this reason a lower price will be paid. Since second-hand goods are 'sold as seen' it is important to examine the goods carefully.

It's important to note that private sales are not covered by the terms of the Sale of Goods and Supply of Services Act. If you buy a second-hand item, for example a car, through a private sale you have no consumer rights as you are not buying from a business.

› The Act makes the **retailer responsible for the goods or services sold**, and so the shop must deal with all legitimate consumer complaints. Since this is a contractual issue, they cannot pass responsibility on to manufacturers. If faulty goods need to be returned to the manufacturer, it is up to the retailer to do so, having first provided appropriate redress to the consumer.

› **Signs limiting consumer rights are illegal:**
The conditions outlined above are statutory entitlements. This means the consumer has very clear rights which are set out in law (statutory rights) and retailers cannot attempt to diminish these. Consumers have the same rights shopping in the sales as they do at any other time of the year. If an item is faulty, your consumer rights do not change just because it was on sale. The only exception would be in situations where sale price is reduced due to clear faults or defects in the goods.

What makes the first sign legal is the statement which recognises that consumers have statutory rights. While the retailer may not ordinarily have a policy of offering a replacement or a refund for goods, they realise that customers are well within their rights to receive these where the goods are faulty or unfit for purpose.

Legal notice:

No refunds or exchanges. This does not affect your statutory rights.

Illegal notices:

No refunds.

Goods will not be exchanged.

Sorry, no refund or exchange on sale items.

› Consumers are also entitled to **redress for faulty or damaged goods** even where the items were purchased in a sale.

› Guarantees from manufacturers and retailers can offer **extra protection** to consumers but cannot limit or remove statutory rights.

› The retailer must have the legal right to sell goods and the consumer is entitled to **ownership and quiet possession**.

› **Inertia selling** refers to a situation where goods are sent to a person who has not ordered them and a demand for payment is later made in respect of those goods. This type of practice was common with book or music clubs which regularly sent unsolicited goods to people 'on approval'. The Act outlaws this practice and allows for the customer to keep these goods free of charge after thirty days, provided they have written to the seller asking them to collect the unwanted goods.

> In every contract for the sale of a motor vehicle there is an **implied condition** that, at the time of delivery, the vehicle must be free from any defect which would render it a danger to the public, including persons travelling in the vehicle.

Redress for consumers

In circumstances where the retailer has broken any conditions of the sales contract, the consumer has legitimate grounds for complaint and would therefore be entitled to suitable redress. This means that consumers are entitled to any of the three R's:

> Refund   > Repair   > Replacement

The Sale of Goods and Supply of Services Act makes no legal provision for the issuing of **credit notes** and consumers should only consider accepting a credit note in circumstances where they have no legal entitlement to redress.

A consumer has no right to redress where the goods are not faulty, where the goods were damaged due to misuse by the consumer or where the consumer has simply changed their mind. Retailers also tend to offer credit notes in situations where customers have received duplicate goods, often as a gift. In these circumstances the offer of a credit note should be accepted by the consumer and seen as a gesture of goodwill by the retailer, who is under no legal obligation to offer any type of redress.

Consumer Protection Act, 2007

« syllabus signpost 1.3.4

One of the most recent pieces of consumer legislation to be enacted in Ireland is the Consumer Protection Act, 2007. The Consumer Protection Act seeks to update and modernise consumer law while also establishing the **National Consumer Agency (NCA)**. The NCA replaces the Office of the Director of Consumer Affairs and has taken on many of its functions.

National Consumer Agency

www.consumerconnect.ie

The **main functions** of the National Consumer Agency are:

> To **promote and protect** the interests and welfare of consumers.
> To **enforce** and encourage compliance with the relevant consumer law.
> To **investigate suspected offences** under any of the relevant laws.
> Where appropriate, to **refer cases** to the director of public prosecutions.
> The NCA has an **advisory role** and can make recommendations or raise concerns about consumer protection legislation.
> The NCA also has the power to make **proposals for new legislation.**
> Since 2010 the National Consumer Agency has taken over the Financial Regulator's responsibility to provide consumer **information on financial services.**

The Consumer Protection Act, 2007, deals with unfair business-to-consumer commercial practices; it does not apply to dealings between businesses. Amongst other things, it sets out various rules that apply to:

1 Claims made about goods and services
2 Claims made about prices

3 Aggressive retail practices

4 Prohibited practices

5 Price controls

6 Codes of practice

7 Enforcement

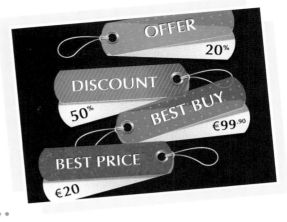

1 Claims made about goods and services

This Act protects the consumer from misleading advertisements and requires that the information in advertisements is fair and accurate. For example an advert which features a top-of-the-range car alongside the price for an entry-level model would be clearly misleading, since in reality the featured vehicle cannot be purchased for the price shown.

The provisions of the Consumer Protection Act apply to all types of communication that promote goods or services, including advertisements, shop notices and claims made by a sales assistant about a product or service.

Under the terms of the Act, it is illegal for an advertiser to make false or misleading claims about goods, services or prices. A claim that a product is waterproof when it's not, or attributing some unproven health benefit to a product, are both breaches of the Consumer Protection Act. For example, claims that a product is effective as a cure for migraine must be borne out by scientific evidence.

The withholding of material information is also considered to be a misleading practice.

The provisions outlined above recognise that **advertising** can be very persuasive and that customers are entitled to know exactly what they are buying.

A **false claim** is one which is simply untrue; for example, advertising a jumper as 100 per cent wool, when in fact it contains some acrylic fibres.

A **misleading advertisement**, on the other hand, may not be entirely untrue, but is deceptive because it presents an unfair impression of a good or service. Misleading adverts tend to focus on one or two aspects of a product. They usually highlight the positive features of the product while playing down or ignoring the less appealing aspects. By being 'economical with the truth' they do not paint the full picture and can mislead consumers.

Case Study

A builder targeting families for a new housing development advertises its proximity to local primary and post-primary schools. The advert clearly states that the new development is 'within walking distance of local schools'.

Taken at face value the advert seems to be accurate since there is indeed a new primary school in the village and a post-primary school less than ten minutes' walk from the new houses. The advert fails, however, to tell potential purchasers that the secondary school in question is a fee-paying school and the nearest non fee-paying school is twenty minutes' drive away.

Potential buyers who rely on the information provided by the developer are certainly in danger of being misled.

There has also been a great deal of controversy in recent years about the misleading claims made by cosmetics companies in relation to hair and beauty products. Many adverts have featured pictures of celebrities who have used the product to attain a particular 'look'. It later emerged that this flawless appearance was in fact achieved by post-production changes to the picture or through the use of additional products. All of this suggests that the average consumer may not be able to achieve that appearance simply by using the product alone and that the adverts may mislead consumers.

Claims about usage and prior history must be true and accurate. This would clearly outlaw a claim by a motor dealer that a used car had one previous owner, when there is evidence to suggest the vehicle has had several owners.

2 Claims made about prices

In addition to misleading claims about the nature and characteristics of products, the Act also addresses their availability at a particular time, place or price.

If a product or a special offer price is only available in a limited number of retail outlets, this must be clearly stated. For example, chain stores like Dunnes Stores, which operate in both the Republic of Ireland and Northern Ireland, need to inform customers that certain special price deals apply to Northern Ireland stores only.

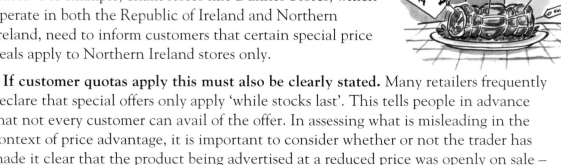

If customer quotas apply this must also be clearly stated. Many retailers frequently declare that special offers only apply 'while stocks last'. This tells people in advance that not every customer can avail of the offer. In assessing what is misleading in the context of price advantage, it is important to consider whether or not the trader has made it clear that the product being advertised at a reduced price was openly on sale – and at the same location – for a reasonable period of time.

Example

It would be an offence under the Act to claim that a HD TV now 'on sale' for €450 is a genuine reduction unless the same TV was previously offered for sale at a different price (say €600) at the same place (Dundrum town centre) for a reasonable period of time. The law does not specify the exact time period required, but guidelines suggest it should be at least twenty-eight consecutive days in the previous three months.

The advice given to shoppers is always to shop around and not to engage in impulse buying. The Latin phrase '*caveat emptor*', meaning 'let the buyer beware', is very relevant in these situations.

3 Aggressive retail practices

The Consumer Protection Act also prohibits a number of aggressive practices by traders, including **harassment** and **coercion**. This means forcing someone to do something against their better judgement. Some consumers may feel pressurised or even threatened by aggressive sales tactics and agree to the sale simply to escape a stressful situation. The reality is that the salesperson has been guilty of exercising undue influence and has put unfair pressure on the customer.

« *syllabus signpost*
1.3.6

The law offers specific protection to consumers when the trader knows their judgement is impaired, since the trader is effectively taking advantage of a consumer's misfortune or circumstances. The use of **threatening or abusive language or behaviour** by the trader is also outlawed.

You have probably seen TV programmes that feature 'secret filming' and highlight salespeople targeting older customers with products which are inappropriate for the customer or which are extremely expensive. In order to secure a sale they may spend several hours in the home of a vulnerable customer and refuse to take 'no' for an answer.

Not only are these aggressive practices outlawed by the Consumer Protection Act, but it could be reasonably argued that any contract entered into is illegal as the customer did not consent freely to the agreement.

4 Prohibited practices

The Consumer Protection Act, 2007, prohibits or forbids the following practices:

> **Making false claims about cures for illnesses.**
> **Offering free prizes when it costs money to claim the prizes.** This type of tactic is common when consumers win unsolicited prizes and may be required to forward a small payment in order to receive their 'free gift' or prize.
> **Running promotions or competitions when the top prize is not available.** If holding a lottery, raffle or some similar promotion the trader must ensure that the top prize is a genuine one and that consumers have a real opportunity to win it.

unit 1

> **Persistently cold calling, having been asked to leave or stop.** Cold calling occurs when the customer has had no prior contact with the seller and the salesperson arrives unannounced and without an appointment.
> **Demanding payment for unsolicited goods.** Unsolicited goods are those which the customer has not actually ordered. Sometimes companies send products to customers 'for approval'. Some customers may feel obliged to keep and pay for the goods, so yet again this is a type of pressurised selling. This is also called 'inertia selling'.
> **Pyramid schemes are prohibited.** A pyramid scheme is defined as one where a person pays money, but their primary benefit derives from the introduction of other persons into the scheme, rather than the supply of a product.

 **Example**

You receive a letter from someone asking you to send them €10 in return for a promise of €90 profit. It is further explained that this profit will accrue to you when you send the same letter to ten of your friends.

If each of these friends sends you €10, you will have made a €90 profit on the scheme (€100 received – €10 paid out). The scheme continues with each of your ten friends passing on a similar letter to ten of their friends and so on.

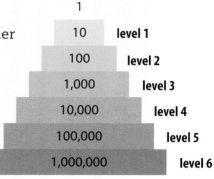

1	
10	level 1
100	level 2
1,000	level 3
10,000	level 4
100,000	level 5
1,000,000	level 6

The problem is that the number of people required to keep this scheme going increases in multiples at each level. A pyramid scheme initiated by one person will require 1 million people by the time it reaches stage 6 and this will rise to 10 million at stage 7. Pyramid schemes are ultimately unsustainable and will inevitably collapse. Those near the top are likely to gain the most, while many who join the scheme later will make losses. To all intents and purposes, it is a scam and is justifiably outlawed under the Consumer Protection Act, 2007.

5 Price controls

Price controls can only be introduced in emergency situations and must be by decision of the government and not just the Minister for Jobs, Enterprise and Innovation

Price display regulations: The Consumer Protection Act, 2007, gives the minister the power to make regulations requiring that the prices of certain products be displayed in a specific manner. For example, they could provide that prices of certain products, including airline fares, must be displayed inclusive of charges, fees and taxes.

6 Codes of practice

The Consumer Protection Act, 2007, provides for the recognition of codes of practice drawn up by traders or groups of traders and for the National Consumer Agency to approve such codes. It also provides that the NCA may issue guidelines to traders about consumer protection and welfare, commercial practices, quality assurance schemes and codes of practice.

7 Enforcement

The Consumer Protection Act, 2007, provides for the following enforcement mechanisms to be available to the NCA:

> The NCA can accept a **written undertaking from the trader** that a prohibited practice will cease. The undertaking may contain whatever terms and conditions the NCA thinks are appropriate, e.g. refrain from the activity, compensate consumers, publish a corrective statement.

> The NCA can apply for a **prohibition order** from the circuit/high court. This will require the offending trader to stop their illegal behaviour.

> The NCA can serve a **compliance notice** on a trader whom it considers to have engaged in a prohibited activity. The trader has fourteen days in which to appeal the notice. If the trader fails to comply, the NCA may take criminal proceedings.

> The National Consumer Agency has the power to impose **on-the-spot penalties** for offences relating to the display of prices and staff carry out regular spot checks on business premises to ensure they are in compliance with legal requirements.

 Pubs and other licensed premises are required to display price lists in clear view and are not permitted to charge higher prices without notifying consumers. This measure is designed to prevent consumers being charged excessive prices, particularly on days where demand levels are high.

national consumer agency
gníomhaireacht náisiúnta **tomhaltóirí**

putting **consumers** first

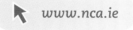
www.nca.ie

> Publication of a **consumer protection list:** a list of traders convicted of criminal offences, subject to court orders, bound by an undertaking, served with a compliance notice, or subject to a fixed payment notice is compiled by the NCA. The list is updated regularly and posted on the NCA website.

Redress

1 The Consumer Protection Act allows consumers to apply to the courts for damages if they suffer loss due to misleading practices by a business.

2 The National Consumer Agency may also apply to the court for an order that requires a business to pay compensation for any loss or damage to the consumer resulting from an offence.

COMPENSATION

The Consumer Protection Act effectively replaces the Consumer Information Act, 1978, which is no longer part of the Leaving Certificate business syllabus. It also introduces the provisions of the EU Directive on Unfair Commercial Practices into Irish consumer law.

unit 1

As outlined in Chapter 1, conflict can be resolved using either legislative or non-legislative methods. The most common avenues open to consumers when seeking resolution to a conflict with retailers are set out below.

Non-Legislative Conflict Resolution

« syllabus signpost 1.3.3

Meet and negotiate

The consumer should return the goods to the retailer and try to negotiate a solution to the problem. If necessary they should ask to speak to the manager and must make their complaint in a manner which is polite but firm. The consumer will be required to provide proof of purchase and having an understanding of their legal rights is helpful to the negotiating position of the consumer.

Write a letter of complaint

If the consumer is unhappy with the face-to-face discussion they should put their complaint in writing. The letter should be sent to the shop manager and a further copy sent to the head office of the company if necessary. This letter, along with any written response from the retailer, may be useful in the event that third-party intervention is required as it will show the extent to which each party has attempted to resolve the issue.

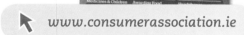

Independent third-party intervention

The most likely sources of non-legislative mediation are from interest groups such as a trade association or the Consumers' Association of Ireland.

Consumers' Association of Ireland

This is an independent, non-profit organisation representing the views and interests of consumers. The association is funded by members and publishes *Consumer Choice* magazine monthly. The magazine reports on goods and services available in Ireland and on consumer rights issues. It highlights current issues facing consumers and lobbies the government in order to seek improvements in consumer protection. Since the CAI is not a statutory organisation, it operates on a non-legislative basis and is independent of the government.

www.consumerassociation.ie

**Oifig an Ombudsman
Office of the Ombudsman**

www.ombudsman.gov.ie

Legislative Conflict Resolution

National Consumer Agency (see p. 22)

Because of its statutory foundation this is a legislative solution.

The Office of the Ombudsman

Set up by the Ombudsman Act, 1980, this office has powers to investigate complaints against government departments and public bodies including local councils, the Health Service Executive (HSE) and An Post.

The Ombudsman, Emily O'Reilly

The Ombudsman will only investigate cases where the complainant has already tried unsuccessfully to resolve the matter with the state body concerned. The Ombudsman will issue a recommendation which is not legally binding. The Ombudsman is appointed by the President and makes an annual report to the Oireachtas.

A separate statutory officer, the **Financial Services Ombudsman**, also exists and deals independently with complaints from consumers about their dealings with all financial services providers. It is a statutory body funded by levies from the financial services providers and became operational in 2005. The existing voluntary ombudsman schemes for credit institutions and insurance schemes were subsumed into it and the number of financial service providers covered by its remit was expanded considerably. The Ombudsman provides a free service to complainants and arbitrates to resolved disputes.

Financial Services Ombudsman

Small Claims Court

Administered by the Small Claims Registrar of the District Court, it deals with consumer claims up to a €2,000 limit. It costs €18 to bring a complaint and there is no need for solicitors. The consumer needs to fill in a complaint form, which can be done online, and the retailer has an opportunity to respond to the claim.

If the retailer accepts liability or fails to contest the claim the court will automatically find in favour of the consumer. If necessary, the Registrar may interview and negotiate with both parties to try to reach an agreement.

The Registrar's decision is not legally binding on either party, but in spite of this the Small Claims Court is very effective in resolving disputes. This is because the verdict can be appealed to the District Court where costs and penalties are higher. A business which loses the legal argument in the Small Claims Court would be well advised to settle the case rather than risk the additional expenses associated with an appeal.

The existence of the Small Claims Court provides reassurance for consumers when dealing with retailers and service providers because the threat of legal action motivates the businesses to act responsibly.

www.smallclaims.ie

This chapter illustrates that consumers in Ireland are well protected by legislation and a range of both statutory and voluntary agencies. However, there still remains a necessity for all consumers to be vigilant and to exercise care when purchasing goods and services. It's important to **shop around** in order to secure the best prices, and this is particularly relevant when buying high-value goods. Those consumers who engage in impulse buying and make hasty purchases may spend a long time regretting their actions. The Latin phrase 'caveat emptor', 'let the buyer beware', continues to be relevant in our day-to-day lives.

Chapter Review Diagram – Conflict Resolution: The Consumer

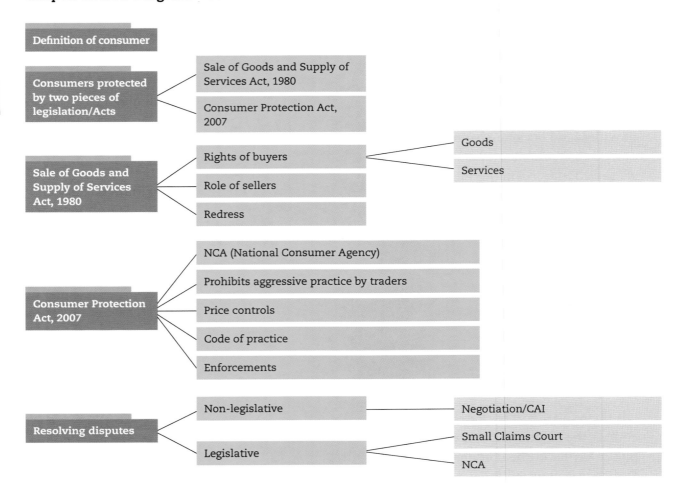

Q Chapter Review Questions

1 What is a consumer?

2 Name two pieces of legislation which offer protection to Irish consumers.

3 Explain the following terms used in the Sale of Goods and Supply of Services Act, 1980. Goods must be:

   › Of merchantable quality
   › Fit for purpose
   › As described.

4 Outline the provisions of the Sale of Goods and Supply of Services Act in relation to services.

5 Explain the redress available to consumers who have a valid complaint.

6 State five functions of the National Consumer Agency.

7 Outline the provisions of the Consumer Protection Act, 2007, as they apply to claims made about goods and services.

8 List six practices prohibited by the Consumer Protection Act, 2007.

9 Name five aggressive practices by traders which are prohibited under the Consumer Protection Act, 2007.

10 Outline how a consumer can resolve a complaint over faulty goods in a non-legislative way.

11 Explain the function of the Small Claims Court.

12 Explain the role of the Ombudsman.

13 Outline two legislative solutions suitable for resolving consumer complaints.

14 Explain the term 'caveat emptor' and outline practical ways in which consumers can follow this advice.

Q Questions · Ordinary Level

1

Paula McCarthy received a birthday present of a new mobile phone from her parents. After one week Paula discovered that the volume control on her mobile phone did not work properly and the phone had to be recharged several times a day. Her parents told her that they had bought the phone in FonesToGo and they gave her the receipt. Her friend Mike, who had studied Business at school, explained to Paula that under the law she had the right to get a phone that was of merchantable quality, fit for its purpose and that she was entitled to redress. *LCOL 2011*

(a) Name the law that protects Paula McCarthy in this case. *(10 marks)*

(b) Explain what Paula should do to try to solve the above situation. *(15 marks)*

(c) Explain the **three** terms 'merchantable quality', 'fit for its purpose' and 'redress', with reference to Paula's situation. *(25 marks)*

2

Tom and Mary Burke purchased a washing machine for €600 from Murray's electrical store. After one week they noticed that the machine did not spin the clothes properly and that water remained in the machine at the end of the washing cycle. They returned to the shop to complain. *LCOL 2010*

(a) Name the law that protects the Burkes in this case. *(10 marks)*

(b) Explain **three** legal rights of the Burke family and one duty of Murray's electrical store under the law. *(20 marks)*

(c) Explain **two** advantages of taking a case to the Small Claims Court. *(20 marks)*

3 Goods sold by retailers must 'be fit for their purpose'. Explain.

4 State, giving reasons, whether the following shop signs are legal:

> No refunds will be given.   > Goods will not be exchanged.

> No credit cards accepted.   > CCTV in operation.

5 List the functions of the National Consumer Agency.

6 What are the rights of consumers when buying services?

7 List **two** possible forms of compensation a dissatisfied consumer may request.

8 Adam Smith put a deposit of €80 on a €300 bicycle two weeks ago. Last week he bought a similar model bicycle for €169 in a sale in a different store. The shopkeeper refuses to return his deposit.

Is Adam entitled to his money back? Yes/No.

Explain your answer.

9 What is the function of the Small Claims Court? *LCOL 2005 (10 marks)*

Q Questions · Higher Level

1 (a) Discuss the rights of consumers under the terms of the Sale of Goods and Supply of Services Act, 1980.

    (b) Illustrate **two** forms of redress available to consumers for breach of the Act.

LCHL 2011 (30 marks)

2 (a) Illustrate the circumstances where retailers would be in breach of the Sale of Goods and Supply of Services Act, 1980.

    (b) Outline remedies available to consumers for breaches of the Act.

LCHL 2008 (25 marks)

3 List the main provisions of the Consumer Protection Act, 2007.

4 What are the functions of the National Consumer Agency?

5 The Consumer Protection Act prohibits a number of aggressive practices by traders; name four of these.

6 Describe a non-legislative method of solving a business conflict. Illustrate your answer with an example.

7 Identify **four** organisations which can assist consumers in trying to resolve disputes they have with retailers. In the case of two organisations describe how they can help the consumer to resolve the dispute.

8 (a) Explain what is meant by 'caveat emptor'.

    (b) Discuss the relevance of this rule, in the light of all the legal protection given to consumers and all the organisations which exist to help them.

9 Outline the role of the Small Claims Court.

STRIKE SHUTS DOWN SERVICES

Chapter 3

Conflict Resolution: Industrial Relations

Syllabus Outcomes

On completion, the student should be able to:

» 1.3.3 Outline non-legislative ways of solving conflict;
» 1.3.4 Outline how a major piece of legislation and the elements of contract law help deal with conflict;
» 1.3.6 Illustrate how legislation affects business relationships (HL);
» 1.3.7 Describe a possible business conflict and show how the law would be used to solve it (HL).

News Flash

ICTU conference opens in Kerry

Pay agreements for low earners, the banking crisis and job creation will be top of the agenda for trade unionists this week.

Up to 800 delegates, guests and observers from Ireland and abroad will attend the biennial conference of the Irish Congress of Trade Unions in Killarney.

Taoiseach Enda Kenny will give the keynote address tonight, with general secretary David Begg due to tackle Mr Kenny on the issue of joint labour committees (JLCs). The Government plans to reform the wage-setting rules used to establish standards for certain lower-paid jobs.

Congress represents 800,000 people working in both the private and public sectors north and south of the border and is the largest civil society body on the island.

More than 40 motions dealing with the economic crisis, the bank bailout, job creation, improved rights in the workplace, the future of the European Union and the Middle East will be debated during the week.

A new report on the structures of the Irish trade union movement with a view to ensuring it is best-placed to meet the challenges of the future will also be discussed.

Tánaiste Eamon Gilmore said the Government has always been willing to engage with the trade unions and employer organisations about the future of industrial

relations in the country...

The Labour Party leader also indicated any social partnership agreement would not be the same as what was in place during the boom years.

"I think that there has to be an understanding which is about getting us to the point of recovery and which ensures that there is a stable industrial relations climate in the country," the Tánaiste added.

"In order for that to happen I think there has to be discussions with trade unions and discussions with employers."

This is an edited extract from **The Irish Times**, Monday, 4 July 2011.

For more up-to-date newspaper articles see www.edcodigital.ie

1 Read the newspaper extract opposite and discuss the issues raised.

2 Can you explain any of the highlighted terms?

Industrial Relations

'Industrial relations' refers to the **quality of the relationship between employers and employees**. In organisations where industrial relations are poor, there will often be conflict between management and staff. Such conflicts are referred to as **industrial relations disputes** and are comprehensively dealt with by the provisions of the Industrial Relations Act, 1990.

Maintaining good industrial relations is important for the following reasons:

> It helps ensure a **positive working relationship** between management and staff. This is very important for overall **morale and productivity** in the business. Productivity measures the output per worker and there is general agreement that happy workers are productive workers.

> Improved morale will increase **staff loyalty and motivation**. Workers will have a positive attitude towards their jobs and levels of absenteeism and staff turnover will be lower.

> > **Absenteeism** occurs when employees are missing from work on a habitual or regular basis. It may indicate that the employee is experiencing personal problems but is also strongly associated with a poor working environment.

> > **Staff turnover** refers to the rate at which employees leave the company. High levels of turnover are also indicative of a negative working environment and increase the costs of hiring and training replacement staff.

> It helps maintain consumer confidence and **customer loyalty**. Consumers may be frustrated by having to deal with constant industrial action and may choose to take their business elsewhere. There have been cases where prolonged industrial action has resulted in the closure of businesses.

> It **encourages investment** and makes it easier to raise finance. Shareholders and investors are more likely to provide capital for a business which enjoys a positive industrial relations climate as they will feel more secure about their investment.

Trade Unions

When employees begin work they receive a contract of employment from their employer. This contract sets out the terms and conditions of employment. Over time it may be necessary to alter the terms of this contract and both sides should negotiate these changes. Employees may be represented by **trade unions** in these negotiations.

Trade unions are interest groups which seek to uphold and improve the working conditions of their members. By acting collectively and in an organised way, workers tend to have greater power and influence when dealing with employers. The largest trade union in Ireland is SIPTU (Services, Industrial, Professional and Technical Union), which has over 200,000 members. Since its members are employed in a wide range of businesses and professions, SIPTU is classified as a general trade union. Other trade unions exist to represent specific professions or groups of employees and these include the Irish Bank Officials Association (IBOA) and the Irish National Teachers' Organisation (INTO).

IBOA

Role of the shop steward

New employees may be approached by the shop steward and provided with information about how to join the trade union. A **shop steward** is a worker and trade union member who has been elected by colleagues as their representative in the workplace.

The shop steward acts as a link between the union members in their place of work and the full-time staff in the union headquarters. They also communicate with employers on issues of concern for union members.

Organisational structure

Most unions have local or regional branches around the country, which provide a forum for elected representatives to meet and discuss issues of mutual concern. In some unions a governing body or national executive may be elected from branch members. Information from these branch meetings is passed on to staff in the trade union head office.

Many of these head office staff are full-time employees of the union and they work on a day-to-day basis to support the interests of members and the functions of the trade union.

They collate information and co-ordinate the union's activities and campaigns. Some of these staff are highly skilled negotiators and are often involved in direct negotiations with employers.

Benefits of trade unions

As outlined in *Chapter 1*, it is better to avoid serious conflict by negotiating a resolution. If a dispute can be resolved without the need for industrial action, this is usually the best possible outcome for all parties involved. The ability to negotiate permitted by the organisation of large numbers of individuals offers a big advantage to workers who are trade union members.

The existence of trade unions can also offer benefits to employers, because once the union and employer reach an agreement it will apply to

all members of that trade union. This process is called **collective bargaining** and helps minimise the time and cost involved in negotiating with each individual employee.

National collective bargaining takes place between interest groups representing the government, employers (IBEC) and employees (ICTU). These national wage agreements are part of the **social partnership** process and seek to establish clear parameters for rates of pay across all sectors of industry.

Industrial Relations Disputes

The main concerns of trade unions are illustrated by examining **the most common causes of industrial relations disputes:**

> Pay and conditions

> Discrimination

> Redundancy

> Promotion

> Demarcation

Disputes over pay and conditions

Employees and the trade unions which represent them will generally seek increased pay in circumstances where conditions of employment are altered. They will also expect to be compensated for **changes to work practices.** Examples of such changes might include extending the working week, the introduction of shift work or the entire relocation of the business.

Ideally, changes to work practices, conditions and pay should be carefully negotiated by the stakeholders involved. Failure to reach an agreed solution will tend to have negative consequences for industrial relations and morale within the business. The exact outcome of the discussions will reflect the bargaining power and negotiating skill of each side. Highly skilled workers who are indispensable to the business will be in a better position to secure a sizeable pay increase than their unskilled or non-unionised colleagues.

The recent economic downturn has seen employees having to accept major changes to their terms and conditions of work without any compensation. This reflects the need for many businesses to cut costs in order to survive. Faced with the threat of job loss many employees and trade unions felt they had no option but to accept the changes. In previous years, where economic growth and profitability were strong, employees expected to be rewarded for their part in the businesses success. Bonuses and profit-sharing schemes were commonplace in many industries.

Types of pay increase

> **Productivity increase:** Workers receive a pay rise to reflect improved output levels. This is effectively extra pay for extra work.

> **Cost of living increase:** Workers often seek wage increases in order to keep pace with the level of inflation in the economy. If prices rise by 3 per cent annually and wages remain unchanged, workers will be 3 per cent worse off in real terms. This means that even if workers maintain the same levels of productivity their wages will buy fewer goods and services than they did last year. Inflation in the Irish economy is measured by the Consumer Price Index (CPI) and this type of wage adjustment is also referred to as being **'index linked'.**

> **Relativity increase:** This type of pay increase is designed to maintain the relative pay differential between employees at different levels of an organisation.

e.g. Example

Consider a business in which the manager is normally paid 40 per cent more than a supervisor. This gap will be reduced to 35 per cent when the supervisor manages to secure a 5 per cent pay increase. If this happens, it is very likely that the manager will seek a 5 per cent increase in order to restore the 40 per cent differential.

Relativity claims can be very expensive for businesses because an award to one category of workers is likely to have a knock-on effect on other grades.

> **Comparability increase:** Employees may seek a pay increase when workers doing similar work in another firm or industrial sector receive an increase.

e.g. Example

If Aer Lingus pilots negotiate a 10 per cent pay rise, there is every likelihood that trade unions representing pilots in other airlines will try to secure a similar improvement.

Disputes over discrimination

Discrimination against an individual or group of workers is illegal (see Employment Equality Act, p. 46) and trade unions will take action to ensure all employees receive equal treatment in the workplace. Differences in pay or conditions between similar groups of workers or between male and female staff illustrate the types of issue involved. The government and trade unions will look to ensure that all employees who carry out the same work will receive the same pay.

Disputes involving redundancy

Redundancy means staff losing their jobs, and it usually happens because a business has decided to close some or all of its operations. Generally a redundancy situation arises if **a job ceases to exist**

and the employee is not replaced. The reason for the redundancy could be the financial position of the firm, lack of work, reorganisation within the firm or the firm closing down completely. Irish law entitles qualifying employees to **statutory redundancy payments** when businesses close down.

Trade unions will seek to ensure that, where possible, redundancies are on a **voluntary** basis. Staff who agree to give up their jobs may receive an improved financial compensation package. This might appeal to senior staff who are already close to retirement and also to the most recent appointees whose statutory redundancy entitlements will be minimal. By using a voluntary approach, businesses and unions hope to avoid the need for **compulsory** lay offs.

Even when a redundancy situation exists, employees may have grounds for complaint if the manner of their **selection for redundancy** was unfair.

In selecting a particular employee for redundancy, an employer should choose selection criteria that are reasonable and apply them in a fair manner. Examples of these situations might include where the custom and practice in a workplace has been 'last in, first out' and an employee's selection does not follow this procedure. Another example would be where a contract of employment sets out criteria for selection which are not subsequently followed.

Disputes over promotion

These have the potential to cause industrial relations unrest within an organisation. Promotion policies can differ across organisations and in particular between the public and private sectors. In the public sector, seniority has been a key factor in securing promotion and there have been cases where the appointment of less experienced staff to management positions has resulted in industrial relations conflicts.

Case Study

In February 2000 civil servants in the Office of Public Works (OPW) took strike action when they placed pickets on offices in Dublin and Kilkenny following a dispute over promotions.

The action was taken by members of the Public Service Executive Union (PSEU). It centred on a claim that the senior management within the OPW had unilaterally changed the system of selecting people for promotion.

Martin Cullen

According to Gerald Flynn in the *Irish Independent*, "Mr [Martin] Cullen, as Junior Minister at the Department of Finance, has two personal secretaries: one in his office in Finance and the other in the OPW. Before Christmas [1999] both were promoted to assistant principal level.

"There were 26 applicants for the two vacancies and Mr Cullen personally interviewed each of them rather than rely on a short-list prepared by senior officials. He selected two new private secretaries, both of whom were working in the Department of Finance.

"About 100 junior and middle-ranking OPW management staff objected to the appointment of [a particular person] as private secretary in the OPW office as he was not an existing OPW employee. Now staff have refused to prepare answers to parliamentary questions or handle letters sent to the minister."

Source: Irish Independent, TUESDAY, 15 FEBRUARY 2000

Disputes over demarcation

« *syllabus signpost*
1.3.7

A **demarcation dispute** is a dispute about who does what job. If this dispute is simply a result of inter-union rivalry then it does not constitute an industrial relations dispute as defined by Industrial Relations Act, 1990. However, if the actions of management bring about this conflict, then staff are entitled to be in dispute with their employer. The HSE 'light bulb dispute' highlights the issues involved in cases of this type.

Light bulb dispute at Cork hospital goes to Labour Court *by Andrew Bushe*

The question of how many electricians it takes to change a light bulb is at the centre of a pay row in Cork's

University College hospital.

The dispute went to the Labour Court when the Health Service Executive (HSE) and the Technical, Engineering and Electrical Union (TEEU) were left in the dark about how to resolve the crux.

What switched on the row was a direction by the hospital authorities that, as part of a work reorganisation, "small, non-essential electric light bulbs" could be replaced as required by

non-electricians.

According to the court, the union objected, maintaining that this was electricians' work and should remain so. "Management contended that this would add considerably to the HSE costs as it would require an electrician to attend on overtime to change a bulb in a bedside lamp, for example," the court said.

The HSE acknowledged that some bulbs in specified areas would need to be replaced by the electricians. The unions are not prepared

to consider any changing of any bulbs by non-electricians, the court said.

As a result of the stand-off, the HSE withheld payments due under a pay agreement. The union said the withholding of retrospective pay increases and bonus payments was "totally unacceptable"...

In a recommendation yesterday, the court found it was "not unreasonable to expect electricians to co-operate" in the proposed bulb changing regime.

Source: The Irish Times, FRIDAY, 3 MARCH 2007

Industrial Relations Act, 1990

The Industrial Relations Act, 1990, defines a trade dispute as any dispute involving people at work which has to do with their employment or non employment or their working conditions. This clearly relates to issues involving employees and employers only and means that inter-union or inter-worker disputes are not covered by the terms of this legislation.

Official vs Unofficial industrial action

In order for industrial action to be official it must be backed by a trade union and ICTU.

Union members on official strike have certain legal protections and cannot be sued by the employer for loss of revenue. Employees who take unofficial action do not have the backing of their union and do not enjoy the same legal protection.

The 1990 Act sets out the procedure to be followed before engaging in official industrial action:

> **Ballot of members:** The union must conduct a secret ballot of all members and the majority must vote in favour of industrial action. In practice, members vote to give their union leaders a mandate for industrial action, which often strengthens their bargaining position when negotiating with employers. Depending on the outcome of negotiations, the union executive may or may not instruct members to take part in industrial action.

> **One week's notice:** Following a vote in favour of industrial action the trade union must give employers a minimum of one week's notice before that action begins. This provides a 'cooling off' period and allows a final opportunity for both sides to reach an agreed solution.

> **Court injunctions:** The law also states that employers cannot get a court injunction to prevent strike action if the trade union has correctly followed the procedures outlined above. An injunction is a court order which forces someone to do something or else to stop doing something. The Industrial Relations Act clearly recognises the legal right of employees to engage in official industrial action and prevents this right being overturned by a judge.

Picketing

Picketing is where employees who are on strike walk up and down outside their place of employment. They carry placards which indicate to customers, suppliers and members of the public that an industrial dispute is taking place. Many people will not pass an official picket and so the business suffers through loss of customers and sales.

Irish law provides for peaceful **primary picketing**. This allows striking workers to place a picket at the business premises of their employer, but picketers are not permitted to engage in violence or intimidation. Picketing at the home of an employer is not allowed. Placing a picket on the premises of another employer is called **secondary picketing** and is only permitted in circumstances where another employer assists in frustrating the strike action.

e.g. Example

Employees of a Dublin-based newspaper are legally entitled to picket the print-works of their own employer during an official strike. If their employer tries to get around the strike action by having newspapers printed by another publisher in Dundalk, the Dublin-based employees are entitled to place a secondary picket on the Dundalk premises.

Closed shop arrangements

Under the terms of the Act **'closed shop'** arrangements are illegal. A 'closed shop' situation occurs when a worker is effectively forced to join a particular trade union once appointed to the job. Workers in Ireland have a constitutional right to join a trade union, but they cannot be forced to join any particular union.

Amalgamation of unions

The Act also provides for the amalgamation of trade unions and sets new requirements for registering a trade union. The intention of these provisions is to reduce the number of trade unions in Ireland. Many trade unionists believe that by organising workers into a smaller number of large unions they will have increased strength and bargaining power. This also simplifies the collective bargaining process for all stakeholders.

The Industrial Relations Act, 1990, also set up the **Labour Relations Commission** and reformed the role of the **Labour Court.**

Types of industrial action

It's important to understand that when employees decide to take industrial action this does not necessarily involve all-out strike action. There are other forms of industrial action also available to aggrieved employees.

› **Work to rule:** Employees perform the duties required of them under the terms of their contracts of employment, but do not carry out any additional duties or overtime. This can impact significantly on a firm's productivity and output. A **go-slow** or **overtime ban** will have similar effects.

These types of action are sometimes used to achieve short-term objectives and are designed to strengthen the negotiating position of the employees.

e.g. Example

The effectiveness of an overtime ban can be illustrated in the prison service, which is prone to staff shortages and relies heavily on prison officers working overtime. If staff refuse to work those additional hours, security levels in prisons will deteriorate and management will be forced to negotiate with trade unions.

> **Token stoppage:** A show of strength by workers, who temporarily stop work for a short period of time. Employees usually choose to walk off the job during a particularly busy time, thereby having the maximum impact on their employer's business. They hope that the action will force their employer to resolve outstanding issues, as failure to do so may result in more prolonged industrial action.

For example, if staff at a supermarket were in conflict with their employer they might have a token work stoppage for two or three hours on Saturday morning. This would result in a significant loss of revenue for the business and would highlight to the employer the seriousness of the staff grievance.

> **Strike:** Workers refuse to carry out any work until the dispute is resolved.

It should be remembered that strikes have short-term costs for employees (lost wages), for employers (lost productivity and sales revenue) and for consumers (loss of services). There is also the possibility that a prolonged strike can seriously undermine the long-term viability of a business. For these reasons, strike action will be seen as a last resort and will only be used where all other channels of negotiation have failed.

As outlined previously, official strikes are those which have the backing and support of the trade union and ICTU. Union members who engage in official strikes are protected from legal action by employers in the event that the business suffers losses.

Those engaging in unofficial strikes have no such protection.

> **Lightning/wildcat strike:** This type of strike takes place suddenly, without any prior notice. While designed to impact on the business, this type of action, because of its unplanned nature, can create serious consequences and inconvenience to consumers. This is particularly true when wildcat strikes involve public transport or utilities. It is for this reason that unofficial action of this type is illegal and employees do not have the support of their trade union.

> **Sympathetic strike:** This occurs when other workers or members of other trade unions take strike action in support of co-workers.

e.g. Example

A bus driver, who has previously been warned about breaches of discipline, arrives late to work and is not in uniform. His manager refuses to let him work and suspends him from duty. All bus drivers immediately decide to cease work until their colleague is reinstated (wildcat strike). Within an hour, other employees including mechanics and inspectors, who are members of another union, decide to strike in support of the drivers (sympathetic strike).

If this action spreads and eventually involves all employees in the company it will be an **'all-out strike'**.

Resolving Conflict

Industrial relations conflicts need to be resolved as quickly as possible, so as to limit their negative impact on all stakeholders. Ideally they can be resolved internally by applying **grievance procedures**.

These are an agreed set of steps which should be followed in resolving all disputes within the organisation. Grievance procedures provide a clear template or pathway towards conflict resolution and mean that all problems and all individuals will be treated in a fair and transparent manner. These procedures help foster a more positive and trustworthy relationship between conflicting parties and should increase the chances of a mutually acceptable settlement.

« *syllabus signpost*
1.3.3

Conflicting parties are also likely to engage in direct face-to-face **negotiations** in order to resolve disputes. This will mean employer and employee representatives sitting down together in order to negotiate some form of compromise agreement.

Sometimes, however, these internal procedures are not successful and it may be necessary to seek **third-party intervention**. This means that some other person or organisation not involved in the dispute is willing to intervene and help the conflicting parties resolve the issue.

Labour Relations Commission (LRC)

The Industrial Relations Act, 1990, gave legal status to the Labour Relations Commission.

> **LRC Mission Statement:** To promote the development and improvement of Irish industrial relations policies, procedures and practices through the provision of appropriate, timely and effective services to employers, trade unions and employees.

The Labour Relations Commission carries out this mission by providing the following specific services:

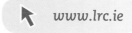
www.lrc.ie

1. **An industrial relations conciliation service:** Conciliation is a voluntary process in which the disputing parties agree to avail of a neutral and impartial mediator to assist them in resolving their differences. The LRC appoints industrial relations officers (IROs) to mediate where the parties cannot resolve the matter themselves.

    Participation in the conciliation process is voluntary, and so too are the outcomes. This means they are not legally binding. All outcomes are reached by consensus.

    Parties to an industrial dispute may request conciliation by writing to the Commission. Where there is a serious dispute situation, and no request for conciliation has been received, the Commission may sometimes intervene and invite both parties to conciliation.

    As a matter of general policy, the Commission does not provide conciliation in unofficial industrial disputes.

2. **Prepares codes of practice:** These represent guidelines for best practice and are designed to help avert, and if necessary resolve, industrial relations conflicts. Since these codes have been agreed with trade unions and employers to help avert conflict, they have proven to be highly effective despite not being legally binding.

3. **Workplace mediation service:** Very often used for issues or disputes involving a small number of employees, the LRC mediation service provides an opportunity for those involved to address the issues, explore options and reach a workable outcome through a mutually agreeable course of action. This voluntary service offers the advantages of being confidential, quick and impartial, since the mediator does not take sides in the discussions

4. The LRC **appoints equality officers** to investigate disputes where discrimination may be involved (see Employment Equality Act, 1998, p. 46).

5. The LRC **nominates rights commissioners** to investigate disputes involving individual, or a small number of, employees. This recognises the fact that some industrial relations problems only affect a tiny minority of employees in an organisation. If left unresolved, however, they may develop into more serious and widespread problems.

    This service is much more formal than the workplace mediation service and tends to deal with issues involving workers' rights in areas such as maternity leave, payment of minimum wages and worker safety. The rights commissioner will listen to both sides before issuing a recommendation. This in turn may be appealed to the Labour Court or Employment Appeal Tribunal.

6. The LRC **researches and reviews developments in industrial relations** and provides an advisory service. It organises regular conferences with employer and employee representatives so as to keep all interested parties up to date on current developments and best practice.

Despite the non-binding nature of LRC agreements it has been very effective in conflict resolution and has a success rate close to 90 per cent. Cases which cannot be resolved by the LRC may be heard by the Labour Court.

Labour Court

The Labour Court was established to provide a free service for the resolution of industrial relations disputes in Ireland. It regularly deals with issues involving equality, organisation of working time, national minimum wage, part-time work, fixed-term work, safety, health and welfare at work, information and consultation matters.

The Labour Court is not a court of law but operates as an industrial relations tribunal. This means it has an independent chairperson as well as employer and employee representatives. It hears both sides in a case and then issues a recommendation setting out its opinion on the dispute and the terms on which it should be settled.

Labour Court recommendations are not legally binding, but there is an expectation that all parties will give them serious consideration. If agreement is reached, it is signed by all parties and registered with the Labour Court. If there is no resolution, responsibility for the settlement of a dispute again rests with the conflicting parties.

In certain circumstances, and particularly when dealing with cases involving breaches of registered employment agreements and employment equality issues, the Labour Court makes legally binding orders.

Since the Labour Court is the **'court of last resort'** for industrial relations matters in Ireland, cases should only be referred to the court when all other efforts to resolve a dispute have failed.

The major functions of the Labour Court currently include:

1. **Investigating disputes** where the LRC has been unable to reach agreement; where the LRC has waived its involvement; or where the Minister for Jobs, Enterprise and Innovation requests Labour Court intervention.

2. **Interpreting codes of practice** and investigating complaints from parties involved, where possible breaches of these codes exist.

3. **Hearing appeals** of decisions made by rights commissioners or equality officers, and issuing binding recommendations.

4. In certain limited situations, and only where both parties agree in advance, the Labour Court decision is legally binding. This is a rare occurrence and is termed **arbitration**. Generally speaking, Labour Court decisions are not legally enforceable but tend to be accepted as this is the final step in the conflict resolution process.

5. The Labour Court also **registers agreements** between employers and employees, and monitors their implementation. Once registered these agreements become legally binding.

▶ *www.labourcourt.ie*

Employment Equality Act, 1998

Discrimination occurs when one person is treated less favourably than another. When deciding whether discrimination has taken place it may be necessary to make a direct comparison between the treatments of different categories of worker, for example male versus female employees.

The Employment Equality Act makes it illegal for an employer to discriminate between workers on nine specific grounds:

1 Gender — MEN WOMEN
2 Marital Status
3 Religion
4 Age
5 Race

All employees must be treated equally in relation to issues like pay and conditions, promotion and dismissal. This legislation also applies to recruitment and selection, so job adverts cannot discriminate against potential candidates. To comply with the provisions of the Act, many job ads clearly state that the business is an equal opportunities employer.

The Employment Equality Act also deals with all areas of harassment, including sexual harassment, and requires all employers to actively prevent or deal with such issues in the workplace.

The law is monitored and enforced by the **Equality Authority,** which also has a role in informing the public of their rights. The Authority will work with all relevant stakeholders and takes a proactive approach to the development of equality policies and codes of best practice.

 www.equality.ie

In September 2011 the government announced its intention to merge the Human Rights Commission and the Equality Authority into a new Human Rights and Equality Commission.

Complaints and breaches are investigated by the Office of the Director of Equality Investigations (the **Equality Tribunal**), which appoints equality officers to deal with specific cases. Having heard submissions from both sides, the equality officer will issue a legally binding decision. This decision may be appealed to the Labour Court.

Unfair Dismissals Acts, 1977 and 2007

«*syllabus signpost* 1.3.4 & 1.3.5

The Unfair Dismissals Acts cannot prevent employees from being dismissed, but do provide them with **a means of correcting the injustice of wrongful dismissal.** The laws apply to all employees (aged 16 to 66), with a minimum of one year's continuous employment with the same employer. The requirement for one year's continuous service does not apply where dismissal results from certain types of leave (including maternity, adoptive, parental or carer's leave) and/or trade union membership. The scope of the legislation has recently been broadened to apply to part-time workers who work fewer than eight hours per week.

The burden of proof in unfair dismissal cases always lies with the employer.

All dismissals are deemed to be unfair unless an employer can clearly show that a worker was dismissed for a valid reason, and that necessary procedures were followed.

Except in serious situations, the employer needs to show **records of verbal and written warnings** to the employee.

Most employers will keep records of employee performance, and responsibility for monitoring and updating information on employees usually rests with the human resources department. This information is subject to the provisions of the Data Protection Acts outlined in *Chapter 6*. If an employee is subsequently dismissed, these records may be used to support the employer's case for dismissal.

Dismissed workers are entitled to be given a written statement outlining the reason for their dismissal and an **opportunity to contest evidence** against them.

Appeals taken under the legislation focus on whether the grounds for dismissal are legal and whether the employer has been fair and reasonable in their treatment of a worker

The following are valid reasons for dismissal:

> **Worker misconduct:** This is quite a wide-ranging category and may include theft, malicious damage, etc.

> **Incompetence:** This covers situations where the worker is incapable of carrying out duties, or is not qualified to do so.

> **Redundancy:** Dismissal is allowed provided the position is being eliminated and an equitable selection procedure has been applied (last in, first out).

Smoker's unfair dismissal case rejected

By Ronan McGreevy

A factory worker who was dismissed after being caught on CCTV smoking in the work canteen, had his case for unfair dismissal rejected by the Employment Appeals Tribunal...

In its ruling published yesterday, the tribunal said it was "satisfied that putting the health and safety of others as well as the safety of the premises, where flammable goods are stored, at risk

constituted gross misconduct and came within the respondent's disciplinary policy".

It upheld the company's decision to dismiss the employee.

This is an edited extract from **The Irish Times,** THURSDAY, 4 AUGUST 2011.

A dismissal is considered to be **automatically unfair** if the employee is dismissed for any of the following reasons:

> Trade union membership or engaging in trade union activities

> Taking legal action against an employer where the employee is either a party or a witness to the case

> Race, colour or sexual orientation

> Religious or political beliefs

> Any matters relating to pregnancy or birth

> Membership of Traveller community

> Unfair selection for redundancy

> Age, other than being under 16 or reaching the normal retirement age for that particular employment

Claims for unfair dismissal are heard by the **Employment Appeals Tribunal.** During the hearing an employer will be required to show that dismissal was necessary and fair. They will also need to show evidence of 'due process' being followed.

In cases of unfair dismissal the decision of the Employment Appeals Tribunal is legally binding. Where a dismissal is deemed unfair the following redress may be available:

> ❯ **Reinstatement:** the employee resumes the same job within the organisation.

> ❯ **Redeployment:** the employee returns to the company but is given a job in a different area or branch.

> ❯ **Compensation:** the employee does not resume employment but receives financial compensation for lost income, up to a maximum of two years' pay.

In practice, compensation is the most likely outcome because most employees are either reluctant to continue with the same employment, or have secured another job in the time taken for the case to be heard.

Constructive dismissal

Constructive dismissal occurs when a worker is not directly sacked from their job, but feels forced to leave and effectively resigns from their position. This often arises where bullying or harassment has occurred and the employer fails to take action to resolve it. By their actions, or lack of them, the employer makes working life unbearable and effectively forces the employee to quit. Constructive dismissal remains the only circumstance where an employee who has not actually been dismissed can claim unfair dismissal against an employer.

Chapter Review Diagram – Conflict Resolution: Industrial Relations

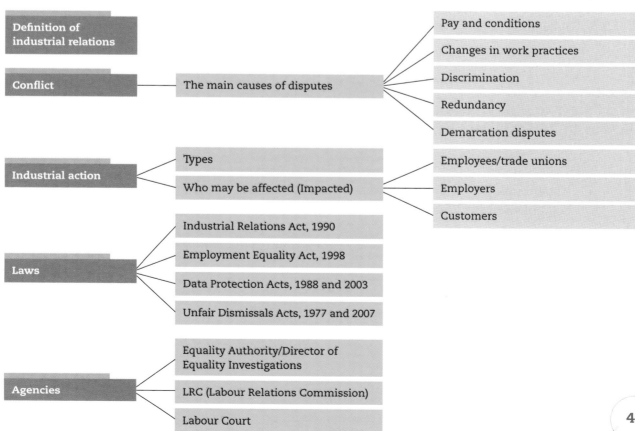

Definition of industrial relations

Conflict — The main causes of disputes — Pay and conditions / Changes in work practices / Discrimination / Redundancy / Demarcation disputes

Industrial action — Types / Who may be affected (Impacted) — Employees/trade unions / Employers / Customers

Laws — Industrial Relations Act, 1990 / Employment Equality Act, 1998 / Data Protection Acts, 1988 and 2003 / Unfair Dismissals Acts, 1977 and 2007

Agencies — Equality Authority/Director of Equality Investigations / LRC (Labour Relations Commission) / Labour Court

Chapter Review Questions

1 Explain what is meant by the term 'industrial relations'.

2 Outline the purpose and contents of a typical contract of employment.

3 Outline the functions of trade unions.

4 Describe the role of a shop steward.

5 Define what is meant by an industrial dispute under the terms of the Industrial Relations Act, 1990.

6 What are the main causes of industrial relations disputes?

7 Explain what a demarcation dispute is and give one example.

8 Define the term 'closed shop'.

9 What does 'work to rule' mean in the context of industrial relations?

10 Distinguish between official and unofficial strikes as defined by the Industrial Relations Act, 1990.

11 List three functions of the Labour Relations Commission.

12 Outline the functions of the Labour Court.

13 List the nine grounds under which employers cannot discriminate against employees.

14 List the reasons for unfair dismissal as set out in the Unfair Dismissal Acts, 1977 and 2007.

15 Name and explain three valid reasons for dismissal.

Questions · Ordinary Level

1
The Employment Equality Act, 1998, outlawed discrimination in the workplace and established the Equality Authority. *LCOL 2011*

(i) List **three** grounds on which discrimination is unlawful under this Act. *(15 marks)*

(ii) Outline the role of the Equality Authority. *(10 marks)*

2
Mark is a public sector worker and a member of a trade union. He has been involved in picketing his workplace as part of a national day of protest. *LCOL 2010*

(i) Explain the term 'picketing'. *(15 marks)*

(ii) Outline **two** functions of a trade union. *(10 marks)*

3

Celine worked as a secretary for J.B. Productions for five years. Recently she informed her manager that she was pregnant and would be taking maternity leave. Her manager informed her that this would not be acceptable to the business and terminated her employment. *LCOL 2009*

Under the Unfair Dismissals Act, 1977/1993

(i) Outline **two** reasons (other than pregnancy) for unfair dismissal. *(15 marks)*

(ii) Outline **two** reasons for fair dismissal. *(15 marks)*

(iii) Explain **one** right that Celine has under the Act. *(15 marks)*

4 What do the letters ICTU stand for?

5 Describe **two** sources of conflict between employers and employees.

6 Explain what is meant by 'collective bargaining'.

7 Explain the role of the Equality Authority.

8 List **four** fair reasons why an employee can be dismissed.

Questions · Higher Level

1 Describe how conflict between an employer and an employee could be resolved in a non-legislative manner. *LCHL 2011 (15 marks)*

2 Outline the procedure by which trade unions can sanction an official strike.

2

The purpose of the Industrial Relations Act, 1990, is to put in place an improved framework for the conduct of industrial relations and for the resolution of trade disputes.

(i) Outline the impact on trade unions of the main provisions of the Industrial Relations Act, 1990.

(ii) Describe **two** types of official industrial action a trade union can undertake as part of a trade dispute. *LCHL 2010 (30 marks)*

4 (i) Explain the term 'employment discrimination' as set out in the Employment Equality Act, 1998. List **four** distinct grounds on which discrimination is outlawed under the Act.

(ii) Evaluate the role of the Director of Equality Investigations in resolving complaints of discrimination in the workplace. *LCHL 2009 (35 marks)*

5 Evaluate the roles of the Labour Relations Commission and Labour Court in dealing with industrial relations conflict.

6 Distinguish between the role of a Rights Commissioner and an Equality Officer.

7 Under the terms of the Industrial Relations Act, 1990, explain the reasons for legitimate trade disputes.

unit 1

Q Applied Business Question

The Big Apple Ltd

Enda O'Mahony set up a fruit and vegetable business some years ago when he was at school. He sourced a good local supplier and was able to supply competitively priced produce to his customers through door-to-door sales. When he left school Enda operated his business on a full-time basis and received some funding from his local County Enterprise Board (CEB).

Over a number of years he expanded the business to meet growing demand and began to employ additional staff. He currently employs ten people who carry out a variety of jobs, from management through to order processing.

Recently a number of customers in the locality have complained about some of the produce being sold to them by the Big Apple Limited. Customers have stated that some produce sold in the shop has been past its 'best before' date. When Enda receives these complaints he refuses to accept responsibility and suggests customers 'could take this problem up with our suppliers'. These customers were not happy and are seeking suitable redress.

Employees have begun to voice opinions about joining a trade union. They spoke to Enda who ruled out the idea and felt it was something he would not entertain. Enda issued a warning to staff on this matter and said he would prefer if staff engaged with him on a one-to-one basis over all employment issues.

The workers were unhappy with this response and four staff subsequently joined SIPTU. When Enda was made aware of this development he dismissed these employees with immediate effect.

(a) Identify **five** stakeholders involved in the Big Apple Ltd.
 In the case of each stakeholder, outline their impact on
 the business. *(30 marks)*

(b) Identify the source of the conflict with consumers.
 Outline a legislative solution to resolving this conflict. *(20 marks)*

(c) Outline the source of conflict with employees. Explain
 the legislative implications of Enda's stance on this issue. *(30 marks)*

Unit Two

Enterprise

Chapter 4
Enterprise

News Flash

Read the newspaper extract opposite and discuss the following:

1 The word 'entrepreneur' is mentioned in the title. What do you think this word means?

2 What type of person do you think is most likely to succeed as an entrepreneur?

3 Based on the information in the newspaper article, list three important pieces of advice you would offer to young entrepreneurs hoping to succeed in business.

4 Can you explain any of the highlighted terms?

Why young entrepreneurs are the way of the future

From fashion-savvy teenagers to confident coders, Ireland's youth are turning ideas into business proposals, writes **Michelle McDonagh.** It was a piece of red confetti stuck to the bottom of her shoe that inspired schoolgirl Tara Haughton to come up with the idea of using stick-on soles to transform any high heel into a designer look-a-like...

Despite being the chief executive of a company exporting to 22 countries worldwide, 16-year-old Haughton was nervous at the thought of having to address a room packed full of her peers at the Brandon Hotel in Tralee, Co Kerry, on Friday...

Haughton was the youngest of a series of Irish entrepreneurs who shared their business success stories to second- and third-level students at the Entrepreneur Blue Sky Day event organised by the co-founder of the Young Entrepreneur Programme and Awards, Kerryman Jerry Kennelly.

Her advice to other would-be entrepreneurs was: "If you have an idea, go for it. Get help, there is help out there, you just need to go and look for it."

She admitted that the downside to being chief executive of her own company – which as it happens has just signed a distribution deal with the United Arab Emirates – is that "there is a lot of work involved and it does take up a lot of time".

James Whelton (19) started his first company, Disruptive Developments, while in sixth year, raising seed capital just after his mock exams.

His company develops Sociero, a social media monitoring and analytic platform.

Whelton came up with the idea for his business when his father, a dentist who had recently discovered the internet, asked him if he could find out what people were saying about him online.

Whelton has since developed software to track what people are saying about a product, person or company through social media and to provide an analytical report based on the comments posted...

Whelton explained that once he had built a small prototype, Enterprise Ireland was "awesome", providing him with a feasibility study grant which was matched by investors. In a short space of time, he was up and running with a business with huge global potential...

[Jerry] Kennelly says he and his co-founders set up the Young Entrepreneur Programme in 2007 to encourage more young Irish people to start their own businesses...

"We are trying to impart the message that you don't need to be a genius or a rocket scientist to be an entrepreneur, you can take control of your own destiny from your own place," he says.

The advice from Bill Liao, co-founder of business social network service Xing, to his young audience was to look for a problem to solve and identify a surprising way to solve it.

"The crucial part is not the idea – you could have 10 good ideas. The hard part is the hard work in the middle. If you put the work in, you can make an idea go global very fast in today's world and you don't need a college degree to make a success of it."

David McCarthy is co-founder of Incidentcontrolroom.com, a cloud-based software application used by large organisations to manage emergency events and crises.

"Businesses do fail but entrepreneurs don't and people don't. If your idea or product doesn't work, drop it and find something else that does work," he advised.

This is an edited extract from **The Irish Times,** MONDAY, 26 SEPTEMBER 2011.

For more up-to-date newspaper articles see www.edcodigital.ie

unit 2

Enterprise

« syllabus signpost
2.3.1

In order to produce goods and services every economy needs four basic elements or **'factors of production'**. These factors of production are land, labour, capital and enterprise. For a detailed explanation of each of these factors see *Chapter 17: Categories of Industry*.

In this particular unit of study the focus will be on just one of those factors of production: **enterprise.**

Enterprise can be broadly defined as **any attempt to do or start something new.** It involves human effort and vision and represents an attempt to combine land, labour and capital in a manner which is both productive and profitable. Enterprise is particularly relevant to business, and without enterprise there would be far fewer business start-ups.

Business enterprise is about spotting an opportunity and taking a risk to make it a reality. It involves combining all four factors of production successfully, and the reward for showing initiative is profit. A person who has this vision and takes such risks is called an **entrepreneur.**

Enterprise, however, is not just about business and profit and it can be applied to many areas of our daily lives, our government and our society.

> **People show enterprise in their personal lives** by getting involved in new hobbies, starting a new health and fitness regime, deciding to undertake further education, etc. You might show enterprise yourself by learning to play a new sport, deciding to start a band or simply embarking on a new study plan. If you were in Transition Year you are likely to have undertaken many enterprising activities and projects including mini-companies and Student Enterprise Awards.

> **People can use enterprise to benefit their community.** Examples of this might include local people starting a new club or community organisation. Community or social enterprise also offers the possibility of creating new jobs and wealth for locals. This aspect of community development will be further discussed in *Chapter 20*, while a profile of Mary Davis, a well-known social entrepreneur, appears later in this chapter.

social entrepreneurs
IRELAND

▶ *www.socialentrepreneurs.ie*

> **A government can also show enterprise** by introducing new laws and policies or by exploring new avenues for job creation. In Ireland, the Department of Jobs, Enterprise and Innovation has responsibility for fulfilling this important role and it describes its mission as follows:

> To drive Ireland's competitiveness and productivity by creating the conditions where enterprise, entrepreneurship and innovation can flourish and quality employment opportunities are grown and maintained.

Recent examples include the jobs created by the development of the International Financial Services Centre (IFSC) in Dublin, the establishment of City and County Enterprise Boards (CEBs), as well as the introduction of a plastic bag levy designed to limit environmental pollution.

Ulster Bank HQ at the IFSC

A government appointed agency, the NCCA, periodically reviews and alters the school curriculum to ensure that students are equipped with knowledge and skills which are relevant to life in a modern society. This is another example of policy makers showing initiative and enterprise.

Entrepreneurs

Here is a list of some well-known **business entrepreneurs**:

> Henry Ford – Ford motor company

> Richard Branson – Virgin Music, Virgin Atlantic airline

> Moya Doherty – Riverdance

> Eddie Jordan – motorsport, Formula 1 racing

> Bill Gates – Microsoft computer software

> Anita Roddick – the Body Shop

> Bill Cullen – Renault (Ireland)

> Nicola Byrne – 11890

> Pat McDonagh – Supermacs

> Cathal O'Connell – Paddywagon tours

Henry Ford

Richard Branson

Moya Doherty

unit 2

Pat Mc Donagh

Anita Roddick

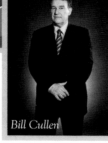

Nicola Byrne

Cathal O'Connell

Bill Cullen

Bill Gates

Eddie Jordan

Case Study

Cathal O'Connell is CEO of Paddywagon tours and creator of one of Ireland's most iconic brands. His business idea developed from his time spent travelling and working abroad and the realisation that the market for 'backpacker tourism' was being ignored in Ireland. When Cathal left UCD in the late 1980s there were very few job prospects in Ireland.

Over the years he held down a variety of jobs, which included working as a chef on a yacht and as a safari driver in Africa. He also amassed a great deal of experience from time spent working in the hospitality industry in New Zealand.

It was during his time in New Zealand that he got the inspiration for the Paddywagon business and set about targeting the backpacker tourism trade. This niche was largely ignored in Ireland at the time but Cathal felt there was a viable business opportunity waiting to be exploited by someone with his vision and work ethic.

Paddywagon was launched in 1998 and has grown to become the second biggest backpacker operation in Europe. With a fleet of 25 buses and almost 90,000 customers each year, Paddywagon is arguably the biggest tour business in Ireland. Cathal brings busloads of fun-loving, budget-conscious young holidaymakers to Ireland from all over the United States, Europe and Australia. His clients are seeking a holiday which is unique, interesting, fun-filled and relatively inexpensive.

Cathal describes his efforts as 'truly entrepreneurial' and outlines how hard work and belief were used to compensate for his lack of experience in the transport sector.

While Cathal is willing to delegate responsibility to his staff he understands that the success of his business hinges on his ability to keep an eye on all aspects of the operation. Cathal takes a very hands-on approach and is willing to play a variety of roles in the business. He still drives buses on a regular basis; he answers the phones at Paddy's Palace in Dublin and also cooks at their Killarney hostel.

Cathal describes himself as 'an ideas guy' and someone who 'comes up with good ideas and tries to make them happen'. His enthusiasm and passion for the business is infectious and he has enormous belief in the business concept.

Characteristics and skills of entrepreneurs

Characteristics are innate abilities which people are born with, whereas **skills tend to be learned over time**. The question of whether entrepreneurs are born or bred continues to be a source of debate. Some would say that entrepreneurs are instinctive people who have a natural ability and flair which ensures their success. Others would argue that it is possible to learn to be enterprising.

While there is no definitive answer to the question, it's likely that the truth lies somewhere between these two points of view. Certainly there are many people who exhibit an enterprising streak from a very early age. These are the people in your family, your class or your community who are always trying to develop some new idea or scheme.

Very often they fail in their objective, but this is rarely the end of them. Most will learn from their mistakes and will try again and again before eventually succeeding. This suggests that experience or learned behaviour also has an important role to play in entrepreneurial success.

If we look at the profiles of successful entrepreneurs they tend to exhibit many similar traits and skills, some of which include:

Enterprise characteristics	Enterprise skills
Creativity	Inner control
Innovation	Reality perception
Risk-taking	Risk management
Confidence	Decision-making
Decisiveness	Planning and goal setting
Determination	Time management
Flexibility	Ability to delegate
Resilience	Human relations management
Hard-working	Problem-solving

The above is certainly not an exhaustive list and there are many other examples of skills and characteristics associated with successful entrepreneurs.

Successful entrepreneurs tend to possess the following natural abilities:

« *syllabus signpost*
2.3.4

1 Being creative

Creativity involves developing genuinely new ideas or adding new impetus to old ideas.

Some entrepreneurs succeed by having a 'eureka moment' in which they make an unprecedented breakthrough. This allows them to bring a totally new and innovative product or service to market.

The German electronics company Philips pioneered the development of the compact disc in 1985, and its joint efforts with Sony revolutionised the way in which music was recorded and played. CDs utilised the most innovative laser technology which enabled the disc to be read without any direct physical contact. This produced a far superior sound quality to that offered by vinyl records and led to the dominant market position of the CD for over two decades.

When MP3 became a recognised industry standard in the mid 1990s it paved the way for a range of new innovations, including Windows media player, Napster (file sharing) and Apple iTunes.

Most entrepreneurs achieve success by improving on an existing idea, but this again requires a creative approach to product development and marketing. While Philips and Sony were the inventors of the CD, many copycat ('me too') products quickly emerged and brought commercial success to rival entrepreneurs.

This serves to highlight **the difference between an inventor and an entrepreneur.**

Inventors tend to be good at coming up with new ideas, but may not have the other skills required to successfully bring a product to market. Entrepreneurs, on the other hand, possess a broader range of skills which allows them to take an idea and turn it into a commercial success.

2 Being realistic risk-takers

There is a need to take calculated risks which, on the basis of careful analysis, seem likely to succeed. Starting and maintaining a profitable business involves a high degree of ongoing risk, so people who are risk-averse are unlikely to succeed as entrepreneurs simply because they dislike or are unwilling to take those risks. On the other hand, those who engage in unrealistic gambles are equally likely to fail. Sooner or later they will get it wrong and the business will suffer. A carefully considered and planned approach is the most likely route to success but this does not ignore the need to take realistic commercial risks.

Case Study

In 1986 Bill Cullen bought the Irish franchise for Renault car distribution for just £1. While the purchase price seems extraordinarily low, the deal also entailed taking on a debt burden of £18 million.

This was undoubtedly a massive risk for the entrepreneur, but Bill clearly felt it was one worth taking and succeeded in restoring the ailing franchise to profitability. Within ten years the business achieved a record turnover of €350 million.

Although the franchise was once again taken under Renault's direct control in 2006, Bill Cullen continues to own Ireland's largest Renault dealership, CityGate Motor Group. He also owns the Muckross Park Hotel in Killarney as well as the Europa Academy (training centre) in Swords, Co Dublin, which houses his famous 'Apprentice' boardroom.

3 Being flexible

The ability to adapt plans as circumstances change is a vital element of successful entrepreneurship. The business environment is very dynamic and this makes it highly unlikely that everything in a developing business will go exactly according to plan. For that reason a flexible approach is needed

Recall and Review

Why, do you think, did the Renault franchise have a purchase price of £1 and why was it not just given to Bill Cullen free of charge?

so as to meet the new reality. Entrepreneurs who fail to modify their approach are unlikely to meet the needs of the market, their investors or their customers.

4 Being resilient

This highlights an entrepreneur's ability to take a knock and keep going. It reflects the motto 'If at first you don't succeed, try, try and try again.' It is closely linked to the need for flexibility in the face of changing circumstances or unexpected barriers.

Case Study

James Dyson originally hoped to sell his idea for a bagless vacuum cleaner to existing manufacturers. Following constant rejection of his idea by industry leaders he set up his own manufacturing plant. This example clearly illustrates the flexibility and resilience which turned this prolific inventor into a genuine entrepreneur.

5 Being proactive

Just as important as a visionary approach is a willingness to take action or instigate change, rather than waiting for someone else to do it. This involves **showing initiative.** While there are obvious risks involved in fledgling industries, they are frequently outweighed by the increased market share and profitability available to early adopters. Those who choose to enter these markets at a later stage are said to be 'reactive'.

Successful entrepreneurs will need to learn the following skills:

« syllabus signpost 2.3.3

1 Being future-focused

Successful entrepreneurs need to look at future demand and formulate plans to stay ahead of competitors. They have a sense of vision which allows them to anticipate customer needs and therefore steal a lead on rivals. Think of the entrepreneurs who pioneered the mobile phone industry. At the outset, the technology was futuristic and impractical. Over time, however, their foresight proved to be realistic and well founded, leaving them in an ideal position to reap the rewards of a developing global industry.

In 1989 Charles Dunstan, a UK mobile phone retailer, established the first Carphone Warehouse shop. Even though the fledgling industry was in its infancy and had a very uncertain future, Dunston and his partner David Ross decided to act on their business instincts. Their instincts and actions have since proved to be well justified and the Carphone Warehouse is now Europe's largest independent mobile phone retailer. The group operates over 2,000 stores, including 70 here in Ireland.

2 The ability to delegate

The workload involved in developing a business can be overwhelming for many would-be entrepreneurs. Some, however, have developed the skill of delegation, which allows them to pass some responsibility to others and thereby reduce their own personal workload. The key to successful delegation is to prioritise the needs of the business and to offload less critical tasks to those who are capable of fulfilling them. This leaves the entrepreneur free to focus on the most important aspects of business development. Richard Branson, the head of the Virgin Group, adopts this approach when managing a highly diversified business, spread across several industry sectors.

3 Decision-making ability

A capacity to be decisive and take necessary action is also an important criterion for successful entrepreneurs. They should have an ability to act on the spot and a willingness to take responsibility for decisions. Failure to make important decisions or unreasonable delays when making decisions can be very costly in terms of missed opportunities.

Since many entrepreneurs become successful business managers, they are generally competent at carrying out the tasks associated with management, i.e. planning, organising, controlling, leading, motivating and communicating. While this illustrates some similarities between managers and entrepreneurs, there are also a number of differences and these are outlined more fully in Unit 3.

Motives for entrepreneurship

People often decide to start their own businesses for some of the following reasons:

> **Independence:** The opportunity to be their own boss, and be in a position to make important decisions can be very appealing.

> **Income:** The earnings potential offered by business ownership is a strong motive for some entrepreneurs.

> **Challenge:** Some entrepreneurs constantly seek to test themselves and see if they have what it takes to succeed. This is similar to Maslow's 'self-actualisation'.

> **Redundancy:** The loss of employment may cause some people to contemplate creating a job for themselves and also provide them with the finances to achieve it.

> **Creativity:** A new business enterprise may provide an outlet for individual creativity and expression which isn't possible in paid employment.

Intrapreneurship

This occurs when an employee within an existing organisation acts in an enterprising way for the benefit of that organisation. These employees choose to remain with their current employer rather than attempting to set up their own business. Many companies encourage employees to show enterprise in their existing jobs, and will generally provide financial rewards for the most effective ideas. Examples include an employee who develops a new and more efficient production technique for an existing product, or develops an idea for an entirely new product.

Case Study

Sticky 'Post-it' labels were the brainchild of Arthur Fry, an employee of the 3M company who was tired of losing important information written on bits of paper. He first developed the idea as a bookmark using a revolutionary low-tack glue invented by a colleague. Post-it note products are now sold in over a hundred countries worldwide.

Cadbury's 'Time Out' bar was developed by employees at its plant in Coolock in Dublin.

Four years of research and development were needed to turn the original concept into a marketable product, but the product quickly became the most successful ever developed by Cadbury in Ireland.

Both of these examples clearly illustrate the potential benefits to a business of harnessing and promoting 'intrapreneurship'.

The importance of enterprise

For individuals:

> Enterprise provides a pathway to self-employment for those who have lost their jobs or who have ambitions to run their own business.

« syllabus signpost 2.3.5

For business:

> Enterprise enables an existing business to become more efficient and can result in cost savings. This is achieved by redesigning products and operating systems or adopting innovative approaches to production.

unit 2

> Intrapreneurship also provides existing businesses with a source of new ideas and products.

> Enterprise can provide existing businesses with a competitive advantage over rivals. This is especially true when it results from innovative new products and is reinforced by intellectual property (IP) rights such as patents and trademarks.

> Enterprise and innovation can also help overcome competitive disadvantages, such as higher costs or poor brand identity. Customers will often seek the latest technology and will be less concerned about issues like pricing and tradition.

 **e.g. Example**

> The enterprising approach taken by Nokia enabled that relatively small company from Finland to become the world's largest producer of mobile phones. This was in spite of the market presence of technology giants from both Asia and the USA.

For society:

> Commercial enterprise can improve the economic wellbeing of entire nations and offers the prospect of increased employment and wealth. This is because innovation tends to improve competitiveness and this in turn boosts economic growth.

« syllabus signpost 2.3.2

In recognition of this benefit, successive Irish governments have focused their efforts and resources on the creation of a 'smart economy'. This type of economy is driven by enterprise and innovation and relies on using knowledge and education to create high-value products.

> Enterprise helps to provide society with a means of improving the position and status of its citizens. Social innovators have the potential to fundamentally alter the way in which services are delivered to some sections of society.

Social entrepreneurs possess the same characteristics, skills and ambition which we associate with business entrepreneurs, but rather than pursuing profit or personal gain they direct their efforts towards making positive changes to our society.

Social entrepreneurs tend to work closely with community groups and see these organisations as vehicles for achieving social improvement.

Case Study

Social enterprise in action

Mary Davis is a social entrepreneur and was given a Person of the Year award in 2003 for organising the hugely successful Special Olympic Games in Dublin. The 2003 Games were the largest sporting event in the world that year and Ireland was the first country outside of North America to host the Games.

Mary Davis began working with children with special educational needs at St Michael's House, Ballymun, in the 1980s and was appointed chief executive officer (CEO) of Special Olympics Ireland in 1989.

She was appointed to the Council of State (a presidential advisory board) in 2004 and was a candidate in the 2011 presidential election. During the campaign she repeated her call for a wide-scale national debate which would enable the reform and renewal of Irish society.

unit 2

Chapter Review Diagram – Enterprise

- **Definition of enterprise** — Enterprise
  - Personal (life)
  - Business
  - Government
  - Community
- **Entrepreneurs**
  - Role
  - Characteristics
  - Skills
- **Motives for entrepreneurship**
- **Enterprise at work**
  - Intrepreneurship
  - Examples
- **Importance of enterprise**

Q Chapter Review Questions

1 Explain the four factors of production.

2 Explain the term 'enterprise'.

3 Identify three areas of life where you can find enterprise in action.

4 In enterprise, explain what is meant by having a vision.

5 Explain the term 'entrepreneur'.

6 Name four entrepreneurs in the world of business.

7 Name five characteristics and five skills which an entrepreneur should have to demonstrate authority.

8 Describe three enterprise skills required by an entrepreneur.

9 What are the motives of entrepreneurs?

10 Explain, using an example, what is meant by the term 'intrapreneur'.

11 Outline the term 'proactive' associated with entrepreneurship.

12 What are the reasons for the growth of enterprise in Ireland over the past decade?

Q Questions · Ordinary Level

1

Jason saw a business opportunity in January 2010 when snow and bad weather hit the country. He recognised that there was a huge demand for snow to be cleared from housing estates, pavements and private driveways.

He set up in partnership with his friend Gerry. They got financial help from their parents and a loan from the bank. They imported three mini road sweeper machines from Sweden, which could be used to clear snow and ice in winter.

During the major snowfall before Christmas 2010, Jason and Gerry had to employ two part-time staff to help them with the extra workload. Jason decided to attend night classes to learn more about being an employer and about taxation.   *LCOL 2011*

(a) Outline three enterprising characteristics/skills displayed by Jason.   *(15 marks)*

2

Andrew Roche, a qualified plumber, has recently set up his own business. He provides services for households and small businesses in his local area. He has rented premises and is considering the purchase of a van. He intends to employ other staff as his business expands and knows that this may require focus on the area of human resource management.   *LCOL 2007*

(a) Outline **four** characteristics of an entrepreneur.

(b) Describe **three** enterprising skills/characteristics that
Andrew has as an entrepreneur.   *(15 marks)*

3 Distinguish between an entrepreneur and an intrapreneur.

4 List **two** enterprise skills and illustrate how they could be used
in the home and the community.

5 Entrepreneurs need confidence, decisiveness and motivation. Explain the importance of each of these characteristics and use an example in each case to support your answer.

6 Describe **two** benefits of enterprise: (a) in the community, (b) in the home,
(c) in the public sector.

7 Explain what is meant by being a 'realistic risk-taker'.

Questions · Higher Level

1 Read the information supplied and answer the question which follows.

Colm has decided to form a tidy towns committee in his local village and enter the 'tidiest village' category of the National Tidy Towns competition in 2013.

Discuss **four** entrepreneurial skills that Colm will require in developing this local community initiative.

LCHL 2011 (20 marks)

2

'Being decisive, creative and being prepared to take risks are personal characteristics often associated with entrepreneurs.'

Discuss these characteristics and support your answer with examples.

LCHL 2008 (15 marks)

3 Describe **three** enterprise skills required of an entrepreneur.   *LCHL 2007 (15 marks)*

4 Using examples, analyse the importance of **four** different enterprising skills and relate **two** to business and two to the community.   *LCHL 2006 (20 marks)*

5 Describe your understanding of the term 'entrepreneurship'.

6 Compare and contrast entrepreneurship and intrapreneurship.

7 'Enterprise does not only happen in business.' Illustrate, using examples, the importance of enterprise in other areas of life.

8 Using examples, distinguish between risk taking and risk management.

9 Describe the impact of enterprise on the development of the local economy.

10 Identify the personal characteristics normally associated with entrepreneurial business people.   *LCHL 2003 (20 marks)*

11 Illustrate how entrepreneurial skills might be used to enhance either
(a) the local community **or** (b) a government department.   *LCHL 2003 (30 marks)*

unit 2

Q Applied Business Question

Adventure Ireland Ltd

John and Edward Smyth realised a lifetime ambition in 2006 by setting up their own outdoor pursuits business called Adventure Ireland Ltd. The dream of owning their own business was first conceived in school when their innovative business teacher had encouraged all of her students to take part in a student enterprise competition. While they did not win any prizes that year, John and Edward began to develop their business plan and had an opportunity to explore the benefits and challenges of business ownership. In the decade prior to setting up their business, they had both qualified as outdoor pursuits instructors before setting off to gain valuable work experience in New Zealand, South Africa and Canada.

They had always shown themselves to be independent-minded and adventurous young men and they relentlessly pursued their career ambitions while travelling abroad. The brothers worked very hard and their commitment and enthusiasm eventually brought promotion to managerial positions. While in New Zealand Edward took the opportunity to put some of his innovative ideas to the test and was well rewarded by his employer when market share and profitability of the business increased.

Despite these successes, however, the Smyths made a decision to return home and start their own business in Ireland. John and Edward had great belief in their own abilities and were confident of success despite the economic slowdown and the competitive nature of the industry.

Their local County Enterprise Board (CEB) was able to provide them with a small grant, which enabled them to conduct a feasibility study. After a detailed analysis of the opportunities and risks in the market they opened Adventure Ireland Ltd close to their hometown of Naas.

They had great difficulty raising finance, but thanks to a loan from their parents, their own savings and a further capital grant from the CEB, they were able to get the business up and running. The business grew rapidly and after six years now employs fifteen people, in different areas of the business.

John and Edward have worked hard for their success and are pleased to be back home in Kildare. As the economy continues to struggle through a recession they have noticed the negative impact it is having on the local community. They are currently working with the local VEC to see if they can provide a much-needed facility or club for young people in the area.

(a) Outline your understanding of the term 'intrapreneurship' and illustrate how it was effectively employed in the case study above. *(20 marks)*

(b) Describe the enterprising skills/characteristics displayed by John and Edward in their business Adventure Ireland Ltd. *(30 marks)*

(c) 'Entrepreneurship can have a positive impact on many areas beyond commercial businesses.' Outline briefly the important role played by enterprise and innovation in the public sector and the local community. Illustrate your answer with appropriate reference to the text outlined above. *(30 marks)*

Unit Three
Managing I

Chapter 5
Introduction to Management and Management Skills: Leading and Motivating

Syllabus Outcomes

On completion, the student should be able to:

» 3.4.1 Define management;

» 3.4.2 Identify the importance of management skills in areas such as home, school, local community, government departments and business start-up;

» 3.4.3 List the characteristics of managers;

» 3.4.4 Explain the basic management skills;

» 3.4.11 Differentiate between enterprise and management (HL);

» 3.4.12 Explain the contribution of both managers and entrepreneurs to business (HL).

Introduction to Management

What is management?

Management is **the process of achieving results through resources.** These may include:

> **Natural resources**

> **Capital resources:** machinery, equipment and vehicles

> **Human resources:** staff (see *Chapter 11: Human Resource Management*)

> **Financial resources:** money (see *Chapter 8: Household and Business Management: Finance*)

« syllabus signpost 3.4.1 & 3.4.2

The job of a business manager is to combine these resources in the most effective way in order to achieve corporate goals. As outlined in previous chapters, the overriding objective for most businesses is profitability.

Management and the skills associated with it are relevant to many areas of our lives and our society:

> On a personal level, we commonly focus on **time management**, and sticking to a study plan is an example of time management in action. Managing your time carefully represents an important step towards your overall goal of exam success.

> Your school has a **Board of Management** and a principal who implements its management policy on a day-to-day basis.

> If you play sport, your **team** will almost certainly have a **manager**, and it is his or her responsibility to get the best results possible out of the players.

In the very same way, every household, organisation and government tries to manage its resources so as to maximise its results and live within its means. These examples all illustrate the fact that management is an integral part of our everyday lives.

The **management process** involves:

> **Management Activities:**
  planning – organising – controlling

> **Management Skills:**
  leading – motivating – communicating

It has already been mentioned that managers exist in **business,** in **government,** in the **community** and in **schools,** but no matter what type of organisation they are running these are the things that managers do.

If we examine the behaviour of successful managers we can see a range of skills and characteristics that seem to provide optimal results.

« *syllabus signpost*
3.4.3

Management characteristics

In all walks of life managers typically show the following characteristics:

> **Decisiveness:** This is the ability to make decisions and take appropriate action.

> **Flexibility:** This means being able to alter one's approach or goals when circumstances change. Sometimes things do not go according to plan and managers need to be able to 'think on their feet'.

> **Innovation:** Managers need to be capable of adopting a fresh approach to their work. They need to be willing to try innovative approaches when it comes to issues like motivation and communication.

> **Hard work:** Managers must be prepared to put in long hours in order to make the business a success. They must inspire their staff and are often required to lead by example. This also reflects the fact that the actions of management set the tone for the culture within an organisation.

> **Good with people:** Managers spend a great deal of their time working with other people. For this reason they need to have the type of personality which enables them to interact well with others.

> **Charisma:** This is the ability to attract, inspire and influence people. Some leaders have extremely charismatic personalities and people seem to be drawn to them and take on board their values and beliefs. In business this characteristic is particularly useful for a salesperson or a manager. Examples of well-known charismatic leaders include Ghandi, Martin Luther King, Adolf Hitler and Steve Jobs.

Many of the characteristics listed above are similar to those displayed by **entrepreneurs;** however there are also a number of **differences between the two roles.** These are evidenced in the following ways:

« *syllabus signpost*
3.4.11 & 3.4.12

Idea generation

Entrepreneurs come up with new ideas and attempt to develop new businesses. For many entrepreneurs the goal of bringing their idea to market is a major source of motivation and satisfaction.

Managers, on the other hand, are charged with implementing the ideas of entrepreneurs and they achieve this through the management of resources. While managers need to display innovation in their co-ordination of these resources it is not the same as the creative process pursued by entrepreneurs.

Risk-taking

Entrepreneurs who attempt to bring their ideas to market run the risk of personal financial loss or bankruptcy. This is especially true for sole traders, who have unlimited liability. This means they risk losing personal assets in order to pay off business debts. Poor decision-making can impact on profitability and can have far-reaching consequences for the business and the entrepreneur.

Managers who perform poorly jeopardise performance-related bonuses and ultimately risk losing their job and reputation. While this has serious short-term consequences, it is arguably not as significant as the risk borne by entrepreneurs.

Communication

Entrepreneurs are self-driven, and often seek to carry the business idea single-handedly. The may lack the need or ability to motivate others, and as such may not develop the necessary communications skills.

Managers, however, must be able to co-ordinate the actions of others in order to achieve goals. Since communication is such an integral part of this process it's fair to say that excellent communications skills are critical to managerial success.

It should be noted that in some organisations the roles of entrepreneur and manager are combined, while in others an entrepreneur might need to assume the role of manager as their business expands.

Management Skills: Leadership

« syllabus signpost 3.4.4

Leadership is the art of getting someone else to do something you want done because he wants to do it.
Dwight Eisenhower

Leadership reflects a person's ability to **influence the actions and behaviour of others**. Leaders try to direct this behaviour in the pursuit of certain goals.

Brian O'Driscoll

While leaders often 'lead by example' it is unlikely that the efforts of one person alone will enable the organisation to achieve its goals, so the real power of effective leadership lies in the ability to have a positive impact on the behaviour and actions of others. A team captain, for example, tries to direct the efforts of all players towards the goal of winning the competition, and in a similar way, business managers will direct staff members towards improved efficiency and profitability.

Pope Benedict XVI

In large organisations it may not be possible for a leader to manage all available resources and in these circumstances effective leadership may also involve some degree of **delegation**.

Delegation means passing on responsibility for certain decisions or outcomes to others. For example, a marketing manager may have overall responsibility for a marketing strategy, but may choose to delegate responsibility for the market research element to a subordinate. Delegation is not only effective as a time-management tool, it also provides other staff with an opportunity to improve their skills and levels of motivation.

Enda Kenny

There is evidence to suggest that several clearly identifiable **leadership styles** exist and each is closely linked to a manager's personality.

Activity

Discuss the leadership roles played by all of the above people. Make a list of any similar skills or characteristics that they display or possess.

Autocratic leaders:

'My way or the highway'

This type of leader is very **controlling,** and often motivates through fear and intimidation.

Autocratic leaders are seen as being **undemocratic.** They prefer to make all key decisions themselves and don't tend to give much responsibility to employees. They frequently dictate instructions to staff and tell them exactly what to do. Employees who fail to follow these clear instructions run the risk of serious sanctions or dismissal.

unit 3

Example

In a sporting context Jack Charlton and to a lesser extent Giovanni Trappatoni can be seen as examples of an autocratic type of leadership approach. Jack Charlton managed the Republic of Ireland soccer squad between 1985 and 1995. He wanted his teams to play a particular style of 'high pressure' direct football and insisted that all players must fulfil very specific roles within the team.

Jack Charlton

Henry Ford (automobiles) and John D. Rockefeller (oil) were two giants of American industry who displayed similarly autocratic characteristics when building their business empires. They rarely delegated responsibility and those who opposed their vision for the business were ignored or sacked.

John D. Rockefeller

Both men tended to surround themselves with like-minded individuals as this limited the need for debate and democracy. Ford in particular placed too much value on his own leadership and made no attempt to prepare a successor. This rigid leadership style caused problems for the business at a time when a dynamic automobile industry called for a more flexible management approach. He was eventually sidelined by his own board of directors.

Henry Ford

There are very few examples of 'old school' autocratic leadership in the modern world of business and this leadership style might be best suited to organisations where strict standards of service are required or in the media industry where production deadlines are rigidly enforced.

Case Study

Steve Jobs is an interesting case study in business leadership and while his leadership style has variously been described as 'unique', 'iconic' or 'transformational', he certainly seemed to display some autocratic elements.

His death in October 2011 is likely to increase the amount of material written on the topic, but there is already clear evidence that Jobs's leadership style followed a vertical, top-down approach. Decision-making at Apple was always swift, sometimes instinctive, with communications always coming from the top.

There are many reports to suggest that Jobs was both a visionary and a perfectionist and, while teamwork (a feature of democratic leadership) played an important role in Apple's day-to-day operations, staff often struggled to meet the targets and exacting standards of their leader.

Joe Nocera, writing in the *New York Times*, observed that Steve Jobs "violated every rule of management. He was not a consensus-builder but a dictator who listened mainly to his own intuition. He was a maniacal micromanager. He had an astonishing aesthetic sense, which business people almost always lack. He could be absolutely brutal in meetings: I watched him eviscerate staff members for their 'bozo ideas.'... He never mellowed, never let up on Apple employees, never stopped relying on his singular instincts in making decisions about how Apple products should look and how they should work."

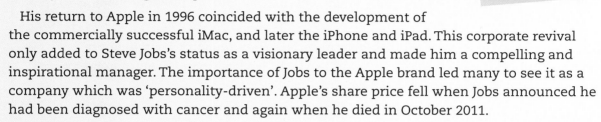

Steve Jobs suffered the same fate as Henry Ford and left the company he had founded having lost a power struggle with the board of directors in 1985. Apple's commercial fortunes declined in the years following his departure.

His return to Apple in 1996 coincided with the development of the commercially successful iMac, and later the iPhone and iPad. This corporate revival only added to Steve Jobs's status as a visionary leader and made him a compelling and inspirational manager. The importance of Jobs to the Apple brand led many to see it as a company which was 'personality-driven'. Apple's share price fell when Jobs announced he had been diagnosed with cancer and again when he died in October 2011.

It remains to be seen how the company will develop in his absence, but what Steve Jobs succeeded in doing was to create successful teams of workers who produced visionary products which are loved by millions of consumers worldwide.

Whether his autocratic approach was driven by his exacting vision or his overpowering ego is a matter for debate, but he appears to have taken strong autocratic traits and successfully applied them to a modern business environment.

unit 3

In a wider social context, the **armed forces** represent the most obvious example of an overtly autocratic style of leadership, and this is based on the need for soldiers to follow orders in an unquestioning manner. Can you imagine a situation where soldiers take 'time out' to discuss all orders given to them by superiors? It's likely that their response would be slow and uncoordinated and would be rendered ineffective.

Benefits of an autocratic leadership style:

› **Effective in routine situations:** Autocratic leadership can be successfully applied to routine tasks, or where staff has little scope for creativity anyway. Managers may also find that some employees are more comfortable with a work environment where they follow instructions since they may be unwilling or unqualified to innovate. Although these staff are unlikely to develop to their full potential, they may be very competent and productive in the limited roles they play.

› **Helps reach quick decisions:** Autocratic leaders are also useful where a quick decision is required. This would apply to a situation where a short-term opportunity arises and an immediate response will allow a business to benefit from it.

Drawbacks of an autocratic leadership style:

› **De-motivates staff:** A common criticism of autocratic leadership is that by denying staff opportunities to express an opinion or act creatively, it may leave them feeling unfulfilled and unmotivated. This has implications for both staff morale and productivity.

› **Over-reliance on management:** In an environment where staff are used to receiving orders from management or where they fear punishment for bad decisions, employees are likely to avoid making decisions at all. This increases the level of dependency on management and may result in decision-making 'bottlenecks'. As overloaded managers struggle to cope with every aspect of business operations they are likely to become stressed and are prone to making poor decisions.

For these reasons and because of a higher regard for their human resources, most modern businesses have rejected autocratic styles of leadership in favour of more inclusive and collaborative approaches

Democratic leaders

Democratic leaders are more likely to **seek the opinions of others** when making decisions.

Decisions made democratically tend to be better as they take on board all available opinions and advice. As a result of being consulted and listened to, workers are often more compliant, more motivated and more likely to display intrapreneurship.

Democratic leaders also have a much higher degree of trust in their subordinates and frequently **delegate authority**.

 **Example**

Japanese workers are encouraged to develop their sense of loyalty to the company in a culture which values both teamwork and intrapreneurship. This culture of teamwork and collective responsibility is facilitated by regular discussions between management and subordinates.

Bill Gates

Quality circles also allow employees to discuss their specific roles within the organisation and enable them to make suggestions about how best to improve the operation of the business.

Bill Gates, Chairman of the Board of Directors at Microsoft has adopted this participative style of leadership and decentralises authority by involving his subordinates in decision-making.

When asked about his own particular leadership style, Jerry Greenfield (a co-founder of Ben & Jerry's ice cream), describes himself as being 'a pretty laid-back kind of guy' and someone who tries to run his business on the basis of 'give and take'.

Jerry Greenfield

Benefits of a democratic leadership approach:

› **Better decisions:** Democratic leadership means that managers are willing to consult widely and take on board the views of others before making a decision. By listening to all of the available information managers can make more informed decisions.

› **Improved participation and motivation:** Workers like to feel valued and are more likely to accept decisions if they feel they've been part of that process. There is also likely to be an increased level of motivation and intrapreneurship in the organisation.

› **Improved industrial relations:** The industrial relations climate in the business is likely to improve as the culture of transparency and consultation eases employee concerns and reduces their mistrust of management.

Drawbacks of a democratic leadership approach:

› **Slower decision-making:** The time taken to consult with others is very likely to delay the decision-making process and this can be a problem in a very dynamic business environment where swift action is required.

› **Poor outcome:** There is some fear that the eventual outcome or decision may be poor, as it tries to accommodate the views of so many. There is a danger that in trying to keep everybody happy, the end result may not be ideal. The cliché which suggests that 'a camel is a horse designed by a committee' illustrates this difficulty and highlights the potential pitfall of too much consultation.

Overall, however, despite these concerns, a democratic approach is a far more inclusive and more popular approach than autocratic leadership.

Laissez-faire leaders

This type of leadership approach provides subordinates with **greater levels of freedom** when it comes to setting and pursuing goals.

> *The best executive is the one who has sense enough to pick good people to do what he wants done, and self-restraint to keep from meddling with them while they do it.*
> *Theodore Roosevelt*

Laissez-faire managers act as **facilitators rather than dictators** and provide general targets and resources, before stepping back to allow subordinates get on with it themselves. This is sometimes called **spectator leadership.**

unit **3**

In order for this leadership approach to succeed **workers need to be highly capable and motivated**, otherwise results can be off-target or inconsistent. It tends to be used in high-tech industries which rely on well-educated and highly autonomous employees.

It also lends itself to a business environment which supports teamwork. For example, a company producing computer software may allow a team of engineers and programmers to develop a new application. Management will set the overall objectives, provide the necessary resources and monitor progress, but the employees will be given the freedom to operate creatively on a day-to-day basis.

e.g. Example

In his highly diversified Virgin group of businesses, Richard Branson admits to having a 'hands-off' approach. Branson sets and co-ordinates overall corporate policy, but he delegates a high degree of responsibility to professional business managers right throughout the group. While this type of leadership approach clearly reflects Branson's personality and business philosophy, it was partly developed out of necessity as he began to move the focus of his business away from its origins in the music industry. Faced with managing a diverse array of business interests, many of which he had little practical experience of, the entrepreneur had little choice but to rely heavily on his capable management team.

Benefits of a laissez-faire leadership approach:

> **High levels of intrapreneurship:** Since staff are not told exactly what to do all the time there is a requirement that they be able to 'think on their feet'. This offers the possibility of innovative solutions to everyday problems.

> **Improved motivation:** Greater autonomy and worker participation help increase the levels of staff motivation and build a stronger sense of loyalty to the business.

> **Effective decision-making:** As decisions are made by those directly involved in the tasks and there is less dependency on management input, the decisions taken are likely to be more informed and should be arrived at more quickly.

Drawbacks of a laissez-faire leadership approach:

> **Lack of control:** Suitable management control systems need to be put in place in order to ensure that employees stick to the overall objectives. This may involve regular progress meeting or audits designed to ensure that targets are being met.

> **Not suitable for all staff:** A flexible leadership style is not suited to all businesses and all employees and so managers need to utilise it appropriately. For example, staff who are not used to making decisions or who lack decision-making skills will tend to struggle in this type of environment. This will lead to poor decision-making and will have negative consequences for the business.

Conclusion

The leadership style adopted by top management tends to reflect the **organisational culture** of the firm. This describes the overall atmosphere and values throughout a business and has been defined as 'the way we do things 'round here'. Modern, high-tech business tends to adopt more flexible styles as it suits the dynamic world in which it operates.

It should also be borne in mind that not all employees respond equally well to a chosen leadership style. Effective managers need to consider a range of factors when choosing a leadership approach. These include the personalities and needs of their staff, the culture of the organisation and the urgency of the situation.

The best managers are those who are capable of using the most appropriate leadership style based on their analysis of these variables.

« syllabus signpost 3.4.4

Management Skills: Motivation

Motivation is about what makes people do things. In business terms, it's what makes people work!

There are two general theories of motivation which help explain the issues involved:

> Maslow's Hierarchy of Needs

> McGregor's Theory X, Theory Y

Maslow – Hierarchy of Needs

Abraham Maslow produced a theory of human motivation which suggests that people seek to satisfy several different types of need as they grow and develop. Maslow's hierarchy of needs is generally portrayed in the form of a pyramid, with the most basic needs at the base and the higher-order needs closer to the top.

As each need is satisfied it ceases to motivate and is replaced by a higher-level need.

> **Physiological needs** are basic bodily needs which have to be satisfied in order to keep a person alive. They include the need for food, clothing and shelter.

unit 3

Workers satisfy these needs by spending their wages on goods and services, so businesses can motivate staff by providing them with adequate pay.

When you start working for the first time you may use your wages to pay rent, buy food, maintain a car and have a social life. You may view your job simply in terms of the lifestyle it supports and so long as your income level meets these needs you will be happy to keep working.

> **Safety and security needs** represent our desire for stability and consistency in our lives. We like to feel that our health and wellbeing are secure and employers can meet these needs by ensuring a safe and comfortable working environment.

Once your basic physical needs are met, you may begin to look for job security. This might reflect changed circumstances in your life. Perhaps you have aspirations to settle down in a long-term relationship or buy a property. This new reality might cause you to re-evaluate your job and it may cause you to shift your focus away from the monetary rewards and on to the long-term job security it offers. With a mortgage to pay and a family to support a job with good pay and long-term prospects becomes a necessity. A manager who realises this may be able to motivate you with the offer of a long-term contract.

> **Social/acceptance needs** are about love and a sense of belonging. When we join an organisation we need to feel we will fit in. This is really about shared goals and our ability to get along with our peers or co-workers. If staff do not get this reassurance they will begin to feel isolated and vulnerable. Eventually this will undermine their belief in the organisation and may result in a decision to leave. Few people are willing to stay in a job when they feel unwanted.

Many employers spend a great deal of time and money on looking after the social wellbeing of staff. Corporate team-building and the development of sports and social clubs illustrate the lengths to which employers will go to ensure staff feel a sense of affinity with their company.

> **Esteem needs** represent human desire for recognition and status. We try to develop a strong sense of self-esteem which may be enhanced when other see us as important. It's necessary for employees to be assured about their importance to the organisation and employers can satisfy this need by adding status to a worker's position. Being given a promotion or getting your own office might be clear indicators that your employer holds you in high regard. Companies which have a policy of internal promotion provide staff with a ladder to achievement and this can have a very strong motivating effect on those with management ambition.

> **Self-actualisation** is about striving to fulfil your full potential. It involves being all we can possibly be. A company wishing to hold on to senior staff will need to ensure that they are provided with work that is both challenging and fulfilling. Failure to do so is likely to leave them feeling unmotivated and may cause them to seek new challenges. After many years of senior management in a business an employee may decide to go it alone and set up their own business. For many, this represents both a dream and an immense challenge.

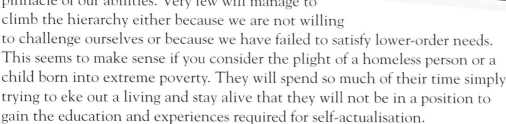

While we are all capable of great things, Maslow's theory suggests that many of us will never reach the pinnacle of our abilities. Very few will manage to climb the hierarchy either because we are not willing to challenge ourselves or because we have failed to satisfy lower-order needs. This seems to make sense if you consider the plight of a homeless person or a child born into extreme poverty. They will spend so much of their time simply trying to eke out a living and stay alive that they will not be in a position to gain the education and experiences required for self-actualisation.

Evaluation

When evaluating Maslow's theory it's important to understand that human needs and motives will vary over time and also with each individual. While Maslow's is a useful general theory which recognises this individuality, it certainly cannot be applied to all people in all situations.

For managers, the key to using the theory involves trying to identify the stage at which each employee finds him- or herself. Once this is established they can set about providing suitable rewards. Managers also need to recognise that money may not motivate all people in all situations.

Despite its limitations, Maslow's hierarchy provides human resource managers with useful insights into the needs and desires of employees as they develop their careers. Businesses which match these needs with appropriate rewards will be most likely to retain the loyalty and commitment of staff.

McGregor – Theory X and Theory Y

The American social psychologist Douglas McGregor first proposed his famous X–Y theory in his book *The Human Side of Enterprise* (1960). This well-known theory of motivation suggests there are two broad approaches to the management and motivation of employees.

According to McGregor, **Theory X managers believe most workers are lazy**; that they **dislike work**. Managers also hold the view that staff are **resistant to change** and are **untrustworthy**.

This set of beliefs about workers allows managers to justify close control of their staff. It implies that managers who seek to motivate their employees using a Theory X approach are likely to rely on fear and intimidation.

Employees are given very little autonomy, and can only be motivated by financial rewards. All in all, this rather bleak view of staff justifies the imposition of an autocratic style of leadership, and for that reason **Theory X managers are often referred to as 'controller' managers**.

An opposing view is taken by **Theory Y managers**, who believe that **workers can enjoy work, can be trusted, and can be flexible**.

These managers argue that employees who are provided with interesting and challenging work will prove themselves capable of very high levels of motivation and productivity.

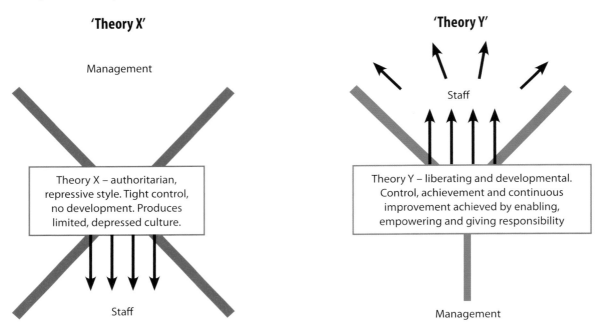

© Alan Chapman 2001-4. Downloaded from www.businessballs.com September 2011. Diagram Alan Chapman, based on Douglas McGregor's X-Y Theory. Used with permission of www.businessballs.com. Not to be sold or published. More information at http://www.businessballs.com/mcgregor.htm

Their beliefs appeal to higher-level motivators and justify increased delegation, empowerment, flexibility and training. In contrast to their Theory X counterparts, Theory Y managers favour more democratic or laissez-faire styles of leadership. **Theory Y managers are regarded as 'facilitator' managers.**

Evaluation

McGregor again provides a useful general theory that recognises worker differences and attempts to offer guidelines to management. A major criticism of this approach is that it seems far too simplistic to suggest all managers fit into two broad categories, but it nonetheless illustrates two contrasting approaches to managing and motivating staff.

The overall suggestion is that Theory X managers are likely to create a climate of hostility and resentment within the organisation and this will be reflected in poor levels of employee motivation and productivity.

Theory Y seems to offer a more enlightened and modern approach, which recognises the value of staff and seeks to nurture their intrinsic desire to work hard and develop.

 www.businessballs.com/mcgregor.htm

Chapter Review Diagram – Management Skills: Leading and Motivating

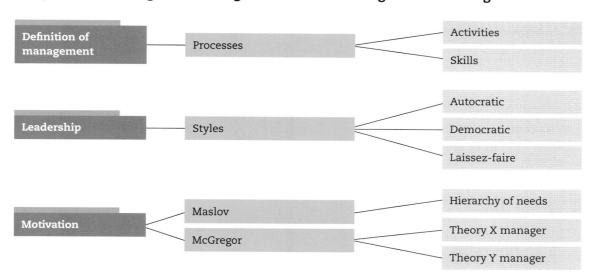

unit
3

 Chapter Review Questions

1 Define management.

2 What are the key characteristics of effective managers?

3 Discuss the statement: 'Management is relevant in many areas of life'.

4 Outline two differences between the roles of managers and entrepreneurs.

5 Distinguish between management skills and management activities.

6 Several clearly identifiable leadership styles exist and each is linked closely to a manager's personality.

   (i) List three leadership styles that managers may have.

   (ii) Outline the main characteristics of each leadership style.

7 Describe what is meant by the term 'organisational culture'.

8 Illustrate Maslow's Hierarchy of Needs.

9 Distinguish between the motivational approaches of Theory X and Theory Y managers, as set out by Douglas McGregor.

Q Questions · Ordinary Level

1

> Brady's Hotel is a family-run business, situated in a seaside town. It provides accommodation, restaurants and bar services. Mark Brady has overall responsibility for managing the hotel. He wants to upgrade the hotel. Despite his plans for the hotel, Mark has noticed that some of the hotel staff lack motivation. His focus now is to try and improve staff motivation.
>
> *LCOL 2011*

(a) Outline **three** methods that Mark could use to improve staff motivation.   *(20 marks)*

(b) Maslow's Hierarchy of Needs is presented below:

   (i) Physical Needs, (ii) ……………………………, (iii) ………………………………,

   (iv) Esteem, (v) ……………………………

Briefly explain **two** of the five levels.   *(20 marks)*

2

> Roisín Murphy worked as a hairdresser in her home town for six years. She left her job as a result of poor employer–employee relationships in the workplace. She believes her former boss Michael was an autocratic leader.
>
> Roisín is an enterprising person and has just opened her own hair salon employing three staff. She completed a start your own business course, planned her business well and organised the finance. She regularly consults with staff over business issues and values their opinions. She pays her staff well and praises the high standard and quality of their work. She is an excellent communicator and believes in McGregor's Theory Y on motivation.
>
> *LCOL 2010*

(a) Explain the term autocratic (authoritarian) leader.   *(10 marks)*

(b) Outline **three** enterprising skills/characteristics displayed by Roisín.   *(15 marks)*

(c) Explain McGregor's Theory Y on Motivation, with reference to the above text.

   (15 marks)

3 Outline **two** characteristics of a democratic leader.   *LCOL 2009 (15 marks)*

4 Autocratic, Democratic and Laissez-faire are three styles of leadership.

Describe the characteristics of **two** of these leadership styles.   *LCOL 2007 (20 marks)*

Q Questions · Higher Level

1 (i) Explain Maslow's Theory of Motivation.

(ii) Illustrate how a manager could motivate workers by applying Maslow's Theory in the workplace. *LCHL 2011 (20 marks)*

2 Analyse the implications for a business of a manager adopting a Theory X approach to managing. *LCHL 2009 (30 marks)*

3 Discuss **three** styles of leadership. *LCHL 2006 (30 marks)*

4 Evaluate the motivational theories of Maslow and McGregor *LCHL 2005 (25 marks)*

5 Illustrate the importance of management skills in each of the following areas:

(a) The home

(b) The local community

(c) A government department

(d) A business start-up *LCHL 2002 (20 marks)*

6 Differentiate between enterprise and management. Illustrate your answer.

7 Describe **five** important characteristics of effective managers.

8 Entrepreneurs and managers share many characteristics but their roles are essentially very different. Discuss.

unit **3**

unit 3

Syllabus Outcomes

On completion, the student should be able to:

» 3.4.5 Explain the central role of communications in business and management;

» 3.4.6 Identify and explain the main barriers to effective communications;

» 3.4.7 Demonstrate business data in the following written forms: memos, reports and business letters; draft a visual presentation from given data;

» 3.4.8 Identify the duties of a chairperson and secretary and draft an agenda and minutes of a meeting;

» 3.4.9 Distinguish between the methods of communication;

» 3.4.10 Discuss the importance of general communication skills (HL).

News Flash

Pleased to meet you, virtually

By Niall Byrne

Videoconferencing is coming into view for more and more businesses as prices fall and quality improves.

Recently, 240 employees of the Revenue Commissioners from 11 regional offices attended a seminar on VAT. In the past, this would have involved a mass exodus of staff to a central location such as Dublin, an administrative hassle trying to accommodate the numbers in one room and thousands of man-hours lost as workers made the journey.

Upon finishing the recent seminar, however, employees were back at their desks in minutes. Videoconferencing technology enabled the workers to link in from the meeting rooms in their offices and partake in the information seminar with minimum disruption to productivity…

The upgrade of the videoconferencing technology is providing tangible benefits for Revenue, says Paul McDonald, business operations manager, Revenue… "There are benefits vis-à-vis savings in travel costs and at some stage we'd be looking to reduce carbon emissions, but better communication is the main driver."

A lot of Revenue's work is based on legislation so any changes to the law and the knock-on effects for the tax system have to be communicated to all staff at the same time to avoid regional discrepancies. Videoconferencing smooths the passage of this information through to those at the coalface.

For Icon Clinical Research, improving productivity and keeping on top of vital relationships are the benefits of videoconferencing. "One of our drivers for using videoconferencing technology is to ensure we maintain necessary relations with staff, peers and customers without travelling all the time to do so," says Joe Daly, IT director, EU and rest of world, Icon Clinical Research…

"We're a global company and we do have quite high travel costs, particularly for client visits and general meetings," explains Daly. Videoconferencing has reduced the number of trips executives make, freeing up time and curbing expenses.

This is an edited extract from the **Irish Independent,** THURSDAY, 13 MARCH 2008.

For more up-to-date newspaper articles see www.edcodigital.ie

1 Read the newspaper extract opposite and discuss the issues raised.

2 Can you explain any of the highlighted terms?

Management Skills: Communication

Communication involves **exchange of information,** and we now live in what we have learned to call the **Information Age.** This suggests that this period of human history will be defined by our ability to transfer information freely, and to have instant access to knowledge that would have been difficult or impossible to find previously.

It is estimated that managers can spend up to 75 per cent of their time communicating and this reflects the way in which access to information and the need to transfer it effectively is increasingly vital to business success.

The communication process allows people to exchange not just information, but ideas and opinions as well.

Importance of good communication in business

1 Gets work done

The simple reality is that communication is such a vital part of everyday life that **it would be impossible to run a business without communication.** For example, workers need to communicate in order to complete tasks and assignments; managers need to communicate with superiors, with subordinates and with each other. Businesses also need to communicate with suppliers, with customers and with shareholders.

« syllabus signpost 3.4.5 & 3.4.10

2 Improves co-ordination

Managers rely on effective communication systems in order to co-ordinate all of the business activities and resources and this is especially true as companies develop and expand.

As the world's economy is becoming increasingly global, transnational companies in particular could not operate effectively without excellent communications systems. See also *Chapter 24: Global Business.*

3 Benefits industrial relations

Ineffective communication with employees may lead to industrial relations problems. If minor problems are left unresolved they may develop into more serious conflicts. The existence of effective channels of communication between management and subordinates will enable all staff to discuss issues of concern before they escalate.

unit 3

4 Avoids costly mistakes

Failure to communicate information correctly leads to mistakes being made and can create problems with suppliers and customers. Repairing the damage caused by misinformation has a financial cost as well as a reputational one.

5 Reflects a changing work environment

Modern workplaces are becoming increasingly complex and this makes communication even more important. Greater use of teamwork has made communication essential to organisational success.

This is all part of a process by which autocratic management has been replaced by participatory management styles which empower workers. Under these more modern approaches communication is a key element in building trust, promoting understanding and motivating staff.

Methods of communication

Businesses communicate with all of their stakeholders, using a variety of methods both internal and external.

« *syllabus signpost* 3.4.9

Internal communication

This type of communication takes place within an organisation and involves communication between internal stakeholders or their representatives. Examples include management meetings, staff meetings and the use of intercoms, notice boards and newsletters.

A local network of computers, usually accessible only to employees of a specific business is called an **intranet.** It is quite possible that the computers in your own school are part of an internal network of this type. Each computer is connected to a server which allows users to access and share information across the local area network (LAN).

External communication

This takes place with stakeholders outside an organisation, for example customers, suppliers and government departments.

Methods of external communication:

> Letters > Email > Websites
> Telephone > Fax

Channels of communication is the term which describes the pathways along which information flows through an organisation. The most common channels of communication include:

> **Downward communication:** Information travels from top levels of the management structure, downwards via supervisors to subordinates.

> **Upward communication:** Subordinates report to those higher up the chain of command.

> **Horizontal communication:** This involves communication between those on same level of organisational structure, e.g. finance manager and production manager.

Businesses also need to be aware of the flow of information through formal and informal communications channels.

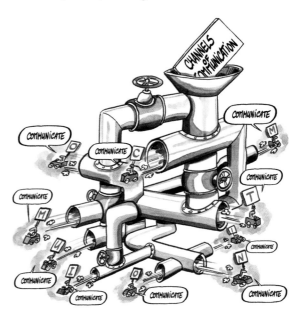

> **Formal communication:** This includes information passed through approved channels (e.g. letters, formal meetings).

> **Informal communication:** Organisations need to recognise that an unofficial network of communications ('the grapevine') co-exists within their business. Informal discussions and resulting rumours can sometimes undermine more formal ones and conflicts with stakeholders can result.

 **Example**

A rumour may circulate among staff of possible job losses or changes to work practices. These can take hold and spread very quickly, and if the business fails to address the issues in a clear and unequivocal manner they may result in mistrust and suspicion from employees and trade unions.

Types of Communication

« syllabus signpost 3.4.7

> **Verbal/oral communication:** Making use of telephones, meetings, intercom systems and press conferences are all examples of verbal communication in action.

They generally involve a quick and direct means of communicating information to others. On the negative side, they may not always provide a record of the information transferred and this may lead to confusion or misunderstanding about what was actually said or agreed.

> **Written communication:** Letters, memos, reports, newsletters and email are all examples of written communications. Since they can be re-read at a later stage they are particularly suited to complex or detailed messages. They also offer the advantage of providing a record of the communication. Examples of letters and reports are provided at the end of this chapter (see p. 103).

> **Visual communication:** Graphs, charts and pictures are the most commonly used types of visual communication. They tend to be used to reinforce a message delivered using oral or written communication. Statistical information or sales figures can be difficult to understand, so managers frequently prepare trend graphs, pie charts or bar charts to add clarity to a verbal presentation. Visual communication is effective because sometimes 'a picture paints a thousand words'.

unit **3**

Regional Sales 2010

Region	Sales Revenue €
Leinster	140,000
Munster	70,000
Ulster	40,000
Connacht	60,000

**Regional Sales 2010
Sales Revenue**

- Leinster
- Munster
- Ulster
- Connacht

Pie chart

Quarterly Sales Revenue: Leinster Region

Quarter	Sales Revenue €
Q1	25,000
Q2	40,000
Q3	55,000
Q4	20,000

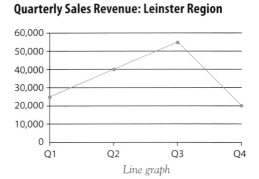

Quarterly Sales Revenue: Leinster Region

Line graph

Information and Communications Technology

Information and communications technology (ICT) refers to a growing range of technologies which enable people to access, manipulate, store, retrieve and transfer vast quantities of information very quickly. These new and innovative technologies now play an increasingly significant role in personal and business communications.

In a business context, ICT tends to fit into two broad categories:

1 Traditional **computer-based technologies.** Examples in this category include the use of computer programs (database, spreadsheets and word processing) and some internet applications (email, web pages, broadband).

2 More recent and more dynamic **digital communication technologies.**

Examples in this category include digital music, digital television and digital storage systems which are capable of sorting, storing and retrieving enormous amounts of information.

The development of more efficient information and communications technologies has also been a major factor in the growth of transnational and global businesses. The availability of up-to-date information now makes it easier to manage a business which operates in many parts of the world.

ICT has also been a positive development for many sectors of the Irish economy since it has created a huge number of additional jobs, especially in the computing and telecommunications industries.

Global web giants get together at Dublin events *by John Collins*

Chad Hurley, Niklas Zennstrom, Michael Birch and Jack Dorsey certainly are not household names.

But YouTube, Skype, Bebo and Twitter, the web companies they started certainly are and rank among the most influential and most valuable web companies of the last decade.

These four will be joined by over 100 other web innovators, investors, academics and social entrepreneurs in Dublin over the next three days for an invite-only get together called Founders.

Aimed at the founders of the world's most successful and most promising internet ventures the event runs between today and Saturday at venues around the city.

Giving the event some added gravitas former president of Ireland Mary Robinson, Goldman Sachs International chairman Peter Sutherland and the World Bank's chief economist Dr Justin Lin will also speak.

In tandem with the private event, some of the high profile attendees including YouTube chief executive Mr Hurley, Twitter inventor Mr Dorsey and Skype co-founder Mr Zennstrom will speak at the Dublin Web Summit...

The international speakers will be joined by Irish web experts who will address a sell-out crowd of 500.

Both events are the brainchild of Paddy Cosgrave who... says the event features "the fastest growing companies of the 21st century".

Despite many of the attendees being multimillionaires whose services touch the lives of millions, the vast majority are under the age of 40...

While technology dominates the panel discussions at Founders the state of the world economy and providing educational opportunities for the socially disadvantaged will also come under the microscope.

Early arrivals today include representatives of the world's business and technology media, will also get the chance to visit the Irish offices of Google and Facebook, as well as indigenous success story Jolt Online Gaming...

This is an edited extract from **The Irish Times**, THURSDAY, 28 OCTOBER 2010.

unit
3

Uses of ICT in business

Word-processing

Businesses use word-processing packages such as Microsoft Word for a whole variety of applications. It's useful for preparing formal letters, memos, agendas and minutes of meetings. The major advantage is that documents can be changed or formatted very quickly.

Databases

A database is very similar to a computerised filing system and enables the user to store, update and manipulate huge amounts of information. Obvious benefits come from the ability to store large amounts of information on computer discs and also the efficiency with which the information can be sorted. Preparation of customer and staff databases are common uses for this technology. Microsoft Access is a widely used database package.

Mail-merge

This useful application combines both word-processing and databases and is used by businesses to support their customer service and marketing efforts. It enables a business to produce 'personalised' letters for clients. A single standardised letter is prepared using word-processing software and the computer can print this letter for each customer, using names and addresses stored in the database.

Spreadsheets

Spreadsheets are utilised when dealing with accounts, budgets and other financial information. They are ideal for budgets and cash flow forecasts, as the computer can be programmed to carry out the calculations and will update totals when figures are changed. Microsoft Excel is one of the most commonly used spreadsheet packages.

Internet

The Internet is an international network of computers which can access and share enormous amounts of information online. It is often called the World Wide Web (WWW). The Internet is an example of a wide area network (WAN).

Businesses frequently use the Internet for market research, email, advertising and online sales. Most businesses have **websites** which allows them to interact in a virtual way with their stakeholders. Websites allow the business to promote and sell their products twenty-four hours a day, without the need to employ additional staff. This has a major cost-saving benefit for a company and the possibility of online sales means they are never closed for business. Customers can view online catalogues and fill virtual shopping baskets before proceeding to cyber checkouts. Electronic fund transfers are used to pay for the goods and are facilitated by a variety of debit, credit and charge card companies.

Some companies have established a highly successful business model which relies totally on a website and online sales. Examples of these **'dot com' companies** include Amazon and eBay. In recent years businesses have also availed of social networking sites such as Facebook, LinkedIn and MySpace to raise awareness and improve their profile with consumers. The Internet also allows businesses to send electronic mail (email) to thousands of customers simultaneously and at a very low cost.

Videoconferencing

Videoconferencing is a method of interactive telecommunication which allows people in two or more locations to interact using two-way video and audio transmissions. The development of Integrated Services Digital Networks (ISDN) in the 1980s made this possible and it has been refined and improved ever since. Broadband services currently enable users to transfer very complex information streams which can include text, audio and video content.

Businesses use this technology to allow staff in different geographic locations to interact and share information in 'virtual meetings'. It is especially useful for global companies since they no longer need to waste time and money flying senior managers to one location for important meetings. It also adds a visual element to meetings and presentations which is not available using audio methods alone. Free Internet services like Skype have made videoconferencing part of everyday life for many people.

Electronic Data Interchange

Electronic Data Interchange (EDI) is a communications system which uses computers to transfer information directly from one business to another. It is used by companies who deal with each other on a regular and ongoing basis and requires each business to install compatible software. Once in place the system allows for goods to be automatically re-ordered, as well as facilitating the transfer of invoices, credit notes and statements of account. It is efficient and cost-effective because it means that the entire transaction from ordering goods, right through to payment, is conducted electronically.

Cloud Computing

Many businesses in the ICT industry have recently begun to focus attention and resources on the potential of **cloud computing.** Cloud computing enables data to be stored in offsite locations or servers ('clouds'), which minimises the need for expensive hardware and onsite storage capabilities.

The information in the cloud can be retrieved at any time by multiple authorised users and is usually password protected or encrypted. Dropbox.com is an example of a company which is exploiting this type of technology to offer an enhanced email service to its client.

Case Study

In September 2009 Microsoft invested €350 million in a data centre in Dublin. This was the first data centre of its kind to be built outside the US and represents a huge investment in the Irish economy. The data centre has been used to improve Microsoft's cloud computing capabilities and enable it to gain a larger share of a growing market.

Paul Rellis, managing director of Microsoft Ireland, said recently that cloud computing represented the future of Microsoft's business and it was only through embracing and developing this new technology that Microsoft could ensure its own survival.

The technology benefits businesses by allowing them to cut operating costs and also making optimal use of technology without the need to worry about issues like storage capacity.

Former Minister for Communications, Energy and Natural Resources, Eamon Ryan, had the following to say on the likely impact of cloud computing: 'The Irish Government has identified cloud computing as a key driver of our economic renewal. Not only does this emerging technology afford our ICT sector huge opportunities, but it has the potential to transform the way we, in Government and in the wider economy, do business.'

Source: Institute of International and European Affairs

Challenges of ICT

The growth of online business has been spectacular in recent decades and is likely to continue at an ever-increasing rate. This provides a number of challenges for both businesses and governments, which must facilitate and regulate the emerging industries.

Key challenges associated with ICT include:

Infrastructure

There has been a lot of talk recently about the 'smart economy' and the potential for modern high-tech jobs, but the reality is that failure to put in place fast, high-volume broadband could seriously undermine our attempts to develop this type of business in Ireland.

Broadband is regarded as 'high speed' Internet access as it allows a high rate of data transmission across the Internet. Almost every business in Ireland relies on ICT to some extent and the government has a very important role to play in developing the necessary infrastructure. This can be achieved by direct government intervention, by private-sector investment or in some cases by a joint effort between the public and private sectors. These joint efforts are called public–private partnerships (PPPs) and have also been used to provide roads and schools. See also *Chapter 19: Business, Government and the Economy.*

While broadband access is important to most businesses, it is of particular significance when it comes to sustaining and developing Ireland as a location for Internet-based businesses and international call centres. Internet search engine Google has already made a significant commitment to Ireland and has an operations headquarters here which serves Europe, the Middle East and Asia.

Security

Many businesses and consumers have concerns about the security of Internet transactions and many fear that personal information may be stolen (**hacked**) or used inappropriately. It is difficult to guarantee data protection for individuals since the Internet is not as easy to police or regulate as traditional marketplaces. Many customers make use of online banking and payment services and these have been prone to a variety of computer **viruses** and scams, including phishing.

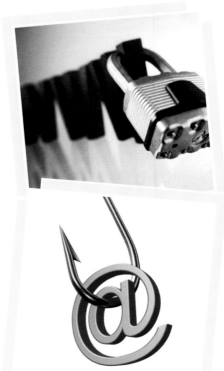

Phishing is an attempt to gain access to sensitive information such as passwords and account numbers by directing users to a fake Internet site which has been set up to look exactly like a legitimate site. Unsuspecting users believe they are using a genuine site and pass on their password or bank details to the fraudsters. So long as consumers have concerns over this type of activity, many will be reluctant to trust and avail of e-commerce.

Consumer protection

Questions of consumer protection are also an impediment to e-commerce and many potential customers are uncertain about their legal rights and entitlements for goods purchased online. Consumers are unclear about the level of protection and right of redress available to them if goods are faulty or not fit for purpose. The National Consumer Agency provides a detailed guide to shopping from home (distance selling) on its website: www.consumerconnect.ie

For businesses themselves, the Internet throws up potential problems, especially when it comes to intellectual property issues. It can be very difficult to protect patents and copyrights in an online environment, and this makes a risky and expensive step for some businesses.

For example, peer-to-peer (P2P) file-sharing technologies, such as those popularised by Napster, have been used to illegally download music and video files. This is just one development from a range of similar issues which have given rise to increased worries and costs for businesses.

Data Protection Acts, 1988 and 2003

The fundamental principle governing data protection is that everybody should be able to control how information about them is used.

These laws apply to all information kept on computer and in manual files. The laws are designed to protect the person whose information is on file. This person is the **data subject**. The law places specific responsibilities on the holder of that information (the **data controller**). Data controllers are often employers, government agencies or financial institution, and all have the capacity to hold large amounts of sensitive information relating to staff or clients.

The **Data Protection Commissioner** is responsible for enforcing the Acts, and individuals who feel their rights are being infringed should complain to the Commissioner, who will investigate the matter and if necessary take action to resolve it.

The Commissioner is appointed by government but operates independently and presents an annual report to the Oireachtas.

Rights of data subjects:

> **Right to access information:** having made a written request the information must be supplied within 40 days.

> **Right to correction of errors:** this might include details of qualifications or experience and could affect an employee's prospects of promotion.

> **Right to complain:** where breaches of the Acts have taken place, complaints should be made to the Data Protection Commissioner.

> **Right to compensation:** where damage has been suffered due to misuse of information held. A worker who was passed over for promotion because of inaccurate information held on file may seek compensation for loss of opportunity and pay. Court action is required when seeking compensation.

> **Right to have human input into important decisions:** data subjects should not be subjected to automated decision-making.

unit
3

> **Right to prevent your data from being used for direct marketing purposes:** this is put into effect by writing to the data controller and directing him/her to stop using your information for this purpose. Providers of telecommunications services often pass on this information unless instructed otherwise. This can lead to unsolicited phone calls from sales reps.

Obligations of data controllers:

> To obtain information in an honest and fair way.

> To secure the information safely and prevent unauthorised access to it.

> To correct and update information as necessary and to delete or destroy it when it is no longer needed.

> To provide a copy of information to a data subject upon request.

> To ensure information is only used for the purpose for which it was provided.

Hogan reassures public on household charge website

by Elaine Edwards

Minister for the Environment Phil Hogan has insisted the website set up for payment of the new household charge adheres to "the required data protection and privacy standards", despite concerns raised today.

Mr Hogan was responding after Data Protection Commissioner Billy Hawkes described as a "disturbing development" the proposal to use information held by the ESB in order to pursue payments.

Mr Hogan… committed to working with the commissioner "to make sure that we comply with information and respect the privacy of individuals".

Mr Hawkes said there was a certain expectation there would be some data sharing between government agencies, this was "extending the tentacles of the State into the commercial area".

"Obviously, when we give information to a commercial body, data protection law says that it can only be used for the purpose we gave it. So it has to be an issue of concern that it's now potentially being used for another purpose."…

"We have had urgent contact with the Department of the Environment and have agreed with them that if there is to be any access to ESB data it will be on the basis of a strict protocol…"

This is an edited extract from **The Irish Times,** Thursday, 5 January 2012.

Role of Data Protection Commissioner:

> Provides information in relation to the requirements and provisions of the Data Protection Acts.

> Develops codes of practice, so as to allow organisations to comply with their obligations under the Act.

> Maintains a list of data controllers who are required to register with the Commissioner.

> Investigates complaints against data controllers for breaches of the Act. Where breaches are found the Commissioner can issue enforcement orders or instigate court action.

Benefits of ICT to business

> **Improved efficiency:** The speed at which routine transactions can be carried out is greatly improved. Computers are very efficient at completing repetitive tasks and will continue to perform to the same high standards without getting tired or bored.

> **Faster communication:** Communication of information is also quicker and more efficient. As outlined previously, it is quicker and cheaper to send large volumes of information via email rather than by post.

> **Lower staff costs:** ICT will reduce the need for staff and will therefore lower payroll costs for businesses.

> **Increased sales potential:** Company websites are effective for raising the profile of businesses and facilitate online sales and advertising twenty-four hours a day.

> **Market research benefits:** Businesses can also use the World Wide Web to carry out market research. This can be achieved by looking at competitors' websites and also using their own websites to get feedback from their target market.

Effective communication

Effective communication should be:

> **Accurate**
> **Brief**
> **Clear**
> **Suitable**

> **Open to feedback**
> **Fast**
> **Economical**
> **Recorded**

Accuracy

Accuracy is important because decisions may be taken on the basis of information provided in meetings, letters or reports. If this information is factually incorrect, then bad decisions will be made and this can have huge consequences for a business and its stakeholders.

Brevity and Clarity

Messages and reports should be kept as short as possible and need to be clearly laid out in a language which is understood by the receiver. Too much information may confuse the issue and result in key information being overlooked.

Suitability

It's also important that a suitable medium is chosen to reflect the nature and confidentiality of the message. It would seem appropriate to communicate private information in a formal letter and have it delivered directly to the person involved.

Feedback

In order to ensure that the information was understood correctly, effective communication should try to allow the receiver to provide feedback. This will enable any misunderstandings to be eliminated immediately.

Speed

Most modern communication takes place in a very dynamic business environment, so it must be passed on quickly in order to be effective. Managers need information updates in order to formulate policy and make decisions.

Cost

At the same time communication has cost implications for a business and they will need to examine the overall financial impact. Where the audience is large, meetings or email may prove cost-effective.

Record

Finally there are clear advantages where a record is kept of important correspondence as future confusion and misunderstandings can easily be resolved. Most written forms of communication provide for a record to be kept on file.

A failure to meet any of the above criteria will reduce the effectiveness of communications.

Factors affecting choice of communications medium

> **Cost:** Each medium has different cost implications and a company will need to examine its impact on spending. Emails, for example, are effectively free, while posting letters to thousands of customers can be very expensive.

> **Nature of message:** It is usually best to put long or detailed messages in writing. This allows for re-reading and should improve understanding.

> **Urgency:** Messages sent via the postal system will travel relatively slowly over long distances compared to a phone call or email which are instantaneous.

> **Confidentiality:** A company would not post confidential information about employees on a notice board or broadcast it over an intercom system. They should instead choose a face-to-face meeting or personal letter.

> **Technology available:** A communications medium should only be chosen when it is available to both the sender and the recipient. If the receiver does not have access to email or a fax machine, they are simply not an option, no matter what other advantages they might offer.

> **Record:** Is a record required? Telephone conversations and face-to-face meetings are not generally recorded whereas most written forms of communication offer this advantage. Orders for goods should always be put in writing.

> **Legal requirements:** In order to be valid insurance contracts for the purchase of land and insurance policies must be in writing. In contract law, this is called legality of form. There is also a legal requirement to provide employees with written contracts of employment.

Barriers to communication

> **Language used:** A poorly composed message or overuse of technical language (jargon) will frequently result in confusion and lack of understanding.

« *syllabus signpost* 3.4.6

> **Wrong medium:** The medium chosen must suit both the message and the audience. Businesses have a wide choice of communications media at their disposal, including letters, faxes, email, meetings and so on. Choosing the most appropriate medium for each message will enhance the effectiveness of the communication process.

> **Organisational structure:** Lack of clear channels of communication within an organisation can impede the flow of information. In some instances there may be too many contradictory instructions.

> **Noise:** Any outside interference, including background noise from machinery or vehicles, can distort the message. Other types of interference can include emotional or mental barriers. If you are in disagreement with somebody you might choose to ignore what they say, even though they may clearly deliver the instructions.

> **Poor timing:** Messages may be delivered at inappropriate times or perhaps without enough time to consider or understand the information. If a teacher starts calling out homework just as the bell rings for lunch, it's very likely that some students will be too busy leaving the classroom to take notice.

> **Lack of feedback:** Feedback allows the sender to verify that the message was understood.

Meetings

Meetings play an important role in the running of many organisations, including businesses. Board meetings allow directors to plan strategically, while department managers will meet very regularly to formulate tactical plans and co-ordinate activities. Staff meetings allow all employees an opportunity to engage with management while the AGM provides a forum for shareholders to comment on the performance of senior managers.

AGM: Annual General Meeting

Companies are required by law to hold this meeting once every year. It gives shareholders a chance to question the directors about the performance of the company. Shareholders also receive updates on key areas of the business including its financial performance. Other important issues decided at the AGM include dividend policy and the election of directors.

unit 3

EGM: Extraordinary General Meeting

By definition, an annual general meeting can be held only once per year. If a major issue arises after the AGM has already been held, the directors may have to convene a second shareholder meeting to discuss and resolve the issue. This subsequent meeting is called an EGM and recognises that it has arisen due to extraordinary circumstances. An EGM might be required if a takeover bid threatens the future of the company.

Virtual meetings

By using audio-visual and Internet technology, business managers can employ videoconferencing to hold meetings involving staff in different locations. Employees can be linked to each other using webcams, which enables them to interact in real-time meetings.

Ad hoc meetings

Ad hoc meetings are held on an occasional basis to deal with a specific issue or problem facing the business. The term 'ad hoc' means 'for that purpose'. If the issue cannot be resolved by the meeting a decision may be made to set up an ad hoc committee which will investigate and discuss the problem before presenting a report at a later date. Once that specific issue has been dealt with the committee will be disbanded.

Procedure for conducting meetings

The **notice** and **agenda** must be sent out by secretary in advance. The notice informs all interested parties that the meeting will take place; it also sets out the date, venue and time of the meeting.

The agenda is a list of topics for discussion at the meeting. It's a bit like a menu for conducting a meeting and will be followed in a strict order.

Sample notice

NOTICE OF ANNUAL GENERAL MEETING

Notice is hereby given that the AGM of Loot Ltd will take place in the Priory Hotel, Stillorgan, Co. Dublin, at 3pm on 30 August 2012.

All shareholders are invited to attend.

Signed:

A. Murtagh

A. Murtagh

(Company Secretary)

Sample agendas

AGENDA FOR ANNUAL GENERAL MEETING OF LOOT LTD

1. Minutes of previous AGM
2. Matters arising
3. Managing Director's report
4. Election of directors
5. Auditor's report
6. Declaration of dividend
7. Any other business

AGENDA FOR AGM OF COOTEHILL ATHLETICS CLUB

1. Minutes of previous AGM
2. Matters arising
3. Chairperson's report
4. Election of committee members
5. Treasurer's report
6. Fundraising & sponsorship
7. Any other business

Exam Tip

Note the differences between the agenda for a company and a club. In exam questions on this topic it is important that the items listed in the agenda are relevant to the type of organisation under discussion.

Always ensure that the agenda has a minimum of **five** relevant items. Items 1, 3 and 5 must always be included. (See sample agenda opposite.)

Before a meeting begins the chairperson must ensure that a quorum is present. A **quorum** is the minimum number of people required for a meeting to be valid. Most organisations have a clear rule governing the minimum attendance and this is intended to prevent a small minority from having their views and policies approved on the basis of a very low turnout. If a quorum is not present for the meeting any decisions taken will not be valid and the chairperson would have no option but to postpone the meeting.

unit 3

The **minutes** of a meeting are a written account of what was actually discussed and decided at the meeting. These are taken by the **secretary.** The minutes of the previous meeting are always read and adopted (agreed) at the start of the next meeting.

Sometimes it may be necessary to follow up on an item mentioned in the minutes and this is provided for under the heading of 'matters arising'. For example, during a previous meeting the marketing manager may have been asked to clarify the costs involved in an advertising campaign. If this information was not immediately available, the question will be noted in the minutes but will remain unanswered. At the start of the next management meeting the item will be mentioned when the minutes are read. If the marketing manager is now in a position to clarify the cost issue, she is entitled to provide the necessary information at this point in the meeting.

Sample minutes

MINUTES OF LOOT LTD AGM

The secretary provided all shareholders with copies of the minutes from the previous AGM which was held in August 2011. All agreed they were an accurate account of events and the minutes were formally adopted.

There were no matters arising.

The Managing Director, Declan McAnespie, addressed the meeting and outlined the success of the company during the past year. He briefly outlined the challenges ahead and predicted the business would continue to grow.

He thanked all the directors for their hard work throughout the year and paid tribute to the contribution of Austin O'Malley who was retiring as a director after 12 years' service.

Barbara O'Malley was elected to the Board of Directors to replace Austin O'Malley who was retiring. All other directors were re-elected for a further two-year term.

The auditors provided a summary of the company's financial accounts to all shareholders and they outlined key issues. They reported that annual pre-tax profits had risen for the third consecutive year.

The directors proposed a dividend of €1.20 per share and this was approved by a majority of those in attendance.

As there was no other business to be discussed the meeting concluded at 4.20 p.m.

Role of the secretary

« *syllabus signpost*
3.4.8

› **Send out notice and agenda.** This informs interested parties when and where the meeting will be held. It also lists the topics for discussion.

› **Arrange the venue and facilities** for the meeting. A suitable venue needs to be organised in advance and requirements for ICT must be met. Some speakers may require laptop, PowerPoint or data-projection facilities.

› **Read minutes from previous meeting.** When the meeting commences the secretary will provide a reminder of the last meeting by reading the minutes.

› **Read out any relevant correspondence** received since last meeting. Letters and notices are usually sent to the secretary of clubs and companies and some of the more important issues may need to be highlighted and discussed at the meeting.

› **Take notes and write up minutes of meeting.** As each item on the agenda is discussed, the secretary will take note of key issues and decisions. These notes will later be used to write up a more detailed account of the meeting.

Role of the chairperson

› **Ensure that the meeting has been properly convened.** The rules for meetings, called **standing orders**, may require that the notice is sent up to fourteen days in advance. If the meeting has not been properly convened it may not be valid.

› **Ensure that there is a quorum present.**

› **Have the minutes of the previous meeting** read and adopted.

› **Follow the agreed agenda.** Each topic needs to be discussed in turn. The chairperson needs to ensure that where possible all those who wish to speak are given an opportunity to do so. The chairperson should also make sure that all contributions are relevant to the topic under discussion.

› **Ensure that the meeting is run in an orderly manner** and according to the standing orders.

› **Conduct votes** where necessary. In order for a decision to be made a topic (or motion) may be put to a vote. The chairperson has the responsibility for overseeing the vote and should follow standing orders when deciding on the type of vote (e.g. secret ballot, show of hands) or the majority required for a motion to be carried. Some organisations may have rules requiring a two-thirds majority in favour when making major changes to policy. If the standing orders provide for it the chairperson may have the deciding or casting vote in the event of a tie.

Written Communication: Samples

Formal letter

A formal letter should contain:

> ❯ Sender's address
> ❯ Recipient's address
> ❯ Date
> ❯ Opening salutation (Dear —)

> ❯ Main body (use paragraphs)
> ❯ Closing salutation (Yours faithfully)
> ❯ Sender's signature and title

Sample

Ryan Insurance Ltd
12 Lesson Street
Limerick
Ireland
Tel: 353-61-386666   Fax: 353-61-386444
E-mail: RyanInsurance@eircom.ie

Letterhead outlining name of company and contact details.

Our Ref: PF1
Your Ref: FB
Date: 30/9/2012

Date

Ms Frances Burton
Manager
Shop Electrics
High Street
Dublin 2

Complete title, name, address of person/ company to which letter is being sent.

Dear Ms Burton,

Salutation – where possible it's better to address to a particular person.

Re: Non-Disclosure of a Material Fact

What the letter contains.

Further to our recent correspondence in regards to your Buildings Insurance it has been brought to my attention that your business premises has a thatched roof. From our records this appears to be contrary to the original insurance application form.

May I bring to your attention two principles of insurance relevant to your insurance situation.

Body of letter

Utmost Good Faith

This requires all material facts to be disclosed so that the insurance company can fully assess the risk and calculate an appropriate premium. I must point out that failure to disclose a material fact can render the contract void.

Average Clause

If a Premises is underinsured, i.e. insured for less than its worth, compensation will only be paid by the company in proportion to that fraction of the loss which was covered.

I look forward to hearing from you to discuss this issue further.

Yours faithfully

To close a letter, use 'Yours sincerely' when using a personalised salutation; use 'Yours faithfully' when using a more impersonal salutation.

Peter Fry

Peter Fry
Manager – Assessor Unit
Enc. Original Insurance Application Form

Author's signature

Enclosures – these are the attachments to the main letter.

Chief Executive Officer: Mary Sutton

Directors: Alan Osbourne, David O'Hara

Senior management names

Report

A report should contain:

- Title
- Prepared for
- Prepared by
- Date
- Terms of reference (topic for report)
- Introduction
- Main body
- Conclusions/ recommendations
- Signature

Sample

Title: A report on the implications of introducing new ICT to Lloyds Ltd

To: Chief Executive Officer of Lloyds Ltd

From: Conor O'Shea, ICT Consultant

Date: 10/10/12

Terms of Reference: To outline the implications of introducing new ICT to facilitate decision-making in the firm.

Procedures: All staff were surveyed in order to obtain their views on the needs of the firm.

A representative sample of technology available from three large suppliers was examined and the views of the firms installing the technology were sought.

Terms of reference:
Sets out the reasons why the report is being written and the issues it intends to address.

Body of Report:

Findings: Introducing new ICT systems to the firm will have the following implications.

Benefits:
- Information will be processed faster.
- Decisions will be made faster.
- Accuracy of record keeping and accounts will improve.
- Closer contact will be kept with customers.
- Fewer staff will be needed.

Difficulties:
- Installation costs will be high.
- Training costs will be expensive and ongoing.
- Redundancy costs will be incurred as staff levels are reduced.
- Industrial relations difficulties can be anticipated.

Body of Report:
This sets out the information and factual part of the report.

Conclusions: It would seem that the benefits outweigh the difficulties involved in introducing the technology to the firm.

Conclusions:
A statement of what the author believes is true about the issue.

Recommendations: Further advice should be sought on costing an ICT System appropriate to the firm's needs before the decision to proceed further is made.

Recommendations:
The actions to be taken.

Signed:

Conor O'Shea

Conor O'Shea

ICT Consultant

Appendices: Staff Survey on needs of the firm

Appendices:
The material that is not suitable for the main body of the report: question-naires, names and references, etc.

Memo

A memo should contain:

> Title (Memo)
> To:
> From:
> Date:
> Re: (topic)
> Main body (message)
> Signature

Sample

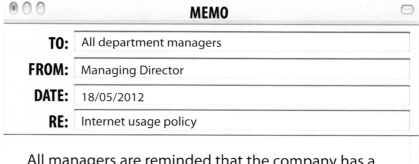

MEMO

TO:	All department managers
FROM:	Managing Director
DATE:	18/05/2012
RE:	Internet usage policy

All managers are reminded that the company has a clear policy on Internet usage and that this policy prohibits access to social networking sites. Following some recent breaches of policy I request that all managers remind staff in their department of their responsibilities in this area. This is a matter of some urgency and your co-operation is appreciated.

T. McCarthy
Managing Director

unit 3

Chapter Review Diagram – Management Skills: Communication

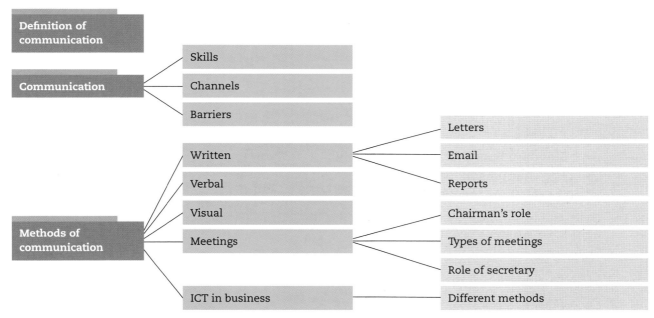

- **Definition of communication**
- **Communication**
  - Skills
  - Channels
  - Barriers
- **Methods of communication**
  - Written
    - Letters
    - Email
    - Reports
  - Verbal
  - Visual
  - Meetings
    - Chairman's role
    - Types of meetings
    - Role of secretary
  - ICT in business
    - Different methods

Q Chapter Review Questions

1 Define the term 'communication'.

2 Outline the importance of good communication in business.

3 List three internal and three external forms of communication.

4 Illustrate three channels of communication.

5 Outline four factors which will influence a manager's decision when choosing the most appropriate method of communication.

6 Illustrate the use of ICT in business today.

7 Explain the following terms: ISDN, EDI, ICT, WWW.

8 Analyse the benefits of ICT to business.

9 Outline the main provisions of the Data Protection Acts, 1988 and 2003.

10 Outline the rights of data subjects under the Acts.

11 Describe the role of Data Protection Commissioner.

12 List five barriers to effective communication.

13 Define the term 'quorum'.

14 In the context of a meeting, explain the terms 'notice', 'agenda' and 'minutes'.

15 Outline the role of both chairperson and secretary of a meeting.

Q Questions · Ordinary Level

1

Glendarn Sports Club in Galway will hold its AGM in a local hotel next month. The chairperson Joanne O'Boyle and the Secretary Michael Brown are planning the meeting and discussing items for the agenda.   *LCOL 2010*

(a) Using today's date draft the Notice and the Agenda for the AGM of Glendarn Sports Club.   *(25 marks)*

(b) Outline **two** duties of a Chairperson at a meeting.

(c) Outline **two** duties of a Secretary at a meeting.   *(20 marks)*

(d) State **two** advantages of meetings as a method of communication.   *(10 marks)*

2 Outline **two** advantages of meetings as a method of communication.

LCOL 2009 (10 marks)

3 Explain **three** advantages of meetings as a method of communication.

4 Draft the Notice and Agenda for the upcoming AGM of a local sports club. Include at least **five** items on the agenda.

5 Write up the minutes of the AGM mentioned in question 4 above.

6 Describe **two** functions of the Data Protection Acts, 1988 and 2003.

Questions · Higher Level

1 Describe the barriers to effective communication in a business enterprise and suggest methods a business might consider to overcome **two** of these barriers.

LCHL 2008 (25 marks)

2 'On average, managers spend over 75 per cent of their time communicating.'

Explain the factors that ensure managers communicate effectively. Use examples where appropriate.

LCHL 2005 (25 marks)

3 Explain what is meant by a 'virtual' meeting.

4 Explain the role of the following:

(a) Secretary

(b) Chairperson.

5 Draft the Notice and Agenda for the upcoming AGM of Fresh Foods Limited. Include at least **five** items on the agenda.

6 Write up the minutes of the AGM mentioned in question 5 above.

7 The Data Protection Acts, 1988 and 2003, sets out the following:

(a) The rights of Data Subjects

(b) The obligations of Data Controllers and

(c) The functions of the Data Protection Commissioner

Explain any **two** of the above.

LCHL 2007 (25 marks)

Chapter 7
Management Activities: Planning, Organising and Controlling

Syllabus Outcomes

On completion, the student should be able to:

» 3.4.13: Discuss the nature of management activities and their linkages (HL).

Management Activity: Planning

Planning is all about establishing goals and then setting out policies or pathways to achieving them. In simple terms a plan is a bit like a roadmap for success. It shows where somebody wants to go and also how they expect to get there. Think about planning in your own life. Students often make study plans to help them achieve their exam goals. These plans are an attempt to map out blocks of study on a day-by-day basis, and if everything goes according to plan all necessary material will be revised and a better exam grade will result.

In your home, either you or your parents might make use of spending plans or household budgets. These are examples of financial plans and are helpful for avoiding overspending and cash shortfalls. *Chapter 8* will deal with this issue in greater detail.

The motto 'fail to plan and plan to fail' is often used to highlight the potential consequences of poor planning. It suggests that those who make inadequate preparations are destined to fail, and there are many examples which seem to support this view.

Case Study

One well-publicised situation from the sporting world concerns the now infamous training camp established by the FAI in Saipan. The training camp was part of the squad's preparation for the 2002 FIFA World Cup in Japan and Korea.

Roy Keane

Mick McCarthy

As he departed from the camp following a disagreement with manager Mick McCarthy, Roy Keane was very critical of the location and in particular the lack of preparation by the FAI.

He said that important training equipment was not available, either because it had not been provided or because it was delayed in transit. It seemed that planning was inadequate and no thought had been given to alternatives. Whatever the truth of the matter, the perceived lack of planning was enough to undermine the squad preparations and divert focus and energy from their primary goal.

The importance of planning

Since planning provides such a foundation for success it's often argued that it is the most important management function. Here are some reasons to support this view:

Planning reduces uncertainty

Once clear goals have been set out they will provide direction for the business. Those working at all levels of the organisation should have a clearer understanding of what's expected of them.

Senior management will play a major role in setting these corporate goals and these will form the basis for more specific plans of action within each department.

Planning provides greater unity

This reduced uncertainty should also translate into a more unified approach. Since everyone knows exactly what's expected they'll try to work towards the same goals. This really involves **co-ordination** of efforts and it should help to reduce wasteful inefficiencies.

In much the same way as a rowing boat moves more quickly through the water when its crew are all rowing together, a business will operate most effectively when all staff 'pull in the same direction'.

Planning helps raise finance

The existence of clear and realistic plans is an absolute necessity for businesses seeking finance or additional capital. Investors, venture capitalists and financial institutions will expect to see a detailed **business plan**. This will set out the aims and objectives of the business and will provide cash-flow forecasts and profit projections.

Planning facilitates change

Plans reflect the future direction of the business and this often requires changes to operating policy and procedures. By making plans available to staff, or better still, involving them in the planning process, it allows workers to see the need for change and plan its implementation. Changes which have the support of all staff are more likely to be accepted. See also *Chapter 12: Managing Change.*

Planning improves control

The link between the management activities of planning and control is fundamental to business success. As we've already illustrated, planning is about setting goals and targets whereas control involves comparing actual outcomes to those targets. If the goals have been achieved employees can be rewarded, or in situations where results are off target, corrective action can be taken. To put it simply, without plans there would be little chance of effective control. Control is discussed in greater detail later in this chapter (see p. 121).

Planning requires realistic situational analysis

Planning is also important because it forces management to focus on the business's current situation. Before looking too far into the future they will need to consider the realities of their current position and take into account the positive and negative features of both the company and the wider business environment. Managers will utilise some form of situational analysis to assist them. Conducting a **SWOT analysis** is an example of how this might be achieved. The letters **SWOT** stand for **Strengths, Weaknesses, Opportunities** and **Threats.**

SWOT analysis

The overall aim here is to focus on internal strengths and weaknesses while also looking at issues or changes in the external environment that may be positive or potentially negative for the business.

This type of analysis is important because it allows a business to play to its strengths and try to compensate for any negative aspects.

Strengths

Internal strengths are things which the business is particularly good at and which can be developed into a competitive advantage. Examples include strong brands, intellectual property rights such as patents and trademarks or even the availability of a highly skilled workforce.

Weaknesses

Weaknesses are any aspects of the business which are deficient or underdeveloped and which have the potential to undermine the overall success of the company. Possible weaknesses include being undercapitalised, ongoing industrial relations problems or over-dependence on a single product.

Opportunities

Opportunities are things outside the business which have the potential to benefit the company. When considering external factors, businesses might regard access to an enlarged EU market as an opportunity.

Threats

External factors which are likely to have a negative impact on a business can be regarded as threats. Examples in this category include increased competition or legislative changes that could present major threats to the market share.

In 2004 the Irish government introduced the workplace smoking ban, a change in legislation that was a major threat to owners of cigarette-vending machines. The ban was also feared by many publicans who were concerned that the new law might encourage some customers to stay at home. Some publicans, however, saw the creation of a cleaner environment as an opportunity to appeal to a different target market.

Families with young children were more inclined to visit pubs in the aftermath of the smoking ban and this was particularly the case where the pub offered good quality food. So in this instance, what had been perceived as a threat by some business-owners also provided the opportunity to diversify their business and reach a new group of consumers.

Mission statements

Who we are; what we do; where we're going.

A mission statement is a brief statement outlining the most important aims of an organisation and what it sets out to do. For example, it might set out the reason for establishing the organisation and detail its core values and commitments. Very often mission statements focus on the relationship with key stakeholders, including staff, customers and the community in which the organisation is based.

The mission statement is very important because it provides a framework within which all organisational plans are developed.

Mission Statement: Google

Google's mission is to organise the worlds' information and make it universally accessible and useful.

 www.google.com

unit 3

111

Types of plan

Strategic plans

Strategic plans are long-term plans which set out the vision for the whole business. They cover a time period of up to five years and deal with issues like market share, profitability and diversification.

An Irish company may plan to expand its business into the UK market, and as a strategic goal might seek to gain a 10 per cent market share within five years.

Strategic planning is of vital importance to a business as it establishes key priorities for the organisation and determines the focus of its operations for the years ahead. It is a function of the board of directors and senior management to develop and implement strategic plans. Business plans, which are prepared for start-up or expanding businesses, are another example of strategic planning.

Tactical plans

Tactical plans represent an attempt to break strategic goals down into more manageable one- or two-year plans. Taking into account the overall strategic vision, these shorter-term tactical plans will be implemented across every department and can be seen as important stepping-stones on the way to achieving longer-term goals.

For an Irish business contemplating expansion into the UK market, appointing a UK agent for their products or opening their first UK retail outlet might represent a tactical plan for the current year.

This important distinction between long- and short-term plans is exemplified in many areas of our everyday lives. For example, you may have a long-term goal of starting your own business, or of being a doctor. If you do, you'll no doubt realise that there are many steps along the way to achieving these goals. For that reason, the study plans you make in sixth year are a type of tactical plan designed to get you the coveted college place which will in time enable you to achieve your strategic goal.

Similarly, if you play sport your team is likely to have a strategic goal of winning a championship or gaining promotion to a higher division. During the course of several seasons you will need to employ tactical plans for each individual game, but each is simply a step along the path to achieving your primary objective.

unit 3

> *Strategy without tactics is the slowest route to victory. Tactics without strategy is the noise before defeat.*
>
> **Sun Tzu,** The Art of War

Operational plans

Operational plans are short-term plans for specific events or departments. They are concerned with daily or weekly issues. They are usually conducted by front-line supervisors who are in a position to implement budgets, targets and supervision of an area.

Good operational planning will be reflected in high turnover of products, no wastage of raw materials and optimum usage of labour. Poor operational planning will be reflected in low turnover of products and an oversupply of labour.

Contingency plans

Contingency plans are back-up or emergency plans which are formulated to protect the business in the event of unusual or unexpected circumstances. They are in effect the proverbial 'Plan B' and will only be utilised if something goes wrong.

For example, a business may have to consider locating alternative sources of raw materials if a major supplier is crippled by strike action and unable to fulfil its orders. Serious loss or damage to machinery as well as the impact of strike action by its own employees are other issues which may require contingency plans.

Effective plans

Effective plans are **S.M.A.R.T. plans**:

> Specific   > Measurable   > Agreed   > Realistic   > Timed

Specific

Plans need to establish very clear and precise aims. If plans are not specific enough they are likely to confuse staff or might be misinterpreted. Outcomes which are vague are also difficult to evaluate in terms of future success or failure. Setting out to be 'the best' is an example of an unclear objective. Does this mean having the largest market share? The best customer service? The highest turnover? The biggest profit? If the aim is to have the biggest market share in the industry by 2020, then it is much more specific and easier to verify.

unit **3**

Measurable

It's also important to set a target which can be evaluated. Without ongoing evaluation it will not be possible to identify weaknesses or deviations. In a competitive business environment companies cannot afford loss-making ventures and need to spot problems as early as possible.

The criterion of having the biggest market share in a particular industry is clearly a more measurable objective than simple aiming to be 'the best in the business'.

Agreed

Plans which are supported by all members of staff or by all major stakeholders are far more likely to be implemented successfully than those which are simply imposed by senior management. Where possible, stakeholders should be involved in the formulation of plans as well as their implementation.

Performance appraisal, which is a function of human resource managers, would be an example of this approach to management by consensus.

Realistic

Objectives which are difficult or impossible to achieve may de-motivate staff rather than inspire them. Management needs to set goals which reflect the capabilities of the business, and in particular the staff who will be expected to achieve these goals. If staff see little realistic hope of success they are likely to become demoralised and will rarely associate work with any sense of positivity. It is better to improve a business with small gradual steps rather than risk the failure of unrealistic leaps.

Timed

Setting a clear time frame for achieving the goals is also a characteristic of effective planning. Plans should not be open-ended as this not only causes delays but once again makes it difficult to evaluate and control the outcome.

The previous example of a business which aims to have the largest market share by 2020 is a strategic objective which is specific, measurable and timed. For a business which already has an established market presence or which has innovative new technology, this should not be unrealistic. It would therefore be up to management to agree a set of tactical plans aimed at making the objective a reality.

Management Activity: Organising

This management function involves bringing people and capital resources together to achieve a common goal. It is really about co-coordinating the activities of a business in a systematic or structured way. Once plans have been made, managers must set about making the best use of the resources available in order to achieve them.

Organisational structure

An organisational structure sets out the ways in which these resources and tasks will be divided. It also clearly defines areas of responsibility, the chain of command and span of control.

Businesses employ a number of clearly identifiable organisational structures and it is up to each company to choose the type of structure which best suits its culture and needs. It also needs to be recognised that a business may decide to alter its structure as circumstances change. This might occur, for example, when a business expands or diversifies its operations. The implications of changes to the organisational structure will be set out in *Chapter 16: Business Expansion*.

Functional structure

Departments are organised on the basis of what function or role staff perform in the organisation. All staff who do the same job are assigned to the same department; therefore all marketing personnel are bundled together in a marketing department, all production staff in a production department and so on.

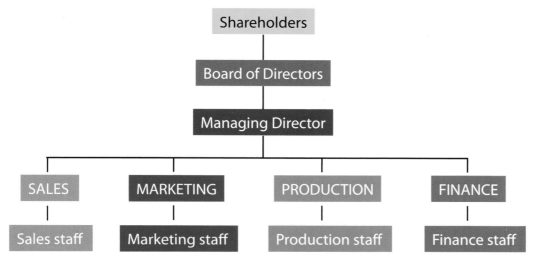

> ❯ The **advantages** of this type of structure are that each department is effectively a **pool of expertise** for each function. This makes the operation more efficient and also helps when training new staff. It may also be possible to benefit from economies of scale associated with group activities.

> ❯ **Economies of scale** arise when carrying out activities on a large scale. As a result of efficiencies generated through bulk-buying and pooling of resources, the unit costs of production are often lower despite the increase in the scale of the operation.

> ❯ The main **disadvantage** of a functional structure is that employees often see themselves in **isolation** from the rest of the business and fail to recognise 'the bigger picture'. They focus exclusively on their own departmental issues and consequently may ignore the more important organisational goals.

> This lack of awareness and 'inward looking' approach can also lead to **problems with communication** right across the organisation.

Product structure

A product structure divides business operations on the basis of its product lines, and would suit a business like Sony, which makes several different types of product.

Each product area or division will have its own compliment of sales, marketing, production and finance staff who deal only with product-specific issues.

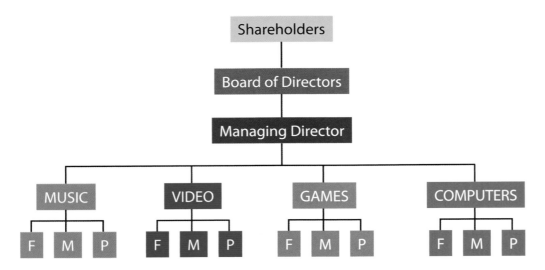

F – Finance
M – Marketing
P – Production

> There are once again **advantages** in terms of **specialist expertise**. For example, sales staff who operate in the computer division will have a very detailed knowledge of these types of product and will be in a better position to meet the needs of their customers.

> This type of structure also opens up the lines of **communication** between staff in different functional areas. In order to be successful high levels of co-operation and mutual understanding are needed between staff involved in design, production, sales and finance.

> The main **disadvantage** of a product structure is that it is likely to involve some **duplication** of work. With functional staff being spread across several divisions of the business, the overall number of staff required will increase.

Based on the example above, each product division may require three finance staff to meet its needs. This is a total of twelve staff in all. Using a functional structure it may be possible for just ten finance staff in a dedicated finance department to carry out the same work for the entire company.

> In some instances this duplication may even turn into **competition between different product divisions**. For example, sales and marketing staff in the music division will be competing against sales and marketing staff from the computer division for the same customers.

› Product structures also mean that a high level of specialisation may **limit the firm's scope to transfer employees** from one division to another. In situations where transfers are possible they are likely to involve training costs.

Geographic structure

A geographic structure is very similar to a product structure, except that corporate divisions are based on geographic locations rather than the type of goods produced.

A geographic structure is most likely to be employed by a transnational company which has operations and cost centres across the globe. Each division is responsible for a full range of activities including production, marketing, finance and sales and each division may also produce a range of goods.

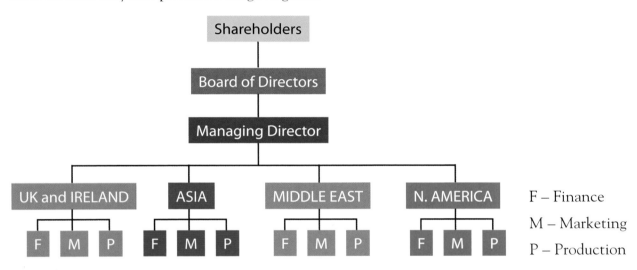

F – Finance

M – Marketing

P – Production

› One **advantage** of this type of structure is that it allows the company to **meet the needs of each market** in which it operates and adapt its business model to suit the needs of a local target market.

› A geographic structure also allows **senior management** to examine the operating costs and profitability for each location. This is important for TNCs which are concerned with overall corporate profitability and have a high degree of mobility when it comes to business location.

› The **disadvantages** of a geographic structure again relate to **duplication of resources** and also the need for senior managers to employ considerable time and effort on the co-ordination of activities at corporate level.

Matrix/team structure

A matrix structure combines both a functional structure and a team approach to business operations. Staff are assigned to a functional department but can also be selected to take part in project teams when a specific need arises. A matrix or team structure is particularly suited to companies which operate in very dynamic industries or business environments, and is commonly utilised by technology companies.

unit

3

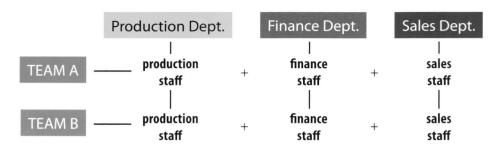

Project teams can be set up on an ad hoc basis and team members appointed with the appropriate skill set or expertise for the project.

Some companies may utilise a laissez-faire style of management and allow the team to complete its assigned task with little interference from management.

A computer software company may decide to set up a project team in order to develop a new game or programme. Employees with backgrounds in programming, manufacturing, finance and marketing may be chosen to make up this team. Given the level of expertise it would seem appropriate for senior management to set a clear objective and time frame while also facilitating the project through the provision of resources. Provided they stick to the brief, the budget and the time frame, the project team will have a great degree of autonomy when developing the software.

> One of the **advantages** of a matrix structure is that it gives a business a great degree of **flexibility**, as it enables managers to deploy staff with the appropriate expertise to meet dynamic business needs.

> **Co-ordination and communication** within the business is improved as team members with different skills and areas of expertise are required to work more closely together.

Bee hives operate on a matrix structure

Staff with different functional backgrounds gain a much greater understanding of how their individual jobs meet the overall needs of the business, as well as gaining useful insights into the role of their colleagues.

> On account of the increased communication and transfer of skills there are likely to be major benefits to the business in terms of **innovation**, **problem solving** and **motivation**. Team members may also have the opportunity to become team leaders.

> The possible **disadvantages** of adopting a matrix structure arise from the **divided roles** and loyalties which some employees may experience. For example, a member of the marketing department may be accountable to both his functional manager and his team manager. If these relationships are not managed carefully, they may create confusion and frustration for staff.

> Teamwork is a skill which can be improved with training and experience and so a matrix structure **may not be suitable for inexperienced staff**. It is very likely that a

business wishing to use this type of structure will need to invest time and money in appropriate staff training.

> Businesses which seek to move from a very traditional functional structure may also experience some **resistance from staff**, especially where it is perceived as a threat to their jobs or existing working conditions.

Choosing and changing an organisational structure

The choice of which organisational structure to adopt rests with senior management in a business. They need to choose a structure which suits both the needs and culture of the organisation. They need to be mindful of the company's mission and its strategic goals before opting for the organisational structure which is most likely to achieve these objectives.

The chosen structure needs to be easily managed and must allow information to be communicated to all parts of the organisation.

Two other important issues which may influence the choice of structure are the **chain of command** and the **span of control**.

Chain of command

The chain of command establishes the hierarchy in the business and shows how instructions flow through an organisation, from top to bottom. It also illustrates how many levels (layers) of management are involved.

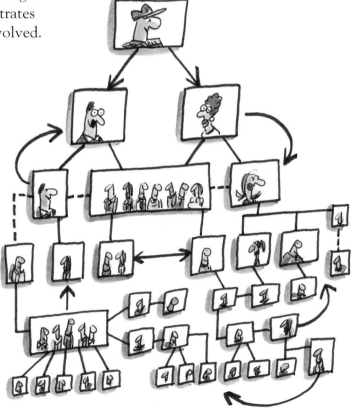

If the chain of command is too long or has too many levels there is a danger that information transfer will be slow or distorted. If you have ever played 'Chinese whispers' you will have experienced this effect.

Over time a company may decide to remove some of these management layers. This process of stripping away layers of management is called **delayering** and is usually an attempt to improve the speed at which information is communicated throughout the business.

In recent years many companies have begun to evaluate the role and impact of their organisational structures and in some cases have decided to make major changes to it.

Unfortunately the term **'restructuring'** has become all-too-synonymous with job losses in some businesses.

Case Study

In October 2011 the European insurance giant Aviva embarked on a major restructuring programme which combined Aviva Ireland with Aviva UK to form a new UK and Ireland region. The company explained that the move was part of its 'ambition to become the most competitive insurance provider in Ireland'. They went on to explain that the Irish business would benefit from Aviva UK's investment in technology, underwriting capability and significant purchasing power, enabling Aviva Ireland to offer more competitive pricing and to introduce new products and services.

The cost in employment terms was in the region of 950 jobs, to be lost over a two-year period.

The span of control

The 'span of control' refers to the number of workers reporting directly to each manager. A **wide span** would be one where a manager is responsible for a large number of subordinates. A wide span suits highly motivated and autonomous staff, or those whose jobs are routine and require little decision-making. In both of these situations it should be possible for a single manager to oversee the work of a relatively large group of employees.

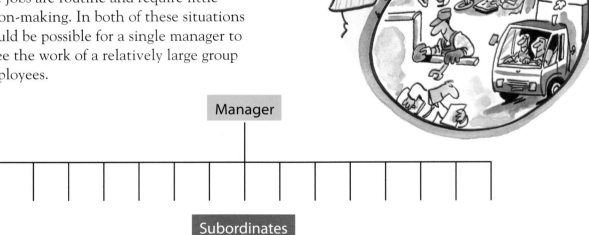

A **narrow span** of control refers to a situation where a manager has responsibility for a much smaller group of employees. It is suited to areas where workers need close supervision or constant guidance from their manager.

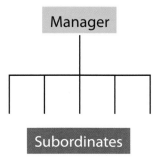

unit **3**

Management Activity: Controlling

Controlling is really about **measuring performance** and is carried out by **comparing actual outcomes to plans,** and taking corrective action if necessary. As outlined previously, it's important for business plans to set out specific and measurable outcomes and the reason for this is to facilitate this important control procedure.

For businesses there are **four key areas** which need to be controlled:

> Stock   > Credit
> Quality   > Finance

Stock control

Businesses need to control stock (inventory) levels for finished goods and raw materials and managers need to establish an optimum or ideal stock level for both. Decisions will also need to be made in relation to minimum, maximum and re-order levels.

Minimum stock levels represent the smallest amount of stock it is necessary to hold, whereas the **maximum stock level** is the upper limit. The **re-order level** is the point at which new stock needs to be ordered. It takes into account the expected time period from day of ordering to delivery of the goods. This is called the **lead-time.** The re-order level will also depend on projected daily sales.

A business which sells 150 units a week should never hold fewer than 300 units if the lead-time is two weeks. This means that 300 units is the minimum stock level.

In practice, the business will probably allow for a small level of safety stock (or **buffer stock**), and will re-order when stock levels drop to 400 units. This will allow the business to avoid stock-outs in the event that deliveries are slow or sales surge unexpectedly.

A decision to allow for buffer stock is an example of **contingency planning.**

There are costs associated with both overstocking and under-stocking and some businesses use **just-in-time (JIT)** stock-control systems in order to minimise these costs.

A just-in-time system aims to limit the stock levels for raw materials and finished goods by ensuring raw materials arrive just as they are needed for production. Companies like Dell Computers also seek to ship finished goods immediately after production so as to minimise their storage and insurance costs. This type of system requires very careful planning and excellent logistics and is only possible where suppliers and customers have a very close working relationship. The use of **Electronic Data Interchange (EDI)** is an important factor in ensuring the success of this type of stock-control system.

Modern businesses use ICT to assist them in stock control and a number of specialist software packages are available commercially. For businesses making use of Electronic Data Interchange (EDI), the process of monitoring and reordering stock can be carried out using sophisticated computer systems.

unit 3

Increased storage and insurance costs, as well as the danger of obsolescence, are the most obvious consequences of excessive stock levels.

The major cost associated with inadequate stock levels is a loss of sales. When a stock-out occurs customers may choose to fill their orders from another supplier. If they go elsewhere and are happy with the new supplier there is a danger that the original supplier will lose the customer permanently.

Quality control

All businesses must ensure that the goods and services they provide meet legal requirements and customer expectations. The Sale of Goods and Supply of Services Act, 1980, requires products to be of merchantable quality and fit for their intended purpose. Businesses which fail to meet these standards are in breach of contract and will need to provide suitable redress to consumers.

Companies which adopt the marketing concept and produce goods to meet the needs of their target market are more likely to boost their sales and profits. For modern businesses, it's important to realise that issues of quality are no longer just about the finished product. There is increased emphasis on **Total Quality Management (TQM)**, which stresses quality at every step from sourcing of raw materials right through to after-sales service. TQM is discussed in greater detail in *Chapter 12: Managing Change*.

Implementing a quality control system

> **Focus on TQM:** The most effective systems of quality control will focus attention on all business inputs, activities and outputs. In effect this is a description of Total Quality Management and it seeks to ensure that every single aspect of the business succeeds in meeting very stringent quality standards.

> **Regular inspections:** Effective quality control requires regular checks to ensure standards are being met. Raw materials should be checked when they arrive, systematic checks should be made during the production process and finished goods need to be checked before being dispatched to retailers and customers.

> **Staff training and teamwork:** Since staff members are ultimately responsible for ensuring all goods and services meet the required quality standards, it is essential that they are made aware of the standards and provided with regular training in order to maintain their skill levels.

If a TQM approach is adopted by the business, it relies on the collective efforts of all employees to ensure that quality is an overriding concern. This requires excellent teamwork and may even involve more formal interactions, such as quality circles.

Quality circles are discussion groups made up of workers who meet on a regular basis to discuss their jobs and to make suggestions about how the quality of their work can be improved.

Benefits of effective quality control

> **More satisfied customers:** Customers will be happy to buy goods and services once they are satisfied that the quality meets their expectations and the legally acceptable standard.

> **Cost savings:** Imperfect or substandard goods are extremely wasteful of business resources and will result in defective items being reworked or dumped. By eliminating waste and costly errors a business can make huge financial savings.

> **Better quality and improved reputation:** Businesses which gain a reputation for poor quality are unlikely to attract repeat business. By the same token, a reputation for high quality enhances the long-term sustainability of a business. Profitability may also increase as higher quality may allow a business to charge higher prices. This is called a **premium pricing policy**.

Recognised quality standards

> The **International Standards Organisation (ISO)** sets out clearly defined quality standards across a range of industries. These standards are voluntary but are internationally recognised.

In order to receive accreditation businesses must meet the stringent standards set out for their industry. These high levels of quality must be independently verified by ISO inspections.

ISO certification is particularly beneficial for companies involved in international trade since it serves to reassure potential customers about the high quality of the goods and services on offer.

> The **Q Mark** is a quality standard available to businesses operating in Ireland only. It is broadly similar to the ISO certification and is awarded by the Excellence Ireland Quality Association.

Credit control

Buying goods **on credit** means 'buying now and paying later'.

The central issue for credit controllers is effective management of debtors and creditors.

Debtors are other businesses which owe us money, usually because we have sold them goods on credit or have loaned money to them. **Creditors are businesses to which we owe money** as a result of buying goods on credit or borrowing from them.

In simple terms, a business needs to collect debts from its debtors before paying its creditors. If they cannot achieve this position, they need to consider getting a bank overdraft or perhaps even factoring some debts. **Factoring** involves the sale of some debts to a third party at a discount (see *Chapter 8: Household and Business Management: Finance*).

The first step in effective credit control is to **evaluate the creditworthiness of potential customers**. It may be possible to achieve this by getting a bank reference or by contacting other suppliers who have dealt with them in the past (**a trade reference**).

Most lenders pass details of customer loans on to the **Irish Credit Bureau (ICB)** and this information is used to generate credit reports and credit ratings for each business or individual. Customers seeking credit can also be asked to provide a recent ICB credit report to support their request.

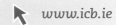
www.icb.ie

Having established their creditworthiness the next step is to **set realistic credit limits** for each customer. These limits will reflect the need to generate sales but will also take into account the customer's credit history and ability to repay.

A firm needs to enforce these credit limits and should ensure that invoices and reminder notices are issued to customers as promptly as possible.

Debtors who are slow to pay create **liquidity (cash flow) problems** and may need to be offered discounts, or charged interest to encourage prompt payment.

The major benefit of effective credit control is that it helps to minimise **bad debts**. A bad debt occurs when a debtor is unable to pay some or all of the money they owe. That part of the debt which cannot be recovered is effectively a loss and needs to be written off as an expense in the profit-and-loss account.

Financial control

Financial control (also called **budgetary control**) deals with key issues like cash-flow management and budgeting. It aims to ensure the business always has sufficient money available to carry out its day-to-day activities.

Financial controllers are likely to avail of the following management tools to ensure effective financial control:

> Budgeting (see *Chapter 8*)
> Cash flow forecasting (see *Chapter 8*)
> Ratio analysis (see *Chapter 10*)
> Break-even analysis (see *Chapter 13*)

The steps involved in **effective financial control** are as follows:

1 **Set targets:** This generally involves preparing departmental budgets. A **budget** is a financial plan which sets out projected income and expenditures. Budgets are normally based on previous patterns of income and expenditure but may be adjusted to reflect increased business activity in some departments.

2 **Compare results to targets:** Managers will need to keep accurate records of actual income and expenditure and these figures can then be compared with the targets set out in the budget.

3 **Investigate reasons for differences:** If there are differences between budgeted and actual figures, the financial controller must uncover the reasons why these have arisen.

4 **Take corrective action:** Based on their investigation and analysis of the differences, managers must set out measures to eliminate these discrepancies and ensure that future cash flows are in line with targets.

The bottom line for any business is that they must have enough money available to pay bills as they fall due. If they cannot generate this finance from day-to-day operations, they will need to look at borrowing the money. In these situations the job of the financial controller may extend to sourcing the cheapest and most suitable source of finance to meet the short-term needs of the business.

Benefits of control

Control procedures are beneficial to businesses for the following reasons:

> Effective control helps **eliminate costly mistakes**. The sooner a mistake is identified, the sooner it can be rectified and the less costly it will be.

> Controls are necessary for the purpose of **evaluation**. Managers need to know how effectively a business has achieved its planned objectives.

> Control mechanisms also help **reduce waste**, especially in areas like product quality. Businesses that adopt a Total Quality Management approach are likely to improve business performance right across their organisation.

> Controls can also be used to **motivate staff** and keep them focused on the task in hand. If staff realise that their performance is subject to some form of evaluation or control they are more likely to carry out the task in a careful and diligent manner.

**Chapter Review Diagram –
Management Activities: Planning, Organising and Controlling**

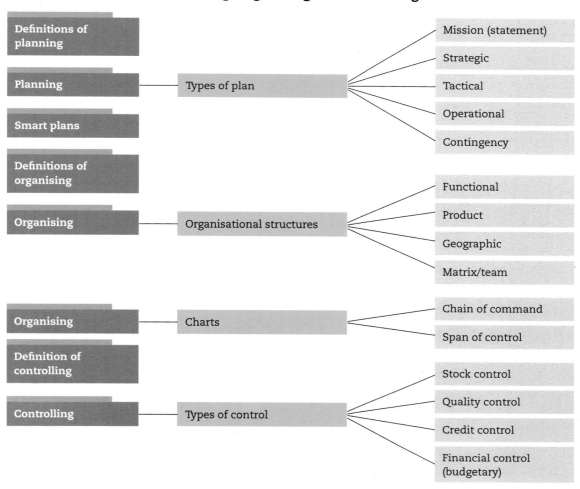

125

Q Chapter Review Questions

1 What is planning?

2 What are the potential consequences to a business of poor planning?

3 Explain two benefits of planning.

4 Explain the term 'SWOT analysis'.

5 Explain the purpose of a mission statement.

6 Distinguish between a strategic plan and a tactical plan.

7 Illustrate the importance of contingency planning to a business.

8 'Effective plans are SMART plans.' Discuss this statement.

9 (i) List four common types of organisational structure.

   (ii) Use a diagram to illustrate any three of these structures.

10 Outline the benefits of a clearly defined organisational structure to a business.

11 Define what is meant by the chain of command in an organisation.

12 What is 'delayering'?

13 Explain the term 'span of control' and use a diagram to illustrate both wide and narrow spans of control.

14 Controlling is measuring performance and is carried out by comparing outcomes to plans, and taking corrective action if necessary. What four key areas need to be controlled in a business?

15 Outline the benefits of an effective quality control system in business.

Q Questions · Ordinary Level

1 (a) Name **two** types of plans used in business.

   (b) Explain **two** benefits of planning for a business.   *LCOL 2009 (25 marks)*

2 List the three management activities.   *LCOL 2004 (10 marks)*

3 Explain the following terms:

   (i) chain of command

   (ii) mission statement

4 An effective plan is supposed to be a SMART plan. Describe four features of an effective plan.

5 Outline the importance of stock control to a company. *LCOL 2002 (10 marks)*

6 Draft and label a matrix structure for a manufacturing organisation.

7 Name **one** type of organisation structure.

8 Draw a chart of an organisation structure of your choice.

Q Questions · Higher Level

1 (a) Explain the term span of control.

(b) Outline **two** factors that affect the width of the span of control in a business.
LCHL 2011 (10 marks)

2 (a) (i) What is meant by the term SWOT analysis?

(ii) Conduct a SWOT analysis on a business of your choice *(20 marks)*

(b) Analyse the contribution that strategic and tactical planning can make to the successful management of a business. Use examples in your answer and include two points under each heading. *(20 marks)*

(c) Discuss the benefits of a functional organisational structure in a business. Refer to the Chain of Command and Span of Control in your answer. *LCHL 2010 (20 marks)*

3 Define 'organising'. Illustrate the importance of good organisation for the success of a business enterprise. *LCHL 2004 (15 marks)*

4 Evaluate how **two** different types of planning contribute to the success of a business or community enterprise. Use examples in your answer. *LCHL 2004 (20 marks)*

5 Draft a typical span of control for an organisation of your choice. *LCHL 2002 (10 marks)*

6 'Planning is the most important management activity.' Explain why many managers would deem this statement to be true. Support your answer with reasons and examples.
LCHL 2001 (25 marks)

7 Define 'controlling' in a business context.

8 Contrast the **three** most common types of control in a business.

unit **3**

Q Applied Business Question

Tech-Fixers Ltd

Tony and Lucy had long thought about setting up their own business. Both were ambitious and very well educated with degrees in computer science. They had both worked in a number of companies in Ireland and abroad and gained an immense amount of experience in the development and maintenance of information and communications technology. Both were aware of the challenges to be met when starting a new business, but felt that they had lots of good ideas and were excited about getting down to work. Their sense of confidence and their analysis of the growth prospects for the ICT industry encouraged them to make the decision to set up Tech-Fixers Ltd. The company provides domestic customers and small businesses with maintenance and technical support over the phone or at the client's workplace or home.

Their business has expanded to include four retail outlets nationwide and Lucy and Tony owed much of this success to the preparation of detailed and realistic business plans at the outset. While this ensured that the business was able to start its development on a secure footing, it had become increasingly difficult to develop a strategic vision for the business.

Both Tony and Lucy work extremely hard but despite this are always rushing to achieve deadlines. Lucy has highlighted her concern that the company may not be sufficiently proactive and therefore lacks vision for the future.

The work environment is highly pressurised and all their employees are beginning to feel the strain of meeting tight deadlines. Some customers have complained about poor standards of workmanship and customer care.

Neither Tony nor Lucy has ever asked staff for their opinions or ideas that might improve the level of service and morale at the company. Staff turnover is unusually high and Lucy is very keen that this issue be addressed by adopting a more democratic and inclusive management style. Tony, however, has recently taken to issuing orders to employees and some staff have seen their hours of work reduced without explanation or compensation.

In a recent meeting Tony and Lucy discussed ways of increasing sales, improving the quality of service to customers and boosting staff morale. They both agreed that the achievement of better outcomes in their business would require better use of resources and a more formal organisational structure.

They also discussed the idea of rewarding staff performance based on the attainment of clearly defined goals and targets. While this might require the introduction of routine performance appraisal for employees, no final decision has been made on this issue yet.

(a) Illustrate the enterprising characteristics displayed by Tony and Lucy.   *(20 marks)*

(b) Evaluate how this couple might succeed better in the business if they improved their management skills. Support your answer with reference to the text.   *(30 marks)*

(c) Discuss how management activities can help Tony and Lucy improve the performance of the business.   *(30 marks)*

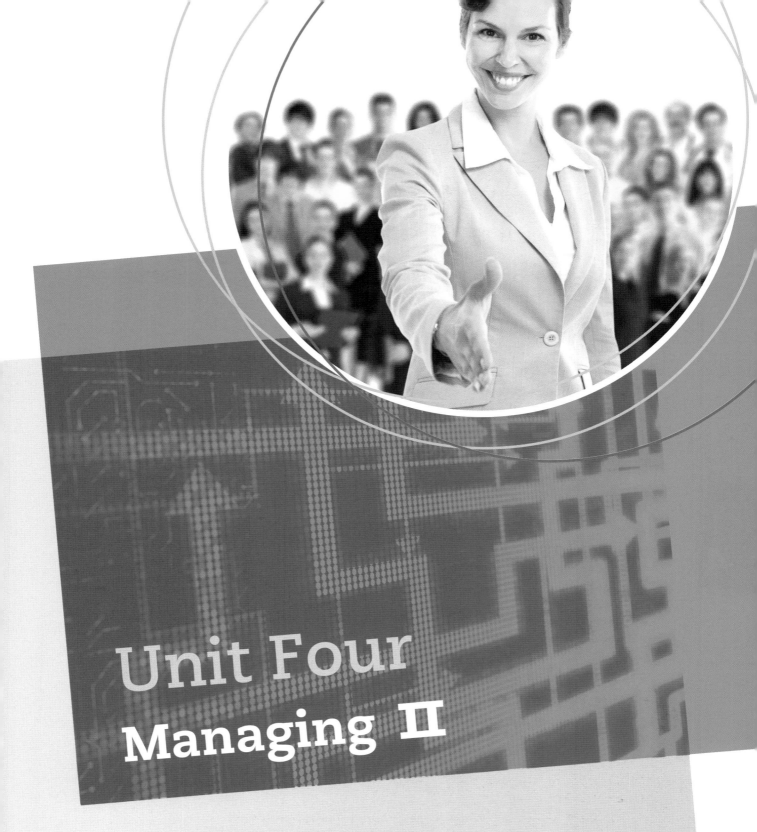

Unit Four

Managing Ⅱ

Chapter 8
Household and Business Management: Finance

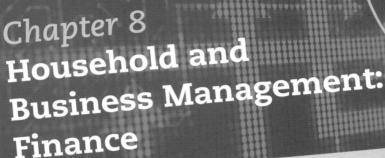

Syllabus Outcomes

On completion, the student should be able to:

» 4.5.1 Outline the differences between managing a household and managing a business;

» 4.5.2 Explain the importance of finance, insurance and tax implications for business.

News Flash

1 Read the newspaper extract below and discuss the issues raised.

2 Can you explain any of the highlighted terms?

Credit review office underused

by Simon Carswell

The state office set up to review why small businesses have been refused loans is one of the most "under-utilised" parts of the financial system, according to the Department of Finance's head of banking supervision John Moran.

Addressing the banking conference, Mr Moran said he found it disappointing and frustrating that there were not more applications to the Credit Review Office, despite the criticism that the banks were not lending.

There needed to be "spot-checking" across the banks to determine lending levels, he said.

The department plans to survey 1,500 businesses to determine the level of credit supply and demand, and to repeat this exercise every six to eight months.

Mr Moran said banks had to move away from lending on property and "hard assets" as collateral to understanding the business models and cash flows of firms.

There were levers the department could pull to force banks to meet their lending targets, he said.

Lending decisions had become more centralised at the banks and they need to delegate more authority to local levels, he said.

He called on more tie-ups between businesses and venture capital funds to fund enterprise.

Brian Hartzer, chief executive of UK retail, wealth and Ulster Bank at Royal Bank of Scotland, warned that higher capital and liquidity demands on banks would inevitably reduce the amount of loans and increase their cost.

Greater demands by state regulators were creating "parochialism and protectionism" in banking and that this was "a very dangerous development", he said.

Danny McCoy, director general of employers' group, Ibec, said that there was a risk of a swing towards over-regulation after the crisis and "more emphasis on box-ticking than on management".

The Irish Times, THURSDAY, 13 OCTOBER 2011.

Finance

Budgets and cash flow forecasts (CFF)

A **budget** is a financial plan. Household budgets and cash flow forecasts show expected monthly income and planned expenditure. It is important for both businesses and households to manage their cash flow since this allows them to live within their means. **Cash flow forecasts** also help identify future surpluses and deficits. A **surplus occurs when income exceeds expenditure** and a **deficit is the term used to describe a month which has excess expenditure**.

Once identified it should be possible for the household or business to arrange additional finance to overcome a deficit, or place surplus funds on short-term deposit with a financial institution.

Turnover is vanity, profit is sanity but cash flow is reality.

Banker's mantra

A cash flow forecast is a plan, drawn up by a business, to ensure that there is ample liquidity available each month. **Liquidity** is about making sure there is enough money coming into the business each month in order to pay bills and expenses as they fall due. Poor liquidity is perhaps the single biggest reason for business failure, so maintaining a balance between total income and total expenditure should be a key priority for business managers. Many businesses get into financial difficulty because they try to grow too rapidly. Entrepreneurs often pursue additional profit by increasing sales revenue, but fail to realise that extra sales usually mean extra costs for things like materials, transport and wages.

Failure to collect payment quickly from customers will cause problems with bill payment. This in turn will lead to increased reliance on borrowing or eventual bankruptcy. This sequence of events is sadly all too common in business and only serves to underline the importance of cash flow management.

« *syllabus signpost* 4.5.2

Importance of cash flow forecasting

> Cash flow forecasting creates estimates of income and expenditure and allows managers to identify periods of excessive cash inflow or outflow.

> Once identified, managers can formulate plans to deal with excess income or expenditure. For example, the household or business may need to arrange for a short-term loan to cover cash shortfalls or may invest cash surpluses to earn deposit interest.

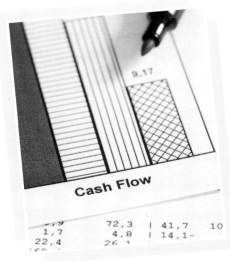

unit 4

> Cash flow forecasts are intended to help businesses and households to make the most out of the cash resources available to them. They are particularly useful for predicting future problems. Cash flow forecasts and household budgets focus on two specific areas:

> **Receipts (Income)**
> **Payments (Expenditure)**

Some of the main sources of income and items of expenditure for both households and businesses are listed below:

« syllabus signpost
4.5.1

Household Income	Business Income
Wages and salaries	Sales income
Unemployment benefit	Investment income/deposit interest
Pension	Receipts from debtors
Child benefit	Income from grants
Interest on savings	Borrowings
Lottery winnings	Share capital
	VAT refunds

Household Expenditure	Business Expenditure
Mortgage/rent	Purchase of raw materials
Insurance	Purchase/rental of fixed assets
Groceries	Dividends
Travel expenses	Taxation (VAT, PAYE, etc)
Light and heat	Payments to creditors
Entertainment	Overheads
School costs	Loan repayments

Interpreting cash flow forecasts

A cash flow forecast of Albatros Ltd is shown below. It outlines **receipts** and **payments** of this company.

Cash flow forecast of Albatros Ltd

2007	July	August	September	Total
Receipts (A)	60,000	65,000	80,000	205,000
Payments (B)	70,000	55,000	55,000	180,000
Net cash (A–B)	(10,000)	10,000	25,000	25,000
Opening cash	3,000	(7,000)	3,000	3,000
Closing cash	(7,000)	3,000	28,000	28,000

Deficit   Surplus

When analysing and interpreting cash flow forecasts it's important to recognise 'problem months' for the business. Any figure in brackets is a minus amount. This represents a deficit and will result in a net cash outflow for that month. This is never an ideal situation for any business, but it may be sustainable in the short term, provided the deficit can be made up from available cash reserves (opening cash).

If you examine the CFF for Albatros Ltd it indicates they expect to receive a greater income in August and September than they plan to spend. This will leave them with net cash surpluses of €10,000 and €25,000 respectively.

July, however, presents a different scenario, since a net cash deficit is expected. This planned overspend of €10,000 cannot be met out of opening cash reserves and this means that Albatros Ltd will face an overall (closing cash) shortfall of €7,000 at the end of July.

A closing cash deficit is *always* a problem for a business, since this money will need to be made up from borrowing. A business which has an ongoing liquidity problem of this type will face difficulties paying bills and is very reliant on short-term borrowings. In recent times many businesses in Ireland have struggled to survive, as they have been unable to secure adequate overdraft facilities during the credit crunch. A **credit crunch** (or credit squeeze) describes a situation where there is a shortage of funding available in financial markets and consequently banks tighten their lending criteria. In effect, financial institutions are unable or unwilling to lend.

Fortunately for Albatros Ltd, their liquidity problems are short-term ones and the CFF indicates that they will have overcome the deficit by the end of August and will add to their cash reserves with a healthy surplus in September. This CFF could be used to support their application for an overdraft as it should satisfy the bank manager as to the longer-term viability of the business.

Even with the best financial management available it is almost inevitable that businesses and households will not always be in a position to meet their needs from their own financial resources. When this happens they will need to avail of some of the sources of finance set out below. Short-term sources will be repaid in less than one year, medium-term sources between two and five years, while long-term finance will be repaid over a time period which exceeds five years.

unit
4

Sources of Finance

Short Term	Medium Term	Long Term
(<1 year)	(1-5 years)	(>5 years)
Creditors	Leasing	Share capital*
Bank overdraft	Medium-term loan	Debentures*
Accrued expenses	Hire purchase	Retained earnings*/savings
Factoring*		Venture capital*
Credit cards		Grants
		Mortgages
		Sale and leaseback*

*Available to businesses only.

What factors influence households and businesses when choosing sources of finance?

> **Purpose of the finance:** First and foremost a household or business needs to consider the reason for the finance. Is it for working capital (day-to-day) purposes or is it to fund longer-term assets or strategic objectives? The answer to this question will determine the time frame involved and will allow managers to apply the matching principle.

   The matching principle requires that each need is matched by a suitable type of finance. Short-term needs should be financed from short-term sources and longer-term needs require longer-term finance. Failure to do so will result in increased borrowing costs and may have unwelcome consequences for cash flow.

> **Amount of finance required:** Long-term sources tend to be more appropriate for large amounts as this allows a business to spread the cost of borrowing over a longer time period. Consequently, monthly repayments will be lower and this helps with liquidity. Trying to pay off borrowings too quickly can lead to cash shortfalls for other essential items and this is rarely in the best interests of the household or business.

> **Cost of finance:** Compare the **Annual Percentage Rate (APR)** of each possible source and lender. Since the APR is a standardised measure of borrowing cost, it allows managers to evaluate the cost implications of each option.

   Share issues and use of retained earnings are beneficial because they avoid the need for monthly repayments.

unit 4

> **Control:** The business will need to examine the impact of some sources of finance on business ownership and control. Issuing new shares will allow new shareholders to invest in the company but will also give them a say in how the business is run, as well as a share of future dividends.

> **Security required:** What collateral will be required to protect the lender in case of non-payment?

Some sources of finance, specifically mortgages and debentures, may require business assets to be set aside in the event of default. This will limit the ability to cash in on these assets by selling them at a later date.

> **Risk involved:** This requires an overall assessment of the level of risk associated with each source of finance. This risk may be financial, reputational or may reflect the risks associated with default.

Students are frequently asked to compare, contrast or evaluate sources of finance, so make sure you understand the relative advantages and disadvantages of each. To assist you with this type of question, each source of finance outlined below will be evaluated on the basis of:

> Cost   > Impact on control   > Security required   > Risk

unit 4

Short-term sources of finance

Creditors

A trade creditor is an individual or company to whom money is owed, very often because goods were purchased on a 'buy now, pay later' basis. Most businesses avail of this type of credit arrangement and hope to sell the goods quickly. If they succeed with these quick sales they will be in a position to pay for the goods within the agreed credit term, usually thirty to sixty days.

As most businesses do not have sufficient cash available to pay for goods immediately, the availability of credit from suppliers is hugely important to their survival.

Households avail of credit terms when purchasing utilities like gas and electricity. They consume whatever quantity they need and receive a bill at the end of the month. Households which have 'bill pay' phones are also making use of credit terms offered by their service providers.

> **Cost:** No direct cost involved, but cash discounts may be lost and late payment may be subject to interest charges.

> **Impact on control:** No impact on control.

> **Security required:** Security not required. In business situations the seller retains legal ownership until goods have been paid for.

> **Risk:** Little financial risk involved although some reputational damage may occur for households and businesses which miss payments. This will cause their credit rating to disimprove and will make it harder to get credit in the future.

Bank overdraft

A bank overdraft is permission from a bank to withdraw more money from a current account than is actually in the account. An overdraft facility is subject to an agreed limit and interest is charged on the overdrawn balance. The rate of interest charged is much higher than for medium- or long-term lending and reflects the fact that a bank overdraft is only designed to be a short-term facility.

Banks will not allow a business to have a continuous overdraft and will insist their customers clear their overdraft for at least one full month each year. Bank managers are normally the decision makers when clients are seeking overdraft approval from their bank.

> **Cost:** The APR varies from one lender to another. In general short-term finance carries a higher rate of interest than longer-term sources.

> **Impact on control:** No direct impact on control but a lender may take court action to recover unpaid debt. In these situations the court could appoint independent financial managers (called receivers) to manage the business.

> **Security required:** Some lenders require security but most rely on ability to repay and will consider household or business income.

> **Risk:** Relatively low risk. The lender can recall or terminate the overdraft facility at short notice and this will have serious financial consequences for the business.

Accrued expenses

These arise when households or businesses delay or fall behind on the payment of bills like electricity bills or VAT. As a result of this delayed payment these expenses are due from a company or household at the end of an accounting period.

They are a source of short-term finance because by delaying the bill payment money is made available for other uses. This approach carries considerable risk for the business or household concerned. Failure to pay may result in interest penalties, reduced credit rating, loss of services and perhaps even liquidation following legal action by creditors.

> **Cost:** No direct cost involved. Cash discounts for prompt payment may be lost.

> **Impact on control:** No impact on control.

> **Security required:** No security required.

> **Risk:** Failure to pay bills on time runs the risk of reputational damage and in extreme cases can result in bankruptcy proceedings.

unit 4

Liquidator appointed to McFeely firm

A High Court judge has made an order winding up a construction company of which developer Thomas McFeely is a director over its failure to pay the Revenue Commissioners some €144,000 for unpaid VAT and PRSI.

Ms Justice Mary Laffoy yesterday appointed a liquidator to Coalport Building Company Ltd, Holles Street, Dublin, after being informed the company had failed to satisfy the Revenue demand…

The Revenue had petitioned the court to have the company wound up on grounds its demand had not been satisfied and it was of the view Coalport was insolvent.

During yesterday's proceedings, the judge was told Coalport had a cheque in court to satisfy the Revenue's demand. Revenue's counsel asked for an adjournment to allow time for the cheque to clear.

Ms Justice Laffoy said that she was not prepared to grant a further adjournment of the matter.

She had already granted one adjournment and, in keeping with the policy of the court in relation to winding-up petitions, was not prepared to delay matters again.

When the matter was before her last month, she had warned that if the Revenue demand was not dealt with by yesterday, she would have no option but to make an order winding up the company.

It was up to Revenue to either withdraw the petition or proceed with its application to have the company wound up, she said.

The judge said she had also wanted to see an affidavit from the company's directors showing it was solvent but no such affidavit was presented to the court.

Following the judge's comments, Dermot Cahill, for Revenue, applied to proceed with the petition to wind up the company and the cheque was returned.

The judge made the winding-up order and appointed Derek Earl as liquidator…

This is an edited extract from **The Irish Times,** TUESDAY, 22 FEBRUARY 2011.

Factoring

This is the selling of debt to a debt management company at a discounted rate. Sometimes companies which are owed large amounts of money by debtors find themselves short of cash to meet their ongoing expenses. One solution to this liquidity problem is to sell the debt to a debt management company for a figure which is less than the book value of the debts.

 **Example**

ABC Ltd owes €100,000 to Elite Ltd for goods bought on credit. ABC Ltd is slow in paying the debt and Elite Ltd is concerned about the possible bad debt which would arise in the event of non-payment.

Elite Ltd approaches a factoring company which agrees to take over the total debt of €100,000 but at a discounted price of €80,000. The difference of €20,000 is a direct cost to Elite Ltd and since it's a bad debt it will impact on their annual profit. On the other hand, Elite Ltd no longer has an outstanding debt and has improved its liquidity position by receiving an €80,000 payment up front.

From the point of view of the factoring company the difference of €20,000 is their charge for taking over the risk of the debt. Most commercial banks offer factoring services to their business customers.

> **Cost:** Factoring is very expensive as debts are often sold at a big discount. This is the price which must be paid for immediate cash.

> **Impact on control:** No impact on control.

> **Security required:** No security required.

> **Risk:** There is a risk of alienating customers since some debtors do not like to have their debts 'sold on' to a third party and may be unwilling to do business with a company which regularly raises finance by factoring debts.

Credit cards

Households and businesses can utilise credit cards to buy goods now and pay for those goods at the end of each month. Each credit card has a spending limit which is set by the bank and is based on the customer's income and ability to repay. The cardholder enters their personal identity number (PIN) at the point of sale and does not require cash to purchase goods. The credit card company or bank issues a bill to the cardholder at the end of each month.

The bill sets out all items purchased on the credit card for the month in question, as well as any balance due from previous months. If the bill is paid *in full* by the holder no interest will be charged. However if the credit card account is not paid within the specified period the bank will charge a very high rate of interest on the outstanding amount. Many cardholders make the mistake of just paying the minimum payment requested by the bank (sometimes as low as 1 per cent of the outstanding balance) and incur higher interest charges.

Credit cards are a major source of household and business debt and need to be used and managed very carefully. Since it is very easy to buy goods without the immediate availability of cash, there is a danger that cardholders will run up large debts through impulse buying.

Ideally cardholders should only use a credit card to overcome temporary cash shortfalls, or perhaps to buy goods online. The golden rule with credit cards is not to spend more than you can afford to repay at the end of each month. By sticking to this rule you will avoid overspending, interest charges and the erosion of future spending power.

Case Study

In early 2011, the collective credit card debt of Ireland's 2.1 million cardholders stood at almost €3 billion. Many had run up huge personal debts during the boom years of the Celtic Tiger and are facing huge problems with repayments in recessionary times.

Bear in mind that a debt of €10,000, where the cardholder only makes the minimum monthly repayment, would take more than twenty years to pay off and would incur interest charges of over €9,000. This also assumes the card is not used to purchase any additional items during that period.

> **Cost:** As the example above illustrates, credit cards have the potential to be a very expensive source of finance. On the other hand, a customer who can clear the balance each month will benefit from up to fifty days' interest-free credit. The key to keeping costs down is knowing how to use credit cards effectively.

> **Impact on control:** No impact on control.

> **Security required:** Security is not required, although banks will issue cards and set spending limits according to a customer's perceived ability to repay.

> **Risk:** As it is easy to buy goods without the need for cash, there is considerable risk of running up large debts.

Medium-term sources of finance

Leasing

Leasing is essentially the renting of an asset by a household or business. The lease agreement, which is a contract, allows a household or business (the lessee) to have possession and use of the asset provided they make fixed and regular payments to the leasing company (the lesser). **Ownership is never transferred** and the asset remains the property of the leasing company.

For the lessee this offers the advantages of immediate use of the asset without the large capital outlay involved in a purchase agreement. It may also be possible to amend the contract terms at a later date so as to allow more modern equipment or larger premises to be leased. Businesses and households frequently enter into leasing arrangements for property and vehicles. Despite the short-term benefits they offer to cash flow, leasing assets can be expensive over a longer time period and it is likely that the rental cost will greatly exceed the initial purchase price of the asset.

Some lease agreements involving vehicles may provide for outright purchase of the asset at the end of a fixed period. The lessee may have the option of paying a once-off 'balloon payment' in order to secure ownership of the vehicle. The alternative is to return the vehicle to the leasing company.

> **Cost:** The total cost of leasing can be expensive, especially considering the lessee will never own the goods. Leasing does offer the benefit of lower monthly payments and this is beneficial for cash flow.

> **Impact on control:** No impact on control as ownership always remains with the leasing company.

> **Security required:** Security is not required.

> **Risk:** There is no real risk associated with leasing, although the lessee will have a contractual obligation to make regular payments for a fixed time period.

Medium-term loan

A medium-term loan is a source of finance which can be accessed by households and businesses through high street banks. The bank manager has the responsibility to assess the customer's ability to repay the loan over a maximum period of five years. The bank manager will also consider the suitability of the client by way of past credit history and any collateral which may be available. **Collateral** involves the borrower putting up some form of security, usually a valuable asset, against defaulting on repayments. In the event of non-payment, the lender can sell that asset in order to recover the debt.

This medium-term source of finance is very suited to businesses as the repayments are fixed but the loan itself can be redeemed at any time should the business have access to sufficient funds. For businesses, the interest charged on this type of loan can be written off as an expense in the profit and loss account. While this will reduce their annual profit, it will also mean a lower bill for corporation tax. This tax advantage does not apply to households or individuals using medium-term loans.

> **Cost:** The APR is usually cheaper than a bank overdraft.

> **Impact on control:** As with a bank overdraft, failure to repay the loan can result in legal action and loss of control.

> **Security required:** The lender may require some assets be provided as collateral.

> **Risk:** Failure to repay the loan can result in reputational damage, loss of credit rating and legal action.

Hire purchase (HP)

Hire purchase is a source of medium-term finance in which the purchaser pays an initial deposit followed by an agreed number of fixed regular instalments. Unlike leasing, **ownership of the asset will eventually pass to the hirer**, but not until payment of the last instalment has been made. There is no security required but the APR is very high.

Many people buy furniture using HP

Hire purchase agreements can be held with banks, building societies, finance companies and certain retail stores, for example, garages. The retailer is not actually providing the loan. It is acting as an agent for a finance company and earns commission from the finance company for arranging the loan. For example, if a Ford customer chooses to avail of the dealerships finance options the purchase will be financed by Ford Credit, which is a registered trading name of Bank of Ireland Leasing Ltd.

It is advisable to read a hire purchase contract very carefully before committing yourself to any agreement.

How does a hire purchase agreement work?

Here's an example to illustrate the how the HP agreement operates.

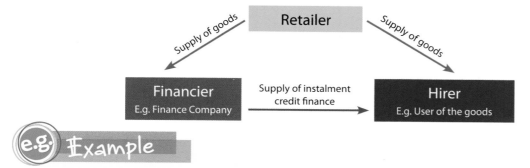

Example

Minico Ltd, a small printing business, needs a photocopier which costs €7,000, but is not in a position to finance this from its own cash resources or from borrowings.

Copyrite Ltd, a retailer of photocopying equipment, outlines a possible hire purchase (HP) agreement, with a finance company called Fastcash Ltd. This would involve an initial deposit of €700 followed by 36 monthly instalments of €220.

Minico Ltd agrees to the deal, pays the initial deposit to the finance company, and receives the photocopier it needs. The finance company will pay the full purchase price of €7,000 to the retailer (Copyrite Ltd).

The finance company (Fastcash Ltd) now owns the photocopier but enters into a contract which allows Minico Ltd to rent it from them. Fastcash Ltd will collect all future payments from Minico Ltd. Ownership of the photocopier will only pass to Minico Ltd at the end of the rental period, provided all payments have been made.

On the face of it, this seems like a mutually beneficial arrangement since all three parties to the agreement have secured some benefit. The small business has the copier it needs; the retailer has secured the sale of an expensive piece of equipment; while the finance company will receive payment on an ongoing basis.

The one issue to highlight here is the actual cost of the photocopier to Minico Ltd. Taking into account the deposit and the sum of all the instalments, the total cost is €8,620. This represents an interest payment of €1,620 and an APR of 23 per cent.

This is very expensive and Minico Ltd will need to weigh this cost up against the revenue the photocopier can generate. They will also need to consider the ongoing cash flow implications of the monthly instalments.

What is in a hire purchase agreement?

The hire purchase agreement states:

> The goods the agreement refers to – for example, a car or computer.
> The cash price of the goods.
> The hire purchase price, which is the total sum payable over the life of the loan in order to complete the purchase of the goods.
> The amount of each instalment. Sometimes the last instalment required to end the agreement is much larger than all the others. This is called a 'balloon' payment and will have to be paid to clear the loan and allow the consumer to become the owner.
> The date each instalment is to be paid.

unit 4

> The number of instalments.

> The names and addresses of all the parties to the agreement.

> A statement that the hirer has the right to withdraw from the agreement within ten days of receiving a copy of the agreement. This is known as a **'cooling off' period**. Consumers should try to take some time to read all the terms of the agreement and to ensure they understand these fully before signing this or any other part of the agreement.

> A statement that the hirer (consumer) must inform the owner (finance house) as to the whereabouts of the goods to which the agreement relates.

> The words 'Hire Purchase Agreement' must be stated clearly and in a prominent position on the agreement form.

> The fees and penalties that apply. Some examples of these include documentation fees, interest surcharge for missed repayments and penalty fees for missed or late payments.

Unless all of these requirements are contained in the agreement, and the hirer receives a written copy of the contract, the agreement itself may not be enforceable. (See 'legality of form' on page 13.)

Can a consumer terminate a hire purchase agreement?

A consumer (the hirer) can terminate the agreement at any time by giving notice in writing to the owner of the goods (the finance company). Consumers should be aware that breaking a hire purchase contract before its normal end date usually involves penalties. The consumer can either:

1 Pay half the amount of the total hire purchase price and return the goods to the owner.

Or

2 Buy the goods earlier than planned. The consumer can own the goods by paying the difference between the amount already paid and the total hire purchase price.

Can the owner (finance company) repossess the goods?

The finance company can only repossess the goods under certain circumstances. If the consumer has not yet paid off one-third of the total hire purchase cost, the owner can repossess the goods at any time without taking legal action against the consumer.

However, if the consumer has paid one-third or more of the total hire purchase cost, the owner cannot repossess the goods without taking legal proceedings.

❯ **Cost:** Hire purchase is usually a very expensive source of finance and the APR could be well in excess of 20 per cent. Taking out a medium-term loan is likely to be cheaper, but may not be possible if the customer has a poor credit rating. For that reason HP is often used as a last resort by households and businesses which cannot obtain loan finance.

❯ **Impact on control:** No loss of control.

❯ **Security required:** Since ownership is not transferred until final payment is made no security is required. In the event of non-payment the HP company can repossess the asset.

❯ **Risk:** Hire purchase holds little risk, although failure to meet the payment schedule will result in the assets being repossessed.

Long-term sources of finance

Share capital

Capital is the money invested into a business by its owners. These owners are called shareholders. The payback to the shareholder is by way of a dividend. Dividends are paid normally on an interim basis and at the end of the financial year.

A business is authorised by the Companies Registration Office (CRO) to issue a certain amount of shares depending on its size and its ability to grow over time. The size of a company's authorised share capital is decided when the company is being set up and is included as an item in its memorandum of association. For private limited companies these shares represent the capital invested into the business by the owners, while for public limited companies shares can be bought and sold on the stock market by private or institutional investors.

If a public limited company (plc) requires an injection of capital it can go to the market and raise more money by selling further shares. The extra capital can be used to recapitalise or expand the business.

❯ **Cost:** There are no fixed-interest payments involved in share issues. Shareholders are entitled to a share of company profits (dividends). If no profit is made no dividend needs to be paid.

For public limited companies the cost of issuing shares on the stock exchange can be very high.

❯ **Impact on control:** Issuing extra shares may reduce the control of existing shareholders as all new shareholders will have a say in the running of the business.

For plcs in particular, issuing additional shares increases the possibility that their business might be a target for a takeover bid.

> **Security required:** No security is required for share issues.

> **Risk:** Share issues hold little risk for businesses and are a popular source of finance.

Debentures

These are long-term loans with a fixed interest rate and has a specific maturity date. For example, a €5 million, 7 per cent debenture (2018) allows a firm to borrow €5 million immediately and pay 7 per cent interest per annum with the lump sum due for repayment in 2018.

This type of loan is sanctioned by a financial institution on the basis of fixed collateral like property deeds. The borrower must submit to the bank a detailed business plan outlining all areas of budgeted income and expenditure and indicating its medium-to long-term growth prospects.

The fact that a debenture carries fixed-interest payments means that a business will be under pressure to generate sufficient levels of income to meet this annual debt. These fixed-interest payments must be met before shareholders can make a claim for dividends.

> **Cost:** Fixed-interest payments must be made and the amount borrowed must be repaid in full.

> **Impact on control:** Debentures involve no loss of control although some assets may be used as security.

> **Security required:** The lender is likely to require security in the form of fixed assets.

> **Risk:** Failure to repay the lump sum or to meet the annual interest payments means that any assets offered as security will have to be surrendered. Defaulting on the loan also presents a serious risk of bankruptcy for the borrower.

Retained earnings (business) or Savings (household)

This source of finance involves ploughing a portion of annual profits back into the business. This reinvestment of earnings can be used to purchase fixed assets or to fund expansion.

For a business, this type of policy requires ordinary shareholders to forego short-term dividends in the expectation that long-term returns will improve. It is a cheap source of finance as the money used already belongs to the business shareholders. It does not involve fixed annual repayments, which are a major feature of long-term loans, and minimises the level of external debt taken on by a business.

For households, savings are a type of retained earnings and allow the household to purchase assets without the need for borrowing.

> **Cost:** Cheap. Using one's own money means no interest payments are involved. There will, however, be an opportunity cost as money cannot be spent in other areas.

> **Impact on control:** No impact on control.

> **Security required:** No security required as own money is being used.

> **Risk:** This source of finance is risk-free.

Venture capital

Venture capital companies invest in new or high-risk businesses, often taking an equity stake and a seat on the board of directors. They hope that the business will succeed and the value of their investment will grow. If the business is successful it may be sold to a competitor at a much higher value and this will provide a large profit for the venture capitalist. The 'dragons' on the TV programme *Dragons' Den* are venture capitalists. Most of the commercial banks also have venture capital divisions which specialise in financing business start-ups.

 **Example**

The AIB Seed Capital Fund, which is co-owned by the AIB bank and Enterprise Ireland, was established in 2007 and a total of almost €7 million had been invested in eighteen projects by June 2009. The average initial investment made by the Fund is in the order of €250,000 but smaller investments of €100,000 have also been made.

The venture capital fund provides money for investment in innovative enterprises in exchange for a stake in the enterprise.

Following a successful period of venture capital investment there is normally a stock exchange flotation, a merger, an acquisition or a buy-out. (See *Chapter 16: Business Expansion*.)

> **Cost:** Venture capitalists will look for a significant return on investment and this may come in the form of a shareholding in the business and dividend payments.

> **Impact on control:** If venture capitalists take shares in the business they will have some control over the business.

> **Security required:** Security is not required.

> **Risk:** Apart from the loss of control, venture capital offers little risk to the business seeking finance.

Grants

Businesses often receive grants to help them set up, create employment and stimulate economic activity within the area in which they are based. The money is usually provided by the government, local authority or the European Union (EU).

145

Grants normally carry no interest or repayment conditions provided they are used for their intended purpose. They are provided for several different reasons but typical uses include payments for training or the purchase of machinery. Households can receive grants for improving the energy rating of their homes and for installing solar panels.

› **Cost:** Grants are free from interest charges and do not normally have to be repaid. Some terms and conditions may be attached to their use.

› **Impact on control:** The agency providing the grant will set strict conditions governing the use of the grants. In some cases the grant may be drawn down in stages and is subject to certain criteria being met. For example, a business gives a commitment to create 100 jobs and is set to receive grant aid of €2 million. The agreement may allow for €0.5 million to be paid for every 25 jobs created.

› **Security required:** Generally no security is required.

› **Risk:** Little or no risk is involved. If not used for the intended purpose, they may have to be repaid.

Mortgages

Mortgages are long-term loans which are taken out by both households and businesses and specifically used to purchase property. Security for the loan is the value of the property itself. Lenders will also consider a borrower's ability to repay and this will depend on an individual having secure employment and a sustainable level of income. For businesses, lenders will base their decision on audited final accounts and projected future earnings.

The rate of home ownership in Ireland is very high compared to other countries in Europe, so most Irish households have some level of mortgage debt. There are almost 800,000 mortgage-holders in Ireland with a combined mortgage debt of €117 billion.

This has had negative economic implications in recent years following the collapse of property prices. With property prices falling by up to 50 per cent in some cases, many homeowners found themselves in **negative equity**. Negative equity refers to a situation where the market value of a property is less than the value of the outstanding mortgage on that property. This is not an ideal situation for either the homeowner or the lender, especially if there is a need to sell the property. In financial terms it will mean that the seller will not receive sufficient cash to clear the debt.

e.g. Example

A couple take out a 95 per cent mortgage in order to purchase a property valued at €300,000. This means they borrow €285,000 and intend to repay the loan over 25 years. Shortly after they buy the house the property market crashes and the market value of their home falls to €250,000. The couple are now in negative equity, since the value of the loan exceeds the value of the property.

While this is not a good outcome for the couple in this case, being in negative equity does not present them with any *immediate* financial problem. In fact, if house prices rise again and they continue to pay off the loan this financial situation is likely to be reversed over the 25-year term.

Negative equity really only presents a problem if the couple decide to sell the property before prices rebound. This may arise because they need to trade up to a larger property in order to meet the needs of a growing family or because unemployment makes the current mortgage repayments unsustainable. If they are only able to sell the property for €250,000, they will have a repayment shortfall of almost €35,000 on the mortgage.

This type of situation faces many Irish households who bought property at peak prices, only to see them devalue very rapidly during the property crash. In effect, they are stuck with these properties and have very little prospect of selling or trading up.

The scale of the negative equity problem in Ireland is also a major worry for financial institutions, as they have provided loans where the security (i.e. the house) is not sufficient to cover the value of the outstanding loan. This means that if the borrower defaults, the lender will suffer a loss (a bad debt) on the transaction.

unit
4

Case Study

The government established an Inter-Departmental Working Group on Mortgage Arrears which estimated (in its October 2011 report) that it would cost in the region of €14 billion to clear the negative equity in the Irish mortgage portfolios.

The report also cited a dramatic rise in the level of mortgage arrears in the previous two years and this trend is continuing with approximately 45,000 households more than 90 days in arrears, of which approximately 32,000 households are more than 180 days in arrears. Numbers in the 180+ days arrears category have doubled since the end of 2009.

The report says there are also approximately 56,000 households with restructured loans.

The repayment schedule on a mortgage will depend on the term of the mortgage and the type of interest payable. A **variable rate of interest** allows the lender to adjust the rate of interest up or down at their own discretion. From the borrower's viewpoint this adds an element of uncertainty to the situation.

If a **fixed rate of interest** is applied, it will usually be higher than the variable rate, but the lender cannot alter the interest rate for an agreed time period. This provides far more certainty for the borrower. This is very useful to businesses as they can plan their future finances better when preparing cash flow forecasts.

In recent years some lenders offered **tracker mortgages** whereby the rate of interest is linked to changes in the base rate set by the European Central Bank (ECB). The rate is set out in the contract and will track increases or decreases in the ECB rate. While this type of product is no longer offered to new customers, approximately 40 per cent of mortgage holders in Ireland have tracker mortgages.

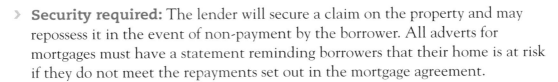

> **Cost:** All mortgages must be repaid and have annual interest payments. While the APR for mortgages is lower than for short- and medium-term finance, the length of the loan makes the overall repayment cost very high. For example, a mortgage of €200,000 is likely to incur interest in excess of €200,000 over the life of the loan, meaning total repayments of over €400,000.

> **Impact on control:** Ownership of the business or home will not be directly affected unless the borrower defaults and the lender takes court action to recover the debt.

> **Security required:** The lender will secure a claim on the property and may repossess it in the event of non-payment by the borrower. All adverts for mortgages must have a statement reminding borrowers that their home is at risk if they do not meet the repayments set out in the mortgage agreement.

> **Risk:** As outlined above, the major risk associated with a mortgage arises from non-repayment of the loan.

Sale and leaseback

Sale and leaseback is a long-term source of finance available to businesses. A business may decide to 'cash in' on the value of its premises by selling them to an investor and simultaneously signing a long-term lease with the new owner. This new arrangement allows the business to continue operating from the same premises while also providing them with a large amount of extra capital.

This approach has been taken by Bank of Ireland, which sold its headquarters and a lot of its branch network before leasing back these same premises.

> **Cost:** The cost involved is the annual rental charge.

> **Impact on control:** Once the asset is sold the business will lose control over it. This will reduce the value of the company's fixed assets.

> **Security required:** No security is required.

> **Risk:** There is no risk to the business from sale and leaseback as they can continue operating from the same location.

unit 4

Banking issues

Current account

This type of account can be opened in all commercial banks in Ireland and is available to both businesses and households. Current account holders can use this account for day-to-day spending. Traditionally no interest is received on current account balances.

Account holders get a chequebook and an ATM card. Most banks also offer facilities for overdrafts, Laser cards, phone and Internet banking, direct debit, credit transfers, and Paypath. **Paypath** allows an employer to pay wages directly into employees' bank accounts.

Bank Account Statement (example)

Account Holder (fictional)
Peter Lacey
12 The Crescent
Dundrum
Dublin

Statement Reference: **123456**

Date of Statement: 25 September 2013

Date	Details	Cheque Number	Debit €	Credit €	Balance €
1 Sept	Balance C/F				100.00
10 Sept	Paypath			2,000	2,100.00
14 Sept	ATM		400		1,700.00
16 Sept	FBD Insurance	DD	55		1,645.00
17 Sept	Cheque	142	150		1,495.00
24 Sept	Volkswagan Bank	SO	200		1,295.00
26 Sept	Bank charges		22.50		1,272.50

Deposit account

This is a savings account which is available from all financial institutions. Account holders receive interest on their deposits. A deposit account is useful for large sums of money which are not required for day-to-day spending. If the account holder agrees to deposit their money for a fixed term they are entitled to a higher rate of interest. This type of deposit account is used by individuals who are saving for longer-term needs, including retirement, and who are willing to sacrifice liquidity for a higher return on their investment. Savers need to compare the **Annual Equivalent Rate (AER)** on offer from several financial institutions before committing to this type of arrangement.

Loan applications

What factors will a lender consider before agreeing to a loan?

> **Purpose of loan:** The lender will need to establish what exactly the household or business intends to do with the money. Is it going to be utilised in the best manner possible and, in the case of a business, will it be used for a productive purpose?

   A household might use the money to purchase a car, extend a house or replace a kitchen.

   A business might use the money for business expansion through a buildings programme, other business acquisitions or the purchase of capital items.

> **Ability to repay:** The bank must be convinced that all customers have the capacity to repay any loans issued to them. The bank assesses the borrower's ability to repay by examining pay slips, P60s and bank statements.

unit 4

Businesses seeking loans will need to provide audited accounts for several years as well as realistic cash flow and profitability forecasts.

Prudent lenders often complete their vetting process by **stress testing** each client's ability to repay the proposed loan. Stress testing a loan application allows both the lender and the borrower to consider the impact on monthly repayments if interest rates were to increase. If a very high proportion of disposable income is committed to loan repayments the lender may conclude that a smaller loan or longer time period is more appropriate.

> **Security/collateral:** Lenders need some means of recovering their money if borrowers default. They will accept deeds of property, insurance policies and personal guarantees.

> **Credit history:** Financial institutions under the supervision of the Financial Regulator are obliged to check the credit history of all prospective borrowers. A borrower with a good track record has a higher credit rating and is more likely to repay the loan. The Irish Credit Bureau compiles a database which allows financial institutions to check a borrower's previous banking and loan history.

> **Own investment:** Banks are more likely to lend to households and businesses if the risk is shared. This usually requires the borrower to part-finance the project with some of their own money. Banks may be fearful that borrowers are willing to take bigger risks with bank money than with their own funds. They may also be less concerned with failure and default if the money at risk is not their own.

During the property boom in Ireland competing banks were willing to offer 100 per cent mortgages to house buyers. This had the effect of increasing property prices but also left banks very vulnerable to the price crash which followed. As prices fell sharply, borrowers were in negative equity and lenders were unable to recover the full value of outstanding loans. In recent years banks have returned to the more traditional practice of extending finance up to a limit of 90 per cent of the purchase price.

> **Business plan:** Businesses need to support their loan applications with detailed and realistic business plans which the lender will closely examine before making a decision. Business plans outline future sales projections, planned expenditure and profit forecasts.

Recent developments

The Credit Review Office

Do not confuse this with the Companies Registration Office (CRO) whose role is outlined in Chapter 18: Ownership Structures.

The Credit Review Office was established by the government in 2010. Its main function is to assist sole traders, small and medium-sized enterprises (SMEs) and farm enterprises that have been refused credit from banks and feel that the bank's decision is unjustified.

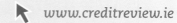 *www.creditreview.ie*

It also examines credit policy to assist the minister in deciding what further actions may be necessary to increase the flow of credit in the economy.

The Credit Review Office review process operates only after the borrower has unsuccessfully appealed through the bank's own internal appeals process.

Upon receiving an application from the borrower, the Credit Review Office will carry out an independent and impartial review of the bank's decision. The review process will review decisions to refuse, reduce or withdraw credit facilities (including applications for restructured credit facilities) from €1,000 up to €500,000.

The Credit Review Office will also look at cases where borrowers feel that the terms and conditions of their existing loan, or a new loan offer, are unfairly harsh or have been unreasonably changed to their disadvantage.

On reviewing an application, the Credit Review Office will provide the bank with an opinion on whether it agrees with the lending decision or not. The bank then responds to this opinion and confirms the next steps in response to the recommendations set out by the Credit Review Office.

The Credit Review Office has no regulatory or mandatory powers over the opinions it gives on applications. In practice, however, where the Credit Review Office has suggested the lending should be made, the banks usually respect and comply with that opinion.

The Credit Review Office also collates the outcomes of the appeals into a regular report for the Minister for Finance to inform the government how the credit system is operating in the participating banks.

At present, the participating banks are those engaged with **NAMA**:

> Allied Irish Banks   > Bank of Ireland   > EBS
> Irish Bank Resolution Corporation (IBRC) (formerly Anglo Irish Bank)
> Irish Nationwide Building Society

Other banks may opt to enter the review process voluntarily.

NAMA

The National Asset Management Agency (NAMA) was established in December 2009 as one of a number of initiatives taken by the Irish government to address the serious problems which arose in Ireland's banking sector as the result of excessive property lending.

The Agency has acquired loans (land and development and associated loans) with a nominal value of €72.3 billion from participating financial institutions. The loans were bought for €30.5 billion, an overall discount of 58 per cent. NAMA's objective is to obtain the best achievable financial return for the state on this portfolio over an expected lifetime of up to ten years.

Source: www.nama.ie

Chapter Review Diagram – Household and Business Management: Finance

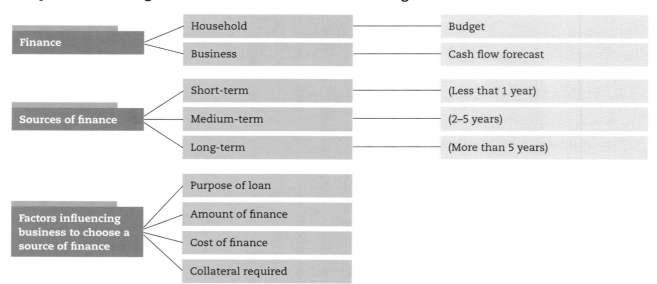

 Chapter Review Questions

1 What is a household budget? How does it differ from a cash flow forecast prepared by a business?

2 Outline the importance of cash flow forecasting.

3 Complete the cash flow forecast (CFF) of Astro Ltd.

2007	Jan	Feb	March	Total
Receipts	130,000	165,000	280,000	
Payments	110,000	155,000	295,000	
Net cash				
Opening Cash	18,000			
Closing cash				

4 List three sources of finance under each of the headings 'short-term sources', 'medium-term sources' and 'long-term sources'.

5 Outline four factors which influence households and businesses when choosing the most suitable source of finance.

6 Explain why a business may use factoring as a source of finance. Outline the costs and benefits to the business of this source of finance.

7 Outline the advantages and disadvantages of leasing as a source of finance.

8 Distinguish between a medium-term loan and a bank overdraft as sources of household and business finance.

9 Outline the impact on existing shareholders of a company's decision to raise additional finance by issuing more shares.

10 Explain what is meant by a debenture.

11 Explain the role of venture capitalists in financing business start-ups or expansions.

unit 4

12 Explain the term 'negative equity'.

13 What is the main function of the Credit Review Office.

Questions · Ordinary Level

1 Distinguish between short-, medium- and long-term sources of finance, and list **three** examples of each.

2 Explain the term 'bank overdraft'. *LCOL 2010 (10 marks)*

3 Name **two** long-term sources of finance and explain **one** of them. *LCOL 2009 (20 marks)*

4 Outline the benefits of hire purchase as a source of finance.

5 Explain how sale and leaseback operates.

Questions · Higher Level

1 Outline **two** reasons why a business should prepare a cash flow forecast.

2 Describe the difference between debt capital and equity capital.

3 Define 'accrued expenses' and give **one** example.

4 The business cash flow forecast of Irish Garden Furniture Ltd is set out below:

	July	August	September	Total
	Euro	Euro	Euro	Euro
Receipts	16,000	15,750	14,850	46,600
Payments	28,000	13,000	24,500	65,500
Net cash	(12,000)	2,750	(9,650)	(18,900)
Opening cash	8,500	(3,500)	(750)	8,500
Closing cash	(3,500)	(750)	(10,400)	(10,400)

(a) Outline **two** reasons why Irish Garden Furniture Ltd. prepared the above cash flow forecast.

(b) Analyse the cash flow forecast. Explain, and offer solutions to, any **two** problems you think the business may have. *LCHL 2002 (20 marks)*

5 Describe the criteria a bank will apply to a loan application before making a decision.

6 Identify **three** medium-term sources of finance for a business and evaluate the benefits of each of the three sources.

7 Distinguish between fixed-rate mortgage and a variable-rate mortgage and outline the benefits of each to a borrower.

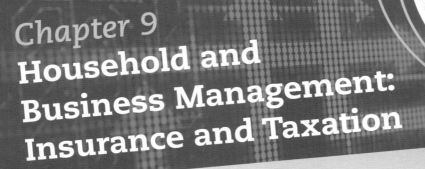

Chapter 9
Household and Business Management: Insurance and Taxation

Syllabus Outcomes

On completion, the student should be able to:

» 4.5.1 Outline the differences between managing a household and managing a business;

» 4.5.2 Explain the importance of insurance and tax implications for business;

» 4.5.3 Identify activities common to managing a business and a household, including completion of relevant forms;

» 4.5.4 Understand the similarities and differences between these activities in a household context and in a business context.

News Flash

1 Read the newspaper extract below and discuss the issues raised.

2 Can you explain any of the highlighted terms?

Survey shows €5,000 difference in life insurance costs

by Cathal Hanley

Consumers could save between €595 and €5,000 over the term of a life insurance policy

by shopping around and quitting smoking, according to the latest survey by the Financial Regulator.

The survey covers the monthly costs for life and mortgage protection insurance for people of different ages, both smokers and non-smokers...

Comparing the most extreme examples at each end of the scale the survey finds that the monthly costs for a 28-year old taking out a €200,000 policy over a 35-year term range from €15.65 a month for a female non-smoker to €45.83 a month for a male smoker. The total difference in payment over 35 years for this example is €12,675...

Consumer Director, Mary O'Dea said, "At this time of year, many people think about their personal finances. One of the things you might want to consider is whether you need life insurance, or indeed, if you have enough life insurance."

She added, "If you are thinking about taking out a mortgage this year you will probably be offered mortgage protection insurance by your mortgage lender.

"While this may be a discounted rate for the first few years, it is worthwhile looking at our survey to see who offers the best mortgage protection rates to make sure you are getting the best deal you can. Remember, you do not have to buy your mortgage protection insurance from your mortgage lender."

This is an edited extract from The Irish Times, WEDNESDAY, 11 JANUARY 2006.

For more up-to-date newspaper articles see www.edcodigital.ie

Insurance

Insurance is a protection against a possible loss. Under this system a large number of people who face a similar risk pay a relatively small amount of money, called a **premium,** into a fund. The fund is administered by an insurance company or underwriter. If any of the insured parties suffer an insurable loss they are entitled to claim compensation from the insurer. The fund is used to pay compensation to claimants, and should also cover the administration costs of the insurance company. Any remaining funds represent a profit for the underwriter.

Assurance is protection against certain future loss. For example, life assurance provides a payment when a person dies, or in some cases when a person reaches a specified age. In both of these situations there is an element of certainty around both the event and the payment.

Its aim is to minimise the impact on future cash flows by setting aside money from current income.

Businesses use insurance as an important element of their **risk management** strategy. Risk management is a process by which a household or business seeks to minimise the impact of unexpected events. It involves a number of steps:

1 **Risk assessment:** An important first step is to identify the areas where there are high levels of risk or where accidents are likely to occur. A business may view chemical stores as a potential source of high risk.

2 **Risk reduction:** Once these risks are identified, management can take appropriate steps to eliminate or minimise the risk involved. The chemical stores may be placed in isolated and secure locations. Staff may be trained in risk reduction techniques and may be provided with protective clothing and safety equipment when dealing with chemicals.

3 **Insurance:** Any risks which cannot be eliminated will continue to pose a threat to the business or household and need to be insured against. While nobody wishes to suffer serious unexpected losses, it is wise to protect a home or business against their worst effects. Insurance companies will look favourably on all risk reduction efforts when determining the premium. Households and businesses which have alarms, sprinklers and other safety devices are likely to have discounts applied to their premiums. A **discount** is a reduction in the cost of a basic premium and is a reward for lower-than-average levels of risk.

Insurance is also important to business for the following reasons:

> **Survival:** Insurance enables a business to cope with difficult or unexpected situations. Serious damage to uninsured premises may result in closure of business.

unit
4

€35m insurance payout over gutted C&D pet food plant

Money to fund recovery of firm but not all workers will return

by Tom Lyons

Insurance compensation of around €35m will be paid out to pet food company C&D Foods following a raging fire last month.

The money… will be used to fund the recovery of the factory in Edgeworthstown, Co Longford after the fire which seriously damaged not only its buildings but also its lofty status as a €100m a year business.

One of the largest pet food companies in Europe, C&D has been forced to lay off most of its 500 staff.

But management at the plant led by the family of former Taoiseach Albert Reynolds have been working hard to put it back on track.

The exact amount of compensation has not been finally agreed but following estimates by loss adjustors, the Irish Independent understands it will be in the region of €35 million.

All efforts are focused on ensuring everything is in place for the return of 173 of the original 500 staff… It is estimated parts of the plant could be out of action for 16 months leaving the future uncertain for the 300 staff not due to rejoin the company next Monday.

The bill for the fire, reported to have been started by an accidental electrical failure, will be divided between three insurance companies: FBD, Hibernian and British-based Aspen Insurance… C&D's claim is made up of two main elements. The first is for buildings and capital equipment, which is based on the assets' net book value and is usually straightforward to agree.

The second, based on loss of profits, can be trickier and is the part of the claim still being worked on by insurers of the Longford company.

This is an edited extract from the Irish Independent, FRIDAY, 3 FEBRUARY 2006.

> **Liquidity:** Insurance can also help a business to meet its cash flow requirements, as compensation alleviates the financial consequences of unexpected damage or accidents. If a business has consequential loss insurance, this may also maintain weekly income even while the business is closed for repairs.

> **Safety:** As part of overall risk management, firms will generally improve safety standards in a bid to reduce premiums. This can be done in the following ways:

> Stricter monitoring of production and quality

> Better health and safety procedures

> Training of staff on safer work methods

> Installing safety and security devices

> Reducing the amount of stock on hand at any moment in time

Insurance removes the need for businesses to worry about risks on a daily basis and allows them get on with their core objectives of trading and meeting consumer demands. Paying for insurance clearly involves a financial cost and some might question the benefit of paying it. The reality is that buying insurance is really about buying 'peace of mind'.

While no business wishes to have its premises destroyed by fire, managers realise that the consequences of this type of mishap would be potentially disastrous, so choosing not to pay for insurance might represent a false economy.

Key terms

The following are some of the key people, paperwork and payments involved in insurance:

Insurance broker

A broker is a person who sells insurance policies on behalf of several insurance companies. They receive income in the form of commission which is based on the number of policies sold. This commission is paid by the insurance company.

Households and businesses seeking insurance use brokers to find the most suitable and cheapest policy to suit their needs. Brokers will effectively 'shop around' on behalf of their client and should offer free and impartial advice to households and businesses.

Some brokers only sell policies on behalf of one insurance company and are therefore called **'tied agents'**.

Proposal form

This is the application form for insurance. The rules of insurance require that it be completed truthfully by the person seeking insurance. This will enable the insurance company to make a realistic assessment of the risk involved and determine an appropriate premium.

Policy

The policy document is a legal contract outlining what exactly is insured and in what circumstances. A house insurance policy sets out which specific property is insured, the insurable value of the building and contents and the types of losses which merit compensation. It also contains details of any exclusions and policy excesses.

Exclusions are specific items or risks which are not insured. By excluding certain high-risk activities it may be possible for insurance companies to lower the average level of premiums.

 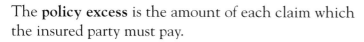

Injury caused by skiing or skydiving may be excluded from the terms of travel insurance policies. Holidaymakers who wish to insure themselves for these activities may need to pay additional premiums to reflect the higher level of risk involved.

The **policy excess** is the amount of each claim which the insured party must pay.

 Example

A motor insurance policy may require that the insured driver pay the first €200 of any claim. This money would be deducted from the compensation and is supposed to cover the administration cost of each claim, but also has the effect of discouraging small claims.

Policyholders may voluntarily agree to a higher policy excess in return for a lower premium.

Premium

This is the amount of money paid by the insured to the insurance company to cover a particular risk. The premium is calculated by an actuary and depends on the likelihood of a risk occurring and the expected financial cost of that loss.

Loading

Insurance companies sometimes add an extra amount to the basic premium to cover increased risk.

 **Example**

> A learner driver's insurance premium always carries a loading which reflects the higher level of risk associated with an unqualified and inexperienced driver.

Actuary

An actuary is the person responsible for calculating insurance premiums. In order to pay compensation and generate profits, the insurer must make an accurate calculation as to the likelihood of a particular event occurring. They must also be able to calculate the likely level of compensation when setting the rate for insurance premiums. Actuaries rely heavily on careful analysis of statistical information and mathematical probability. In situations where an actuary is unable to evaluate the level of risk, an insurance company is unlikely to insure against that risk.

Compensation

This is the amount of money paid out by the insurer in the event of a successful claim. When processing claims the insurer will look closely at the nature and value of the loss and will check if it is actually covered by the terms of the policy. Compensation is designed to put the insured party back in the same financial position they were in before the loss occurred. Less compensation will be paid where assets have depreciated in value or where the insured party was partially responsible for the loss.

Example

> A car owner who fails to lock their vehicle is likely to receive a reduced level of compensation if the car is stolen since their own negligence was a factor in the theft.

Assessor

This is a person who inspects damage and calculates the compensation to be paid to the insured party for the loss suffered.

unit 4

When assessing liability for the loss it is important to determine the **proximate cause.**

This refers to the actual cause of the loss and insurance companies will need to establish if this event is covered by the terms of the policy. If it's excluded in a policy, the insurance company will not pay compensation.

e.g. Example

Tom has third-party, fire and theft insurance on his car. He crashes his car and as a result it catches fire and is destroyed. No compensation will be paid since the proximate cause of the loss (the initial crash) is not covered by terms of this particular policy.

Principles of Insurance:

> Insurable Interest
> Utmost Good Faith
> Indemnity
> Subrogation
> Contribution

Insurable interest

In order to insure something you must benefit by its existence, and suffer (financially) by its loss. You can only insure items whose destruction will cause you financial suffering or loss.

For example, an individual can only insure their own property but not their neighbour's property.

Utmost good faith

The insured must disclose all material facts to the insurance company when applying for insurance. A material fact is anything that is likely to alter the decision to grant insurance, or to affect the level of premium charged. Failure to do so may invalidate the contract.

e.g. Example

An applicant for motor insurance fails to inform the insurance company that they have eight penalty points on their licence. Since this information is relevant to the application and will impact on the premium, it is regarded as a material fact.

If uncertain, it is always advisable to disclose information which might be relevant, since failure to do so may invalidate future claims for compensation.

Indemnity

The insured party cannot make a profit from insurance. This is a most important rule of insurance and recognises that insurance exists to put the insured person back in the same financial position as they were in before suffering the loss.

An insured driver involved in a car accident damages his five-year-old car beyond repair. The compensation paid should allow him to replace the damaged vehicle with one of a similar age and model. If the compensation allowed him to purchase a brand new vehicle, he would be better off after the accident and this would breach the principle of indemnity.

This is a fundamental rule which applies to all insurance contracts and has implications for the insurable value of many household and business assets. Assets which are over-insured will not receive additional compensation, but will have excessive insurance premiums. It is important therefore to insure assets for a realistic replacement value.

Both **subrogation** and **contribution** are based on the principle of indemnity.

Subrogation

There are two aspects to subrogation.

Firstly, when an insurer has paid full compensation they are entitled to any remaining scrap or salvage value from the insured asset.

Secondly, an insurance company is also entitled to sue a third party who may have been at fault for the loss.

John Smith was involved in an accident in which his car was a write-off. He subsequently received €18,000 in full compensation from his insurer (Allianz Ireland). Following an investigation of the incident it became clear that another driver, Mary Roche, was responsible for the accident. Based on the principle of subrogation, Allianz Ireland will take action to recover the €18,000 compensation from Mary Roche, or her insurance company.

Allianz Ireland is also entitled to receive €700 scrappage from the sale of the damaged vehicle.

Contribution

Where the same risk is insured with more than one insurer, the insurers will divide the cost of the claim between them. The total compensation paid will not exceed the value of the item, and the amount paid by each will be proportionate to the risk insured by each insurer.

unit 4

A premises worth €120,000 is fully insured with two separate insurance firms. If the building is totally destroyed in fire, how much will each insurer pay?

To comply with the principle of indemnity, the maximum compensation must not exceed €120,000. Since the building is equally insured with both insurers, each will pay half the total. The answer therefore is that each insurer will pay €60,000 compensation to the insured party.

Average clause

Average clause is a rule used by insurance companies to calculate compensation in situations where an asset is underinsured and has suffered partial loss. It is based on the principle of indemnity and the following **formula** is used to calculate compensation:

$$\frac{\text{Value insured}}{\text{Actual value of item}} \times \text{Loss suffered}$$

Consider the following situation:

A premises valued at €100,000 is insured for only €80,000. A fire at the premises causes €50,000 worth of damage. The owner applies to the insurance company for €50,000 compensation. How much compensation will be received?

$$\frac{€80,000}{€100,000} \times €50,000$$

Compensation will be €40,000.

In this instance the owner would receive 80 per cent (or 4/5) of the financial loss sustained. This proportionality is vital in resolving this claim.

Note also that had the entire premises been destroyed, the maximum compensation payable would have been €80,000, as this is the insured value, and the amount on which the premium is based. If €100,000 compensation were to be paid, the insured party would be better off after the fire and this breaches the principle of indemnity.

Impact of insurance valuations

If we apply the principles and rules outlined above, they highlight the importance of insuring assets for realistic replacement values. Since insurance will only return the insured party to the same financial position they were in before the loss, it's important that households and businesses are able to calculate realistic replacement values for their assets.

Assets which are over-insured will be charged higher insurance premiums to reflect these inflated values. If a loss does occur they will not receive compensation beyond the reinstatement value, since to do so would break the principle of indemnity.

On the other hand, assets which are undervalued and underinsured may have lower premiums but this will lead to lower compensation when the average clause rule is applied. In these circumstances the level of compensation will be insufficient to cover the replacement cost, so the saving on the premium represents something of a false economy.

Types of household insurance

Buildings and contents insurance

Buildings insurance covers the actual building against accidental structural damage due to circumstances such as fire, storm damage and burst pipes.

The insurable value should be based not on purchase price or current market value, but on current replacement cost. Insurance companies are able to advise householders on typical values based on the prevailing economic conditions.

It is also possible to insure all of the contents including furniture, fittings and household possessions, up to an agreed total value, for example €40,000. It is not necessary for a householder to declare and value each individual item, but some policies may require individual items valued in excess of, say, €2,000, to be specifically declared. In addition to accidental damage, contents would also be insured against theft.

It's important to note that the specific terms of each policy will vary, so householders need to read the details carefully and ensure the policy suits their needs and circumstances. They need to pay particular attention to exclusion clauses.

Motor insurance

By law anybody driving a vehicle in Ireland must have adequate motor insurance. This means that **third-party insurance** is the minimum legal requirement.

When an insurance contract (policy) is taken out, the insured driver and the insurance company are both parties to that contract. Third-party motor insurance protects all other parties who suffer injury or loss due to the careless actions of the insured driver. This type of policy specifically excludes claims from the insured driver for injury or loss caused to themselves or their vehicle.

This ensures that all drivers can, at the very least, compensate innocent third parties for their losses and suffering. These third parties might include other drivers or road users injured in an accident and they may also include passengers in the insured driver's vehicle.

Some insurers offer **third-party, fire and theft** policies, which are an extension of the basic policy and provide compensation to insured drivers in situations where their vehicle is stolen and/or destroyed by fire.

Comprehensive motor insurance provides compensation for all injured parties including the insured driver, but the increased cover and risk involved is reflected in a much higher premium. Additional risks may also be reflected in the addition of loadings to the basic premium.

Where a driver has a proven track record of claim-free driving they are likely to benefit from a **no-claims bonus.** This is a discount off their premium and is a reward from the insurer to its customers who make no claims on their policy over a number of years. It typically takes five years to build up a full no-claims bonus and some or all of the bonus will be lost if the driver makes a claim. The loss of this bonus will obviously cause their premium to increase, so there is a strong incentive for drivers to drive safely. Some insurers allow minor claims or compensate for windscreen damage without impacting on a driver's no-claims bonus.

Health insurance

This type of insurance is used by households and individuals to help cover the financial impact of injury or serious illness. Companies such as VHI, Aviva and Quinn offer a range of policies to suit the needs and budget of many families. Many of these policies cover the cost of medical treatment and hospital visits, while some even provide for ongoing day-to-day care by GPs.

Life assurance

Assurance is protection against a certain future loss, and life assurance is the most common example. It aims to minimise the impact on future cash flows by setting aside money from current income. Individuals who choose to take out life assurance can select from a number of different types of policy, including whole life assurance, term life assurance and endowment policies.

> **Whole life policies** cover an individual until their death, provided premium payments are kept up to date. In effect this type of policy provides money to cover funeral expenses and to meet some of the financial needs of the next of kin.

> **Term life policies** cover a named individual for a specific period of time and no compensation can be paid if the insured person lives beyond this date. A policy of this type might be taken out when undertaking a risky project or expedition. Term policies can also be used to cover the insured person's life until such time as they have paid off a large debt like a mortgage. The policy can be timed to cease whenever the mortgage debt is paid off.

> **Endowment policies** are designed to pay a lump sum after a specified term (on its 'maturity') or on earlier death. In a similar way to term policies, endowment life assurance policies are frequently tied in with the payment of mortgage debt. For example, a person obtains a twenty-year mortgage and also

unit
4

takes out a twenty-year endowment life assurance policy. They make interest payments on the mortgage and also pay an insurance premium each month. At the end of twenty years, the endowment policy matures and the lump sum is used to pay off the mortgage. If the insured person dies before twenty years have elapsed, the life policy will also cover the outstanding mortgage debt.

An endowment policy can also be used to save for a retirement, with the policy due to mature when the insured person reaches retirement age. If the insured person dies before retirement age the compensation is paid to next of kin, but if they live to retirement the insured person benefits from the payment of a lump sum. Since this type of policy has a guaranteed payment, the insurance company will charge a higher premium for an endowment policy.

Pay-Related Social Insurance (PRSI)

This is a statutory payment for insurance and is therefore required by law for all those in paid employment. It is paid by both employers and employees. Employees who have paid the required amount of PRSI contributions qualify for a range of benefits. These include Jobseeker's Benefit, Illness Benefit, Maternity Benefit and a State Pension.

Mortgage protection insurance

A policy of this type is designed to protect both a policyholder and a mortgage-lender in certain circumstances where the mortgage-holder cannot repay the loan. Most mortgage protection policies provide a lump sum equivalent to the outstanding loan in the event that the insured party dies or suffers a specified critical illness.

Mortgage protection policies are not compulsory, but it is very unlikely that a bank will agree to a mortgage unless the borrower has first taken out insurance against these risks.

Income protection insurance

This is designed to protect household income in the event that a wage-earner is unable to continue in paid employment, usually as a result of a serious illness or injury. If an uninsured worker becomes incapacitated in this way, they will suffer a severe loss of income and this will have a negative impact on their standard of living.

If they choose to pay income protection insurance, they agree to set aside a certain percentage of current income on an ongoing basis. In the event that they suffer an insurable loss, they will be entitled to claim a specified proportion of their normal income until such time as they are fit to resume work, or they reach retirement age.

Travel insurance

Many households and individuals avail of this type of protection when travelling abroad. Most travel insurance policies cover losses due to cancellation of flights, lost or stolen luggage, as well as the costs incurred due to illness abroad. Loading will be added to the premium to cover additional risks, especially those involved in skiing or adventure holidays.

Types of business insurance

Buildings and contents insurance

Business premises are subject to the same risks as homes and also additional risks from business activity. Some business premises contain hazardous or flammable substances and these heighten both the risk of damage and the need for insurance.

Businesses also need to protect expensive stocks of raw materials and finished goods which are stored in their warehouses and factories.

Motor insurance

The legal requirement for motor insurance applies equally to businesses and households, and many companies will take out fleet policies to cover a large number of vehicles and drivers. The costs to a business of insuring very expensive and very large vehicles such as trucks and buses can be considerable.

Public liability insurance

Businesses need to take out public liability cover to protect themselves from claims made by members of the public (including customers) who may be injured or suffer loss while on their premises.

It specifically applies to situations where a third party has sustained property damage or injury arising out of the negligence of that business or its employees and/or sub-contractors.

The potential for large compensation claims is high and public liability insurance adds to the costs of operating a business.

 **Example**

> A customer trips on an uneven floor surface in a retail premises and suffers back and hand injuries. The injured customer may feel the accident resulted from the retailer's negligence and may seek compensation for the injuries they've suffered.

The insurance costs associated with having large crowds of people in a relatively confined location has led to far greater public liability costs for concert promoters in recent years. Increased insurance costs are inevitably passed on to the all concertgoers in higher ticket prices.

Product liability insurance

This protects the business from claims made by customers who are injured or killed by the firm's products. A product of the business can include anything manufactured, installed, altered, repaired, etc.

This type of insurance might be particularly important for manufacturers of vehicles, food products or pharmaceuticals, as well as for some service-providers.

Example

An electrical contractor carries out some work on a property which is being renovated. He fails to notice that a number of live wires have been left exposed in the utility room. Some weeks later, when the house is again occupied by a family, a child is injured after receiving an electric shock from the exposed cable. The owners of the house contact their solicitor and initiate legal action against the contractor.

Employer's liability insurance

This is designed to protect the employer from claims made by employees who are injured while at work.

Despite health and safety guidelines, there are many workplace accidents and even some fatalities in Ireland each year.

According to the Health and Safety Authority's (HSA) annual report for 2011, there were 55 workplace fatalities recorded compared to a record low of 43 in 2009. The majority of all fatal incidents recorded occurred in the farming, forestry and fishing sector, which collectively accounted for 28 deaths. There were six recorded fatalities in the construction sector, the lowest since the authority records began in 1989. Falls from height were the most common cause of workplace deaths in 2011, the majority of which occurred in farming and construction where roof repair and maintenance was taking place.

This type of policy will provide cover for defence and/or settlement costs where an employee (or his/her estate) takes legal action against the employer, resulting from injury, illness or death sustained whilst working for the employer, and which they believe is the fault of the employer.

Example

A factory employee sustains a hand injury whilst working on a machine. He brings a claim against his employer for pain and suffering, loss of earnings, future loss of earnings and special damages.

Pay-Related Social Insurance (PRSI)

Employers pay a PRSI contribution in respect of each member of staff.

Consequential loss insurance

This type of insurance provides compensation for businesses which suffer loss of earnings as a result of an insurable risk, such as a fire. While buildings and contents insurance will compensate for damaged premises and stock, it may be necessary to close the business temporarily in order to clean and renovate the premises. While this closure will damage income and profits, consequential loss insurance can be used to claim for loss of earnings which result from the closure. Insurance companies will generally set upper limits on the size of each claim and will rely on audited accounts from previous years' trading when estimating the level of compensation.

The previously mentioned case involving C&D Pet Foods Ltd (see p.156) included the payment of compensation for consequential loss in respect of a fire at the canning factory.

Cash/goods in transit insurance

If goods are stolen or damaged whilst being transported from one location to another, this type of policy will cover the loss. This type of policy also covers money stolen in transit.

Fidelity guarantee insurance

This is a type of insurance which provides compensation to businesses which find they have been defrauded by employees. Some employees may be in positions of responsibility and may have access to large sums of company money. In some cases they may steal or embezzle money from the business and use it for their own personal spending.

 **Example**

> In March 2011 a former assistant manager of FÁS was sentenced to four years in prison for defrauding the state agency of over €600,000 between 2003 and 2008. The money was spent on foreign holidays, home improvements and a new car and the court was told that all of the money had been spent.

Underestimating the importance of business insurance could prove to be a costly error for both start-up and established companies.

« syllabus signpost
4.5.2

The importance of insurance for business

> **Business protection:** Having business insurance is one way of protecting all the hard work that has gone into developing a business. Insurance protects a business from closure due to catastrophic losses caused by fires and natural disasters. The existence of adequate insurance should mean that any closures or losses are only temporary.

> **Legal obligation:** Some types of business insurance are required by law, for example motor insurance and PRSI.

> **Legal liability:** Some types of insurance will protect the business in situations where it may be liable for losses to others. We live in a society where legal action is increasingly common and where even the most frivolous lawsuit can be costly to defend. In the event that a business loses a lawsuit, the damages awarded could exceed its abilities to pay. Some types of insurance, including public liability, employer's liability or malpractice insurance will cover some, if not all, of any damages.

unit 4

> **Cash flow implications:** Large and unexpected losses can cause great difficulties for a business and are impossible to plan for. Insurance therefore involves the planned payment of a premium in the hope of avoiding these large and unexpected losses.

Comparison of household and business insurance

« *syllabus signpost*
4.5.3 & 4.5.4

Similarities

> **Risk management:** Both households and businesses need to engage in the process of risk management. This involves risk assessment, risk reduction and insurance.

> **Statutory insurance:** Some types of insurance are legal requirements for both households and businesses. Examples include motor insurance and PRSI.

> **Form-filling:** Having shopped around for the most suitable types of insurance, households and businesses need to complete insurance proposal forms. When a policy is received it should be analysed and filed away for future reference. If a claim for compensation is made at a later date, it will also be necessary to fill in a claim form.

Differences

> **Scale of potential losses:** The level of risk and potential losses associated with businesses is far greater than those for a household. For that reason the amounts of money involved in business insurance greatly exceeds those of household insurance.

> **Types of insurance:** The scale of business risk also means that businesses need to avail of a far greater range of insurance policies than households. Examples of business-only insurances include product and public liability, as well as fidelity guarantee insurance.

> **Business expenses:** A business can legitimately write off insurance costs as a business expense. This effectively reduces the liability for corporation tax. Households are not entitled to this type of write-off.

Taxation

Taxation is a compulsory payment to the government (Exchequer) to meet its expenses. In Ireland, the state agency responsible for tax collection is the Revenue Commissioners. Our government uses these taxes to fund both current and capital expenditure in the economy. It also uses these taxes to ensure that there is a more equitable distribution of wealth within the economy.

unit 4

Types of tax

Direct taxes

These are taxes imposed directly on income and usually deducted at source. This means the tax is deducted from income by an employer or financial institution and paid over to the Revenue Commissioners. Examples include Pay-As-You-Earn (PAYE) income tax and Deposit Interest Retention Tax (DIRT). A system where those earning the highest income pay the highest taxes is said to be **progressive**.

Indirect taxes

These are taxes imposed on goods and services, e.g. VAT. The rate of tax is the same for all and therefore the burden of tax falls most heavily on those on low incomes. This type of tax is **regressive** – impacting more severely on the people or households with relatively low income levels. For this reason, some basic goods may be exempt from VAT or may only be taxed at minimal rates.

Taxes paid by households

Pay-As-You-Earn income tax

This is a direct tax on income and all employees must pay tax on their wages and salaries. Tax is levied at a standard rate (currently 20 per cent) and a higher rate (currently 41 per cent) on all income above the standard rate cut-off point.

Employees qualify for a range of allowances which reduce their tax liability. These allowances are called **tax credits.** Tax credits currently available include PAYE tax credit, personal tax credit, lone parent tax credit and home carers tax credit. The tax credits available to each person reflect their personal circumstances and can change from year to year.

All employers in the state have a duty to collect these payments and submit the returns to the Revenue Commissioners.

Examples of income tax calculation are outlined on pages 174–6.

Self-assessment income tax

This is tax system whereby individuals who are self-employed (e.g. sole traders) calculate their own tax liability and make a return themselves to the Revenue Commissioners. They are obliged to make a tax payment after July in each tax year. This initial payment is known as **preliminary tax.** The remainder of the tax must be submitted before the end of the tax year.

In order to ensure that correct assessment and payment of tax is made, the Revenue Commissioners carry out spot checks on self-employed taxpayers. If they suspect incorrect payments have been made a **tax audit** may be conducted. This is where the tax authorities carry out a very detailed examination of a taxpayer's financial affairs.

Universal Social Charge (USC)

This is a relatively new tax, which replaced existing income and health levies. Where an individual earns more than €10,036 per annum (€193 per week) the USC is charged at an ascending rate on all income. Current rates are 2, 4 and 7 per cent. At present the USC does not provide any direct benefit for those who pay it.

Value Added Tax (VAT)

This is a tax on goods and services sold. It is intended to tax the value added to the product at each stage of its channel of distribution, but businesses can effectively pass the full burden of this tax on to consumers.

> Essential goods such as basic food items, medicines and children's clothing have a VAT rating of zero.

> A new 9 per cent reduced rate of VAT for tourism-related activities including restaurants, hotels, cinemas, hairdressing and newspapers, was introduced by the government to assist economic growth and job creation. It applies for the period 1 July 2011 to 31 December 2013.

> A standard VAT rate of 23 per cent is levied on all goods and services that do not fall into the reduced rate categories. Consumers are often unaware of the VAT element when buying goods as the tax is included in the purchase price. VAT increases the price paid by consumers and also adds to business costs since they are required to account for the tax and make VAT returns every two months.

How VAT works

Value Added Tax derives its name from the way it is levied and the fact that the tax is based on the value added to goods at each stage of their production and distribution. For example:

Stage 1:

A furniture manufacturer sells a small table to a wholesaler for €100 and charges him VAT at 23%. This means the wholesaler pays €123 for the table. The furniture manufacturer keeps €100 and pays VAT of €23 to the government.

Stage 2:

The wholesaler later sells the table to a furniture retailer for €200. He again adds VAT at 23%, so the retailer must pay a total of €246.

The wholesaler owes the government the VAT of €46, but can reclaim the €23 VAT he has already paid to the manufacturer. This effectively means he'll pay just €23 to the government.

Stage 3:

When eventually the retailer sells the table to a consumer, he must also add on VAT to his selling price. He sells the table for €300, plus VAT at 23%, making a selling price of €369 to the consumer.

The retailer must also pay the VAT to the government but can claim back the €46 VAT that he paid to the wholesaler, leaving €23 for the government.

In conclusion:

The government has now received 23% (or €69) on the price paid for the television by the consumer.

The retailer, wholesaler and manufacturer only paid the amount of VAT they charged to the next group down the line.

The consumer is not in a position to pass on this tax and effectively bears the full burden of the VAT being levied. VAT is an example of a regressive tax as it impacts equally on all consumers irrespective of their level of income.

Deposit Interest Retention Tax (DIRT)

DIRT is a tax on interest earned on savings accounts in financial institutions in Ireland. It is deducted at source, which means the banks calculate the tax payable on savings accounts and submit a return to the Revenue Commissioners. This tax is currently levied at a rate of 30 per cent.

Capital Gains Taxes (CGT)

These are taxes on profits earned from sale of assets such as property and shares. Such profits (capital gains) arise where the value of these assets increases above their original purchase price. For example, on shares bought for €5,000 and later sold for €7,000, the capital gain of €2,000 is taxable. Capital gains from the sale of a primary residence are exempt from tax. The current CGT rate is 30 per cent.

Capital Acquisitions Tax

This is a tax paid on gifts and inheritances. Transfers between spouses and charitable donations are exempt. The current rate is 30 per cent.

Customs and excise duties

Customs duty is a tax on goods imported from non-EU countries.

Excise is an internal tax on certain products such as tobacco, alcohol and oil sold in Ireland.

Motor taxation

This is a compulsory tax paid annually on all vehicles. It is paid to the local authority.

Taxes for business

Corporation tax

This is a tax on company profits. At present, corporation tax in Ireland is 12.5 per cent. By international standards this is a relatively low rate, but it is seen by the

unit **4**

government as essential for attracting foreign businesses to set up operations in Ireland. It also helps provide a good incentive for Irish entrepreneurs.

Value Added Tax (VAT)

Charged by businesses on the value added at each stage of production, it is accounted for and submitted to the Revenue Commissioners every two months. Almost all businesses are required to register for VAT and only those whose annual turnover (sales) is very low are exempt.

Commercial rates

These are taxes levied on businesses by local authorities. They are based on the size of the commercial premises and the revenue is intended to fund the provision of essential services like waste disposal, water supply and public lighting.

In addition to the items outlined above, businesses may also have to pay:

> customs and excise duties   > capital gains tax.

« *syllabus signpost*
4.5.2

Implications of taxation for business

> **Production costs:** Taxes on raw materials, particularly customs and excise duties, will increase the production costs for business. In international terms, Irish-produced goods may become uncompetitive.

> **Pricing policy:** Businesses also need to be aware of the impact of specific taxes levied by government since these taxes can also lead to significant price increases. For example, Ryanair led a strong campaign against the Irish government's imposition of a €10 travel tax, which they argued increased airfares and drove tourists away from Ireland.

> **Sources of finance:** Interest payments on some sources of finance (e.g. term loans and debentures) can be written off as business expenses, thereby reducing tax liability. Other sources of finance (including retained earnings and share issues) do not offer this same advantage.

The Business Expansion Scheme (BES) is a tax relief incentive scheme that provides tax relief for investment in certain corporate trades. The scheme allows an individual investor to obtain income tax relief on investments up to a maximum of €150,000 per annum in each tax year up to 2013.

> **Business location:** Businesses may choose to locate their operations in certain regions in order to avail of specific tax incentives. For example, the 1986 Finance Act introduced financial incentives to encourage urban renewal and investment by the private sector. These incentives included a special 10 per cent corporation tax rate for certified companies setting up in the International Financial Services Centre (IFSC). While this tax incentive has now ceased, it succeeded in its

unit 4

objectives of job creation and urban renewal. The centre is host to half of the world's top fifty banks and to half of the top twenty insurance companies.

Similar tax-designated areas have also helped promote Temple Bar in Dublin, Gaeltacht regions and Shannon regional development.

› **Tax collection and administration:** Businesses are required by law to collect and submit a number of taxes to the Revenue Commissioners. These include PAYE income tax and VAT. By law, businesses must also keep proper records and accounts of all taxes collected and paid. Employers provide their employees with an annual summary of their tax deductions (form P60). All of these requirements increase the administration costs for businesses.

› **Cash flows:** Some taxes are collected and returned periodically and managers need to be aware of the impact of these payments on business cash flows. For example, VAT is submitted to the Revenue Commissioners every two months. Failure to submit these payments on time can result in financial penalties and/or court action.

Tax forms

12A: Application for a Certificate of Tax Credits

When an individual begins employment for the first time they need to register for PAYE and should submit a completed form 12A to the Revenue Commissioners. This will enable the tax authorities to determine the appropriate tax credits and rate of taxation for that worker. A notice of tax credits will be issued to both the employee and their employer, setting out the applicable rates and credits. This is reissued on an annual basis and may be adjusted to reflect changing personal circumstances. For example, a recently married taxpayer is entitled to claim a married person's personal tax credit, rather than a single person's credit. First-time employees who fail to submit form 12A before commencing employment may be liable to pay a penal rate of tax called **emergency taxation**.

P60

This tax form is issued by employers to their staff at the end of each full tax year. It shows the total income earned for that year as well as the tax and PRSI deducted. This is an important record of income and taxation and should be kept by each employee. Financial institutions often request P60s to support loan applications since they provide realistic and reliable proof of income.

P45

This is also known as a **cessation certificate** and is issued to employees who end their employment during a tax year. Employment may be ended due to dismissal or redundancy, or simply because a worker chooses to leave a job and pursue their career elsewhere.

unit 4

The information contained on a P45 is similar to a P60 in that it shows income, tax and PRSI deductions, but only up to the date when employment ceased.

Workers taking up new employment should pass the P45 on to their new employer, or where no job is available, will use it to support a claim for Jobseeker's Allowance.

P21

This is a tax balancing statement but it is not issued automatically to each taxpayer. If a person suspects an error has been made on their annual tax submission, they are entitled to request that the Revenue Commissioners examine their income tax liability. If they have overpaid they will receive a rebate, but they will be charged for any underpayment.

Sample tax calculations

Example 1 (PAYE and PRSI only)

Calculate the net annual take-home pay of John O'Brien, using the following information:

Gross salary:	€52,000
Standard rate cut-off point:	€32,800
Standard tax rate:	20%
Higher tax rate:	41%
Tax credits:	€2,575
PRSI:	4% on 52,000

Solution

	Tax Computation for John O'Brien, 2011	€	€	€
Step 1	Gross salary			52,000
Step 2	Calculate PAYE:			
	€32,800 @ 20%		6,560	
	€19,200 @ 41%		7,872	
	Gross PAYE tax		14,432	
	Less tax credits		−2,575	
	Net tax payable (PAYE)		11,857	
Step 3	Calculation of employee's PRSI			
	€52,000 @ 4%		2,080	
Step 4	Calculate Net Income			
	Gross income (Step 1)			52,000
	Less net tax payable (Step 2)		−11,857	
	Less employee's PRSI (Step 3)		−2,080	
	Total statutory deductions			(13,937)
	Net income (take-home pay)			**38,063**

Example : (PAYE, PRSI and USC)

Calculate the net annual take-home pay of Michael Scott, using the following information:

Gross salary:	€75,000	USC rates	
Standard rate cut-off point:	€32,800	€10,036 @ 2%	
Standard tax rate:	20%	€5,950 @ 4%	
Higher tax rate:	41%	Remainder @ 7%	
Tax credits:	€3,300		
PRSI rate:	4%		

Solution

	Tax Computation for Michael Scott, 2011	€	€	€
Step 1	Gross salary			75,000
Step 2	Calculate PAYE:			
	€32,800 @ 20%		6,560.00	
	€42,200 @ 41%		17,302.00	
	Gross PAYE tax		23,862.00	
	Less tax credits		−3,300.00	
	Net tax payable (PAYE)		20,562.00	
Step 3	Calculation of employee's PRSI			
	€75,000 @ 4%		3,000.00	
Step 4	Calculation of USC			
	€10,036 @ 2%	200.72		
	€ 5,950 @ 4%	238.00		
	€59,014 @ 7%	4,130.98		
	Total USC payable		4,569.70	
Step 5	Calculate net income			
	Gross income (Step 1)			75,000.00
	Less net tax payable (Step 2)		−20,562.00	
	Less employee's PRSI (Step 3)		−3,000.00	
	Less USC (Step 4)		−4,569.70	
	Total statutory deductions			(28,131.70)
	Net income (take-home pay)			**46,868.30**

unit 4

Example 3 (PAYE, PRSI and BIK)

Calculate the net annual take-home pay of Michael Scott, using the following information:

Gross salary:	€75,000
Benefit in kind:	€5,000
Standard rate cut-off point:	€32,800
Standard tax rate:	20%
Higher tax rate:	41%
Tax credits:	€3,300
PRSI rate:	4%

Solution

	Tax Computation for Michael Scott, 2011	€	€
Step1	Gross salary		75,000
	Plus benefit in kind		5,000
			80,000
Step2	Calculate PAYE:		
	32,800 @ 20%	6,560	
	47,200 @ 41%	19,352	
	Gross PAYE tax	25,912	
	Less tax credits	−3,300	
	Net tax payable (PAYE)	22,612	
Step3	Calculation of employee's PRSI		
	80,000 @ 4%	3,200	
Step4	Calculate net income		
	Gross income exc. BIK (Step 1)		75,000
	Less net tax payable (Step 2)	−22,612	
	Less employee's PRSI (Step 3)	−3,200	
	Total statutory deductions		−25,812
	Net income (take-home pay)		**49,188**

Note: Benefit in kind is reckonable for both PAYE and PRSI purposes. In the above situation, Michael Scott will take home €49,188 in cash, and will also enjoy a benefit in kind valued at €5,000.

Comparison of household and business taxation

Similarities

« *syllabus signpost*
4.5.3 & 4.5.4

> Both households and businesses are liable for taxation and both must register with the tax office.

> Both must keep tax records in order and ensure that all necessary payments are made to the Revenue Commissioners.

Differences

> **Amount of tax payable:** Businesses will have to pay much larger amounts of taxation simply because of the scale of their operations. Managers need to consider the impact of these payments on cash flows.

> **Types of tax payable:** As with insurance, businesses will have to pay a greater range of taxes. For example, corporation tax, self-assessment income tax and local authority rates do not apply to households.

> **Tax refunds and write-offs:** Businesses can write off legitimate expenses against their profits and as a result can reduce their overall tax liability. Unlike households, businesses may also be in a position to reclaim certain taxes such as VAT.

> **Tax collection:** Businesses must collect taxes such as PAYE income tax from their employees and VAT from their customers. They are required by law to submit these to the Revenue Commissioners.

unit

4

Chapter Review Diagram –
Household and Business Management: Insurance and Taxation

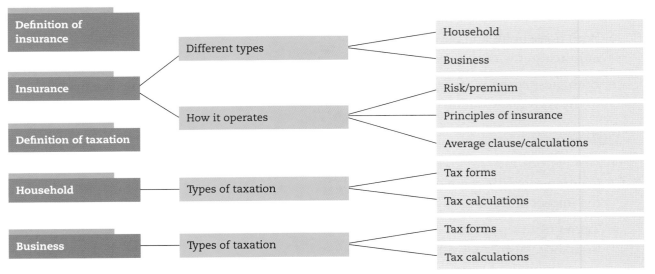

Chapter Review Questions

Insurance

1   Distinguish between insurance and assurance.

2   Distinguish between the following types of life assurance:

> whole life assurance   > endowment life assurance
> term life assurance

3   Households and businesses use insurance as an important element of their risk management strategy. Outline the steps involved in this process of risk management.

4   Outline the role played by each of the following individuals in the insurance industry:

> an assessor   > an insurance broker
> an actuary

5   Explain the terms 'premium' and 'policy' as they relate to insurance.

6   Outline the circumstances which would require a household or business to fill out:

> a claim form   > a proposal form

7   Insurance policies frequently contain the terms 'exclusion clause' and 'excess'. Distinguish between these insurance terms.

8   Name and briefly outline the five key principles of insurance.

9   Outline the circumstances under which an insurance company will apply the 'average clause' rule.

10 A house which is valued at €400,000 is insured under an all-risks policy for €350,000. Calculate the compensation payable in the event that a storm causes damage to the value of €20,000 and the policy excess is €400.

11 Name two types of statutory insurance payments applicable to households and businesses.

12 Distinguish between the following types of motor insurance:

> third-party insurance
> comprehensive insurance
> third-party, fire and theft insurance

13 List five types of business insurance and briefly explain any three.

14 List three types of insurance required by households and individuals.

15 Illustrate the importance of insurance for a business.

Taxation

16 Name the state agency responsible for collecting taxation in Ireland.

17 Explain the term 'direct tax' and give two examples to illustrate your answer.

18 Explain the term 'universal social charge'.

19 In the context of taxation explain what DIRT is.

20 Outline four major implications of taxation for businesses.

21 Calculate the net annual take home pay of Billy O'Driscoll, using the following information:

Gross salary: €70,000

Higher tax rate: 41%

Standard rate cut-off point: €32,800

Tax credits: €3,300

Standard tax rate: 20%

PRSI rate: 4%

22 Calculate the net annual take home pay of Mary Higgins, using the following information:

Gross salary: €42,000

Standard rate cut-off point: €32,800

Standard tax rate: 20%

Higher tax rate: 41%

Tax credits: €2,750

PRSI rate: 3%

unit

4

Questions · Ordinary Level

Insurance

1 Name and explain two common types of motor insurance.

2
> Jack Sullivan, a sole trader employing five staff, runs a small bakery and coffee shop in Ennis. He owns his premises and a van which is used to deliver his bread and cakes to local shops in the Ennis area. Jack has seen a decline in his sales and profits due to the downturn in the economy and he has decided to increase spending on advertising. He has also considered using sales promotion methods such as price reductions to increase sales. Jack has applied to the bank for an increase in his bank overdraft limit. *LCOL 2010*

(a) Name three types of insurance Jack should have for his business.

(b) Give one reason for having each type of insurance. *(20 marks)*

3 It is important that a business identifies, assesses and tries to reduce risks before taking out insurance. *LCOL 2008*

(a) Outline four different types of insurance policy you would expect a factory to have. *(20 marks)*

(b) Outline three ways in which a manager can reduce risks in a factory. *(20 marks)*

(c) Name and explain the functions of two documents commonly used in insurance. *(15 marks)*

(d) Explain the following three principles of insurance. Give one example in each case to illustrate your answer.

   (i) Insurable interest

   (ii) Utmost good faith

   (iii) Indemnity. *(20 marks)*

Taxation

4 The following forms are used in PAYE taxation: Form P60, Form P45, Form P21. Outline the purposes of two of these. *LCOL 2011 (10 marks)*

5 Calculate the net annual take home pay of Brendan Tuohy, using the following information:

Gross salary: €60,000   Tax credits: €4,250

Standard rate cut-off point: €40,800   PRSI rate: 5%

Standard tax rate: 20%

Higher tax rate: 41%

unit 4

Questions · Higher Level

Insurance

1 Analyse the relationship between risk and the cost of insurance.

2 Explain the term 'risk management'.

3 Outline three methods that can be used to reduce risk in a business. *LCHL 2008 (20 marks)*

4 Contrast the types of insurance a householder would need with those that a business would need.

5 When seeking insurance, it is important for households and businesses to insure items based on a realistic replacement value.

   Outline the potential risks and costs for households or businesses who fail to follow this guideline.

   In your answer you should refer specifically to the consequences of over-insurance and under-insurance.

Taxation

6 Pay As You Earn (PAYE), Value Added Tax (VAT), and Corporation Tax are examples of taxes relevant to a business.

   (a) Explain each tax mentioned above.

   (b) Evaluate the implications of each tax for a business. *LCHL 2011 (25 marks)*

7 Distinguish between tax avoidance and tax evasion.

8 Outline the main types of taxes common to both households and businesses.

9 Calculate the net annual take home pay of Peadar O'Donnell, using the following information:

(A)	Gross salary: €59,840	(B)	Gross salary: €67,000
	Standard rate cut-off point: €26,000		Standard rate cut-off point: €29,500
	Standard tax rate: 20%		Standard tax rate: 20%
	Higher tax rate: 41%		Higher tax rate: 41%
	Tax credits: €2,500		Tax credits: €3,250
	PRSI rate: 7%		PRSI rate: 6%
	USC: 2% up to €10,000		USC: 7%
	4% on the next €6,000		
	7% on the remainder		

unit

4

Chapter 10
Monitoring the Business (Ratio Analysis)

Syllabus Outcomes

On completion, the student should be able to:

» 4.5.5 Calculate and interpret the main profitability and liquidity ratios and debt/equity;

» 4.5.14 Understand the importance of accountancy and business data in the monitoring of the business enterprise.

News Flash

1 Read the newspaper extract below and discuss the issues raised.
2 Can you explain any of the highlighted terms?

Quinn creditors approve debt proposals

by Barry O'Halloran

Creditors of Quinn Group yesterday approved a proposal to restructure the troubled manufacturing and financial services group's debts that will cut €800 million from the liabilities of its manufacturing business.

The terms of the deal were hammered out early last month and voted on by creditors such as Strategic Value Partners and Silver Point Capital, and banks Barclays, KBC and Danske yesterday.

Yesterday's statement from the group said the creditors approved its restructuring proposals.

The company said the restructuring will see its manufacturing group permanently relieved of more than €800 million of debt. It will cut the group's annual interest bill to €40 million from €60 million.

It added that the vote would pave the way for the sale of the Quinn Insurance business to a joint venture between Anglo Irish Bank and Liberty Mutual. This is expected to be completed in the near future.

Quinn Group chief executive Paul O'Brien said the deal would provide funding and stability for the future. "The group remains profitable at the operating level, but simply could not sustain the level of debt taken on in the past.

"By permanently removing over €800 million of that debt burden, the manufacturing businesses have been placed on a sound financial footing," Mr O'Brien added.

The Quinn Group is the industrial conglomerate formerly owned by Seán Quinn and his family.

The group owes €1.3 billion to banks and bondholders, while Anglo Irish is owed almost €2.9 billion by the Quinn family.

In September, the group's management cut projected earnings for 2011 to €85 million from the previous management's estimate of €115 million, blaming difficult trading conditions.

As a result, it said the interest payments agreed in the original restructuring earlier this year were unsustainable.

This article is taken from **The Irish Times,** Tuesday, 1 November 2011.

For more up-to-date newspaper articles see www.edcodigital.ie

Financial Information

This chapter deals with the calculation and interpretation of **key financial indicators** for a business, and these are important because they provide a good insight into its financial health.

A number of stakeholders are likely to make use of financial information, though they may have different reasons for doing so:

> **Shareholders:** They are the owners of a business and will focus their attention on profitability and return on investment. Profit levels in a business will have a significant bearing on the level of dividends which shareholders receive.

> **Managers:** They need regular information to control expenditure and to aid on-going decision-making. In the longer term, management will be concerned with strategic profit objectives. Managers of commercial businesses who fail to reach profit targets are likely to lose their jobs. Department managers will have a specific need for financial information relating to the performance and liquidity of their own department.

> **Employees:** They will be concerned with all financial aspects of business performance since their jobs depend on the business remaining solvent. Of particular concern to employees will be liquidity and profitability figures, since these are important for both job security and wage levels.

> **Lenders/Investors:** Both of these stakeholders will primarily be concerned with a firm's ability to repay its debts. Banks will seek to ensure that loan repayments are met and that overall debt levels are not excessive. Investors (venture capitalists) are also seeking a return on their investment, so they will compare the returns available across a range of businesses and alternative investments.

> **Suppliers:** Cash flow will be vital if they are to continue providing goods on credit. Concerns over a customer's liquidity may cause suppliers to limit the availability of credit or insist on cash on delivery (COD).

> **Government:** Various government agencies will be interested in business performance, not least the Revenue Commissioners, who will be levying corporation tax on company profits.

unit 4

Financial control and reporting is an ongoing process for all organisations and is carried out systematically using spreadsheets, accounting software and ratio analysis. The information is compiled on a weekly, monthly and an annual basis, with reports and recommendations forming the basis for planning and policy decisions. For this reason it is vitally important that the financial information upon which these decisions are based is gathered in a consistent and reliable manner. Inaccurate information will lead to the wrong decisions being made.

Annual financial statements

Trading account

Used to calculate **gross profit.**

Gross Profit = Sales – Cost of sales

Gross profit is calculated as follows:

Trading Account

Sales	180,000
Less cost of sales	(75,000)
Gross profit	**105,000**

« *syllabus signpost*
4.5.14

Profit and loss account

Used to calculate **net profit/net loss.**

Net Profit = Gross Profit – Expenses

'Overheads' is an alternative name for business expenses.

Net profit is calculated as follows:

Profit and Loss Account

Gross profit	105,000
Less expenses	(45,000)
Net profit	**60,000**

If the expenses are greater than a firm's gross profit, they will have a **net loss**.

unit 4

Profit and loss appropriation account

Shows **how profits are distributed.**

Typically a portion is given to shareholders in the form of dividends and the remainder kept by the firm as retained earnings or reserves.

Profit and Loss Appropriation Account	
Net profit	60,000
Less dividends	(20,000)
Retained earnings/reserves	**40,000**

Balance sheet

Illustrates the year-end value of company assets and liabilities, as well as details of its capital structure. Important items in the balance sheet include:

> **Fixed assets:** items owned by business and intended for long-term use, e.g. premises, equipment, vehicles.

> **Current assets:** cash, or any asset which can be converted to cash in the short term (one year), e.g. bank deposits, debtors, stock of goods.

> **Current liabilities:** short-term debts owed by the business and falling due within one year. Examples include creditors, bank overdrafts, unpaid bills (accruals).

> **Working capital:** the level of cash available to run the business in the short term.

> **Working capital = current assets – current liabilities**

> **Net worth:** also called total net assets, it shows what the business would be worth if it were to sell off its assets and pay its short-term debts.

> **Net worth = fixed assets + (current assets – current liabilities)**

> **Capital employed:** the total of the 'financed by' section of balance sheet, setting out the capital structure of a business. Generally capital comes from two sources: borrowings **(debt capital)** and investments by shareholders **(equity capital).**

> **Authorised share capital:** the maximum amount of shares the company is permitted to issue. It is decided when the company is being set up and is included in the Memorandum of Association.

> **Issued share capital:** the amount of share capital actually issued to date.

unit

4

Sample financial statements

Trading, Profit & Loss and Appropriation Account of P&C Ltd for year ended 31/12/2011

	€	€	€
Sales			180,000
Less cost of sales			(75,000)
Gross Profit:			105,000
Less expenses			(45,000)
Net Profit:			60,000
Less dividend			(20,000)
Retained Profit/Reserves			**40,000**

Balance Sheet of P&C Ltd as at 31/12/2011
Fixed Assets:

	€	€	€
Premises			270,000
Vehicles			40,000
			310,000
Current Assets:			
Cash		3,000	
Debtors		22,000	
Closing stock		10,000	
		35,000	
Current Liabilities:			
Bank overdraft	18,000		
Creditors	7,000	**(25,000)**	
Working capital:			10,000
Total Net Assets (net worth)			**€320,000**

Financed by:	Authorised	Issued
Share capital	500,000	200,000
Debenture loan		80,000
Reserves		40,000
Capital Employed:		**€320,000**

Exam Tip

Leaving Certificate business students may not be required to prepare trading, profit and loss accounts or balance sheets, but you must understand the key relationships involved in these financial statements. For example, you need to be able to calculate net profit if provided with figures for gross profit and expenses.

unit **4**

Cash flow forecasts

These are more regular financial statements and will be used by management to monitor cash flow on a month-by-month basis. They allow potential problems to be identified early, so appropriate action can be taken.

Limitations of financial statements

Financial statements are of limited use in analysing the performance of a business. Here are some reasons why:

> **Absolute figures:** It's important to realise that absolute figures give no real indication of performance. It's impossible to say whether €25 million is a 'good' profit or not. A lot will depend on previous performance, industry norms and economic climate. For that reason we need to **deal with figures in percentage terms** and not absolute amounts.

> **Company-specific:** Comparisons are vital. Taking the figures for just one company is not a useful measure of performance. Again, it's important to compare a set of results with similar figures for competitors or against industry norms, especially when contemplating investment.

> **Non-financial information:** Financial statements deal only with financial information. They give no indication of important underlying issues such as staff morale, productivity or changing economic circumstances. Careful investment requires in-depth research.

« *syllabus signpost*
4.5.5

Ratio Analysis

The ratios provide a useful set of tools which allow all interested stakeholders to evaluate the financial health of a business. The ratios outlined below examine profitability, liquidity and gearing. Each ratio or formula is set out below and worked examples are provided on pages 192–4.

Profitability ratios

Profitability ratios measure profit levels and indicate whether annual profit is improving or declining.

There are three frequently used measures of profitability:

> **Gross profit percentage** (gross margin)
> **Net profit percentage** (net margin)
> **Return on capital employed** (return on investment)

Exam Tip

Frequently Higher Level students are not provided with the names of specific ratios in exams, but are simply asked to evaluate a company's 'profitability', 'liquidity' or 'gearing'. It is therefore vital to know which ratios are classified under each heading.

Who is interested in profitability?

Managers will focus on profitability since they need to meet their annual targets and projections. Managers will also need to meet the expectations of shareholders.

Employees seeking wage increases will also be interested in profitability, as will shareholders and potential investors. Businesses would obviously like to see an increase in annual profits as this reflects improved efficiency and should make it easier to attract additional investment.

Some businesses may be willing to sacrifice short-term profits in pursuit of longer-term strategic objectives, including expansion and diversification.

Gross profit percentage (gross margin)

$$\frac{\text{Gross profit}}{\text{Sales}} \times \frac{100}{1}$$

Illustrates the amount of gross profit earned on sales. For example, a gross margin of 45 per cent means that for every euro of sales revenue, the business is earning 45c gross profit.

Net profit percentage (net margin)

$$\frac{\text{Net profit}}{\text{Sales}} \times \frac{100}{1}$$

Illustrates the amount of net profit earned on sales. For example, a net margin of 20 per cent means that for every euro of sales revenue, the business is earning 20c net profit.

Return on capital employed (return on investment)

$$\frac{\text{Net profit}}{\text{Capital employed}} \times \frac{100}{1}$$

ROI expresses the profit earned as a percentage of the money invested.

Return on investment (ROI) or rate of return is used to measure and evaluate the efficiency of an investment. By comparing the ROI on different investment options potential investors can choose the best possible option.

Liquidity ratios

Liquidity ratios are used to examine cash flow and reflect a firm's ability to pay its day-to-day expenses. Poor liquidity is the single biggest reason for business failure and many profitable businesses are forced to close because they do not have sufficient cash to pay day-to-day bills.

unit 4

Creditors who lose patience can apply to the courts to have their debts paid and this may lead to an illiquid business being wound up.

Liquidation is the term used to describe a situation where a business is shut down and its assets are sold off. The money raised is used to pay all or part of its outstanding debt.

To avoid this type of problem it is very important for managers to prepare cash flow forecasts as this will allow them to identify potential problems before they arise. Once identified, a business can arrange short-term finance to meet the funding shortfall.

During the recent credit crunch, banks were unable to provide overdrafts for their commercial customers and many businesses were forced to close.

A detailed analysis of cash flow forecasting is contained in *Chapter 8: Household and Business Management: Finance.*

Working capital ratio (current ratio)

The working capital or **current ratio** is used to compare the cash available to the business in the short term with the cash needed to pay short-term bills and debts.

If a business needs funding urgently it should be in a position to turn its current assets into cash. In order to ensure that a business will not have a short-term funding problem it is recommended that the value of current assets should be twice that of current liabilities.

Any business which has a negative working capital figure on its balance sheet is showing clear signs of liquidity problems.

Working capital ratio	
Current Assets: Current Liabilities Ideal result is 2:1	*Compares short-term assets to short-term debt: cash available in the coming year versus cash needed in the coming year.*

Acid test ratio (quick ratio)

The **acid test** is a stricter test of liquidity and allows for the fact that it may take some time to turn all current assets into cash. If we list the most common current assets and place them in descending order of liquidity, those which are easiest to convert to cash would be listed first.

Cash:	The most liquid asset.
Bank deposits:	Can be converted to cash in days or weeks if required.
Debtors:	Usually pay within thirty days. Can make use of factoring for immediate cash.
Stock of goods:	Large amounts of stock may take time to sell, even at discounted prices.

unit 4

Given this potential problem with turning stock into immediate cash, the acid test (or the 'real test') of a firm's liquidity is their ability to cover their short-term debts from all remaining current assets.

For that reason the formula is as follows:

Acid Test

(Current Assets – Closing Stock): Current Liabilities

Ideal result is 1:1

Compares short-term assets to short-term debt: cash available in the coming year versus cash needed in the coming year.

Exam Tip

Both liquidity measures must be given in the form of a ratio and marks will be lost where answers are expressed as a percentage.

Gearing ratio

The gearing or **debt/equity ratio** highlights a business's reliance on borrowings or debt capital to finance its operations. A business which has a high proportion of capital invested by shareholders (equity capital) is said to be lowly geared whereas a business which is heavily reliant on borrowings (debt capital) is highly geared. A neutrally geared company has equal amounts of debt and equity capital.

Gearing ratio

Debt Capital: Equity Capital

Illustrates the balance between external borrowings and shareholders funds.

Debt capital = debentures + long-term loans.

Equity capital = issued share capital + reserves.

If debt > equity, company is highly geared

If debt < equity, company is lowly geared

Debt can also be expressed as a percentage of equity by using the formula as follows:

$$\frac{\text{Debt Capital}}{\text{Equity Capital}} \times \frac{100}{1}$$

Low gearing tends to be less risky since the business is under less pressure to meet fixed interest payments. This in turn enables the business to increase its dividend payments to shareholders or to reinvest profits back into the business.

Highly geared companies are those which have a relatively large amount of external debt. This high level of external debt carries increased risk for the business and during periods of slow growth or economic downturn it may struggle to generate sufficient income to meet these repayments. This can lead to liquidity problems, a poor credit rating or even bankruptcy.

Highly geared businesses also find it harder to raise additional funding, since potential lenders and investors may be unwilling to loan money to a business which already has high levels of debt.

During periods of strong economic growth or where interest rates are low businesses may be more inclined to seek additional debt capital. During the boom years of the **Celtic Tiger** (1999–2007) many Irish companies used debt capital to fund investment and expansion projects. A strong economy and healthy sales figures enabled this money to be repaid, but some of this debt became an unbearable burden when the recession began in 2008. The result was failing businesses, huge job losses and a high level of bad debts.

Case Study

The News Flash article on page 182 illustrates very clearly the enormous strain that external debt can have on a business. It also illustrates the consequences for the Quinn Group of failure to meet its financial obligations.

While the business was growing successfully, the company increasingly relied on debt capital to expand its operations. In the initial stages this proved sustainable and the business generated sufficient income to service this debt.

Problems arose when the business and its owners took on very large amounts of debt, primarily from the ill-fated Anglo Irish Bank. When this bank effectively collapsed in 2009, it sought to recover most of this debt and the Quinn Group was unable to pay. As a result, the group was placed into receivership and the business was restructured.

A **receiver** is an external expert appointed by a court or a secured creditor (usually a bank) to take over the day-to-day running of the business. The receiver will replace the managing director and will seek to pay off as much of the business's debts as possible. This is usually achieved by selling off business assets. If possible the receiver will discharge the debt and restore the business to viable operation, but in many cases this is not possible and the business is forced to close down.

This winding-up process is called **liquidation** and is a formal procedure which brings about the legal death of a business.

In the case of the Quinn Group the core business of insurance continues to operate and the receiver sought to protect creditors, clients and employees. Some debts were written off while the remainder were restructured. **Restructuring** means that the repayment terms were altered so as to increase the likelihood that they would eventually be repaid.

Sean Quinn lost control of his business and filed for personal bankruptcy (in Northern Ireland) in late 2011. The insurance business was sold in December 2011.

Exam Tip

Answering exam questions on ratios

1 **Learn the ratios:** This is a vital first step, as this relatively straightforward question becomes virtually impossible if you don't know the correct ratio!

2 **Write down formula:** Marks awarded for correct ratio.

3 **Fill in the figures provided:** Replace items in formula with information given.

4 **Calculate answer:** Now do the sums, using calculator if necessary.

5 **Comment on significance of results:** Compare results with previous year or with rival business. Comment on year-on-year change and try highlighting reasons for change. If ratio has an 'ideal' or target figure, be sure to mention that.

Sample Calculations

P&C Ltd provides the following figures for the financial year ended 31/12/2010:

Gross Profit = 56%

Net Profit = 37%

Return on Capital Employed = 20.7%

Current Ratio = 2.3 : 1

Acid Test Ratio = 1.5 : 1

Gearing (Debt/Equity) Ratio = 1 : 2 (50%)

Using the company final accounts set out on page 186 we can calculate the same ratios for 2011 and can comment on the company's financial performance during the two years.

Gross profit percentage (gross margin)

	2011	2010
$\dfrac{\text{Gross profit}}{\text{Sales}} \times \dfrac{100}{1}$	$\dfrac{105,000}{180,000} \times \dfrac{100}{1}$ $= 58.3\%$	$= 56\%$

This means that for 2011 P&C Ltd made 58.3 cent gross profit for every euro of sales revenue. The results show a small year-on-year improvement in the gross margin and this is obviously a positive development.

Net profit percentage (net margin)

$$\frac{\text{Net profit}}{\text{Sales}} \times \frac{100}{1}$$

2011

$$\frac{60{,}000}{180{,}000} \times \frac{100}{1}$$

$$= 33.3\%$$

2010

$$= 37\%$$

This result indicates that P&C makes 33.3 cent net profit from every euro of sales revenue in 2011. This is a slight disimprovement from the 2010 figure.

With the gross margin improving year-on-year we might expect a similar improvement in net margin but this is clearly not the case. This suggests that P&C Ltd needs to monitor and control its overheads more closely as they are the most likely reason for the disimprovement.

Return on capital employed (return on investment)

$$\frac{\text{Net profit}}{\text{Capital employed}} \times \frac{100}{1}$$

2011

$$\frac{60{,}000}{320{,}000} \times \frac{100}{1}$$

$$= 18.7\%$$

2010

$$= 20.7\%$$

Managers and shareholders will not be happy with the declining return on investment highlighted here. While the return is well above that available on a risk-free bank deposit, no investor likes to see this downward trend. It suggests that the business is being managed less efficiently in 2011 and management will need to take steps to halt this decline.

On the basis of all three profitability ratios, there is some cause for concern with this business. Potential investors will need to examine possible reasons for the decline.

Working capital ratio (current ratio)

Current Assets: Current Liabilities

2011

35,000 : 25,000

= 1.4 : 1

2010

= 2.3 : 1

A disimprovement in the current ratio since 2010 is not a good sign for P&C Ltd and is a clear warning that the business is having liquidity problems. The current ratio was above the target figure of 2:1 in 2010, but has fallen well below that level in 2011. This means that the company may not be in a position to pay all of its short-term debts.

Acid test ratio (quick ratio)

(Current Assets – Closing Stock): Current Liabilities

2011

(35,000 – 10,000) : 25,000

= 25,000 : 25,000

= 1 : 1

2010

= 1.5 : 1

In keeping with the current ratio, the acid test also highlights a worsening liquidity position for P&C Ltd. Some consolation can be taken from the fact the quick ratio has not fallen below the recommended 1:1, but this liquidity issue needs to be addressed immediately.

If no action is taken and the trend continues, P&C Ltd will not be able to pay its day-to-day expenses and running costs.

Debt/equity ratio

Debt Capital: Equity Capital

2011	2010
80,000 : (200,000 + 40,000)	
= 80,000 : 240,000	
1 : 3 (33.3%)	1 : 2 (50%)

Both figures indicate that P&C Ltd is lowly geared and is in fact less reliant on external debt in 2011 than it was in 2010. This would seem to be a positive development, especially in the light of declining profitability and poor liquidity.

Lower levels of debt capital will require smaller interest payments and may enable P&C Ltd to borrow the short-term funding it needs to resolve its liquidity problems.

Chapter Review Diagram – Monitoring the Business (Ratio Analysis)

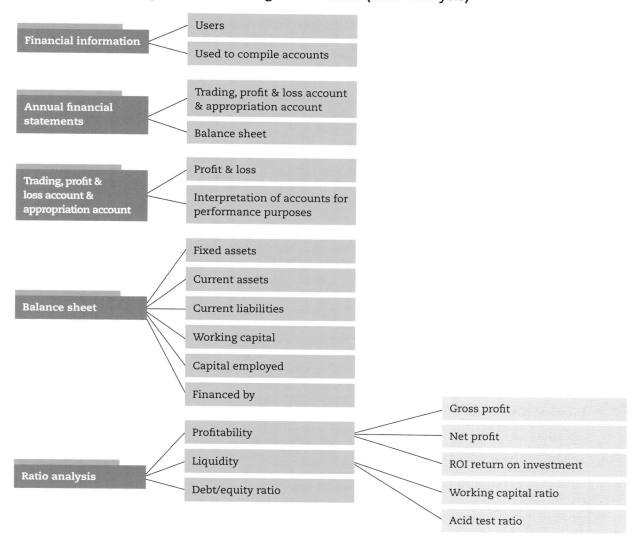

Chapter Review Questions

1 Name five stakeholders who are likely to make use of financial information provided by businesses. In the case of any three of these stakeholders, outline briefly their main reasons for doing so.

2 Use the following figures to calculate both the gross profit and the net profit of Albatros Ltd:

> Cost of sales: €87,000   > Net sales: €175,000   > Expenses: €36,000

3 Identify two fixed assets, two current assets and two current liabilities of a business.

4 Explain the term 'working capital' and outline its importance to business.

5 Explain what 'net worth' (total net assets) means.

6 What formula is used to calculate return on capital employed?

7 Explain the difference between authorised capital and issued capital.

8 Outline three limitations of financial statements as a means of evaluating a business.

9 List all three Profitability Ratios and write out the formula for calculating each one.

10 Explain what is meant by the term 'liquidity'. Outline the consequences of poor liquidity for businesses.

11 The following information is taken from the final accounts of Kenny Ltd on 31/12/2012.

> Sales: €500,000,   > Gross profit: €100,000   > Net profit: €37,500.

Calculate: (i) the gross profit margin, (ii) the net profit margin.

12 Calculate the return on capital employed from the following figures:

Trading, Profit and Loss Account		
	2012	2013
Net profit	€77,000	€87,000
Balance sheet		
	2012	2013
Capital employed	€140,000	€150,000

Show the formulae and all your workings

13 The following information is available from the final accounts of Adams Ltd on 31/12/2012.

> Current liabilities: €100,000   > Current assets: €300,000

Calculate: (i) the working capital, (ii) the working capital ratio.

14 Explain what the debt/equity ratio is and outline its importance to a business.

15 Calculate the debt/equity ratio from the following figures:

> Debentures: €80,000   > Reserves: €45,000

> Issued share capital: €205,000   > Bank overdraft: €16,000

16 Calculate the acid test ratio from the following figures:

> Current assets: €80,000,   > Current assets: €55,000

> Closing stock: €10,000

Questions · Ordinary Level

1 Use the information from below and answer the questions which follow: *LCOL 2011*

Balance Sheet, Brady's Hotel (Extract)		
	2010	2009
	€	€
Current assets	900,000	800,000
Current liabilities	500,000	400,000

(a) Calculate the working capital ratio for 2010 and 2009 (show the formula and all your workings).

(b) Explain whether the ratio had improved or disimproved. *(20 marks)*

2 The following information is available from the final accounts of Doherty Ltd.

LCOL 2009

	2007	2008
	€	€
Sales	600,000	750,000
Gross profit	200,000	300,000
Net profit	120,000	210,000

Calculate the gross profit margin for 2007 and 2008 and comment on the trend. *(20 marks)*

Calculate the net profit margin for 2007 and 2008 and comment on the trend. *(20 marks)*

3 Identify three parties who would be interested in the accounting results of a business, and give one reason in each case.

4 Explain the letters ROI, COD and P & L.

5 Study the information supplied and answer the questions that follow.

Final Accounts	2013	2014
	€	€
Sales	190,000	310,000
Gross profit	70,000	90,000
Net profit	45,000	75,000
Balance sheet	2013	2014
	€	€
Current assets	380,000	570,000
Current liabilities	190,000	400,000
Closing stock	60,000	85,000
Retained earnings	85,000	95,000
Issued share capital	320,000	340,000

(a) Calculate the gross profit margin and net profit margin. Comment on the trend.

(b) Calculate the acid test ratio for 2013 and 2014. Comment on the trend.

(c) Distinguish between 'retained earnings' and 'issued share capital'.

Q Questions · Higher Level

1

RESULTS 2008	
Net profit margin	32%
Current ratio	2 : 1
Acid test ratio	1.1 : 1
Debt/Equity ratio	0.4 : 1

(a) From the figures given below for 2009 calculate the following for CES Ltd:

(i) Net profit margin

(ii) Current ratio

(iii) Acid test ratio

(iv) Debt/Equity ratio   *(20 marks)*

Information for 2009	€
Sales	135,000
Net profit	33,750
Current assets (including closing stock)	84,500
Current liabilities	65,000
Closing stock	39,000
Ordinary share capital	300,000
Long-term debt	192,000
Retained earnings	20,000

(b) Analyse the significance of the trends over the two years (2008/2009) for the following stakeholders:

(i) Investors/shareholders

(ii) Suppliers

(iii) Employees   *(20 marks)*

Note: Results for 2008 are already calculated above.   *LCHL 2010*

2 Explain the importance of good financial information (e.g. financial ratios) to the management team of a business. Use examples to illustrate your answer.

3 Illustrate the usefulness of the debt/equity ratio in helping a manager to monitor the financial performance of the business.

4 Discuss the importance of the following financial statements to the management of a business enterprise:

(i) The profit and loss account

(ii) The balance sheet.

5 From the figures given below:

(a) Calculate for 1999 and 2000 the acid test ratios and the debt/equity ratios.

(b) Analyse any trends you notice from your calculations.

	1999	2000
Current assets	90,500	75,400
Current liabilities	65,100	44,600
Closing stock	47,300	51,200
Equity share capital	240,000	240,000
Long-term debt	150,000	220,000
Retained earnings (reserves)	60,000	62,000

6 Analyse the profitability and liquidity trends in Gracey and Co. Ltd, from the following figures for 1997 and 1998.

	1998	1997
	€	€
Current liabilities	9,400	8,200
Closing stock	8,200	10,100
Equity share capital	85,000	85,000
Gross profit	58,250	42,560
Retained earnings	17,100	16,450
Current assets	13,500	15,450
Net profit	13,500	13,255
Sales	141,500	121,500

7 Study the information supplied and answer the question that follows.

	2000	1999
Long-term loans	310,000	307,000
Ordinary share capital	210,000	150,000
Reserves	98,000	55,000
Overdrafts	56,000	76,500

Calculate the debt/equity ratio for each year and comment on the trend.

8 Distinguish between the following terms:

(i) Working capital and ordinary share capital

(ii) Current assets and current liabilities.

Chapter 11
Human Resource Management

Syllabus Outcomes

On completion, the student should be able to:

>> 4.5.6 Explain the key functions of human resource management;

>> 4.5.10 Understand the relationship between employers and employees and the role of trade unions;

>> 4.5.11 Understand the central role of human resources in management (HL).

News Flash

The people factor

by Gerald Flynn

The recession has forced a shift in human resource management styles at Irish organisations, which are communicating more with their employees even while cutting staff numbers and wages.

A new study of trends and developments in Irish people management shows a shift towards the hard skills with a focus on downsizing, making savings and cutting pay. This is being combined with an emphasis on improved and more intensive internal communications and employee engagement as employers try to keep morale up...

There is a detectable shift in the relationships between employers and employees, with a rise in employment insecurity. Employees are also expected to be more self-reliant and to find their own training and development opportunities.

There is an increasing "marketised" approach to work, with more dependence on performance-related pay and widespread adoption of defined-contribution pension schemes...

Hard human resource management, in general, is reflected in downsizing, tighter attendance management, pay freezes and cuts in any bonuses as well as redundancies and clear attempts to boost productivity to reduce costs and safeguard revenues.

The soft alternative is a series of practices to boost motivation with more intensive communication, staff redeployment to retain and reward high-performing employees...

According to the Irish research, employers have been trying to balance hard and soft practices in response to the recession...

When asked to identify the most effective people

management practices in the recession, the most frequently identified initiatives were: communication and information disclosure; efficiencies and cost control; and engagement and consultation.

This is an edited extract from **The Irish Times,** FRIDAY, 24 JUNE 2011.

For more up-to-date newspaper articles see www.edcodigital.ie

1 Read the newspaper extract opposite and discuss the issues raised.

2 Can you explain any of the highlighted terms?

People are the most valuable resource available to business and therefore need to be managed effectively. The human resource department (or personnel department) is responsible for this vital task.

Human resource management (HRM) seeks to attract the best people and rewards its employees so that they are fully motivated to achieve the overall strategic objectives of the business.

Role/Functions of the Human Resource Manager

« syllabus signpost 4.5.6

A human resource manager has a wide range of responsibilities, which includes:

> Human Resource Planning
> Recruitment and Selection
> Training and Development

> Performance Appraisal
> Employee Welfare and Rewards
> Industrial Relations

Human Resource Planning

HR planning involves **forecasting future staffing needs** based on the firm's strategic goals. An audit of current staffing levels may also be necessary. This will provide senior management with a snapshot of the existing skill set within the business and will assist the planning process by highlighting deficiencies in terms of abilities and staffing levels. This is sometimes called manpower or staff planning.

If expansion is planned in the coming years, the business will need to consider not only the number of extra staff required, but also the types of skills and qualifications they should possess. If the proposed expansion is into overseas markets there will be an obvious need for staff with foreign language skills.

On the other hand, an economic downturn may cause a business to consolidate its operations and this might translate into job losses. The human resource department will need to examine closely the areas to be reduced and will need to negotiate and plan the redundancy process. The initial aim may be to achieve the required cutbacks through **voluntary redundancies**. This requires that staff must agree to give up their jobs and they will expect to be well compensated. A business seeking voluntary redundancies will need to offer severance payments which exceed basic legal entitlements.

unit 4

In a situation where redundancies are compulsory, staff who are laid off are entitled to statutory redundancy payments. The statutory redundancy payment is a lump-sum payment based on the gross pay of the employee. All eligible employees are entitled to:

> Two weeks' pay for every year of service over the age of sixteen, and

> One further week's pay.

The amount of statutory redundancy is subject to a maximum earnings limit of €600 per week (€31,200 per year).

As the issues outlined above clearly illustrate, any decision to alter the number of staff will impact on business costs and for that reason staff planning is a very important HR function.

Recruitment and Selection

This is the process of attracting suitable applicants and then choosing those most suited to the position. The most critical factor in achieving the correct complement of staff with the correct skills is to ensure that careful recruitment is carried out.

From the point of view of the HR department, there are a number of steps involved in performing this function effectively:

1 Prepare job description

2 Prepare person specification

3 Advertise the job

4 Shortlist the candidates

5 Interview

6 Check references

7 Offer job and issue contract of employment

Based on the staffing needs highlighted during the planning process, the HR department will need to prepare job descriptions and person specifications.

A **job description** sets out the tasks and duties involved in the job, as well as the areas of responsibility.

> A restaurant wishes to recruit a head chef. It expects the new recruit will take overall responsibility for the kitchen, will co-ordinate the work of five subordinates and will plan the weekly menu, as well as sourcing all ingredients.

The **person specification** sets out the skills, characteristics and qualifications needed by the person applying for the vacant position.

Example

The restaurant looking for the new head chef decides that the ideal candidate must have a recognised catering qualification and should have a minimum of three years' experience in a similar role.

On the basis of these criteria the firm will formulate advertisements and will choose suitable media in which to place them. Possible media include newspapers, trade magazines and radio ads. Some businesses employ the services of recruitment agencies to assist them with the process while others take a proactive approach by employing graduates direct from colleges and universities.

Adverts must not discriminate against potential candidates on the basis of the nine grounds set out in the Employment Equality Act.

Recall and Review

Can you list the nine grounds upon which discrimination is specifically outlawed?

HEAD CHEF WANTED

A head chef is required for a busy city centre hotel.

Duties and responsibilities include:
- Planning the menus.
- Dealing with the suppliers.
- Supervising inventory and stock control.
- Maintaining the budgetary targets.
- Recruitment, training and supervision of kitchen staff.
- Ensuring that health and safety standards are maintained in the kitchen.
- Reviewing the daily roster of kitchen tasks.

The successful candidate is likely to have the following skills and qualities:
- A degree or college diploma in food and beverage management and/or hotel management.
- A minimum of 3 years' experience in a similar position.
- A passion and love for food.
- Excellent written and oral communication skills.
- Excellent management and organisational skills
- Capable of working well under pressure.

Applications are invited from suitably qualified candidates and Curriculum Vitae should be sent to:

THE HUMAN RESOURCES MANAGER

BOYLAN'S HOTEL

PATRICK STREET

CORK

Closing date for applications is August 20th 2012

Boylan's Hotel is an equal opportunities employer

Having received completed applications and curriculum vitaes (CVs), candidates may be shortlisted before a small number are interviewed. Shortlisting is the systematic process whereby a large number of applicants are whittled down to a smaller number of suitable candidates. When shortlisting candidates, the HR manager attempts to compare each applicant to the criteria set out in the job description and the person specification. These criteria become a checklist against which each potential recruit is evaluated.

Companies also use a variety of other methods to shortlist candidates. These include aptitude tests and personality profiles.

unit

4

Letter of application (example)

The Human Resources Manager

Boylan's Hotel

Patrick Street

Cork

Eoghan Duggan

47 Sycamore View, Parkside, Clonakilty, Co Cork.

Tel: 023 - 93422

eduggan47@gmail.com

Dear Sir/Madam,

I wish to apply for the recently advertised position of Head Chef and enclose a copy of my curriculum vitae for your consideration.

I believe I have the necessary qualifications, experience and passion required for the position and I've had the good fortune to work in some excellent restaurants both in Ireland and abroad.

My time in the kitchen has allowed me to develop my skills and utilise my natural abilities.

I hope you will take time to consider my application and I look forward to hearing from you in the near future.

Yours faithfully,

Eoghan Duggan

Curriculum Vitae (example)

Curriculum Vitae

PERSONAL INFORMATION

Name: Eoghan Duggan

Address: 47 Sycamore View, Parkside, Clonakilty, Co Cork.

Date of birth: 25 April 1986

Telephone: 023 - 93422

Mobile phone: 082 - 7968843

Email: eduggan47@gmail.com

EDUCATION

School: Clonakilty Community College, 1998–2005

University: University of Glamorgan, 2005–2007

    Diploma in Hotel and Catering Management (Honours)

Dublin City University (2007–2008)

    Postgraduate diploma in Food Technology and Innovation

EMPLOYMENT HISTORY

Current employer: Majestic Hotel, Church Street, Dublin 2

Position: Sous Chef

Employment commenced: October 2010.

Previous employment: Oct 2008 – July 2010: The Grand Hotel, Adelaide (Chef de partie)
June–Sept 2008: Franco's steakhouse and grill, Amsterdam (Grill chef)

INTERESTS

Athletics: Member Clonliffe Harriers Athletic Club since 2009. I have completed 2 marathons and 3 triathlons since 2007.

Hockey: Member DCU Hockey Club.

Travel: I travelled extensively during my time in university and have visited Europe, the Americas and Asia.

Once a small number of the most suitable applicants remain, businesses will conduct **job interviews.** Interviews are a very important part of the selection process since they provide face-to-face interaction between the employer and prospective employee. During the interview the employer will have the opportunity to ask in-depth questions of the candidates which will help evaluate their suitability for the vacant position. Interviews also allow employers to assess the interpersonal skills of candidates, as well as assessing how they cope in stressful situations. At some point in the interview, the candidate will get a chance to ask questions about the nature of the position or future plans for the business.

The successful candidate should receive **induction training** and a written **contract of employment.** Induction training helps new recruits to settle into their role, by making them familiar with all of the personnel and operating systems in the organisation. Once familiar with the layout of the building, the health and safety guidelines and their co-workers, an employee is more likely to feel comfortable in their new working environment. This may also help meet their acceptance needs, as highlighted by Maslow in his hierarchy of needs (see p. 79).

Internal Recruitment v External Recruitment

A key consideration for many businesses is whether or not vacant positions should be filled by promoting a current employee, or by looking outside the current workforce for an external candidate. While there is no definitive answer to this dilemma, HR managers need to be aware of the merits and drawbacks associated with each approach.

Advantages of internal recruitment

> **Quicker:** Since the pool of potential candidates is much smaller than with external recruitment, the selection process should be completed more quickly.

> **Less expensive:** Once again, due to reduced numbers and because there is no need for expensive media advertising, the cost of recruitment and selection will be lower.

> **Motivating effect:** If a firm has a policy of internal recruitment and promotion, this provides an incentive for employees to work hard. Making a positive impression on management will improve their career prospects.

> **Familiarity:** The staff member is already well known to management, and will have a track record in the business. This will enable the HR manager to assess the relative strengths and weaknesses of each candidate.

An additional benefit lies in the fact that internal applicants are familiar with the policies and work practices adopted by the firm, so less time and money will be needed for training.

Advantages of external recruitment

> **New talent and skills:** External recruitment provides an opportunity to tap into a whole new pool of talent and perhaps to add skills and experience which do not currently exist within the organisation.

> **Fresh approach:** While external candidates are less familiar to, and with, the organisation this may make it easier to bring with them new ideas and work practices. This is summed up in the old saying that 'a new broom sweeps clean'.

> **Relationship issues:** They have no association with existing staff and may find it easier to assume positions of authority. Current staff will inevitably have personal relationships and 'emotional baggage' which have been built up during their employment. They may find it difficult to impose their authority on former colleagues, who in turn may be resentful of their new role and position.

Whichever method is chosen, the most important thing is to get the **best person for the job**.

Training and Development

This HR function recognises that staff may need ongoing training and development in order to perform at the highest level of efficiency.

Induction training may be required for new recruits. It involves familiarising them with the business, its staff, its culture and its major operating procedures. Health and safety issues and a period of work shadowing may also form part of the induction programme. **Work shadowing** really involves observing others doing a job in order to learn how it's done.

Existing staff may need specific **'on the job' skills training**, particularly when work practices or technology change. This type of training is really about learning by doing and is directly relevant to the type of work the new employee will be required to perform on a day-to-day basis.

In some situations it may be more cost-effective for training to take place away from the work environment. This type of external or **'off the job' training** involves staff being sent to outside agencies who offer specialist training, e.g. colleges and universities offering Masters degrees or similar postgraduate programmes.

Some firms offer financial incentives to staff who return to formal education in order to improve their qualifications. For example, in the accountancy and insurance industries improved qualifications may present opportunities for promotion or increased rates of pay.

Many trainees and apprentices must undertake a combination of college-based study and practical workplace experience before they graduate as fully qualified staff.

Staff development tends to be less job-specific than most training programmes. The aim is to **improve a broad range of general skills** and make the employee more suited to carrying out a whole range of jobs. Staff development days frequently focus on improving teamwork, leadership and communication skills. These are the types of skill which are beneficial to large numbers of staff and enable the HR managers to identify staff with future management potential.

Benefits of training

> **Increased competence and productivity:** Providing staff with the most up-to-date skills will enable them to perform their jobs with greater competence and productivity. They will tend to make fewer mistakes and will rely on the most innovative and efficient techniques.

> **Adapting to change:** As the business world is continuously changing, organisations will need to provide their employees with training throughout their careers. Companies which fail to provide continuous training will find it difficult to stay ahead of the competition.

> **Improved morale/motivation:** Another benefit of training is that it will keep employees motivated. New skills and knowledge can help to reduce boredom and demonstrates to the employee that they are valuable enough for the employer to invest in them and their development.

> **Cheaper than recruitment:** Training can be cost-effective, as it is cheaper to train existing employees than to recruit new employees with the skills you need.

Performance Appraisal

This is a process of **assessing or evaluating the contribution of employees.** It often requires face-to-face meetings between managers and subordinates. These meetings may also be used to set performance targets for individual workers. Future performance can then be measured against these targets and may be linked to pay. For example, sales staff may be set a minimum turnover figure per month and may receive extra commission and bonuses for meeting or exceeding these targets. Staff who perform poorly may be required to engage in extra training.

unit 4

For performance appraisal to be effective, it is preferable that management attempt to negotiate rather than impose performance targets. It is also important that these targets are realistic. Employees are more likely to be motivated by goals which are agreed and achievable. Follow-up meetings will be needed to examine the level of performance and, if necessary, the reasons for under-achievement.

Some businesses have an 'employee of the month' award, which recognises and rewards the best performing staff.

Benefits of performance appraisal for the employee

> Employees will have a **clearer understanding of what is expected** and what needs to be done to meet these expectations.

> They will have **increased motivation and job satisfaction**. This arises from an increased sense of personal value, and is particularly strong in companies where employees are involved in the appraisal process.

> They should achieve **improved working relationships with superiors**. The communication process involved should enable the employees and manager to develop a closer working relationship and improve mutual understanding of their respective roles in the organisation.

> Performance appraisal provides an opportunity for employees to **overcome their weaknesses** by way of coaching and guidance from their superior. It also helps to establish the need for training and development.

Benefits of performance appraisal for the company

> Performance appraisal provides an opportunity to **identify strengths and weaknesses** of employees. Managers are therefore in a better position to identify areas for improvement.

> Effective performance appraisal helps create and maintain a **culture of continuous improvement**. Employees understand that their performance will be evaluated and that new targets will be set after each appraisal.

> It presents an opportunity to **clarify managerial and employee expectations**. This should see an improved performance throughout the company due to a more effective communication of organisational objectives and values.

> Performance appraisal communicates to people that they are valued. This in turn enhances employees' self-worth and **increases their motivation and loyalty**.

Employee Welfare and Rewards

It was pointed out in Unit 1 that disputes over pay and working conditions are a major source of industrial relations conflict.

Health and safety rules are legally enforceable and the **Health and Safety Authority** (HSA) is the state agency responsible for issuing guidelines and enforcing legislation. There are a number of general guidelines which are applicable across all industries; these include the requirement for fire extinguishers and regular fire drills in all workplaces. Some industries also have specific health and safety guidelines, including the requirement for protective clothing in the construction industry. Working conditions have a big impact on employee morale and motivation.

Remuneration refers to all rewards paid to workers. The human resource manager is responsible for agreeing staff remuneration packages. Some reward systems are based on the number of hours worked and are relatively simple to establish, whereas others need to be negotiated on an individual basis. At senior management level, remuneration packages are often comprised of a salary (linked to experience), some non-money extras (perks) and a structured bonus scheme (usually linked to performance). Irrespective of the type of job involved, the HR manager needs to ensure that reward systems are generous enough to attract the best possible candidates and that they will continue to provide employees with suitable levels of motivation. Managers also need to be mindful of Maslow's assertion that financial rewards may not motivate all staff on all occasions.

Businesses can utilise both monetary and non-monetary rewards.

Monetary rewards

Wages and salaries

These represent the normal payment received by employees for carrying out their job.

A salary is an agreed annual payment for a specific job and is linked to qualifications and experience. Salaries tend to be paid on a monthly basis and employees often have the benefit of a salary scale, which provides for regular increases as employees become more experienced or improve their productivity. These increases are called increments.

Employees who are paid a salary do not normally qualify for overtime payments, but may be entitled to performance-related bonuses. Most public sector employees, including teachers and Gardaí, receive a salary.

Wages tend to be paid weekly and **are calculated on the basis of the amount of work carried out by each employee**. They tend to be more variable than salaries and those employees who make an extra effort are likely to be rewarded with an overtime payment or a bonus. Wages are most commonly calculated using a time rate, a piece rate or sometimes a commission.

A **time rate** involves an **agreed rate of pay per hour**. So an employee who works 40 hours per week, with an hourly rate of €20 would earn a gross wage of €800. Gross pay is the employee's wage, before any deductions are made. Statutory deductions are made for income tax (PAYE) and PRSI, while some workers agree to voluntary deductions for savings, trade union membership and health insurance.

If an employee works additional hours they may receive an **overtime payment** with a higher hourly rate. If the overtime rate is 'double time' this would be €40 per hour, while 'time and a half' would mean a rate of €30 per hour.

In order to ensure accurate recording of employee working hours, a business may operate a 'clock in/clock out' system. The weakness of this type of payment system is the inability to measure the effort made by each worker during their time in work. All employees are paid the same rate irrespective of their productivity.

To overcome this problem and to encourage productivity, some businesses use a **piece rate** to calculate staff wages. Under this system staff are paid an **agreed amount per item produced,** provided those finished goods meet necessary quality control standards. A piece rate is particularly suited to manufacturing or clothing industries, where output is very easy to measure. Those who work quickly and accurately are rewarded for their efforts while the employer only pays for items produced.

Commission is a method of payment usually associated with sales staff. Employees receive a payment which represents a **percentage of the value of the goods or services they sell.** For example, a sales person earning a 10 per cent commission on weekly sales of €10,000 would receive a payment of €1,000.

From the employee's point of view the disadvantage of this method is that a low level of sales will obviously result in very poor earnings and as a result income levels can be very unpredictable. For this reason it is rare that staff are paid on a 'commission only' basis, and most will receive a small basic pay, which will at least reflect the time and effort put in by the staff, even where this time and effort does not actually result in a sale.

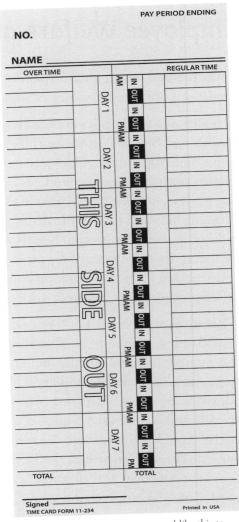

Workers paid by the hour use a card like this to clock in and out

Piece work is where workers are paid for every garment they produce

A car salesman is paid commission for each car he sells

This type of payment is common for employees who sell household appliances, insurance and financial services.

Other monetary rewards

> **Bonus payments** are also used by many firms as an extra incentive for staff. These are payments received in addition to basic pay and are usually given to employees who meet their targets or who display exceptional effort.

> **Profit-sharing schemes** can also be used to motivate and reward staff.

A profit-sharing scheme is where a proportion of company profits is allocated to employees, either in the form of cash or in company stock.

Under normal circumstances it is only the shareholders who receive a dividend payment based on profit, even though these profits have largely been earned as a result of the efforts of staff. By agreeing to allocate a percentage of profit to the staff, the firm provides a stronger incentive to its employees to be productive, because greater effort will tend to yield bigger profits.

Case Study

Google made a decision in 2011 to tie all employees' bonuses to the success of its social strategy. This social strategy really refers to Google's attempts to get a foothold in the growing social networking phenomenon.

Google's latest social networking effort called +1 is a button next to the blue links on Google search results.

When users click the button, Google tells their friends, family, and the rest of the world that it's a recommended link.

At the moment, +1 buttons are only in Google search results, but Google says that they'll soon be elsewhere. This will have a similar effect to Facebook's 'Like' buttons.

In the past, employee bonuses at Google were multiplied against some figure correlated to the overall company's performance. This latest decision is part of a move to abolish this type of bonus and it will tie employee bonuses more closely to individual performance.

Employees who perform well are likely to receive substantial increases whereas bonuses could shrink by 25 per cent if Google doesn't perform.

unit

4

> **Share ownership schemes:** Some companies reward employees by giving them shares in the company. This means that employees have an opportunity to share in the ownership and running of the business and are therefore likely to be more highly motivated.

The employees can make a financial gain either through receipt of an annual dividend or through the sale of their shares

> **Share option schemes** are similar, except that the employees can choose whether or not they wish to purchase the shares at a preferential price. If the market price of the shares increases beyond this discounted price most employees will exercise their option to buy and will make a capital gain.

> **Pensions:** An important financial reward for some employees is the provision of a pension to which their employer makes a contribution. A pension provides an income to employees upon retirement and many workers set aside a portion of annual income in order to generate this future payment. If an employer is willing to contribute to this pension fund, it provides substantial savings to employees and allows them to retain a larger potion of current income.

Non-monetary rewards

A range of **benefits in kind** (BIK) or perks can be given to employees in order to enhance their remuneration package. The most common examples include company cars, petrol allowances, free travel, subsidised meals, rent and health insurance.

While these perks won't directly add any extra income to the employee's pay packet, they have the effect of lowering a person's spending and in this way are seen as financially beneficial. For the purposes of calculating tax and PRSI, most benefits in kind are counted as part of taxable income (see p. 176).

Industrial Relations

« syllabus signpost
4.5.10

Chapter 3 illustrated in great detail the importance of maintaining a positive industrial relations climate between employers and employees, and all of the HR functions set out above are helpful in maintaining this positive relationship.

For most businesses the human resource department will have a formal role in resolving industrial relations problems that arise and also in ensuring grievance procedures are followed.

Human resource managers will engage in discussions with employees and trade unions in an effort to settle disputes quickly and minimise impact on the business. If necessary the HR department may represent the business in more formal discussions at LRC or Labour Court level.

unit
4

Benefits of effective HRM

〉 The firm will have the right staff at the right time and this is important for competitiveness. Poor staffing levels will impact on productivity while overstaffing will add unnecessary costs.

« *syllabus signpost*
4.5.11

〉 A positive work environment will motivate staff to be more productive. Generally speaking, 'happy workers are productive workers'. Good working conditions and rewards will tend to make employees feel they are valued by their employer.

〉 Effective HR management will also help reduce conflict, absenteeism and staff turnover. All of these negative behaviours have cost implications for the business. **Absenteeism** occurs when employees frequently fail to turn up for work, sometimes without a valid reason. **Staff turnover** refers to the rate at which employees leave a business, so a firm with a high staff turnover is not able to hold on to its staff for very long. This leads to increased recruitment and training costs, as well as reputational damage.

If the HR department is functioning effectively, industrial relations problems are likely to be resolved in a speedy and consistent manner.

〉 Good HR management also promotes a positive attitude to staff training and development and helps improve the skill base, morale and staff loyalty.

Ineffective HR management will consequently lead to low morale, prolonged industrial relations conflicts, less productivity and higher staff turnover.

unit
4

Chapter Review Diagram – Human Resource Management

Q Chapter Review Questions

1 List five functions of a human resource manager.

2 Briefly outline the stages involved in the process of 'recruitment and selection'.

3 Distinguish between a job description and a person specification.

4 Explain the purpose of a 'curriculum vitae'. List the main contents of a CV.

5 Outline the importance of interviews to the recruitment and selection process.

6 Outline two advantages and two disadvantages of internal recruitment.

7 Explain each of the following terms:
    > On-the-job training
    > Off-the-job training
    > Induction training

8 Illustrate what is involved in the process of performance appraisal.

9 What is meant by the term 'remuneration'?

10 Use examples to illustrate the difference between the following terms:
    > Monetary rewards
    > Non-monetary rewards

11 Distinguish between the following methods of wage calculation:
    > Time rate
    > Piece rate
    > Commission

12 Explain how 'profit-sharing schemes' work and highlight the motivational impact this type of scheme may have on employees.

13 What are the benefits of effective human resource management for a business?

unit
4

Q Questions · Ordinary Level

1

> Cohan Information Technology Solutions Seeks Web Designer. Cohan IT Solutions is a growing Dublin based company with a current staff of seven. We are looking for a web designer to join our web design team. The position will involve meeting with clients to assess their requirements. Responsibilities include designing and developing unique websites and on-site training for clients. Rewards are negotiable. The ideal candidate must have experience, an ability to work as part of a team, excellent communication skills and problem solving capability.
>
> Apply online: cohanitsolutions.com before 30 June 2010. *LCOL 2010*

(a) Explain the following terms with reference to the above advertisement:

    (i) Job description;

    (ii) Person specification. *(20 marks)*

(b) State **three** ways in which Cohan IT Solutions could reward its staff. *(15 marks)*

(c) State **two** ways, other than the newspaper, Cohan IT Solutions can use to recruit new staff. *(10 marks)*

2 Explain **each** of the following terms:

> ❯ CV
> ❯ Benefits-in-kind
> ❯ Equal opportunities employer *LCOL 2001 (15 marks)*

3 Explain **two** of the following functions of a Human Resources Manager:

> ❯ Recruitment and Selection
> ❯ Training/Development
> ❯ Performance Appraisal *LCOL 2006 (25 marks)*

4

> Anne O'Brien is the human resources manager of Murray's Department Store, a large retail business which employs 76 full-time and 15 part-time staff. Her main functions include training and development, recruitment and selection, and rewarding. *LCOL 2004*

(a) Explain the term 'training and development'. *(15 marks)*

(b) Outline **one** financial reward and one **non**-financial reward that Murray's could give to their sales staff. *(20 marks)*

(c) Outline **two** advantages of internal recruitment. *(15 marks)*

5 State **two** benefits of external recruitment for job vacancies.

6 Explain **two** non-monetary rewards which can be given to employees in order to enhance their remuneration package.

Q Questions · Higher Level

1 Evaluate the effectiveness of a Human Resource Department.　　*LCHL 2011 (30 marks)*

2

　'People are at the heart of every successful business.'

　(a) Performance appraisal, training & development and managing employer and employee relationships are important functions of a human resource manager. Explain the functions underlined above and analyse the benefits of **two** of the functions for the business organisation.

　(b) Outline the different methods of reward used to motivate employees in a business.

LCHL 2008 (15 marks)

3 Explain the steps involved in the recruitment and selection process.

4 Explain each of the following terms:

　❯ On-the-job training

　❯ Off-the-job training.

5 What is meant by 'performance appraisal'?

6 What are the advantages of performance appraisal to an organisation?

7 Name and explain the advantages of internal recruitment.

unit **4**

Chapter 12
Managing Change

Syllabus Outcomes

On completion, the student should be able to:

» 4.5.7 Explain the changing role of a manager from controller to facilitator;

» 4.5.9 Understand how technology changes the role of management;

» 4.5.12 Identify the strategies for managing change (HL);

» 4.5.13 Discuss the importance of Total Quality Management (HL).

News Flash

Kenny urges public service movement on Croke Park

Changes made in the public service under the Croke Park agreement have been "impressive" but are only the beginning of what is required, Taoiseach Enda Kenny has said.

Addressing delegates at the biennial conference of the Irish Congress of Trade Unions in Kerry, Mr Kenny said he shared the view that there had been "much unfair and unreasonable criticism of the Irish public service over recent years".

He acknowledged the "hard work and commitment, and indeed the flexibility and innovation of so many public servants across all the branches of our system".

But Mr Kenny said he was equally aware of the frustration, "and even despair" of many committed public servants at the "outdated structures, the inadequate processes, the fragmentation and arcane work practices which blight their working lives and frustrate our objective to have the highest quality public services available to those who need them".

"That is why nothing less than public service transformation is required. It is why the Government established a new Department of Public Expenditure and Reform to provide effective and focused political leadership for the task of managing change."...

Mr Kenny pledged to get on with the task of fixing the economy "urgently and comprehensively".

He was under "no illusion" about the scale of the challenge. Nothing was excluded from consideration when the Government looked at spending, he warned.

"We will probably conclude that there are some things that the country simply cannot afford, and they will be dropped. There are some things that we cannot afford unless they are done very differently, at a lower cost, and they will be changed."...

"I commit myself and commit the Government to continuing dialogue and discussion with the trade union movement. I think this is very necessary," he said.

This is an edited extract from The Irish Times, Monday, 4 July 2011.

For more up-to-date newspaper articles see www.edcodigital.ie

1 Read the newspaper extract opposite and discuss the issues raised.

2 Can you explain any of the highlighted terms?

Change

The business environment in which modern firms must operate is extremely dynamic, which means it is subject to constant and ongoing change. This new reality requires firms to keep up with this pace of change or risk being surpassed by competitors. A change in the nature of a business or its operations can be a source of huge upheaval and conflict within an organisation. For this reason managing the 'change process' successfully is a vital part of modern business.

What are the major triggers of change for twenty-first-century businesses?

1 **Technology**   2 **Competition**

3 **Consumer demand**   4 **Economic environment**

« syllabus signpost 4.5.9

1 Technology

Technology is uniquely placed to provide not only a trigger for change, but also a method for implementing this change. This becomes very clear when you consider the role and impact of ICT in business and in our daily lives.

Technological change has an enormous impact as it allows the development of:

> New products and businesses (PCs, software development, web design)
> New business methods and operating systems (computer-aided manufacturing, e-commerce)
> Better communication (mobile phones, email, etc)

Technology also impacts on human resource management and marketing.

unit 4

New products

There are many companies in Ireland today which provide goods and services which simply did not exist twenty years ago. The mobile phone and Internet businesses were still in their infancy a generation ago and have now become part and parcel of everyday life. The development of these products and services has led to the creation of vast new industries and new areas of employment.

New operating systems

Computerisation has enabled businesses to develop new production technologies. Computer-aided design (CAD), computer-aided manufacturing (CAM) and computer-integrated manufacturing (CIM) now play a major role in many industries, and allow for the use of technology to assist in the design and development process of goods, including plastics, machinery and cars. The specialist computer software makes the design and development processes quicker and more flexible.

> **Computer-aided design** is useful because it allows designers to make multiple changes to product designs in a virtual environment. In effect, designers can create a computer-generated model of their product, very often in three dimensions, which eliminates the need to build many costly prototypes.

> **Computer-aided manufacturing** uses computers to control machine tools in the factory and is particularly effective for carrying out tasks which are repetitive or which require a high degree of consistency and precision. Unlike human workers, the machines will repeat a specific task following exact instructions and ensuring a uniform level of quality. They do not get bored by the repetitive nature of the tasks, nor do they need constant supervision and motivation.

> **Computer-integrated manufacturing** is closely linked to robotics and involves the use of computers and machinery to co-ordinate the entire production process, including design, purchasing, production and dispatch of finished products. The Nissan manufacturing plant in Sunderland illustrates the importance of this type of technology in co-ordinating the manufacturing process of the Nissan Qashqai. The production of each Qashqai involves 3,779 parts which are sourced from over 200 suppliers.

> www.qashqaiclub.co.uk/qashqai_club_videos_qashqai_in_sunderland..htm

Improvements in manufacturing technology have altered the way in which work is carried out. Many jobs are now more **capital intensive** as work is increasingly carried out by machines and computers. This reduces the need for staff and causes redundancy or downsizing in some organisations.

> **Electronic data interchange** impacts on stock control as well as purchasing and payment policies. The computer monitors and tracks stock levels and allows managers to have the most up-to-date information. It allows goods to be ordered and paid for electronically, thereby lowering administration costs and the amount of paperwork involved.

Improved communication

The arrival of the personal computer, mobile communications and Internet technology has not only changed the way in which businesses operate, but has also provided management with a number of tools to assist them in managing the ongoing transformation of their businesses.

unit 4

Tens of thousands of jobs have been created in these new industries and it is very likely that the next ten years will see new challenges, new developments and new job opportunities emerging. Have you considered the possibility that the job which you may be doing ten or twenty years from now has not even been invented yet?

The challenges for business in this type of dynamic environment are to invest heavily in **research and development** (R&D) and to recruit staff that will have the appropriate skill set to embrace change. Ongoing training and development (**upskilling**) will be a key feature of future employment.

The integration of ICT into the working lives of all employees will be a necessity for business survival. It will facilitate quicker and more effective communication between and across organisations and will include the use of teleworking and videoconferencing.

> **Teleworking** is allowing employees to work from home and then submit completed work via the Internet. It can also be applied to travelling sales reps who work 'on the road'. Teleworking allows greater flexibility for employees and management but it does require managers to monitor the work and ensure that employees meet deadlines.

> **Videoconferencing** is a method of interactive telecommunication which allows people in two or more locations to interact using two-way video and audio transmissions. It is particularly beneficial for global companies as it facilitates communication between staff in different geographic locations. This offers the potential for large savings in terms of both cost and time. See also *Chapter 6: Management Skills: Communication.*

Impact of technology on human resource management

Businesses which recognise the benefits of technology may choose to become more capital-intensive and this will reduce their need for staff. When employees are replaced by machinery the human resource department will need to consider **retraining** and redeploying staff. It may also need to implement a **redundancy** programme.

Technology also improves the administration of employee records and **databases** can be used to store confidential information using only a fraction of the space required by traditional filing cabinets.

unit
4

Electronic fund transfers have led to the widespread use of **paypath,** which enables employees' wages to be paid directly into their bank accounts. This is both quicker and safer for all concerned and yields considerable cost savings to employers.

Many companies are also availing of technologies like Skype to conduct job interviews with shortlisted candidates.

Impact of technology on marketing

The Internet enables businesses to **advertise their products** on company websites and on social networking platforms such as Facebook and Twitter. Some companies are also using wireless mobile phone technology (M-Commerce) to promote their products. This is generally achieved by sending text messages to members of their target market, offering the subscriber a specific incentive, usually a discount, to purchase the goods.

Company websites are also used to **sell products online** and allow a business to remain open twenty-four hours a day.

Selling goods and services over the Internet is called **e-commerce** or e-business and the acronym B2C is used to identify sales from a business directly to consumers. The acronym B2B refers to sales from one business to another.

The Internet also provides a useful tool for **conducting market research** and is particularly suited to gathering secondary or desk research. This is achieved by reviewing online journals and marketing reports and also by accessing the websites of state agencies such as the Central Statistics Office (CSO).

2 Competition

With global markets becoming increasingly deregulated and liberal, modern businesses face an increased threat from global rivals. This requires them to adopt a flexible and innovative approach in order to maintain their market share.

Those businesses which invest most proactively in research and development are most likely to be rewarded with product innovations and competitive advantage over their rivals. On the other hand, those which fail to invest sufficient resources into R&D are likely to lose market share to their competitors.

Innovation can overtake tradition in some industries so firms are under constant threat of elimination. The cutting-edge technology associated with telecommunications has traditionally been developed in the USA or in Asia, but this balance of power was upset in the 1990s when the Finnish phone company Nokia emerged onto global markets. Investment in innovation and a strategic decision to focus its operations only on the telecommunications business enabled this relatively unknown company to become the world's largest producer of mobile phones.

3 Consumer demand

Changing lifestyles create the demand for new and innovative products. As the pace of life has increased for so many people, so has their desire for technology which speeds things up, such as microwaves and personal communications devices. During the housing boom a demand developed in Ireland for American fridge freezers. What started as a specialist import item sold exclusively by a small number of retailers, soon became widely available and was increasingly demanded by house-buyers.

The fact that sales of these fridges declined almost as quickly when the property market collapsed illustrates that many goods can become obsolete as trends and market conditions change. Shorter product life cycles require greater innovation and new product development while also requiring businesses to pay close attention to the needs of their target market.

Consumers have also shown an increased preference for ethically produced goods and services. This has led to pressure on producers to minimise pollution, maximise recycling and engage in socially responsible practices. The Fair Trade label is an example of this in action. See also *Chapter 21: Business Ethics and Social Responsibility*.

4 Economic environment

External changes such as interest rates, taxation, oil prices and market deregulation only serve to make markets more unpredictable and dynamic.

The global credit crunch and a domestic banking crisis were major factors in the decline of the property market in Ireland from 2008. Without access to cheap credit, consumers lacked the financial means to purchase property. The consequences of this collapse were far-reaching and impacted on tens of thousands of jobs right across the economy. Those employed in construction, real estate, house furnishings and architecture were most directly affected, but many other sectors suffered also.

Job losses, business restructuring and in some cases diversification were the solutions put forward by some companies, and each of these involves massive organisational change.

« *syllabus signpost*
4.5.12

Managing the Change Process

Managing change is a very complex process and will require the organisation to employ several strategies including:

> **Training and development**

> **Changing management styles**

> **Teamwork**

> **Communication and consultation**

> **Employee empowerment**

> A commitment to **Total Quality Management**

unit **4**

In *Unit 1*, changes to work practices were listed as a major source of conflict between employers and employees. Resistance to change presents a major challenge to management as they attempt to chart a course towards future business success. Managers will realise that it will not be possible to change work practices or restructure an organisation without the goodwill and co-operation of the workforce. For this reason a number of steps need to taken by management to allay the fears of workers and the human resources department will often play a pivotal role in these efforts.

Communication and consultation

Management need to convince all stakeholders in the business that change is necessary and will need to consult with them to assess and minimise the negative impacts of this change.

For example, suppliers may be affected by changes in purchasing policy, particularly by the introduction of **'just in time' (JIT) procurement**. This will require raw materials to be delivered at very specific times, so as to minimise overall stock levels and ensure goods are available to meet the production schedule.

Similarly, a move to a more automated system, such as EDI, will require very close communication with suppliers.

Employees and the trade unions representing them will also expect to be consulted on proposed changes to work practices. A business needs to be transparent in all of its dealings with staff and this involves setting out clearly the necessity for change and the means by which it will be implemented. Contentious issues like redundancy or changes to pay and working conditions will need to be negotiated, as agreed changes are more likely to be acceptable to staff.

Since change is an ongoing process, it will also be important that **regular reviews** take place to assess the progress to date and to make whatever policy changes are necessary.

Training and development

Training can be used to assist with the process of transition and also to allay some of the fears held by staff. Those facing a new working environment or new operating procedures may be fearful or unwilling to engage in the process due to lack of appropriate skills. This often happens where a high level of automation or computerisation is being introduced.

unit 4

Specific training programmes will have to be devised to meet the needs of the business and its staff. This will improve efficiency and morale amongst the workforce and also help eliminate costly mistakes.

Compensation or changes to wage structures may also be required to gain staff agreement and to reward their efforts. Productivity may be rewarded with bonuses or profit-sharing schemes.

Job enlargement involves making an employee's job 'bigger' by adding extra duties to it. Employees involved in teamwork often find themselves taking on more substantial roles and in some cases they may be required to carry out their functional duties as well as meeting the needs of a project team. In order to avoid staff resistance to this type of change and increased workload it is important that the level of reward increases accordingly.

In some situations, however, particularly where changes are brought about by competitive or economic circumstances, it may not be possible to provide financial compensation to staff. In this situation management will need to convince workers that change is necessary for the very survival of the business. This is the type of scenario which has faced a large number of organisations in Ireland in recent years.

Changing management styles

While consultation, training and communication are important factors in eliminating the resistance to change, businesses may also need to implement a number of strategies to serve the longer-term needs of their organisation. These strategies include a change towards more open and inclusive management styles.

« *syllabus signpost 4.5.7*

A dynamic business environment requires all organisations to be as flexible as possible in their operations. Part of this flexibility may require a move away from a traditional, autocratic approach to leadership and management. Managers are instead expected to take on the role of co-ordinators and coaches.

This facilitative approach allows managers to set the objectives and then provide employees with resources, training and feedback to enable them to achieve these goals. Communication and performance appraisal are likely to be important elements of this approach.

This will involve changes to the chain of command and span of control and will generally result in employees having greater responsibility for their work. Managers will be free from some of their supervisory duties and should able to respond more quickly to ongoing change.

225

Managers can only take on this new role if there is reform of the way in which all employees carry out their work. It is very important to understand that all of the strategies outlined here are designed to work together across all levels of the business. Like pieces in a jigsaw they complement each other and when put together in the right way they help a business to fundamentally alter the way it operates. To be truly successful, the strategies must be accepted and implemented by all stakeholders and 'flexibility' and 'change' need to become part of the organisational culture.

Organisational culture refers to the rules, beliefs and values which underpin all aspects of the organisation. It has been described as 'the way we do things round here'. Cultures can be old and traditional or young and dynamic and each organisation needs to develop a culture which best suits its needs and strategies.

The army has a very autocratic culture and requires members to follow a strict chain of command. There are very traditional reasons for this approach and it has proven successful for hundreds of years.

More innovative cultures tend to be found in modern, high-tech industries such as computing and telecommunications. Flexibility is needed to meet the demands of the industry and of consumers, so businesses need to encourage innovation and intrapreneurship amongst their staff.

Employee empowerment

Empowerment gives employees the power to make decisions about their work as well as the responsibility to implement these decisions.

Quality circles are examples of empowerment, since workers meet to discuss ways to improve the day-to-day operation of their own area of the business.

Empowerment relies on managers as facilitators, as well as the establishment of a very effective system of communications and control.

Job enrichment involves adding extra responsibility to an employee's job so as to improve motivation and morale.

If employees are not provided with clear objectives and adequate training they are unlikely to make good decisions. Management will also need to ensure that adequate control systems have been put in place so as to avoid costly mistakes being made.

On the other hand, a properly implemented system of empowerment offers the following benefits to business:

› Empowerment allows decisions to be taken at the lowest effective level and frees up time for managers to deal with 'bigger issues'. Those who are responsible for carrying out routine tasks are those who make decisions about those same tasks. Managers make more strategic corporate decisions.

> Since employees feel they have some 'ownership' over their jobs they tend to be more satisfied and motivated at work.

> Empowerment also allows a firm to utilise the full array of talents held by its employees. In the longer term this allows employees to gain confidence and decision-making experience, and helps the HR department identify suitable candidates for promotion.

> Empowerment is an important element in creating a culture of innovation and intrapreneurship within a company.

Teamwork

This approach allows for specific tasks or projects to be performed by groups of employees. An extension of the empowerment process, it again provides employees with greater levels of autonomy, responsibility and motivation.

Where team members are drawn from different functional areas of an organisation, it may be necessary to use a matrix structure.

Matrix structure

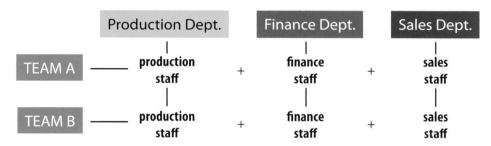

This type of structure reflects the need to utilise skills and expertise across several functional areas. As outlined in a previous discussion on organisational structures (see *Chapter 7*, page 117), a project team may have members from production, finance and marketing departments. Each team member brings a specific skill set and level of expertise which are important to the success of the project. It is only through teamwork and co-operation that the optimal result will be achieved.

Senior management need to consider carefully the composition of each team, as well as the role of team leader. It is also important to monitor and evaluate the work of each team, so as to make sure it is functioning effectively. Sometimes disagreements or personality clashes emerge among team members and these can prevent the group from achieving its objectives.

In some cases the group members themselves will decide on the issues of leadership and assignment of roles. Alternatively, it offers the possibility of **job rotation**, where employees carry out a series of different jobs in succession. The idea is to prevent workers becoming bored or frustrated with their job, thus improving motivation and productivity.

unit 4

Team creation

Creation of teams is a four-stage process:

1 Forming: This involves identifying the members who will form the project team, ensuring they have the necessary skill set, and allowing them to interact. Members need time to get to know each other and focus on developing new relationships. The forming stage is complete when members accept the collective identity and begin to think of themselves as part of a team.

2 Storming: At this stage group members begin to assert themselves and may vie for key leadership roles. Some conflict may arise as individual members resist the loss of individuality and test the boundaries of group control. By the time the storming stage is complete, relatively clear leadership will emerge within the team.

3 Norming: During the norming phase the group establishes its rules of behaviour and assigns roles to its members. The team becomes much more cohesive and this is usually evident in closer working relationships and a strong sense of camaraderie.

When the norming stage is complete the team members will have accepted a common set of expectations and set clear guidelines regarding appropriate work behaviour.

4 Performing: The group now completes the task it was set up to do. Team members are fully committed to the group and all their energy and efforts are directed towards performing the necessary tasks.

Developing teams successfully

The following criteria for the successful development of teams in any organisation are borrowed from an article by Satrina Harvey, Bruce Millett and Don Smith in the *Australian Journal of Management and Organisational Behaviour*, vol. 1, no. 1, 1998:

1 Clear goals

2 Decision-making authority

3 Accountability and responsibility

4 Effective leadership

5 Training and development

6 Resources

7 Organisational support

8 Rewards for team success

unit **4**

1 **Clear goals:** The team needs to be provided with goals which are specific enough to give them direction. These goals should set out the desired outcome and should be measurable. Ideally the methods used to achieve these goals will be left to the team, as this will allow for the greatest level of innovation and creativity.

2 **Decision-making authority:** Teams need to be empowered to make decisions and should be encouraged to experiment with different proposals. There is often more than one way to achieve their goals and team members need the freedom to test their ideas without fear of failure.

   At the same time a company may need to set boundaries for this decision-making authority in order to avoid costly mistakes. Some businesses have found it necessary to increase the decision-making authority of teams on a gradual basis.

3 **Accountability and responsibility:** Closely linked to the empowerment issue is the requirement for teams to be accountable for their decisions and actions. The intention here is to force teams to engage in self-evaluation in order to keep them focused on their primary goals.

4 **Effective leadership:** In the context of team-based structures, effective leadership is more concerned with coaching and facilitating than directing. Team leaders need to understand that democracy and freedom are most likely to bring about innovative solutions and the leader may need to take a less prominent role.

5 **Training and development:** Where team members possess inadequate work skills and knowledge, teams are less likely to succeed. Team leaders may also need training in order to adapt to their new role as facilitators. All team members are likely to need skills training to enable them to work together more effectively. Training and development are enabling factors and should focus on issues like effective communication, conflict resolution and problem solving.

6 **Resources:** In order to operate effectively teams need to have access to adequate resources. These resources may include time, money, equipment, people and information. While it's unlikely that resources will be unlimited, their provision again reflects a sense of trust on the part of the company and responsibility on the part of the team members.

7 **Organisational support:** A culture of support and flexibility right throughout the company is the most conducive environment for the successful development of team structures.

8 **Rewards for team success:** A team-based reward system should be used to reward employees for teamwork and their contributions to team success.

   An emphasis on individual rewards undermines the effectiveness of team-based work and encourages team members to strive for individual performance goals that may be in conflict with team goals.

unit 4

Benefits of teamwork

> **Levels of staff development and motivation improve** as workers experience a variety or roles. This should lead to improved standards of work. Since team members are frequently empowered to handle many of the issues that directly affect their work, teams offer an effective way for management to enhance employee involvement and increase employee morale.

> The **decision-making process improves,** both in terms of efficiency and outcome. This means that better decisions are arrived at more quickly. Most available evidence suggests that teams outperform individuals when tasks require multiple skills, judgement and experience.

> By tapping into the skills and ideas of several employees it may be possible to **improve creativity and intrapreneurship.** Many businesses seeking to compete more effectively turn to teams when trying to restructure themselves. This is because team structures allow them to make the best use of employee talents.

> Many companies have realised the benefits of team structures when it comes to targeting niche markets. In these types of market competitiveness is based on innovation and uniqueness rather than on price or economies of scale. Teams can **maximise organisational innovation** because employees have increased autonomy, increased participation, and ownership regarding decisions. Rather than being told what to do, employees are given goals and are then free to decide how best to achieve those goals

> In a dynamic business environment managers generally find that teams **offer greater flexibility** than traditional functional structures. Teams can be assembled quickly when required, are relatively easy to refocus and can be disbanded when the task has been accomplished.

Total Quality Management (TQM)

« *syllabus signpost*
4.5.13

This is far more than just a quality control system for finished goods.

With TQM the focus is on achieving the **optimum levels of quality for each and every aspect of the company's operations**. From sourcing of raw materials, through a flawless production system and the delivery of excellent products and after-sales care, it is every individual's responsibility to ensure that quality is the organisation's top priority.

The focus of the entire organisation must be on this vital issue as it becomes part of its corporate culture. To this end, workers are empowered to highlight problem areas and if necessary make changes.

TQM incorporates many dynamic practices including empowerment, teamwork, R&D, benchmarking and quality assurance.

Quality assurance

Companies aim to provide consumers with a guarantee that all aspects of their product development and delivery will be of the highest quality. It can only successfully deliver on this claim in an environment which promotes TQM.

Firms which attain continuously high standards may earn certification from the **International Standards Organisation (ISO)**. This internationally recognised standard of excellence is only awarded to businesses which meet strict criteria set out for their industry. This offers huge advantages to businesses involved in exporting since it provides a level of reassurance to customers in relation to the quality of operating systems and finished goods. Overseas customers are more likely to deal with a new supplier if they have obtained the appropriate ISO certification.

A similar system operates for Irish companies which sell only in the home market, using the **Q-mark symbol**. For more information see p. 123.

Aims and benefits of TQM

> The primary aim or benefit relates to the **satisfaction of consumer needs** regarding top quality goods and services. Most businesses realise that satisfied customers are happy customers and a positive experience is likely to develop a sense of loyalty to a business and its products.

> **Flawless production:** Ensuring 'zero defects' will save money on waste and on reworking. TQM focuses on getting it right first time and every time. Poor quality products lead to cost increases, as valuable raw materials need to be discarded or reused.

> **World-class manufacturing:** Many businesses will seek to benchmark (measure) their performance against the industry leaders. **Benchmarking** refers to the highest standards within an industry and the level to which all other firms should aspire. Industry leaders may practise world-class manufacturing and therefore provide a model against which all other firms can be judged. McDonalds, for example, may be regarded as the benchmark for fast-food restaurants.

> **Constant improvement:** The ultimate aim is to improve service to customers, close the gap on industry leaders and ultimately replace them as number one in the business. Businesses engaged in TQM will always seek to develop more innovative and more efficient operating systems. Over time this devotion to quality will become part of the organisational culture.

unit 4

Chapter Review Diagram – Managing change

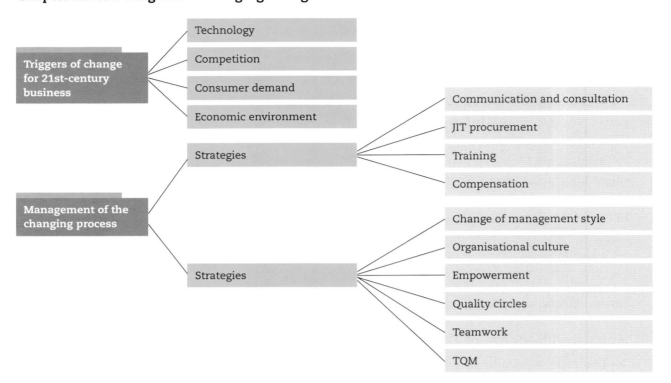

Q Chapter Review Questions

1 List the major triggers of change for 21st-century businesses and briefly outline the impact of any two of these.

2 Outline the impact of technology on human resource management and communication.

3 State what the following letters stand for:
   (i) CAD   (ii) CAM   (iii) R&D   (iv) JIT   (v) TQM   (vi) ISO

4 Distinguish between teleworking and videoconferencing.

5 List five strategies that a business can employ when seeking to implement organisational change.

6 Explain what is meant by a 'just-in-time' system of stock control. Outline the main benefits of this type of system for businesses.

7 Describe how a change in leadership style can impact positively on the process of change management.

8 Distinguish between 'job enlargement' and 'job enrichment'.

9 Explain the term 'empowerment' and briefly outline its benefits to business.

10 Illustrate a matrix (or team) structure for an organisation of your choice.

11 Describe the four stages involved in the creation of successful teams.

12 Outline the benefits of teamwork to a business.

13 Outline the aims of Total Quality Management.

Q Questions · Ordinary Level

1 Outline **two** advantages of teamwork in a business. *LCOL 2011 (25 marks)*

2 Outline **three** advantages of information technology to a business, giving examples. *LCOL 2010 (15 marks)*

3 Explain what 'employee empowerment' means and outline **two** benefits of empowerment. *LCOL 2003 (20 marks)*

4 Describe **two** benefits of Total Quality Management.

5 What are the **four** stages which successful teams go through? *LCOL 2001 (10 marks)*

6 (a) Why do employees in businesses resist change?

(b) How can management overcome this resistance?

7 Explain how the following terms can improve the quality standards of a business:

(i) Quality control (ii) Quality circles (iii) Research and development

8 What do the following letters stand for?

(i) EDI (ii) ICT (iii) CAD

Q Questions · Higher Level

1 Illustrate how the following developments in information and communications technology (ICT) have impacted on business:

(i) Electronic Data Interchange (EDI)

(ii) The Internet and the World Wide Web

(iii) Video-conferencing. *LCHL 2009 (20 marks)*

2 Discuss the benefits of Total Quality Management (TQM) to a manufacturing business. *LCHL 2009 (20 marks)*

3 Describe **two** strategies that a business organisation can use to manage change. Use examples to support your answer. *LCHL 2008 (20 marks)*

4 Using examples, describe **three** ways in which technology has changed the role of management.

5 Illustrate the impact that technology has on an organisation's

(i) Business costs (ii) Personnel

6 Explain how a business benefits by implementing a policy of empowerment.

7 Explain the changing role of a manager from controller to facilitator. Refer to areas such as the empowerment of workers and Total Quality Management in your explanation.

8 Distinguish between the terms 'job enlargement', 'job rotation' and 'job enrichment'.

9 Explain the term 'world-class manufacturing'.

Q Applied Business Question

Moore's Independent Supermarket

In 2009 Gerry Moore took over the independent supermarket from his father who had established the family business and run it successfully for over thirty years. Prior to this venture Gerry trained as an accountant and had worked for five years with a large supermarket chain in Dublin. From the moment Gerry took over the business, he was determined to hit the ground running. He began by instigating a process to upgrade all work practices throughout the supermarket.

One of Gerry's biggest wishes was to improve communications at all levels of the business and he was particularly concerned about the supermarket's failure to develop a web presence. He prioritised the development of a company website and was adamant it would boost branding, advertising and sales.

Gerry also felt that productivity and stock control would be greatly improved by fully automating all checkouts using the latest technology available. By utilising Electronic Data Interchange Gerry could develop a system of automatically reordering goods from suppliers when stock levels fell to a predetermined level. He was also keen to replace the existing manual bookkeeping system with a new computerised version.

Gerry believes passionately in the need for excellent customer service and sees technology as a tool for delivering a better and more efficient service to his customers. Unfortunately he has encountered some resistance to change from a small number of employees and is keen to address their concerns

Gerry is aware that the successful implementation of change is heavily dependent upon careful planning and with this in mind has appointed an experienced human resources manager to help implement his vision for the business. They jointly attended a meeting with trade union representatives, and following a very open and frank discussion, management agreed to adopt a more consultative approach with the workforce.

The HR Manager has already explained the economic benefits associated with greater productivity to all twenty-five members of staff as well as highlighting future opportunities for promotion. He has put together an attractive performance-related rewards package as a motivational tool and to increase sales in the business, which involves a programme of staff training. The aim of this programme is to offer induction training for new staff and to familarise existing staff with the new technology and work practices being adopted.

The new HR Manager immediately set about conducting an audit of current staffing levels and was keen to evaluate the results in the context of the company's strategic plans. The audit revealed that while staff were very experienced there remained some scope for the recruitment of younger employees and he hoped this would improve the prospects for change within the organisation. There was also some evidence to suggest that the current group of staff did not adequately meet the needs of the business and addressing this issue must also be made a top priority.

(a) Discuss the impact that investment in technology has had on Moore's Independent Supermarket. Refer to the above text in your answer. *(20 marks)*

(b) Gerry wishes to implement change. Outline strategies that could be used to facilitate the smooth implementation of change in this business. *(30 marks)*

(c) Evaluate the effectiveness of the human resource management at Moore's Independent Supermarket. *(30 marks)*

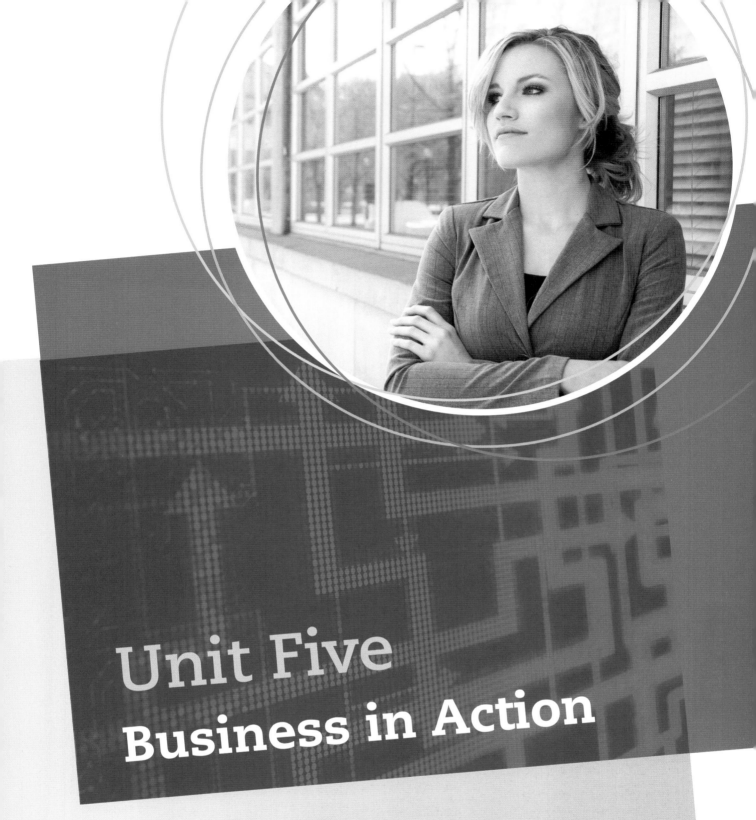

Unit Five
Business in Action

Chapter 13
Identifying Opportunities

News Flash

Business success involves more than coming up with a great idea

by Caroline Madden

"Go for it." That's the key piece of advice Steve Thompson, who runs business training courses with Quality Education Development International, has for aspiring entrepreneurs. "Out of all the entrepreneurs I've worked with, trained and interviewed, I've only ever come across one who regretted giving it a go."

Of course, "giving it a go" is easier said than done. First you've got to come up with a business idea – and a good one at that. However, you don't have to sit around waiting for your eureka moment to strike. According to Thompson, there are plenty of ways to kick-start the ideas-generation process.

A good starting point is to think about what the market wants: "What problems are people having? What are their needs? What are the current trends in Ireland and abroad?"…

If you are still struggling to come up with an idea, try brainstorming, combining old ideas in new ways or reversing the problem, he suggests…

In the experience of Michael Culligan of the Business Innovation Centres network, the startup companies most likely to succeed are those that "respect the market". This means balancing entrepreneurial drive and a never-say-die attitude with an ability to remain "grounded in reality".

"All business must be marketing-centric," Culligan says.

By this he means that entrepreneurs must ask themselves what opportunities exist in the market, whether those opportunities are scalable, who else is competing there, and whether their business will have a competitive advantage.

"One of the things that we would encourage people to do with any product or service is to engage with the market as soon as possible," he says. "The market is the ultimate arbitrator."

Once you have tested out your business idea in the market on a trial basis, it is important to use feedback from this experience to refine your offering before trying again. Businesses that take this approach have a better chance of success.

This is an edited extract from **The Irish Times**, FRIDAY, 5 MARCH 2010.

For more up-to-date newspaper articles see www.edcodigital.ie

Read the newspaper extract opposite and discuss the issues raised.

1 Make a list of the key pieces of advice offered by the experts to entrepreneurs contemplating a business startup.

2 Can you explain any of the highlighted terms?

« *syllabus signpost* 5.5.1

New ideas

Entrepreneurs need ideas when starting a new business. Existing businesses also need to generate new ideas as their current products start to reach the end of their life cycle. Failure to generate new product ideas will lead to loss of market share and eventual decline of the business.

Some business ideas are genuinely new and innovative, but most individuals and businesses take inspiration from the world around them or from their business experiences to date. There is strong support for the view that some of the most successful new product developments emerge from the revitalisation of existing products. The major **sources of new ideas** for individuals and businesses are listed below and include both internal and external sources.

Internal sources of ideas tend to arise from a careful examination of our own strengths and weaknesses. By focusing on the things we do well we are often able to play to our strengths. In much the same way that you might consider the results of aptitude tests when making your subject choices in school, an entrepreneur can choose to develop a business based on the things they know they can succeed at.

External sources of ideas come from the wider world around us. Entrepreneurs need to look at the opportunities and threats in the marketplace and develop a business which will meet an existing need or deflect a potential problem.

SWOT analysis techniques are often used to help with this process.

unit 5

Sources of new ideas

Entrepreneurs	
Internal	**External**
Skills	Neighbours/Friends
Hobbies/Interests	Travel
Innovations	Media
Business experience	State agencies
Brainstorming	Networking/Contacts

Existing Businesses	
Internal	**External**
Customer feedback	Market research
Research and development	Competitors
Staff suggestions/Intrapreneurship	Import substitution
Franchises/Alliances	

Internal sources of new business ideas for entrepreneurs

« syllabus signpost 5.5.2

> **Skills:** Making the most of existing skills and personal strengths is an obvious route to success for many entrepreneurs. Artistic, musical, mathematical or physical skills are developed over several years and may in turn lead to business opportunities.

Sixteen-year-old Patrick Collision, a pupil at Castletroy Community College, won the Esat BT Young Scientist and Technology competition in 2005. His winning entry involved the development of a computer language called Croma. Patrick and his younger brother later used their computing skills to set up a company based in Silicone Valley which they sold to Canadian company Live Current Media in 2009 for €3.2 million.

> **Hobbies/Interests:** In a similar way to skills, an entrepreneur can sometimes turn a hobby or interest into a business opportunity. A person with a strong interest in animal welfare may choose veterinary medicine as a career or a person who takes part in music and dancing as a hobby may develop a business opportunity by teaching younger students.

> **Innovations:** Some business opportunities arise from genuine moments of invention and creativity. These are the 'eureka moments' which enable a person to invent something new or develop a new use for an existing product.

In 1974, Ernö Rubik developed a three-by-three cube designed to help his students to understand 3D objects. This was later patented as the Rubik's Cube puzzle and has become the world's best-selling puzzle game, with over 350 million cubes sold worldwide.

> **Business Experience:** Time spent as an employee in another business may allow a potential entrepreneur to acquire the level of business experience and proficiency necessary to set up their own business.

unit 5

> **Brainstorming:** Brainstorming is a group technique for idea generation. Group members are asked to spontaneously generate a list of ideas on a particular topic with no initial screening of suggestions taking place. This allows for a high level of creativity and enables group members to take inspiration from the thoughts and ideas put forward by others.

Once a comprehensive list of ideas has been generated, it will be necessary to evaluate the suggestions and identify those which are most likely to succeed.

External sources of new business ideas for entrepreneurs

> **Friends and Networking:** Casual day-to-day conversations with friends can sometimes lead to innovative solutions to common problems.

The Stira attic ladder and the Dyson bagless vacuum cleaner were both developed as solutions to common household problems.

In a similar way it may be possible for business ideas and opportunities to develop from discussions or contacts with a wider group of people, including professional bodies or community and sporting organisations. Making use of these contact groups is called **networking.**

> **Travel:** Irish entrepreneurs and consumers who travel overseas are in a position to see the latest product and service ideas available worldwide. If these products are not yet available in Ireland it may be possible to establish a franchise or develop a similar product. Consumer demands can also encourage indigenous firms to develop new product lines.

Niall Fortune, the founder of Eddie Rocket's Diners, claims to have taken inspiration from his travels in the USA and seeing the potential for launching a similar restaurant in Ireland.

> **Media:** Global television, magazines and the Internet provide unprecedented insights into changing trends and fashions. By paying close attention to these emerging trends entrepreneurs can be proactive in getting involved in new areas of business.

Many businesses in the ICT industry have recently begun to focus attention and resources on the potential of **cloud computing.**

unit

5

> **State agencies:** Several state agencies, including Enterprise Ireland, Forbairt and An Bord Tráchtála, have a role in assisting the development and expansion of Irish industry. They are often able to provide statistical and marketing information on indigenous and overseas markets. In this way they assist the development of new product or service ideas.

Internal sources of ideas for existing businesses

> **Customer feedback:** By listening to those who already use their products or services a business can identify problems with existing product ranges as well as developing innovative new goods which will meet the needs of their target market.

> **Research and development:** In order to keep one step ahead of their competitors, businesses are increasing their levels of expenditure on R&D. Many now employ specialist staff whose role is to design and develop new ranges of products or at the very least to redesign existing products to meet the needs of a dynamic marketplace.

 **Example**

> Sony Corporation invests heavily in R&D and recent innovations include the production of the PlayStation 3 and PSP games consoles.

> **Staff suggestions/Intrapreneurship:** An intrapreneur is an individual who is enterprising and innovative and who uses these skills to benefit an existing organisation. Some businesses are very keen to encourage intrapreneurship and offer substantial rewards to employees who develop creative and cost-saving ideas. These innovations may come from design, production or sales staff rather than from specific R&D units. For more information see page 63.

 **Example**

> Cadbury's Time Out bar developed from a suggestion made by an employee at its Coolock plant in Dublin.

External sources of ideas for existing businesses

> **Competitors:** Close monitoring of competitors is another possible source of new business ideas. It is very common for new and innovative products to be replicated soon after their market launch. Rivals are very fearful of losing market share and will be quick to react to new or improved goods and services. When imitating competitors care needs to be taken not to infringe on patent and copyright restrictions. Copycat products which seek to replicate the success of market leaders are known as 'me too' products.

Example

Competing businesses like Sony, Nintendo and Microsoft regularly update their products in order to match the latest developments offered by their rivals. Sony's PlayStation, Nintendo's Wii and Microsoft's Xbox are all targeting the same market.

The groundbreaking Wii controllers were quickly followed by Kinect for Xbox and the PlayStation Move, as rival companies attempted to undermine Nintendo's technological advantage.

> **Import substitution:** Import substitution occurs when an indigenous firm begins to produce a product which had previously been imported. Information on imports is available from state agencies and market research. Import substitution has benefits in terms of job creation and balance of payments.

Example

Based in Drogheda, Irish Breeze Ltd is the only Irish manufacturer of cotton wool and has evolved to be one of Ireland's great success stories since its launch in 1993. Irish Breeze brands include Irish Breeze cotton wool (brand leader) and Irish Breeze soaps (no. 3 in the Irish market).

> **Business alliances/Franchises:** A **business alliance** is an arrangement where two or more independent firms collaborate to develop and market a product. While the businesses always remain independent, they do agree to share resources.

Example

In 1979, Sony and the German electronics firm Philips set up a joint taskforce to design a new digital audio disc. After a year of experimentation and discussion, the taskforce produced the Red Book, which set out the industry standards for the production of compact discs.

A **franchise** is a contractual agreement which allows one company to adopt the business model and product range of another company.

This type of arrangement allows an existing business to broaden its product range or branch out into new markets with minimal risk. A more detailed discussion of franchises can be found in *Chapter 14: Getting Started*.

> **University links:** Businesses are increasingly outsourcing some of their R&D needs by working co-operatively with colleges and universities throughout the country. Most of the major universities have innovation centres which attempt to match the research needs of business with the funding needs of the university.

unit
5

In some cases a large business may sponsor a scholarship programme or research building in a university. In return for the funding, students work on research and development projects which have commercial potential for the business. Below is a perfect example of a co-operative relationship in action.

 **Example**

Invent is a state-of-the-art Innovation and Enterprise Centre based at Dublin City University. Established in 2001, Invent's mission is to transform knowledge into commercial success and to provide the critical link between the university and the marketplace.

Similar facilities exist at other Irish universities and include Trinity College's Innovation Centre, NovaUCD at University College Dublin and UCC's IGNITE graduate business innovation centre.

www.dcu.ie/invent/

› **Market research:** This is the process of gathering and analysing information in order to identify customer needs. For a business, finding out exactly what customers want is an obvious first step in the process of meeting those needs.

Market research is used to gather information on the following important issues:

- › Customer needs
- › Market size
- › Level of competition
- › Future trends

› **Customer needs:** Meeting customer expectations is a requirement for business success and market research techniques help a business to succeed in this important challenge.

This customer-focused approach to product development is part of the marketing concept and is discussed in more detail in *Chapter 15: Marketing*.

Customers also provide invaluable feedback on current products. They can be asked about the strengths and weaknesses of current product offerings, future trends and expectations, as well as possible changes to marketing strategies. A business which fails to consult with this key stakeholder group runs the risk of alienating its customers and losing market share.

 **Case Study**

Coca Cola upset many of its loyal customers in 1985 when it made a decision to change the recipe of its world-famous soft drink. The company was under severe competitive pressure and was losing market share to the rival Pepsi brand. Senior management made a decision to alter the Coke formula, but New Coke was a commercial and marketing failure. Some customers reacted angrily, some boycotted the brand, and a pressure group was set up which eventually forced the company into a U-turn. The old formula was reintroduced under the name of Coke Classic, and over time this effectively replaced New Coke.

> **Market size:** Businesses need some indication of the overall size of both existing and potential markets. If the level of aggregate demand is too low it may not be commercially viable for a company to get involved in a particular market.

> **Level of competition:** Before entering a new market a business will need to assess the level of competition as well as the relative strengths and weaknesses of its rivals. Company websites will provide a lot of useful information about product ranges, prices and market positioning of rival firms.

> **Future trends:** There are lots of variables which will have an impact on the future market for goods and services. The general economic outlook, changes to legislation, taxation and income levels are just some of the issues that need to be considered and analysed. Unless a business has the most up-to-date information on these types of issue it is unlikely to be in a position to accurately assess their impact.

Types of market research

There are two broad approaches to market research:

> **Desk research**   > **Field research**

> **Desk Research:** This technique is used to gather information already available from other sources. Since the information has already been collected by somebody else, desk research is also called 'secondary research'.

It is useful for providing a general overview of a market and would help a business to determine the size of a market, the number of competing firms, demographic trends and consumer spending patterns.

Sources of information

Internal	External
Sales figures	Government publications
Stock movements	Trade journals
Market reports and analysis	Media reports
Reports from sales staff	Company websites

The **advantages** of desk research are that it is relatively cheap and easy to compile and that the information is instantly available.

The **disadvantages** arise from the fact that it may be out of date and is not specific to a particular business. Desk research will not allow a business to gain much insight into the minds of consumers and is unlikely to shed any light on their motives for buying particular products. For these reasons it is usually used in conjunction with field research.

> **Field Research:** This is primary research and requires businesses to gather new information themselves, by asking their own questions.

By making direct contact with customers it is possible to get a greater understanding of their motives and expectations.

This also has the advantage of making it more accurate and relevant to their specific needs.

unit
5

On the negative side, it is far more costly and time-consuming to collect. It also requires a reasonably large sample in order to ensure accuracy.

Various methods can be used to gather primary data, including: personal interviews, telephone interviews, postal surveys, test marketing and direct observation.

> **Postal surveys** and personal or **telephone interviews** all involve the use of questionnaires given directly to members of the **target market**. These are the people a product or service is being aimed at, and for that reason it's important to find out as much information about their needs and spending habits as possible. As it will not be possible to survey all members of the target market a representative subset or **sample** will usually be chosen. Market researchers must be careful that the sample chosen is representative of the overall target market.

This direct contact with customers allows for the collection of detailed information and may enable a business to gain valuable insights into the reasons why consumers like or dislike particular products.

Some consumers are reluctant to take part in surveys and a business may need to offer an incentive in order to entice them to partake. Free gifts and entry to prize draws are some of the methods used by businesses to increase participation.

Note that the questionnaire below contains a mixture of open-ended questions (Q5), closed questions (Q2 & Q3) and multiple-choice questions (Q1 and Q4).

Market Research Questionnaire

Question 1:

Which age group are you in?

Under 10 ☐   15 – 18 ☐   25- 30 ☐

10 – 15 ☐   18 – 25 ☐   Over 30 ☐

Question 2:

Are you: Male ☐   Female ☐

Question 3:

Do you read books as a pastime?   Yes ☐   No ☐

Question 4:

Tick your three favourite categories of books:

Fiction ☐   Biography ☐   Comics ☐

Non fiction ☐   Current affairs ☐   History ☐

Science fiction ☐   Irish language books ☐   Travel books ☐

Horror ☐   Sports ☐

Question 5:

Please take a few moments to tell us what would improve the level of customer service in our bookshop:

_____

_____

_____

_____

_____

_____

> **Direct observation** requires the market researcher to simply look at how members of the target market react in certain situations. For example, a researcher may stand close to supermarket checkouts and count the number of shoppers who purchase a particular product. While this will provide manufacturers with information about purchasing patterns and market share it will again offer little insight into the customers' reasons for buying that particular product.

Due to the problems associated with each of the techniques outlined above, most businesses will use a combination of desk and field research.

unit 5

Product development process

« syllabus signpost
5.5.3

Getting a product to market is a risky and expensive task, so a business should take all reasonable steps to ensure it has the greatest possible chance of success.

Having conducted market research the following steps are necessary in the product development process:

> Idea generation
> Product screening
> Concept development

> Feasibility study
> Prototype development

> Test marketing
> Product launch

James Seddon is the inventor of a waterless egg cooker and boss of **Eggxactly Ltd.**

Before reading the following outline of the product development process, it may prove helpful to visit the company website *(www.eggxactly.com)* and/or view his successful pitch on the UK series of *Dragons' Den*. The company website contains a link to the *Dragons' Den* clip.

> **Step 1: Idea generation** involves identifying a potential business idea. Businesses can use any of the internal or external sources of ideas outlined at the start of this chapter. Ideally they will come up with several ideas from which they can choose the most promising.

James Seddon came up with the idea for the waterless egg cooker following constant complaints from his daughter that he overcooked her boiled egg. James felt that cooking eggs should be as simple as making toast and set about making that a reality.

> **Step 2: Product screening** requires that each idea is evaluated. Based on this initial evaluation, the weakest ideas can be eliminated while the strongest ones will be retained for more detailed investigation. This may involve further **SWOT analysis** and an assessment of potential market size.

James Seddon discovered that many other people shared his problem and that they too struggled to make the perfect boiled egg with any level of consistency. This preliminary and very limited market research did at least offer some hope that his new invention would be well received and was worth pursuing.

unit
5

> **Step 3: Concept development:** During this stage the idea is developed into a saleable product, which will appeal to customers. A business will need to identify key features of the new product and attempt to establish its **Unique Selling Point (USP)**. A unique selling point is what makes a product different from other similar products.

After a lot of experimentation James Seddon hit on the idea of using soft, stretchy heating elements instead of boiling water. By stretching the elements over the egg and controlling them with a microprocessor he was able to cook eggs accurately and easily just the way his daughter likes them.

The uniqueness of James's invention clearly stemmed from the fact that no water was required, and also the fact that the product also offered some measure of consistency when cooking 'boiled' eggs.

> **Step 4: Feasibility study:** This is undertaken to establish whether a product idea is profitable or commercially viable. Issues such as production costs, finance and environmental impact are all considered at this stage. **Break-even analysis** is a tool which can be used to determine the impact of costs and revenues on profitability. It will illustrate the number of products which must be sold in order to cover all the costs associated with production.

Following James's appearance on *Dragons' Den*, over 10,000 potential customers have registered online to express their interest in purchasing a waterless egg cooker once the product is finally launched. This level of demand would make the product commercially viable.

> **Step 5: Prototype development:** At this stage a working model or sample is produced. This allows a firm to see if and how the product can actually be made. It also helps identify possible production or design problems. The finished prototype can be tested and modified if necessary.

James Seddon made several prototypes when trying to prove that the technology worked. Early prototypes were larger and less refined than the final model but they were nonetheless useful as they enabled James to establish the validity of the concept. Later prototypes improved the functionality and aesthetics of the product. During his pitch on *Dragons' Den* (in 2006) James used several prototypes, but each one failed to cook the egg. Despite this setback he managed to secure an investment from two Dragons.

Failure to identify and rectify design problems at the prototype stage can be very costly, both in terms of manufacturing and reputational damage. Mercedes Benz had this misfortune in 1997 when they attempted to enter the compact car market.

Case Study

In the late 1990s Mercedes sought to broaden its target market by introducing the economical A-class. Shortly after its launch the new vehicle hit the headlines for all the wrong reasons when it overturned during a test drive by a Swedish journalist. It failed the famous 'moose test', which is used to determine how a vehicle handles when the driver swerves to evade a suddenly appearing obstacle (such as an animal on the road).

Mercedes made a decision to recall the 2,600 units it had already sold and suspend further distribution. The problem threatened to derail the entire A-class development and cost the German car giant a lot of money and a loss of reputation.

The search for a solution led to the introduction of electronic stability control and proved to be a major step forward for car safety across the entire industry. 'The fact is, we made a mistake,' Mercedes said in a newspaper advertisement when the car was relaunched. 'But we've fixed it and we've learned our lesson.'

› **Step 6: Test marketing:** This is a very important stage in the development process as it brings the new product into contact with consumers for the first time. A relatively small batch of the product is manufactured and given to members of the target market to use and evaluate.

Case Study

Following modifications to the design and production process, Eggxactly Ltd conducted a 'market acceptance test' with a limited edition of the product. This test marketing was conducted prior to large-scale manufacturing of the egg cooker.

Consumer reactions are essential before embarking on a full-scale product launch, so changes may need to be made to the product itself or to the **marketing mix**. The marketing mix is a combination of elements which are essential to market a product successfully. These four key elements are: product, price, place and promotion. A full analysis of the marketing mix can be found in *Chapter 15: Marketing*.

unit

5

> **Step 7: Product launch:** If satisfied with test marketing results, the firm may choose to set up full production facilities and launch the product onto the market. A marketing campaign will usually accompany the product launch.

Case Study

James Seddon expects to launch his waterless egg cooker in 2012.

Evaluation

It needs to be emphasised that the entire product development process is both a lengthy and expensive one. It is, however, necessary since the costs of launching a product that fails to gain market share will far outweigh the costs involved in the process outlined above.

Case Study

In 1979, Guinness launched a low-calorie product called Guinness Light. The ad campaign carried the tagline, 'They said it couldn't be done', and this unfortunately was proven to be the case when the product was withdrawn less than two years later. The *Irish Times* dubbed it 'The HMS Titanic of stout products'.

In the late 1990s Guinness spent over €5 million developing a white wheat beer called Breo. It too proved unpopular and disappeared in 2000.

It should also be remembered that a firm might decide to abandon a product idea at any stage in this process. Business experience suggests that only about 2 per cent of new product ideas actually make it to the market place. The vast majority will not get past the screening stage. This is because development costs begin to increase very quickly beyond this point and businesses need a strong likelihood of success before they will risk further investment.

Protecting intellectual property rights

Businesses and individuals who use their mental efforts to create or develop concepts or products are entitled to protect this **intellectual property (IP)** from imitation. The Irish patent office allows inventors to gain legal protection for a range of intellectual property including patents for inventions, trademarks, industrial designs and copyright.

unit 5

Once a patent is granted, it prevents others from exploiting the invention by making or selling it without the agreement of the patent holder. Patent protection is territorial, which means that an Irish patent will only provide protection in this country. It is, however, possible to acquire additional patent protection for EU and international markets, although this is likely to increase the costs involved. Protection typically lasts for twenty years and is subject to the payment of ongoing fees.

The words 'patent pending' are often used on new products and indicate to users and competitors alike that the inventor has applied for a patent on that product.

www.patentsoffice.ie

Case Study

Since August 2011 Apple and its South Korean rival Samsung have been locked in ongoing courtroom battles which centre on alleged breaches of copyright during the development of innovative smartphones and tablets. Apple claimed that Samsung had copied its hugely successful iPad and its allegations resulted in the removal of Samsung Galaxy tablets from shelves in some countries.

The stakes are very high as both firms seek to dominate these highly lucrative developing markets. In a case which illustrates the dynamic nature of business relationships, Samsung also jeopardises its position as a major supplier of components to its rival. In 2010 Samsung supplied Apple with $5.7 billion worth of components, a figure which represents almost 4 per cent of Samsung's total sales.

Break-even analysis

In order to survive businesses must at least break even, which means they need to generate enough income to cover all of their costs.

Break-even analysis is a financial tool which can be used by managers to determine the impact of costs and revenues on profitability. It will indicate the number of products which must be sold in order to cover all the costs associated with production.

At the **break-even point** total sales revenue is equal to total business costs (**TR = TC**).

TR = Selling Price (SP) x Quantity Sold

TC = Fixed Costs (FC) + Variable Costs (VC)

At this level of sales the firm is not making either a profit or a loss, but is simply recouping the costs associated with producing goods. While this may be sustainable in the short term, it should be remembered that all commercial businesses need to make a profit, so firms will aim to sell more than the break-even quantity. Being able to calculate this break-even quantity therefore represents an important step in achieving this goal of business survival. For a proposed start-up business, break-even analysis can be used to establish whether it is commercially viable or not.

Calculating the break-even point

The break-even point can be calculated mathematically and can also be illustrated using a graph.

In order to work out the break even point a business will need to know its **fixed costs, the variable costs** per unit and the **selling price.**

> **Fixed Costs (FC):** These are expenses which do not change as output changes. They tend to be linked to time rather than output and will have to be paid even when no goods are being produced. Examples include rent, insurance and depreciation. Diagram 1A below illustrates that fixed costs remain the same even as output levels increase.

> **Variable Costs (VC):** These expenses will change as the level of output changes. Examples include raw materials, direct wages and packaging. Diagram 1B below illustrates that variable costs will increase as output increases.

> **Total Costs (TC):** Total costs are calculated by adding all fixed and variable costs. Since fixed costs are paid even when output is zero, total costs will never be less than fixed costs. On a break-even chart TC will not start at origin, but begins at FC level (see diagram 1C).

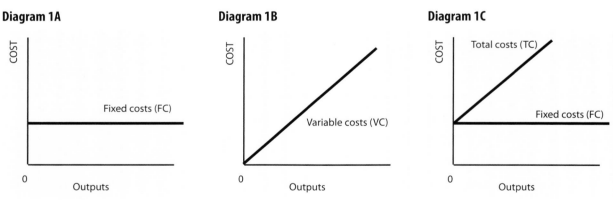

Diagram 1A · COST · Fixed costs (FC) · 0 · Outputs

Diagram 1B · COST · Variable costs (VC) · 0 · Outputs

Diagram 1C · COST · Total costs (TC) · Fixed costs (FC) · 0 · Outputs

Loot Ltd supplies the following details about its activities

> Forecast output (sales): 20,000 units

> Selling price: €200 per unit

> Variable costs: €100 per unit

> Fixed costs: €600,000

Using the formula to calculate break-even point

B/E point (in units) = $\dfrac{\text{Fixed costs}}{(\text{Selling price per unit } - \text{ Variable cost per unit})}$

$= \dfrac{600{,}000}{(200 - 100)} = 6{,}000 \text{ units}$

Exam Tip

When asked to illustrate the B/E point using a break-even chart it is not essential to calculate the B/E point using this formula. It may, however, be helpful to know the break-even point in advance of drawing the chart, as it helps to verify the accuracy of the diagram.

Finding the break-even point using a break-even chart

Set up a chart to examine the revenue and costs involved in selling different levels of output, up to and including the target output. Any output figures can be chosen, but it is generally helpful to analyse what will happen if there are zero sales, if sales reach the target level, and at some point in between. In this example 6,000 units has been used as the interim figure, but sales of 10,000 could also have been chosen and would give a similarly accurate result.

Table A

Sales (units)	Selling price (SP)	Total revenue (Units x SP)	Fixed cost (units x €100)	Variable cost	Total cost (FC + VC)	Profit (TR – TC)
0	€200 each	€0	€600,000	€0	€600,000	(€600,000)
6,000	€200 each	€1,200,000	€600,000	€600,000	€1,200,000	€0
20,000	€200 each	€4,000,000	€600,000	€2,000,000	€2,600,000	€1,400,000

unit

5

Notice that for sales levels below break-even Loot Ltd will make a loss, no profit or loss will be made at break-even, while sales levels above 6,000 units will generate a profit.

Step 1: Use the formula to calculate the break-even point.

> This is a useful check for accuracy.

Step 2: Use graph paper to draw the X and Y axes using appropriate scales.

> Make sure to put a **title** on the graph and **label both axes.** Consider carefully the scale required for each axis before you draw it.

> The horizontal (X) axis will show **output** and should extend to at least the target output level.

> The vertical (Y) axis will show **money values** and can be labelled with a '€' sign. Remember that this axis is used to indicate both costs and sales revenue, and the labelling should show this fact. It would be incorrect to label it simply as costs or revenue.

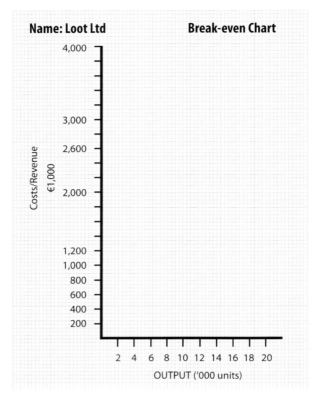

Diagram 2

> The highest amount required on the vertical (€) axis can be calculated as follows:

Target output x selling price per unit

Table A above illustrates that the maximum sales revenue which Loot Ltd will receive is €4,000,000. This will be received if all 20,000 units of target output are sold for €200 each.

> Try to use a scale which will allow you to plot the fixed-cost line easily.

In this case, maximum revenue is €4 million and fixed costs are €600,000 so we've used intervals of €200,000 on the vertical (€) axis. On graph paper this will be very easy to plot accurately, and accuracy is obviously very important when it comes to plotting the break-even chart.

Step 3: Draw the FC line, parallel to horizontal axis, and label it clearly.

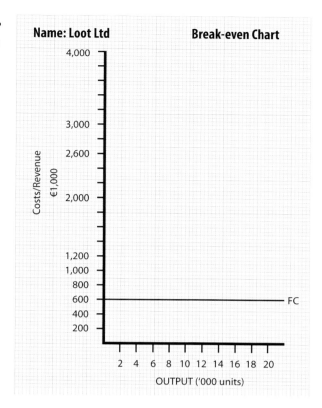

Diagram 3

Step 4: Draw the TC line and label it clearly.

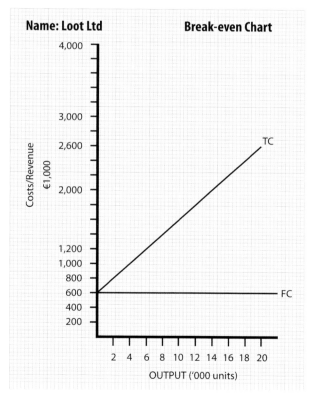

Diagram 4

> Remember that total costs are made up of a fixed cost element plus a variable cost element. When plotting this on the diagram it means that TC will start at the point where the FC line intersects with the Y (€) axis.

> The TC line will extend to the point where output is 20,000 units and TC = €2,600,000. Table A illustrates this mathematically.

> Note that the VC line is not actually shown on the B/E chart but such costs are represented by the gap between FC and TC. As you might expect, this gap gets wider as output increases since variable costs increase in line with output (see diagram 4).

Step 5: **Plot the TR line and label it clearly.**

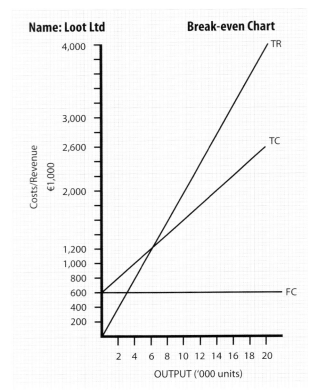

Diagram 5

> The TR line will begin at the origin (0,0) because when output is zero, sales revenue will also be zero.

> The TR line will extend to the point where output is 20,000 units and sales revenue is €4,000,000. Table A again illustrates this mathematically.

Step 6: **Plot and clearly label the break-even point.**

> The break-even point is where the TR line intersects the TC line.

> Check the accuracy against the figure calculated using the formula in Step 1 or by referring to Table A. The break-even output is 6,000 units and both TR and TC are €1,200,000 at this point.

Step 7: **Use the chart to illustrate the margin of safety and the profitability.**

> The **margin of safety** is the difference between the target output level and the break-even output level.

In this example that will be 20,000 units – 6,000 units = 14,000 units.

> The margin of safety indicates the amount by which output (and sales) can afford to decline before the business no longer makes a profit. The bigger the margin of safety, the better.

> The size of margin of safety is a valuable guide to the strength of a business. If it is large, a business can suffer a substantial fall-off in sales and yet make a profit. On the other hand, if the margin is small, any loss of sales may be a serious matter.

> If the margin of safety is unsatisfactory it may be possible to rectify it by increasing the selling price or reducing fixed and variable costs.

> The B/E chart can also be used to interpret or illustrate the level of **profitability** or loss which will occur at any given level of output. In this example we are asked to determine Loot Ltd's profit at target output of 20,000 units.

> This is achieved by placing a ruler perpendicular to the output axis at 20,000 units and shading the triangular area formed by the ruler and the TR and TC lines (see diagram 6).

> This same procedure can be used to illustrate the profit or loss at any level of output.

Remember that for any level of sales below 6,000 units Loot Ltd will make a loss.

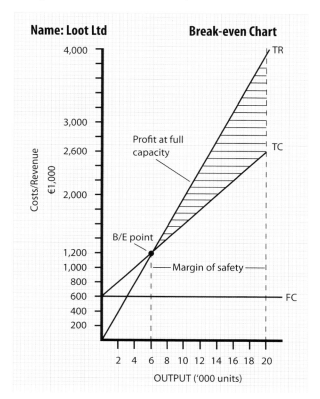

Diagram 6

Changing costs and selling prices

Any changes to costs or selling price will have an impact on the break-even point. If costs increase a greater quantity will have to be sold in order to break even, whereas lower costs will lower the break-even quantity.

In a similar way, an increase in selling price will reduce the break-even quantity and vice versa.

Exam questions involving a change in either of these variables will require students to calculate and/or illustrate the new break-even point.

Depending on which variable has changed, it will be necessary to redraw either the Total Revenue or the Total Cost line.

Let us revisit the Loot Ltd example and consider a situation where variable costs have risen from €100 to €120 per unit.

A helpful first step is to use the formula to calculate the new break-even point

$$\text{B/E point (in units)} = \frac{\text{Fixed costs}}{\text{(Selling price per unit} - \text{Variable cost per unit)}}$$

$$= \frac{600,000}{(200 - 120)} = 7,500 \text{ units}$$

The new TC line (TC2) will again start at the point where the FC line intersects the Y axis. The new total cost at target output is €600,000 + (20,000 x €120) = €3,000,000. Plot this point: 20,000 units of output on the X axis and €3,000,000 on the Y axis. Join it up with the start point to create the TC2 line.

Finally it will be necessary to plot and label the new break-even point, which yet again occurs where TR = TC2 (see diagram 7).

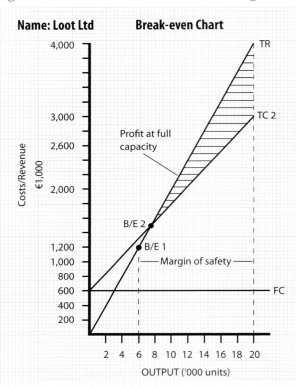

Note

An alternative approach to drawing a break-even chart can be found on www.edcodigital.ie

Diagram 7

[Some students may find this alternative less mathematical and it may be possible to draw it with greater accuracy and speed in an exam situation.]

Break-even analysis, uses and advantages

> It allows a business to determine the level of operations at which it will break even. Based on current cost levels, it helps the management to decide on the number of units which must be sold to recover the costs of production.

> It also helps the management to determine how many units need to be sold to get desired profit on product.

> It allows management to explore the relationship between volume, costs and profits. This is particularly useful as it may be possible to examine the impact of changes to output and costs upon the break-even point and profit levels for the business.

> A break-even chart can be used to show the effect of changes in any of the following profit factors:

> > Volume of sales
> > Variable costs
> > Fixed costs
> > Selling price

> Break-even analysis is used by entrepreneurs to evaluate the feasibility of a proposed business start-up.

Limitations of break-even analysis

> While break-even analysis is a useful tool it is only a model of the real world and for that reason may rely on certain assumptions which are inaccurate or which oversimplify market conditions.

> It assumes all goods produced are sold at the same price. It does not reflect a situation where discounts may be offered to customers who are willing to order large quantities.

> It also assumes that operating costs are static. In reality a business may benefit from economies of scale at higher levels of output.

> It does not allow for stock and it assumes all items produced are sold.

> It is only valid in the short term and where levels of output are relatively stable. In the longer term a successful business may expand its operations and this may impact on fixed costs, particularly where new premises are rented.

Nevertheless, despite these limitations break-even charts are used by management as an efficient tool in marginal costing. They help with forecasting, decision-making and maintaining profitability.

unit
5

Chapter Review Diagram – Identifying opportunities

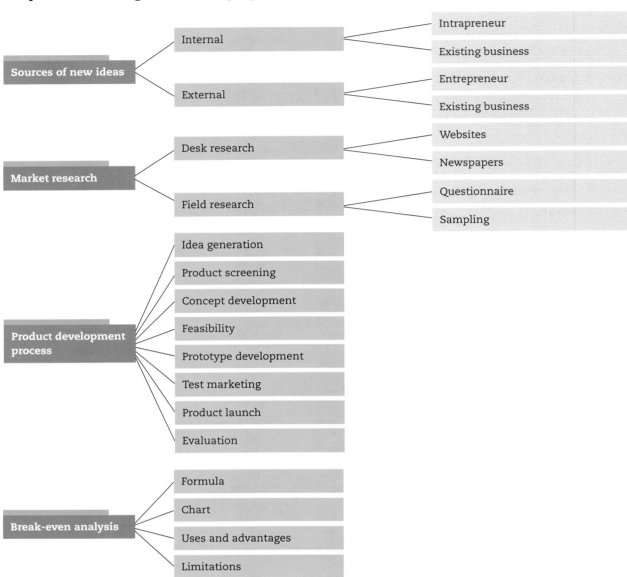

unit
5

Chapter Review Questions

1 Outline two internal and two external sources of new ideas for an entrepreneur wishing to start a business.

2 Outline two internal and two external sources of new ideas for an existing business.

3 Explain the term 'import substitution'.

4 Explain how brainstorming can be used to generate new ideas.

5 Distinguish between a business alliance and a franchise.

6 Define 'market research'.

7 Distinguish between desk research and field research.

8 Outline one advantages and one disadvantage of desk research.

9 Outline three reasons why a business would carry out market research.

10 List the seven steps involved in the product development process.

11 Explain the following:

   (i) Feasibility study

   (ii) Prototype development.

12 Explain how patents and trademarks can be used to protect intellectual property rights.

13 What is 'break-even analysis'? Outline the benefits to a business from using this type of analysis.

14 Illustrate the difference between fixed and variable costs.

15 Calculate the break-even point (in units) for a business which provides the following information:

Fixed costs: €360,000

Selling price: €12

Variable cost per unit: €5

unit

5

16 Study the graph and answer the questions below.

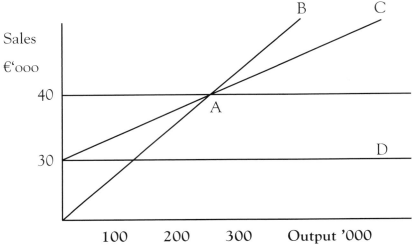

(a) Name point A.

(b) What is the line marked B?

(c) What is the line marked C?

(d) What is the line marked D?

(e) List one reason why this chart is important to a business.

17 Define 'margin of safety' (MOS).

18 Outline the limitations of break-even analysis.

Questions · Ordinary Level

1 Explain the following market research terms and give **one** example of each:

(i) Field research

(ii) Desk research.   *LCOL 2011 (20 marks)*

2 Outline **three** advantages of conducting market research.   *LCOL 2009 (15 marks)*

3 What are the benefits of prototype development?

4 Outline the stages involved in developing a new product.

5 What is meant by 'brainstorming'?

6 Identify **two** benefits to any company of using break-even analysis to assess the feasibility of a new business idea.

7 What is meant by the 'margin of safety'?

8 Outline **three** sources from which an enterprising individual may identify a new business idea.

unit
5

Questions · *Higher Level*

1 As part of its feasibility study for a new product, Moore Ltd supplies the following financial information:
- › Forecast output (sales): 40,000 units
- › Selling price per unit: €20
- › Fixed costs: €300,000
- › Variable cost per unit: €10

(a) Illustrate by means of a break-even chart the following:
  (i) The break-even point
  (ii) Profit at forecast output
  (iii) The margin of safety at forecast output

(b) Outline one other function of a feasibility study for Moore Ltd. *LCHL 2011 (25 marks)*

2

Olympian Ltd is a company that produces a range of high quality branded sportswear. Following a lengthy market research process, the firm is now expanding its business to include a new range of Hoodie Tracksuits, aimed at the teenage market. *LCHL 2009*

Outline the stages involved in the development process of the new range of Hoodie Tracksuits. *(20 marks)*

3

Motor Manufacturing Ltd. is considering the introduction of a new product. The business has provided the following figures:

- › Fixed costs: €200,000
- › Variable cost per unit: €5
- › Selling price: €15
- › Forecast output (sales): 30,000 units

LCHL 2008

(a) Illustrate by means of a break-even chart:
  (i) The break-even point
  (ii) Profit at forecast output
  (iii) The margin of safety at forecast output

(b) Explain 'margin of safety'. *(30 marks)*

(c) Evaluate the importance of 'feasibility study' and 'prototype development' in the development process of a new product of your choice. *(15 marks)*

4 (a) A business supplies the following figures about its activities.
- › Forecast output (sales): 20,000 units
- › Selling price: €50 per unit
- › Fixed costs: €300,000
- › Variable cost per unit: €20

Illustrate by means of a break-even chart:
  (i) The break-even point
  (ii) Profit at forecast output
  (iii) The margin of safety at forecast output

(b) Outline the effect on the break-even point if variable costs increased to €25 per unit. Illustrate your answer on the break-even chart.

5 Name and explain two agencies which assist entrepreneurs to identify business opportunities.

unit

5

Chapter 14
Getting Started

On completion of this chapter, the student should be able to:

» 5.5.4 Identify and explain the elements involved in a new business start-up;

» 5.5.5 Explain the stages involved in setting up a new business;

» 5.5.8 List the main sources of finance available for business start-up;

» 5.5.9 Identify the elements of production processes;

» 5.5.10 Illustrate the central role of the business plan;

» 5.5.16 Apply the main sources of finance available for business start-up (HL).

News Flash

Start-up companies up 6% on last year

by Suzanne Lynch

Some 8,800 start-up companies have been registered so far this year in Ireland, 6 per cent higher than in the same period last year, according to data from visionnet.ie.

However, the number of partnerships and sole trader business names registered so far this year stands at 16,728, down 9 per cent on last year.

Companies in the field of education, health and medical, agriculture and manufacturing have seen the most start-up activity, according to visionnet, an online service which provides information on businesses. The construction, hospitality and retail sectors are showing more negative activity.

Despite the increase in start-up activity so far this year, the number of start-ups is lower than in previous years. 2005 saw 17,300 start-ups in total, while in 2000, 18,200 new companies were registered.

Managing director of visionnet.ie, Christine Cullen said that while the number of start-up businesses is lower than in previous years, the number of operating companies stands at 195,000, up from 175,000 in 2001.

Companies are also now running for longer, she says. "The average age of a business when it runs into difficulty is eight years. Five years ago it was five years. Effectively, companies are staying in business longer than they used to."

Visionnet.ie shows the average age of a company director is 49. There are now 311,000 company directors registered in Ireland, compared to 177,000 in 2001.

The Irish Times, MONDAY, 15 AUGUST 2011

For more up-to-date newspaper articles see www.edcodigital.ie

unit
5

1 Read the newspaper extract opposite and discuss the issues raised.

2 Can you explain any of the highlighted terms?

Why start a business?

In *Unit 2: Enterprise*, we considered the importance of enterprise in business and examined the reasons which motivate entrepreneurs to start their own businesses. The main reasons can be summarised as follows:

> **Independence:** Many entrepreneurs enjoy being their own boss and having the freedom to make their own decisions. They may not be in a position of authority or influence as an employee, or may feel that their current work environment stifles their creativity. Individuals in this position see business start-up as a means of becoming more self-reliant and asserting greater control over their own destiny.

   While this self-determination brings increased risk it also offers greater control and security, especially to those who like to feel they are in charge of their own destiny.

> **Profit:** The opportunity to make a financial gain and secure an income stream for themselves and their family may provide a strong motive for some entrepreneurs, but it is rarely seen as their primary motivating factor. There is no guarantee of business or financial success, but for those who are successful the earnings potential is a welcome benefit.

   Enterprise is a factor of production and profit is the reward for those who take on the risks and challenges associated with entrepreneurship.

> **Challenge:** Some entrepreneurs constantly feel the need to challenge themselves and strive to achieve their full potential. Maslow identifies self-actualisation as the motive for these people.

   Very often they have a proven track record in establishing businesses and have a high level of financial security. On the face of it, they have no reason to take the risks associated with starting new businesses, but are clearly driven by an inner desire for success.

unit

5

Case Study

Richard Branson has often displayed a sense of adventure in both his business and personal life. Having made substantial profits from his music business, he sold it to EMI. He later entered the airline, soft drinks, insurance and rail industries, despite having little previous experience in any of them. This also put him in direct competition with some of the world's biggest brands. Branson has also been involved in world record attempts involving trans-Atlantic sailing and flying challenges. His latest challenge is to provide members of the paying public with space flights.

Tralee native Jerry Kennelly is an Irish entrepreneur who has shown similar motivation. Jerry built up his own stock photography business (Stockbyte), which he subsequently sold to Getty Images for over €110 million. He has since started a new business, Tweak.com, and continues to be active in assisting the Young Entrepreneur Programme.

Jerry also devotes time to voluntary work. Following a challenge from John O'Shea of Goal to set up a sustainable business in Africa, he set up Create Africa.

> **Creativity:** Having developed an innovative concept or business idea, some individuals realise that starting their own business represents the best avenue for achieving their vision. They may find that their current employer is unwilling or unable to see the value in the new idea and as a result it's unlikely to fulfil its potential. If they truly believe in the value of their idea, the inventor may feel compelled to start their own business.

Case Study

James Dyson invented and patented a revolutionary bagless vacuum cleaner, which he showed to existing vacuum manufacturers in the hope that one of them would agree to produce the product under licence. In this way Dyson would avoid the massive development and start-up costs and could earn a living from the royalties.

Unable to convince others of the benefits and commercial viability of his concept, his belief in the product and his desire to bring it to market led him to start his own manufacturing business. The Dyson bagless vacuum was a huge success and since then James Dyson has used his creativity to develop a range of products, including an innovative twin-drum washing machine and the Dyson Airblade hand dryer.

> **Employment:** Sometimes the unfortunate personal circumstances in which people find themselves can be the springboard for future success, as Ireland's recent economic downturn has shown to be true. The loss of paid employment may motivate some individuals to pursue a strategy of self-employment. Faced with the prospect of reduced income and financial insecurity, they may be more willing to take the risks needed to create their own job by starting a business. Redundancy payments and savings may be used to fund the start-up.

« *Syllabus Signpost*
5.5.4 & 5.5.5

unit 5

Key issues for business start-ups

When contemplating a new business start-up, the entrepreneur needs to focus on a number of key issues. Decisions need to be made with regard to:

› The type of **ownership structure** to be adopted
› **Business location**
› Possible **sources of finance**
› The choice of **production methods** employed by the business
› Developing the **marketing mix**

Ownership Structure

What ownership structures are available to start-up businesses?

1 **Sole trader**
2 **Partnership**
3 **Private Limited Company (Ltd)**
4 **Co-operative**

Sole Trader

This is a business which is owned by one person. This type of ownership model is suitable for a whole range of businesses, but is particularly common in the retail and services sectors, which are dominated by small, independent operators. Examples include butchers, barbers, hairdressers and publicans.

Sole trader advantages

› It's **easy to set up** with very few legal formalities. A licence may be required for some businesses, including pubs, pharmacies and bookmakers.

› The owner has **complete control** of the business and makes all major decisions.

› The owner **keeps all the profits.**

Sole trader disadvantages

› **Lack of capital:** Since only one person is financing the business, there is a limit to the amount of capital available.

 Note

A more detailed analysis of these ownership structures is set out in *Chapter 18: Ownership Structures*, but a short overview is provided here.

 Note

Because of the costs involved and the strict criteria set down by the regulatory authorities, it would not be possible for a start-up business to get a stock exchange listing. This effectively means that setting up as a public limited company is not an option for start-up businesses.

unit 5

> **Unlimited liability:** This means that the sole trader's liability for business debts is not just limited to the amount of capital they've invested in the business. In situations where the business debts are greater than the value of the saleable assets, the sole trader may have to sell or forfeit personal assets in order to pay business debts.

Partnership

A business partnership allows for between two and twenty owners, thereby providing greater access to capital and skills needed by a business.

Partners are usually advised to sign a legal agreement called a **deed of partnership** when setting up the business or admitting new partners.

The deed of partnership sets out the following issues:

> Amount of capital each partner will provide
> How profits or losses should be divided
> How many votes each partner has. This is usually in proportion to capital provided.
> Rules for admitting new partners
> How the partnership will be brought to an end, or how a partner leaves

Partnership advantages

> **More capital:** Each partner may bring money and financial resources to the business.

> **Extra skills and shared workload:** A new partner may bring other skills and ideas to the business, complementing the work already done by the original partner.

> **Less risk:** The risk is spread across more people, so if the business gets into difficulty there are more people to share the burden of debt.

Partnership disadvantages

> **Profits shared:** The partnership agreement means that business profits have to be shared amongst the partners.

> **Less control:** Shared decision-making means that each individual partner has less control over the business.

> **Unlimited liability:** General partners have unlimited liability and are 'jointly and severally liable' for business debts. This means they have both a collective and an individual responsibility for all liabilities and this is similar to the position of a sole trader.

> **Disputes:** Disagreements may arise over workload or areas of shared responsibility. Serious disagreements, particularly over the direction of the business, may undermine the relationships and bring the partnership to an end.

Private Limited Company

A private limited company allows up to 99 shareholders to establish a business. Where the number of shareholders is large, they may elect a **board of directors** to run the business on their behalf. Shareholders receive a share of annual profits in the form of a **dividend**. Each share carries voting rights at the Annual General Meeting, so those with the largest shareholding have the greatest say in corporate decision-making.

In Ireland private limited companies must be registered with the **Companies Registration Office**.

www.cro.ie

Key features of a limited company

> **Separate legal entity:** Unlike a sole trader or partnership, the company has a separate legal existence. This means that it is the company itself which owns property and that it is the company which may sue and be sued in respect of the business of the company.

> **Continuity of existence:** The company continues to trade irrespective of director or management changes until it is wound up.

> **Limited liability:** This means that, should the company fail, the shareholders' liability for business debts is limited to the amount of share capital contributed by them. The personal assets of directors or shareholders cannot be seized to pay off company debts.

Formation of a limited company

When setting up a limited company the following documents must be submitted to the Companies Registration Office:

> **Form A1:** gives details of the company name, its registered office, details of secretary and directors, their consent to acting as such, the subscribers and details of their shares.

> **The Memorandum of Association:** sets out the relationship between the company and the general public. It includes details of the company name, its objectives and share capital.

> **The Articles of Association:** sets out the internal rules governing the formation and operation of a company. Key issues will include procedures for electing directors or for conducting company meetings.

Limited company advantages

> **Limited liability:** The protection given by limited liability is perhaps the most important advantage of incorporation. If things go wrong the shareholders' only liability is for the value of their shares.

unit
5

> **Separate legal identity:** A limited company has a legal existence separate from management and shareholders.

> **Continuity:** Once formed, a company can continue indefinitely. They can withstand the replacement, retirement or even the death of directors, management and employees. A company can only be terminated by winding up, liquidation or by order of the courts or the Companies Registration Office.

> **Additional capital:** New shareholders and investors can be easily introduced through the issuing of additional shares or the transfer of existing ones.

> **Taxation:** Ireland's current level of corporation tax at 12.5 per cent is much lower than income tax rates paid by sole traders and other self-employed people.

In addition, there is a wide range of allowances and tax-deductible costs that can be offset against a company's profits.

Limited company disadvantages

> **Set-up procedure and costs:** A very clear procedure needs to be followed when setting up a limited liability company and shareholders must comply with all the legal requirements and submit all relevant documents. The costs associated with setting up this type of business are greater than with most other types of ownership structure.

> **Profits shared:** Annual profits are divided amongst all of the shareholders and each receives a small portion of this profit in the form of a dividend.

> **Disclosure:** All companies are required to make annual submissions to the Companies' Registration Office and the revenue commissioners. Some of this information is available to the public and to competitors.

Co-operatives

Co-operatives involve a group of people working together to achieve shared goals. This type of business is owned by members or shareholders who usually have a common bond and who operate the business for their mutual benefit. Members enjoy the protection of limited liability and decisions at the AGM are on the basis of 'one person, one vote'. As with limited companies, profits shared amongst the owners.

A number of different types of co-op are common in Ireland:

> **Producer co-ops:** Typically seen in the agri-business sector, they engage in the production and processing of crops and farm produce.

 **Example**

The Avonmore and Kerry food brands originated from a producer co-op, although both of these businesses have grown to become public limited companies.

> **Worker co-ops:** In this type of business the workers are also the owners and so their levels of motivation tend to be high. It is an unusual option for a new business start-up.

> **Community co-ops:** This type of co-op is usually set up to fund and provide some important service for members of the local community. Since it is funded and operated by local people for the benefit of their fellow citizens, it is a good example of community enterprise in action.

> **Financial co-ops:** Credit unions are examples of financial co-ops in Ireland. They allow people to pool their financial resources and lend surplus funds to fellow members. The credit union charges interest on loans and any surplus (profit) is reinvested in the co-op or distributed among members.

Business Location

The location of a business is where it is situated, e.g. in Dublin city centre or the Connemara *gaeltacht*. Where to locate a business is a crucial decision because this will have an impact on both its viability and its profitability. Typically businesses will seek locations that maximise revenues and minimise costs.In choosing a business location firms need to weigh up a range of factors. The level of importance attached to each factor will vary from industry to industry and business to business.

> **Proximity to market:** Most businesses need to locate close to their customer base, or at the very least at a location which is convenient to customers.

With the growth of the services sector, business like restaurants, hairdressers, medical and fitness centres need to locate close to their customers. In recent years many urban housing developments have provided commercial premises for community-based retailers including convenience stores and childcare facilities. Most rural towns and villages also support these types of enterprise, as customers insist on convenience. For many service providers the location decision is effectively the 'place' element of the marketing mix, as this is where the service is delivered to the customer.

For large-scale businesses, where it is not cost-effective to offer 'on your doorstep' availability to all customers, selecting a location which is accessible becomes a major priority.

 **Example**

IKEA has only one store in the Republic of Ireland located close to Dublin's M50 motorway. While this is not in close proximity to all members of IKEA's target market, this major motorway can cater for the large volume of traffic generated by the store and also links with the rest of the motorway network serving the north, south and west of the country.

Bulk-forming operations like furniture makers and breweries will also seek to locate close to customers. This is because the bulky nature of the finished product makes transport and distribution both difficult and expensive.

unit **5**

The growth of e-commerce means that not all retailers and service providers need to locate close to customers. Some goods can be purchased online and delivered to the customer. While this obviously relies on good transport infrastructure, it does allow a business to operate from a cheaper 'out of town' location.

> **Proximity to raw materials:** Bulk-reducing industries are those which use large quantities of raw materials in their operation and examples include iron and steel manufacturers. For this type of industry it is more important to locate close to their supply of raw materials or close to a port, as this will minimise transport costs.

> **Transport and communications links:** Many of the examples outlined previously highlight the importance of an adequate transport infrastructure in order to facilitate the delivery of raw materials and finished goods. Access to ports and road networks are all critical factors governing business location. They are of particular concern to businesses involved in international trade, including the transnational corporations which provide so many of Ireland's jobs and exports.

An efficient and cost-effective communications network is equally important for some businesses, especially those which locate away from their customer base or rely on e-commerce.

Problems with the availability of broadband services in rural Ireland have hampered business development efforts in these locations and have become a major focus for government policy.

> **Availability of skilled labour:** Businesses requiring skilled labour will obviously need to locate in areas where they can find it. Very often the chosen location is close to a university as this will provide the business with a steady supply of qualified graduates. If a business is unable to maintain a supply of skilled labour it may be forced to relocate at considerable cost.

Google's search fails to find enough suitable Irish graduates

by Niamh Connolly, Political Correspondent

Google's problems finding suitable Irish graduates with skills in maths and science for top-level jobs at its European headquarters in Dublin was raised by its worldwide boss Eric Schmidt at a meeting with cabinet ministers recently.

The executive chairman of Google told ministers that the world's leading internet search company was forced to recruit graduates from Russia and Ukraine for jobs in Ireland, because of the skills shortage here.

He is also believed to have raised the matter of easing visa restrictions to allow skilled overseas staff to take up posts with his company. Mr Schmidt told ministers that establishing Google's European headquarters in Ireland was one of the best decisions made by the company, but there were also challenges and the country could do better in producing more maths and sciences graduates.

Sunday Business Post, 3 July 2011

unit 5

It is often the case that industries cluster together in a particular location and so benefit from the available supply of labour and economies of concentration. These economies help reduce costs by allowing suppliers and service providers to locate nearby. Intel lies at the centre of a major ICT hub in Leixlip, while Cork has a large cluster of chemical and pharmaceutical firms.

> **Cost and availability of land** is increasingly important today. Land is becoming more and more scarce, particularly in urban locations, forcing rental prices up. Despite the recent slump in property prices, rental costs are particularly high in major city areas and many lease agreements allow only upward changes to rent.

> **Opportunity for waste disposal:** Waste is a significant side-effect of modern industrial processes. Firms that produce a lot of toxic material (e.g. some chemical plants) will seek to locate where there are facilities available for recycling and safe disposal of their products. Indaver Ireland recently sought planning permission to locate a hazardous waste incinerator close to the cluster of chemical plants in Cork.

Under a European Union directive waste must be disposed of close to the area where it is generated and this might end the practice of Irish-produced waste being exported for disposal. Not having a suitable waste facility available locally may force some multinationals to consider locating elsewhere.

> **Government incentives** are important in reducing the cost of locating in certain areas, particularly in less developed regions. These incentives are effectively subsidies provided by the EU Regional Funds and by the Irish government.

The government can also use taxation policy to make particular locations attractive and this is also effective in promoting regeneration of designated areas. The International Financial Services Centre (IFSC) and Temple Bar in Dublin are recent examples of this policy.

> Some businesses, mostly in the services sector, are less constrained than others when it comes to choosing a location. A **footloose business** is one that is not tied down by particular locating factors, meaning it can set up more or less anywhere. Many TNCs are footloose businesses and they are prone to relocating their business operations in order to take advantage of a better trading environment.

unit

5

Case Study

Gay Byrne, writing in the *Irish Independent* recently, described St Mullins as 'a quaint backwater, tiny and quiet, with a eatery/cafe/relaxation area, a place just to do nothing in'.

On the basis of that description, this 'out of the way' location in rural County Carlow, close to the Wexford and Kilkenny borders, seems a most unlikely location for one of the most highly regarded piano shops in Ireland.

But despite its seemingly improbable location, the Piano Gallery has managed to serve the needs of owners and customers alike and has built a strong client base and reputation. In 2003 Chris Jackson became only the second piano tuner in the Republic of Ireland to successfully hold full membership of the Pianoforte Tuners Association.

In recent years he has successfully established a rapidly expanding piano sales and tuning business, tuning for in excess of 70 piano teachers in the region as well as most of the major musical events, including the Wexford Festival Opera and Kilkenny Arts Festival.

When asked to explain the reasons for both their success and their remote location, owners Chris and Marcella Jackson were happy to offer the following insights:

'In the internet age it is possible to have a "virtual shop front" in people's living room, giving them the desire to travel to your business, confident it will be a successful trip. Sites like Google Maps also facilitate the journey, as people are certain of finding you once they have set out.

'People like to buy from a friendly family business – particularly something like a piano which requires an ongoing maintenance relationship. We love the sense of surprise on many customers' faces as they step through the front door. 'It is our experience that people treat their piano purchase as an enjoyable family day out – we facilitate this by recommending local sights, cafés and walks.

'From a cost point of view our rates are many times less than they would be in a city. This allows us to operate at lower margins than our competitors.

'Loading and unloading pianos in a city or town is a logistical nightmare and customers do not like having to search and pay for parking. There are certainly no issues with space at out current location! At the same time we are not too far from the motorway, which allows Chris to serve our client base in Dublin and Cork.'

 www.thepianogallery.ie

Sources of Finance

« *Syllabus Signpost*
5.5.8

Most sources of finance previously outlined in *Chapter 8: Finance for Households and Business* are relevant here, but key concerns for start-up businesses will be around suitable long-term finance and also the issue of liquidity/cash flow. Further discussion on the significance of these issues can also be found in *Chapter 10: Monitoring the Business*.

Short Term	Medium Term	Long Term
(< 1 year)	(1–5 years)	(> 5 years)
Trade creditors	Leasing	Share Capital
Bank overdraft	Term loan	Debentures/loans
Accrued expenses	Hire Purchase	Venture capital
		Grants

Note: Retained earnings is not a relevant source for start-up businesses.

Short-term finance needed for: daily working capital needs including purchase of raw materials, payment of wages, electricity and transport costs.

Medium-term finance needed for: purchase of machinery, equipment, computers and vehicles. These assets tend to have a working life of two to five years.

Long-term finance needed for: purchase of business premises and ongoing business development needs, including research and development.

Failure to accurately estimate the capital requirements of a start-up business is a common and very costly mistake which many entrepreneurs fall victim to. It is generally best for new businesses to rely on **equity capital** rather than on debt. While there may be difficulties in relation to attracting investment from shareholders, a realistic and well prepared business plan will help overcome some of these. **Debt capital** requires regular interest repayments, which may stifle a firm's ability to survive and grow.

It is easier for partnerships and limited companies to get access to larger amounts of equity and to secure loans, so the amount of capital required by the new business may be a consideration when deciding on the best ownership option.

Liquidity

Liquidity is primarily about **cash flow**, and a business that is liquid has enough cash coming in to pay all debts as they fall due. Poor liquidity (and not poor profitability) is perhaps the single biggest reason for business failure. Many businesses have too much money tied up in fixed assets, but these assets may take time to convert into cash. During the recent property crash in Ireland many property developers owned assets, mainly land and buildings, which fell significantly in value and for which there was little demand. This led to insufficient cash being available to pay their debts.

Cash-flow forecasts and **ratio analysis** are important tools in managing liquidity. A huge number of new businesses fail because they do not have sufficient short-term funding to cover day-to-day expenses. Many of them rely on borrowings to meet this shortfall, but in some cases the amount of debt taken on by the business exceeds the value of their assets. A business whose total debts exceed the value of its total assets is **insolvent.**

At the introductory stage of a product's life cycle (see page 296) a business tends to experience a mismatch between its income and its expenditure. Sales revenue is very low and high levels of spending are required for set-up costs, raw materials, wages and marketing.

unit

5

As they have no track record, some new businesses are unable to secure good credit terms and must operate on a cash-on-delivery (COD) basis. This is a major drain on cash reserves and may be amplified where goods are sold on credit to customers. This means that there is a major time lag between cash outflows for raw materials, wages and distribution costs and the cash inflows from sales and debtors. Without the availability of large cash reserves or an overdraft facility many businesses are unable to bridge this gap and struggle to survive.

Factors to consider when choosing a source of finance

> **Purpose:** The business will need to consider the purpose for which the finance will be used. It's very important to apply the matching principle, so that short-term finance is used for short-term needs, etc.

> **Amount:** Long-term sources tend to be more suited for large amounts as the repayment schedule spreads the cost over a longer time period. This results in lower monthly repayments and is beneficial for cash flow.

> **Cost:** If the business plans to borrow money it's important to compare the APR of each possible source and lender. Even small differences in interest rates can have a big impact on the total costs involved, especially when borrowing large amounts over a long time period.

> **Security:** Many lenders will seek to protect themselves in the event of the borrower defaulting on the loan. Some business assets may be used as collateral against non-payment. Hire-purchase and leasing do not require any security.

> **Control:** Some sources of finance, for example a share issue, have the potential to affect the control of a business. New shareholders will be entitled to vote at the AGM and will have a say in how a business is run. They will also be entitled to a share of annual profits.

« Syllabus Signpost 5.5.9

Production Methods

If the new business is involved in manufacturing it will need to use at least one of the following production options:

> **Job production**   > **Batch production**   > **Mass production**

Job production

Job production involves the production of a single product. Very often this product is **made to order** or customised to the specific needs of a client. The uniqueness of this type of production as well as the need for highly skilled and specialist labour means that goods produced using job production will be expensive.

Job production is frequently used by sole traders operating in the craft industries, which are typified by highly skilled workers producing unique hand-made products.

Example

Customers will expect to pay more for a made-to-measure suit than for one which is widely available from a high street retailer. A skilled tailor will be required to make the suit and this employee will need to measure, cut and sew the fabric to meet the specific needs of the customer. Other examples include the production of hand-made glass, ships and designer wedding dresses.

Batch production

Batch production systems allow for a limited quantity of one good to be manufactured, before the same machinery is then used to produce a limited quantity, or **batch,** of a similar product.

Example

A bottling plant provides a good example of batch operation. The factory can be set up to produce and bottle cola for one day, before being reconfigured to allow lemonade to be bottled the next. A similar system operates in most bakeries, which use the same equipment and ovens to produce several varieties of cake and bread.

Generally speaking a batch production system is more automated than job production, while the labour is less skilled. Several employees are likely to be involved in the production of one product and this allows for some **specialisation of labour.** This means that individual workers only need to be trained to carry out a limited range of tasks.

If you choose to buy a suit from a high street retailer, you will find a range of sizes, styles and colours are available for you to choose from. That's because the manufacturer produces batches of similar products to meet the slightly varying needs of consumers. This product may not have the quality and uniqueness of a made-to-measure suit, but it will generally be cheaper.

Mass production

Mass production involves continuous production of very large quantities of identical products. It usually requires a highly automated production process and is therefore very capital intensive. Specialised equipment and the use of **computer-aided manufacturing (CAM)** allows for vast quantities of identical goods to be manufactured on a non-stop basis. Businesses which utilise this type of production tend to operate a shift system for staff, which minimises the downtime for machinery.

unit

5

By producing on such a large scale, the manufacturer benefits from **economies of scale.** These are cost savings which arise from large-scale operations and result from production efficiencies, discounts for bulk buying and the ability to spread research and marketing costs over a huge number of goods. The effect of all of this is to lower the per-unit production costs and provide mass producers with a significant cost advantage over their smaller rivals.

Mass production is used in a whole range of industries where large quantities of similar goods are produced. Examples include the production of ballpoint pens, cars and sweets. The very high capital and mass-marketing costs make mass production an unlikely option for many start-up businesses.

It's important to point out that these production options are not mutually exclusive, and many businesses use a combination of production methods.

A bakery will use batch production for most of its product range but may also utilise job production if personalised cakes are required.

A car manufacturer like Nissan uses mass production techniques for standardised components but batch production techniques when it needs to make variations to vehicle models or colours.

Alternative production options for business start-ups include **franchising** and **subcontracting/outsourcing.**

Franchising

A franchise is an agreement which allows an entrepreneur to adopt an existing business model. The person buying the franchise is called the franchisee while the seller of the business model is a franchisor.

Buying a franchise involves renting the franchisor's trademark and method of doing business. This usually involves a standardised approach to delivering a product or service.

Franchise arrangements exist across a whole range of industries but common examples include McDonald's, Subway, figure8 fitness and O2 mobile phone retailers.

Advantages of buying a franchise

> **Proven business model:** Since a proven business formula is in place and the corporate image and brand awareness is already established there is usually a much higher likelihood of success with a franchise. As consumers are always more comfortable purchasing items from a familiar name or company they trust, this gives the franchise an advantage over other business start-ups.

> **Ongoing support:** A tag line often used to promote franchise operations states that 'franchising allows entrepreneurs to be in business for themselves, but not by themselves'. Most franchisors offer some degree of ongoing marketing and operational support as well as extensive training and support to the franchise owner.

> **Cost savings (economies of scale):** It is also likely that all franchise outlets will benefit from the franchisor's marketing campaigns. Where raw materials are sourced from the franchisor's suppliers, cost savings are also possible due to bulk buying discounts.

> **Exclusivity:** A franchise agreement will allow the franchisee the exclusive right to sell a product or service in a specific location or geographic area. As this is a contractual arrangement they are reasonably assured that no other competing franchise will be permitted to set up in that location. A successful stand-alone business would not have such a guarantee of exclusivity.

Drawbacks of buying a franchise

> **Control:** In order to protect the value and reputation of their business model franchisors will exert some degree of control over the franchise operation and this will clearly limit a franchisee's ability to make changes. A contract will set out the specific requirements and conditions attached to each franchise, and these will often relate to key areas like product range, décor and service provision. If standards are not maintained, the contract may not be renewed.

> **Royalties and fees:** In most cases the franchisee must pay an ongoing franchise royalty fee, as well as an up-front, one-time franchise fee to the franchisor. When considering buying a franchise, an entrepreneur will need to weigh up the impact of these costs and balance them against the increased prospects for success which the franchise may offer.

Subcontracting

Subcontracting (also called outsourcing or licensing) means that a business will pay another supplier to manufacture some or all of its products.

Benefits of subcontracting

> **Lower set-up costs:** Subcontracting production to an outside manufacturer eliminates the need to buy expensive premises and machinery. This is particularly useful for seasonal producers whose costly machinery would operate at low output levels for long periods of time. Anhauser Busch avoided the enormous costs associated with building a brewery in Europe by subcontracting the production of Budweiser beer to Diagio.

> **Increased mobility:** Mobility is increased as the business is not tied to a production facility in any fixed location. Many transnational companies

unit

5

(TNCs), including Nike, see this as a big advantage as it allows a business to shop around for the cheapest supplier.

> **Additional production capacity:** Some businesses use subcontracting to supplement their own production facility and to fulfil customer orders when their own factory is operating at full capacity. The subcontractor is effectively used to deal with the overflow so that customers do not need to be turned away.

Drawbacks with subcontracting

> **Loss of control:** The subcontractor will be responsible for manufacturing the goods, so it is harder to ensure consistent control over quality. Nike appoints quality controllers whose specific role is to spend time in the factories where their goods are produced. They monitor the quality of raw materials and finished goods. Despite the presence of these monitors, factories involved in producing goods for Nike have sometimes been accused of poor standards of production and also of employing child labour. When issues like this arise they reflect badly on the Nike brand.

> **Loss of secrecy:** Subcontractors will need to have detailed knowledge of the products they are making and this may require disclosure of closely guarded design or production secrets. There is also a danger that in the longer term the subcontractor may become a rival by choosing to produce and market similar products under their own brand.

Business Plans

« *Syllabus Signpost* 5.5.10

A business plan is a detailed written plan outlining the key areas of a business proposal. It is used for both business start-ups and expansions.

Unit 3 outlined the importance of planning to the overall success of any business and a business plan is a critical first step for an entrepreneur contemplating a business start-up.

Purpose of a business plan

Sets clear goals

Writing a business plan forces an entrepreneur to focus clearly on the strategic objectives for their new business. They will need to set out realistic targets for key areas of the business including finance and profitability.

The requirement to produce a business plan effectively forces entrepreneurs to focus attention on all the key areas of a business start-up and should ultimately increase the chances of success.

Seeks investment

It allows potential investors or banks to evaluate the level or risk to their investment. For this reason, potential shareholders and investors will insist on a realistic business plan before making a financial commitment to the business. As it is almost impossible to start a business without some form of external investment, a business plan is critical to the viability of the project.

Improves co-ordination

The availability of a business plan allows all managers and employees to adopt a co-ordinated approach to business activities. All stakeholders have a clear blueprint to follow and this will ensure that everyone works towards the same goals.

Assists control

As the business develops, the business plan can be used as a benchmark against which to measure performance. Areas of weakness can be easily identified and management can take steps to get the fledgling business back on track. If, for example, actual sales levels are below those projected in the business plan, management may need to intervene by altering some elements of the marketing mix. A fresh approach to advertising or a price reduction may solve the problem once it has been identified.

Establishes viability of start-up

The business plan would normally include a break-even chart, a cash flow forecast and projections for future profitability. This will allow managers and investors to establish the commercial viability of this potential start-up.

Contents of a business plan

A business plan looks at **what** a business intends to do; **who** will carry out this work as well as **how** exactly these goals are to be achieved.

The plan itself will be divided into several sections, each dealing with a key aspect of the business. When preparing a business plan it's important to follow the required structure and layout and also to remember that the business plan will be used to 'sell the business' to prospective investors. Since many of those reading the plan have no prior knowledge of the business or its aims, the business plan needs to be sufficiently detailed to allow them to make an informed decision. A business plan which is poorly presented or which is missing key information will not create a good first impression and is unlikely to convince investors to part with their money.

What's involved?

> **Nature of business:** Potential shareholders, investors and suppliers will need to be given a brief outline of the products/services which the new business is proposing to bring to market.

In order to establish both the needs and the potential for the start-up business it will be necessary to emphasise its **unique selling point (USP)**. The unique selling point is what makes this new business different from all similar companies.

A business which fails to offer something new or which fails to fill an obvious gap in the market is unlikely to attract much support from customers or investors.

unit

5

279

Who's involved?

> **Ownership:** The business plan should also contain some background information about the entrepreneurs behind the new business. Potential investors or business partners will be keen to establish their qualifications and experience, as these are likely to impact on the success of the new venture.

The importance of the entrepreneurs to the success of the business should not be underestimated and investors are only likely to take a risk when entrepreneurs offer a credible proposal and a strong likelihood of actually delivering on that proposal.

Investors on programmes like *Dragons' Den* frequently comment on their enthusiasm for a product idea, but declare that they are unwilling to make an investment simply because they don't believe that the people behind the venture are capable of making it succeed. This really amounts to saying 'right idea; wrong people' and only serves to emphasise the importance of the personnel involved.

In situations where entrepreneurs lack the personal skills or experience needed to operate the business, they can employ professional managers to bridge the gap and this should be outlined clearly in the business plan.

This section of the business plan should also outline the ownership or legal structure for the new business. This means stating whether it's a partnership, a co-operative or a limited company.

How will goals be achieved?

> **Production plan:** This section of the business plan looks specifically at operational issues such as acquiring suitable premises, machinery and equipment. It also sets out the type of production which the new business will engage in. For most small-scale start-ups this is likely to be a combination of job and batch production.

> **Marketing plan:** The marketing plan outlines the target market for the new goods and services and also deals with vital issues such as product positioning and the marketing mix. A detailed discussion of all marketing concepts can be found in *Chapter 15: Marketing*.

> **Financial plan:** An outline of the capital structure and financial requirements for the new business will be set out in the financial plan. Investors will be able to see the level of debt and equity involved as well as projected cash flow forecasts, sales forecasts and profit projections. This section is vitally important to investors and it needs to be both accurate and realistic.

Sample Business Plan

Paula and Thomas have recently returned to Ireland having worked with transnational companies for 10 years. They wish to set up in business together in Ireland manufacturing a range of new organic breakfast cereals. Paula has particular expertise in production and finance and Thomas in marketing and human resources.   *LCHL 2006 Q6 (a)*

Draft a Business Plan for this proposed new business using five main headings, outlining the contents under each heading. *(40 marks)*

5 @ 8 marks each (2+3+3)

Marks are awarded for listing suitable headings and explaining the type of information which would be contained in each section of the business plan. This is a bit like a mini ABQ, as you have been given details of a specific business proposal upon which to base your answer. All key headings are included and while some basic information was provided in the question, other relevant details have been added in order to illustrate our understanding of each section. While a real business plan may be several pages in length, it's important to remember that in exam situations your time will be limited, so make sure to include the most relevant headings and information.

Suggested Solution

Nature of Business: *(2)* The new business will manufacture a new range of organic breakfast cereals. All ingredients will be sourced from certified organic suppliers. *(+3)* The intention is to produce a top quality premium brand which will initially be sold in health stores and to health spas. *(+3)*

Ownership/Key Personnel: *(2)* The business will be set up as a private limited company in which there will be two shareholders, Paula and Thomas Smith. *(+3)*

Both have worked overseas with transnational companies for ten years. Paula has experience in production and finance and Thomas in marketing and human resources. They intend to employ a full-time production manager with experience in the organic food industry. *(+3)*

Production: *(2)* Initially the business will operate from rented premises which have been fully equipped to meet production needs of the business. *(+3)* As a range of different breakfast cereals are on offer, a batch production system will be used. *(+3)*

Marketing: *(2)* Market research has highlighted a high level of demand for these products and there is strong evidence of annual growth. All competitors currently in the market are small producers, and only one of these is an indigenous firm. *(+3)* The product will be targeted at health-conscious consumers of all ages. Initial distribution will be via health stores and health spas. Contracts have already been signed with two major health resorts in Ireland. This is a top-quality product and this will be reflected in the premium price of the product range. Point of sale promotion will be used extensively and we will run a series of adverts in health and lifestyle magazines. *(+3)*

Finance: *(2)* Owners will each invest share capital of €25,000 and they intend to borrow an additional €40,000 to finance capital needs. *(+3)* Thomas will also contribute an additional €8,000 for working capital needs and this will be supplemented by a bank overdraft when necessary. *(+3)*

unit
5

Chapter Review Diagram – Getting Started

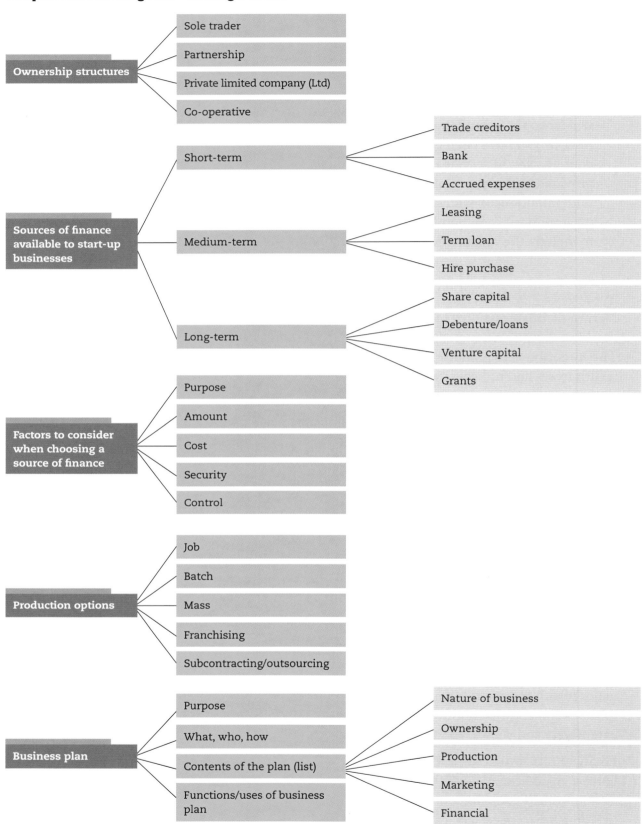

Ownership structures
- Sole trader
- Partnership
- Private limited company (Ltd)
- Co-operative

Sources of finance available to start-up businesses
- Short-term
  - Trade creditors
  - Bank
  - Accrued expenses
- Medium-term
  - Leasing
  - Term loan
  - Hire purchase
- Long-term
  - Share capital
  - Debenture/loans
  - Venture capital
  - Grants

Factors to consider when choosing a source of finance
- Purpose
- Amount
- Cost
- Security
- Control

Production options
- Job
- Batch
- Mass
- Franchising
- Subcontracting/outsourcing

Business plan
- Purpose
- What, who, how
- Contents of the plan (list)
  - Nature of business
  - Ownership
  - Production
  - Marketing
  - Financial
- Functions/uses of business plan

Chapter Review Questions

1 Outline four major reasons why entrepreneurs are motivated to start their own businesses.

2 List four types of ownership structure that are suitable for start-up businesses.

3 Apart from choice of ownership structure, list three other key issues facing start-up businesses.

4 Explain the term 'sole trader'.

5 Outline two advantages and two disadvantages of being a sole trader.

6 Explain the term 'deed of partnership'.

7 Outline the main issues set out in a deed of partnership.

8 Outline two advantages and two disadvantages of partnerships.

9 Outline three key features of a private limited company.

10 Distinguish between memorandum of association and articles of association.

11 Outline the advantages and disadvantages associated with operating as a limited company.

12 Explain the term 'limited liability'.

13 What are the key features of a co-operative ownership structure?

14 List four different types of co-operative that are common in Ireland.

15 What are the factors that a business will consider when choosing a business location?

16 Outline three sources of finance which are available to start-up businesses.

17 Name and explain five factors to consider when choosing a source of finance.

18 Outline three alternative production options for business start-ups.

19 What are the advantages and disadvantages of buying a franchise?

20 List the main contents of a business plan.

21 Outline the main reasons for preparing a business plan.

unit

5

Q Questions · Ordinary Level

1 Explain **two** advantages of a partnership as a form of business. *LCOL 2011 (15 marks)*

2

> **Maria's Design Knitwear Ltd**
>
> Maria has always loved designing and knitting clothes for family and friends. Over the past two years she supplied local boutiques with some of her products and they are proving to be a great success. Maria now wants to turn her hobby into a business. She has received advice from local business consultant Dermot Jones. He advised her to set up a limited company which would give her the advantage of limited liability. He also advised her to conduct market research, to decide on her advertising media, to decide on her target market and to think about a brand name.

What is meant by 'the advantage of limited liability' as referred to above?

LCOL 2011 (10 marks)

3 Outline **two** benefits of preparing a business plan. *LCOL 2011 (10 marks)*

4 State **two** advantages of a private limited company. *LCOL 2010 (10 marks)*

5 State **two** advantages and **two** disadvantages of a sole trader business.

LCOL 2010 (20 marks)

6 (a) What is a Credit Union?

(b) Briefly explain **two** services of a Credit Union to its members. *LCOL 2008 (20 marks)*

7 Identify **two** risks and **two** rewards for a sole trader if they wish to set up their own business.

8 Outline **three** sources of new business ideas for a sole trader.

9 Explain the term 'franchise'. *LCOL 2007 (10 marks)*

10 Outline **two** differences between a co-operative and a limited company.

LCOL 2007 (10 marks)

11 (a) Apart from batch production, name **two** other types of production used in business.

(b) Outline **three** features of batch production. *LCOL 2007 (15 marks)*

Questions · Higher Level

1 Discuss **two** possible challenges associated with starting a new business.

LCHL 2011 (10 marks)

2

Marie Nolan is the owner of 'Marie's Pizzas', a successful pizza restaurant with a home-delivery service. Demand for take-aways has increased, as more people are eating at home due to the economic downturn. Marie is planning to expand her business through franchising and her accountant recommends that a business plan should be prepared before going ahead. *LCHL 2010*

(a) Evaluate franchising (benefits and risks) as a method of expansion for the pizza business. *(20 marks)*

(b) Outline **two** benefits to Marie's Pizzas of preparing a business plan. *(10 marks)*

3 Evaluate 'franchising' as a form of business ownership for a new enterprise.

LCHL 2009 (20 marks)

4 Outline the functions of a business plan.

5 Distinguish between the **three** main production options available to a start-up business.

6 Describe the main factors to be considered when setting up a business.

unit
5

Chapter 15
Marketing

Syllabus Outcomes

On completion of this chapter, the student should be able to:

» 5.5.6 Identify the main elements of a marketing strategy;

» 5.5.7 Explain the elements of the marketing mix;

» 5.5.15 Evaluate the elements of the marketing mix (HL).

News Flash

Brand managers adapt as social media sites put power in hands of consumers

by Siobhán O'Connell

A recent awards show indicated how firms are now using social media to promote themselves

Individuals use Facebook and Twitter to share their lives with friends and family, they don't expect a return on investment.

For businesses, though, the only reason companies invest in social media is to connect with more customers and ultimately sell more stuff...

Singled out for praise at the recent Social Media Awards was mobile phone network Meteor. This wasn't a huge surprise, as Meteor brands itself as "your social network" and the company's primary target market is young people.

It follows that Meteor has to have an impressive digital presence to support the brand identity.

In practical terms, making the most of social media can mean leveraging off mass marketing such as television advertising.

For instance, Meteor's TV commercial last Christmas centred on a Scrooge-type boss. On Facebook, Meteor devised a game using the characters from the commercials and it attracted 20,000 players...

Social media is of most relevance to transactional websites. Social features integrated on the website can improve e-commerce revenues and boost consumer loyalty. Such features include Facebook like, follow or share; e-mail to a friend; share and follow links; product reviews by customers; Twitter tweet or follow and Facebook store.

Web consultancy Amas recently reviewed 100 Irish e-commerce sites, ranking them by how many of 10 social features the websites were deploying. On the Amas criteria, the most social websites are Amazon, HMV, CD Wow and Littlewoods.

Among Irish retailers, the most sociable are Dabs, Elverys, Carrolls Irish Gifts, ESB, Meteor and Micksgarage...

This is an edited extract from **The Irish Times**, THURSDAY, 9 JUNE 2011.

For more up-to-date newspaper articles see www.edcodigital.ie

1 Read the newspaper extract opposite and discuss the issues raised.

2 Can you explain any of the highlighted terms?

What is marketing?

Marketing is a key part of success in modern business, but it can be a difficult concept to define, and for some businesses, a very difficult concept to implement.

A short brainstorm on the topic 'What is marketing?' is likely to unearth words like 'selling', 'advertising', 'market research', 'target market' and 'marketing mix'. All of these words go some way towards explaining what marketing is, but each of these represents just one aspect of marketing and this list is missing some important and relevant terms.

Marketing involves **identifying customer needs,** and attempting to **satisfy these needs** through the production of goods and services. It is a process which begins with market research and incorporates design, manufacture, advertising, selling and distribution as well as after-sales service.

Above all else, **marketing helps businesses to sell goods to customers.** Market research, advertising, sales promotion and the correct marketing mix are all elements in this process and will be examined in more detail throughout this chapter.

While we may struggle to compose a tidy little definition for marketing, we must not underestimate its impact on so many aspects of modern businesses. When you consider the range of activities involved in marketing you can begin to have some understanding of the complexities involved.

What is the marketing concept?

Rather than simply producing goods and then attempting to convince consumers of the need to buy them **(product orientation),** modern businesses tend to be more customer-focused and will utilise the **marketing concept.** This recognises that satisfying customer needs is the best route to success. Businesses which apply the marketing concept in this way are said to have a **market orientation.**

A business which is applying the marketing concept will only succeed if it can clearly identify customer needs and then utilise its resources to satisfy them profitably. This is usually achieved by undertaking market research and this forms the basis for developing a **marketing strategy.**

« *syllabus signpost*
5.5.6

Marketing Strategy and Marketing Plans

The marketing strategy attempts to map out the overall marketing goals for the business. It sets out the manner in which the business can identify and meet the needs of its target market. The **target market** is the particular group of people a product

unit

5

or service is being aimed at. This strategic plan should provide management with direction, co-ordination, financial evaluation and a means of control. A marketing strategy is usually developed with a multi-year focus and will be supported by more product-specific tactical plans. These shorter-term tactical plans need to allow for flexibility and revision because marketing is a very dynamic business activity. This flexibility also reflects the fact that marketing efforts can be hindered by a huge number of variables. These include product issues, customer tastes, the business environment and competitor reactions. A prudent business will also need to prepare contingency plans in case things don't go smoothly.

Case Study

When Sunny Delight was launched in the UK in 1998, the soft drink was stocked in the 'chill cabinet' section of supermarkets and marketed as a healthy alternative to soft drinks. Sales soared and it soon began to challenge Coke and Pepsi as the market leader.

When health watchdogs highlighted the fact that the product contained very high levels of sugar and just 5 per cent juice, consumers were turned off the product in huge numbers, and there were even claims that one girl who drank too much of the product had her skin turn orange.

The bad publicity surrounding these issues proved to be the death-knell for the successful brand. The lack of a credible 'Plan B' led to the demise of Sunny Delight, which was eventually redesigned and relaunched as SunnyD in 2003. Despite these changes, its current sales and market shares are just a fraction of their peak values.

So what exactly are the **strategic aims of marketing**? Possible answers to this question include:

> To increase sales and market share
> To improve profitability
> To enter a new market
> To enhance the product image

Depending on which of these long-term goals is being pursued, the business will need to formulate tactical plans and a marketing mix capable of delivering success.

Key elements of the marketing strategy will include:

> **Identifying the target market**
> **Market research**
> **Market segmentation**

> **Product positioning**
> Development of the **marketing mix**

unit 5

Identifying the target market

The target market is the specific group of people a product or service is being aimed at. For example, the target market for this text book would be Leaving Certificate business students and their teachers. Once a target market has been clearly identified a business can set about identifying and meeting the needs of this particular section of the population. Target markets are often defined by gender, age and income.

Activity

Can you identify possible target markets for these goods?

> Electric cars   > Wetsuits   > Games consoles   > Pre-packed sliced meat

Market research

This is a process of gathering and analysing information in order to identify customer needs. Once these needs have been identified it should make it easier for a business to meet them successfully. It needs to be understood that market research is carried out by entrepreneurs who are contemplating starting a new business but also by existing businesses that need to get feedback from customers on existing product ranges or marketing strategies. A combination of approaches is usually applied:

> **Desk research:** Desk research involves using information already available from other sources. These may include government statistics, media reports and rival companies. This is regarded as secondary research and although relatively easy to compile it may lack accuracy in relation to the questions we want answered.

> **Field research:** Those engaged in field research gather new information themselves, by asking their own questions. This is primary research and is more costly and time-consuming to collect. On the plus side it's likely to be more accurate for their specific needs. Field research generally involves observing consumer behaviour or conducting surveys.

In addition to highlighting consumer needs, market research also provides information on levels of demand, competition, price sensitivity, niche markets and feedback on existing products. All of this helps a business reduce the risk involved in the product-development process and should increase sales and profitability. See also *Chapter 13: Identifying Opportunities*.

Market segmentation

When analysing its target market a business may realise that the total market for a product can be sub-divided into smaller segments, and that each segment may have different needs. In order to maximise profits a firm should attempt to satisfy the needs of each segment.

unit

5

Have you ever considered why most soft drinks are sold in cans and also in 500ml plastic bottles, two-litre multi-packs, in glass bottles, as well as through dispensers?

It's an attempt by producers to meet the needs of individuals, families, publicans and cinema-goers, as each of these represents a **segment** of the overall market for their product.

Drinks manufacturers have realised that if they only sell their product using a 'one size fits all' approach, they will not maximise their sales and profits. Similar thinking has led to the development of diet, low-sugar and low-caffeine versions of these popular drinks.

Businesses use a whole range of measurable consumer characteristics when attempting to segment their target market. Examples include age, nationality, gender, location and income. Here are some common methods of segmenting a market:

Geographic segmentation

According to:

> Region of the country
> Urban or rural

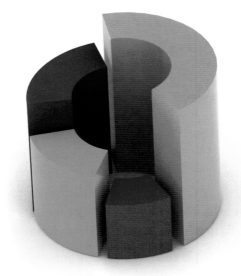

This type of segmentation is common in the media and publications business where local radio stations and local newspapers seek to target people in a specific geographic area.

Demographic segmentation

According to:

> Age, gender, family size
> Income, occupation, education
> Religion, race, nationality

An enormous number of markets are segmented on a demographic basis, and examples include the food and drinks industry, which provides goods for small and large family units. The clothing industry also produces goods which are gender-specific.

Psychographic segmentation

According to:

> Social class   > Lifestyle type   > Personality type

Products like cars and newspapers use these criteria to help segment their customers. Some newspapers, like the *Irish Times,* are aimed at readers in the upper social classes while most of the tabloids tend to target working-class readers.

Cars are also produced to suit lifestyle needs and often reflect the buyer's personality. Can you think of a car which would suit a person with an adventurous personality? What car might suit a conservative driver?

unit
5

Behavioural segmentation

According to:

> Product usage (light, medium, heavy users)
> Brand loyalty (none, medium, high)

As outlined previously, multipacks are manufactured to cater for the needs of customers who have ongoing heavy demand for a product. Some manufacturers also produce smaller portions of their product, which suit those with light usage or occasional demand.

Heinz and Bachelors baked beans can be bought in family multipacks and also in half-size tins.

Activity

Having previously identified possible target markets for electric cars, wetsuits, games consoles and pre-packed sliced meat, can you identify different market segments which might exist for these products?

Market analysis may also highlight the existence of **niche markets.** These are small, specialist segments of a larger market. Very often a small producer may be able to profitably serve these 'gaps' in the market. Markets for specialist sports equipment and bridal footwear would be examples. As job or batch production techniques are often used to manufacture these products, they tend to be more expensive than mass-produced goods.

The term **product portfolio** is used to describe the range of products a firm produces in order to satisfy the needs of each market segment.

Example

Kellogg's have an extensive product portfolio which includes Coco Pops, Rice Krispies, Corn Flakes, Bran Flakes, Start and Special K. This recognises that consumer needs vary in the breakfast cereal market and it is more profitable to serve each segment rather than just produce one type of cereal for all.

Product positioning

This identifies where a firm chooses to place its product relative to those of its competitors. For example, in the car market a BMW might be positioned at the luxury or 'executive' end of the market, while a Fiat Punto is positioned as an economy family car.

« *syllabus signpost*
5.5.7

unit
5

Marketing mix

The four P's

In order to maximise sales and profits businesses need to find the optimum combination of four key elements:

> **Product**   > **Place**

> **Price**   > **Promotion**

If any one of these elements is deficient it will undermine the entire mix, so it's important to recognise the pivotal role of each of these four individual elements. A successful marketing mix is about having the 'right product', at the 'right price', available in all the 'right places' and also ensuring that people in the target market are aware of its availability. This is achieved by using the most suitable types of promotion.

Getting the **optimal blend of elements** is a very difficult task and is complicated by a number of variable factors relating to each element of the marketing mix. These major issues are outlined in the pages which follow.

The Marketing Mix – Product

The product element deals not only with the provision of goods but also with services which meet the needs of the target market.

In the entertainment industry it is even possible that people, or more specifically artists, could be classified as 'products'. Most pop stars and bands produce music which is sold on CDs or via download; they also perform live shows for which fans buy tickets. The artists are heavily marketed in an industry where image is vitally important. Different types of music and artists are used to target different segments of the market.

For more traditional products, market research should provide a starting point by highlighting the needs of consumers. From there it's necessary to implement the product development process (see *Chapter 13: Identifying Opportunities*).

The main product issues will relate to:

> Developing a **unique selling point** (USP)

> **Design**   > **Packaging**   > **Branding**   > **Product life cycle**

Unique selling point

A unique selling point is what makes the products of one company different from its rivals and each business will try to implant this uniqueness in the minds of consumers. Marketers will also attempt to convince buyers that this uniqueness also makes their product better than competitors' products. If successful they will increase brand loyalty and sales.

e.g. Example

For many years Volvo used superior safety features as a unique selling point before this advantage was copied and eroded by rivals.

Toblerone uses its unique shape to distinguish it from other chocolate products.

Lyons have used innovative pyramid-shaped tea bags to give an element of uniqueness to their brand.

Cadbury emphasise the 'glass and a half' in every half pound of their chocolate which suggests to consumers that it is the 'milkiest' milk chocolate available.

Design

The product or service will have the greatest chance of commercial success if it fulfils the needs of its target market. Companies spend a huge amount of time and money trying to understand the buying motives of consumers.

The **'core product'** refers to the primary function of the product, and represents the main reason why consumers will choose to buy a product. A lawnmower, for example, is bought to cut grass while a car is seen as method of transport. Any goods or services which don't fulfil their core function will be rejected by consumers. A business can usually satisfy consumer concerns by ensuring its product is 'fit for its purpose' and is safe and reliable. For example, a person buying a car will have a wide range of makes and models to choose from but ultimately they will choose a car which will start reliably and will enable them to transport their family safely.

It would, however, be simplistic to assume that reliability will be the only factor affecting a consumer's choice of vehicle, especially since most cars will meet this criterion. For that reason manufacturers will need to find other ways to enhance their product or service offering in the eyes of the consumer. The **augmented product** includes all of these extras which help to sell a product. They include extra features, brand name, image, style, quality, packaging, guarantees and so on.

In our car example, brand name, style and image may also be important. Manufacturers can also augment their vehicles by adding alloy wheels, high spec music systems, air conditioning and additional safety features.

It is this combination of functionality and form which will be used to create a unique product offering. **Packaging** can also play a role in developing this product identity.

unit

5

Packaging

From a marketing point of view the packaging used on a product is more than just a container. It often fulfils several different roles.

> **Protection:** All products need to be protected from damage and from contamination. Manufacturers do, however, need to be mindful of the additional costs and environmental impact associated with extra packaging.

> **Presentation:** From the manufacturer's point of view, attractive, eye-catching packaging is a necessity in order to make their products stand out. The colours used on packaging often reflect the target market. For example, Kellogg's Coco Pops have bright yellow packaging with cartoon imagery, whereas products like Corn Flakes and Bran Flakes have much more 'grown up' colour schemes.

> **Information:** Very often there are legal requirements which oblige manufacturers to include certain information on product packaging. Examples include lists of ingredients on food products, 'use by' dates and storage instructions, as well as health and safety guidelines. While serving suggestions and operating instructions are not legal requirements on most products, they are often added by manufacturers as they enhance the consumers' experience of the product.

> **Identity:** Some products use their packaging as an identifying feature. Toblerone is an obvious example of a confectionery product which uses unique packaging to help it stand out from the crowd. How do the makers of After Eight chocolates use packaging to create a unique identity for their product?

This attempt to provide a unique identity for a particular range of products using packaging is a vital step towards developing a **brand.**

Branding

A brand name is a primary identifying feature and is usually registered with the Controller of Patents, Trade Marks and Designs, in order to protect against imitation. This has the effect of making it a legally protected USP.

Functions and benefits of a brand name

> **Makes a product recognisable** and helps customers to choose between similar products. The brand name and logo used by Adidas make their products instantly recognisable. This is an important advantage in a very competitive and crowded market.

> **Differentiates product from rivals** and promotes brand loyalty. Manufacturers want their goods to stand out and they also want consumers to make brand-specific purchases. Ideally they hope consumers will have already decided on choice of brands before entering the shop. When you decide you're thirsty and in need of a cola drink, both Pepsi and Coca Cola will be hoping that you will enter the shop with their specific brand in mind.

> **Conveys an image and supports the price.** This is usually an image of quality which reflects the premium price. This suggests that consumers will often be

prepared to pay a higher price for a branded product and it arises from the perceived reliability or image of the product. There is often an assumption, sometimes incorrect, that branded goods are of better quality. Producers will certainly do nothing to discourage this perception and will claim that the higher price justifies their investment in the brand.

> **Helps introduction of new products.** Once consumers are familiar with a brand and recognise what it stands for, they are more likely to be positive towards latest releases. Consumers who have bought O'Neills sportswear in the past and have been happy with the product will be willing to buy other products from the O'Neills range. The manufacturer will not have to launch additional advertising campaigns to support new products.

Own brands

Own brands are brand names which have been registered by retailers rather than manufacturers. Examples include the Savida brand used by Dunnes Stores, the Per Una brand developed by Marks and Spencer and a range of own-brand products by supermarket multiples such as Tesco and SuperValu.

These represent a range of goods which are sold exclusively in their shops and are usually produced by independent manufacturers who are under contract to the retailer.

Benefits of own brands

> **Retailers** benefit from cheaper products which helps attract extra customers. The retailer also receives a huge advertising benefit because of their association with the brand.

> **Consumers** benefit from lower prices and a greater choice of products.

> **Producers** benefit from extra sales which are achieved with lower manufacturing and marketing costs.

Underpinning all of this product and brand development is an understanding of the **product life cycle.** Businesses need to understand that products, like people, have a natural life cycle and the age of a product will have a bearing on the marketing effort required.

Product life cycle

This concept is based on the principle that all products brought to market go through the same five-stage life cycle. It should be noted, however, that the duration of this life cycle differs with each product. That is to say that some products, like Wrangler jeans or Kellogg's Corn Flakes, have very long life cycles, whereas seasonal products tend to come and go very quickly.

unit

5

The diagram below shows the level of **sales** achieved by a typical product over **time.**

Product life cycle

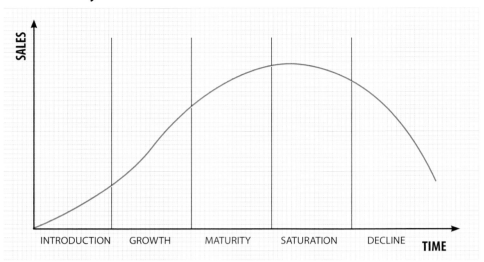

Stage 1: Introduction

At this point in its life cycle the product has successfully negotiated the product development process and has just been launched onto the market. Consumer awareness and sales are both likely to be low. For this reason a business will tend to focus its efforts on distribution, advertising and sales promotion in order to improve awareness and sales. The business will need to decide on a suitable marketing campaign and will need to adopt an appropriate pricing strategy. Depending on the pricing strategy chosen and the overall level of sales, the new product may be loss-making at this stage. It is important to manage cash flow very carefully at this stage since the costs associated with raw materials, manufacturing and marketing are likely to far outweigh the ability of the new product to generate sales revenue.

Stage 2: Growth

If the marketing and distribution efforts are successful sales should rise sharply during the growth phase. Media advertising, merchandising and word of mouth can be very effective in creating interest in a new product. Once consumers try the product they will hopefully be convinced of its benefit and value and continue to purchase it. Improved sales and lower marketing costs bring improved profitability.

For some products, where sales grow too rapidly, the business is unable to fulfil orders and runs the risk of **overtrading.** This means the business cannot support the level of business being generated. For example, there may not be enough cash to buy raw materials and pay variable production costs like wages. If borrowings are used to address the shortfall in working capital this may lead to liquidity problems.

unit 5

Stage 3: Maturity

At this point in its life cycle sales of the product are still growing, but at a much slower rate. Most sales are repeat orders rather than first-time purchases. The product is now well established and may need updating. The business will need to ensure it's not over-reliant on this single product, which is now ageing and facing competition. If it has not already done so, the business will need to develop new products.

The cash flow situation should be greatly improved at this stage since a well-established product requires less advertising and is capable of generating high levels of sales revenue.

Introduction → Growth → Maturity → Saturation → Decline

Stage 4: Saturation

During this stage there is no more room to expand the market for a product. Sales level off and reach their peak during the saturation phase. The only way to increase sales is to take customers from rivals. A business may choose to introduce competitive promotion and pricing policies to achieve this objective. Some businesses might try to extend the life cycle of their product by using an **extension strategy** (see below).

Stage 5: Decline

Eventually the product is overtaken by rival products and demand falls. A firm may try to upgrade or re-launch the product or may simply decide to cut advertising and maximise profit. This is called **product harvesting**.

When a product has reached the end of its life cycle it becomes obsolete and will be replaced.

Extension strategies

The aim of these strategies is to prolong the life cycle of a product and businesses often use them during the maturity and saturation stages. Most extension strategies involve either **product development** or **market development.**

> **Product development strategies** seek to modify and revamp the existing product to make it more appealing or to develop the number of products in the product line. If you consider the number of product innovations which take place in the washing powder industry you get some idea of what's involved. Each 'new improved' version of the product is designed to outperform its predecessor and its rivals. Over the years we've seen a progression from powder to liquids, then to non-biological and concentrated liquids, with each claiming to leave clothes cleaner and fresher than anything which had gone before.

> **Market development strategies** attempt to find new markets or new uses for existing products and are really an attempt at market segmentation or niche marketing. Tobacco companies may choose to market heavily in developing countries to counteract declining sales in Europe and the United States.

unit 5

Example

Lucozade was traditionally given to people who were ill, on account of its high level of glucose. As it became less popular and sales began to decline, the makers of Lucozade decided to market a related product, Lucozade Sport, to athletes.

The Marketing Mix – Price

For this element of the marketing mix, it is important to understand the factors which influence prices for goods and services as well as the pricing strategies adopted by businesses.

Factors influencing price

Production costs

Commercial businesses need to make a profit, so in the long run their pricing strategy must allow them to recoup production costs. While it may be possible for businesses to sell at or below cost for a short period of time this is not a sustainable position for a commercial business. Management obviously need to be able to calculate production costs accurately if they are to succeed in this objective.

Demand

When demand for a product exceeds the available supply, prices will tend to increase. You will know all about this if you have ever tried to get tickets for a concert or football match after they'd sold out. This also gives us an understanding of why regulatory authorities are unwilling to allow companies to dominate a particular market. Once a firm has a near monopoly position it can restrict supply and force prices upwards. This is not a positive development for consumers.

Competitors

Firms may also need to set prices in line with rivals or they will risk losing market share. Compare the premium pricing policy adopted by Aer Lingus in the era before Ryanair emerged as a rival with the low-cost model it was forced to adopt to compete with the budget carrier. Do you think it's just coincidental that rival cola brands have identical prices, or does it suggest each is aware of the price sensitivity of consumers?

Consumer expectations

The willingness of consumers to pay for certain goods will be influenced by their perception of 'value for money' as well as overall income levels. During the property boom from 2000 to 2007, Irish consumers expected to pay very high prices for property and were willing to commit to large mortgages partly because they expected prices to continue rising. It may

unit 5

seem somewhat subtle, but there is a difference between the price of a three-bedroom semi-detached house and what that three-bedroom semi is actually worth. Following the property crash, house buyers have been more focused on 'worth' and now insist on value for money. Sellers have been forced to reduce prices to reflect this change in consumer sentiment.

Type of goods/services

Price sensitivity can vary depending on the type of goods involved. For basic goods such as bread and milk, consumers will often switch brands to avoid price increases.

Smokers, on the other hand, are less likely to quit or switch brands when prices rise. Services which are non-transferable (e.g. hairdressing, medical costs) are also less price sensitive.

Pricing strategies

Bearing in mind the factors outlined above, the following pricing strategies are commonly used by businesses:

Cost plus (mark-up pricing)

This simply involves adding a certain percentage to production costs in order to satisfy the desired profit level. For example, if a 50 per cent mark-up is used, goods purchased for €10 would be sold by the retailer at €15.

Each business will need to decide the percentage mark-up to charge and whether to use a single mark-up on all goods or whether it should apply different percentages to different types of products.

Premium pricing

This involves charging a high price for goods which are deemed to be of high quality or value, e.g. designer clothing. Many branded goods are marketed as being 'exclusive' or desirable and therefore carry a premium price. While the quality and originality of the goods may justify some of the price increase, many believe that consumers are willing to pay more for particular brands. This once again illustrates the value of a strong brand to the business which has developed it.

Penetration pricing

This strategy is used by firms who wish to break into a new market quickly. It achieves this by initially charging a low price in order to build up market share for a new product. Once established, prices may rise to industry norms. This strategy is often used by publishing firms who sell the first issues of a magazine at a low 'introductory' price. Prices will later rise to meet industry norms.

unit 5

Competitive pricing

This means setting prices in line with rivals in order to remain competitive in the market. Aer Lingus and Ryanair or Aldi and Lidl are examples of companies which compete closely on price. Coca Cola and Pepsi set identical prices for their products too.

Sometimes a business will use a very competitive pricing strategy in an attempt to force its rivals out of the market. This means dropping prices to very low levels which weaker competitors may find unsustainable. When businesses compete by lowering prices in this way, they are engaging in a **price war.** The strategy employed is called **predatory pricing.**

Below-cost selling

Now legal in Ireland, this practice allows firms to sell goods at less than cost price. Goods sold in this way are called 'loss leaders'. The aim here is to use these cheap products to attract customers to the business in the hope they will buy other goods on which profit can be made.

Example

> A supermarket decides to sell a range of meat and dairy products below cost price for a limited time. Advertising and word of mouth will hopefully succeed in attracting extra customers from rival supermarkets. Many of these new customers will buy all of the groceries they need there, not just the discounted meat and dairy products. Overall sales will increase and the profit made on other items should more than compensate the retailer for the losses on the meat and dairy.

While these low prices may appear to benefit the consumer, this practice is controversial.

There is a danger that pressure from low-cost retailers can force producers to supply goods at unprofitable levels. Since the producer may not be in a position to recoup these losses from other products, some producers may be forced out of the market, with resulting job losses.

There are also concerns about the types of products which retailers choose to sell below cost. The licensed vintners association and medical experts are united in their criticism of below-cost selling of alcohol. There are obvious health and social consequences of overconsumption, while pubs which are unable to compete with the low prices may be forced to close.

Case Study

In September 2011 Lidl was criticised by the Minister of State for Health for selling wine below cost and the incident raised the possibility of a minimum price being imposed for alcohol sold in the state.

The price of alcohol in Irish supermarkets has fallen dramatically since the abolition in 2006 of the Groceries Order, which had outlawed below-cost selling. The alcohol market in Ireland is worth more than €6 billion a year and off-sales are frequently used as a loss leader by supermarkets.

Peak-load pricing

A strategy of maximising profits by charging a higher price on goods for which there is strong demand. Flight costs and hotel prices tend to increase during peak season. Obvious examples include travel costs during school and summer holidays and also in the run-up to major sporting or cultural events. The travel industry knows the level of demand will enable them to fill all available flights and hotel rooms even at higher prices. Lower prices will typically apply for off-peak travel.

Price skimming

This practice occurs where high prices are charged on new product ranges, and prices will eventually be lowered as competition increases. Manufacturers will justify this as an attempt to recoup development costs for expensive technologies, e.g. PlayStation 3, Nintendo Wii.

It may, however, be the case that lack of competition allows for an initial high price and also that some consumers are willing to pay a premium price for trend-setting and innovative technology. This group of consumers are known as **early adopters.**

Adoption of innovations over time

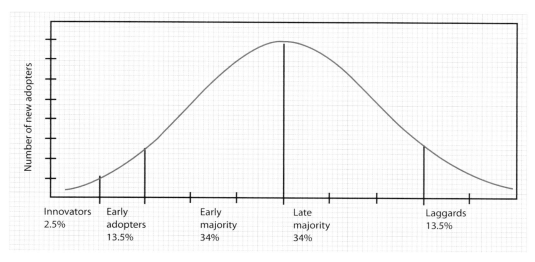

unit

5

> **Innovators:** a small minority of people who always seek to have the latest technology or product.

> **Early adopters:** opinion leaders who also like to try out new ideas. They approach new innovations in a more sceptical and considered way than innovators.

> **Early majority:** a large percentage of the population who are willing to embrace new technology ahead of most people. They are willing to buy new products once they have started to have a more established market presence.

> **Late majority:** another large percentage of the population who eventually embrace the new technology once it has become very popular and its continuity is assured.

> **Laggards:** a section of the population who tend to embrace tradition and are reluctant to adopt innovative technology or products. They may eventually be forced to accept mainstream ideas once traditional products have become obsolete.

The Marketing Mix – Place

The place element of the marketing mix is really about distribution and getting goods to customers. It's important to choose a **channel of distribution** which is accessible to members of the target market.

The following channels of distribution are commonly used:

a	**b**	**c**	**d**
Manufacturer	Manufacturer	Manufacturer	Manufacturer
⇩	⇩	⇩	⇩
Wholesaler	Retailer	Consumer	Agent
⇩	⇩	*e.g. mail order goods, craft items*	⇩
Retailer	Consumer		Consumer
⇩	*e.g groceries/ clothing*		*e.g. imported goods, cosmetics*
Consumer			
e.g. sweets			

> **Channel (a)** is a very traditional one and the role of the wholesaler is to break bulk. This means they buy in large quantities from the manufacturer and sell in smaller quantities to retailers. In this model retailers are typically small independent shops.

> **Channel (b)** reflects the situation where large retailers (supermarkets) buy in bulk direct from manufacturers, before selling on to consumers. As there is no longer a need to break bulk the wholesaler is not part of this channel. By 'cutting out the middle man' retailers will benefit from a cost saving which can either be used to sell at a lower price to consumers or to increase the retailer's profit margin.

> **Channel (c)** illustrates a situation where there are no intermediaries between producer and consumer and it is also regarded as a cost-saving approach.

  Goods sold through catalogues, over the Internet, fresh from the farm or made to order are suited to this approach. Dell sell the vast majority of their computers in this way. Customer orders are taken online or over the phone and each computer is individually made to meet the specific requirements of the customer. It is only in recent years that Dell has also started to sell standardised machines through PC World retail outlets.

> **Channel (d)** replaces the traditional retailer with an agent who sells goods to consumers, e.g. Avon cosmetics. In the services sector this type of distribution might involve the use of franchising.

The Marketing Mix – Promotion

This aspect of the marketing mix involves communicating information about the business and its products to consumers. The overall message is frequently delivered through a variety of methods which collectively are called the **promotional mix.** While each business or product will have a unique combination of promotional elements, those most commonly employed include direct advertising, sales promotions, personal selling, public relations and sponsorship.

Advertising

This is where businesses communicate directly with consumers in an attempt to convince them to buy certain products. Since advertising uses high-profile media and involves direct contact with customers it is regarded as above-the-line marketing.

Functions/types of advertising

The following are the main **functions** of advertising and from each we get a specific **type** of advertising. Note that some adverts are capable of fulfilling more than one function, thereby making them more effective.

> **To inform:** Advertising is frequently used to provide factual information about a firm and its products. It may be as simple as 'sale now on' or may include detailed technical information (e.g. car brochures, computer catalogues). This is **informative advertising**.

> **To persuade:** In this instance marketers try to convince consumers they 'must have' a particular product. This can be a very emotive type of advertising and frequently uses glossy images in an attempt to link the product to a successful or fashionable lifestyle (e.g. perfume, designer watches). Celebrity endorsements are often used to support the advertising campaign. The overall message being conveyed is that 'buying this product or service will allow the consumer to enjoy this type of lifestyle or appearance of success'. This is **persuasive advertising**.

> **To compete: Competitive advertising** attempts to show customers that one firm's products are better than those of its nearest rivals. The reference to rival products may be indirect ('another leading brand') or, in the case of a price war, may be very

unit

5

specific (e.g. Aer Lingus vs Ryanair). Great care needs to be taken not to make libellous statements about rival producers, so most businesses tend to avoid direct comparisons with competitors.

> **To remind:** This represents an attempt to keep the product fresh in the minds of consumers and is often used to support products in the mature or saturation stages of their life cycle. Kellogg's recently ran a TV ad campaign to promote Corn Flakes to adults, using the slogan 'Have you forgotten how good they taste?' This is also called **reminder advertising**.

> **To sell:** All successful advertising will ultimately succeed in selling products and services. While advertising is normally used by a particular business to promote its merchandise, there are some examples of advertising which has a wider benefit right across an industry. Where advertising seeks to promote the produce of an entire industry it is called **generic advertising**. A campaign urging us to 'drink more milk' would be an obvious example. Generic advertising is usually paid for by all the firms in the industry or in some cases by a state-sponsored body set up to promote that industry. For example, Failte Ireland promotes Ireland as a holiday destination. It does not promote the services of any particular airline or hotel, but simply seeks to increase tourist numbers in Ireland. If it is successful, many tourism-related businesses will benefit.

Effective advertising

Think of an advertisement which you saw or heard recently and which you regard as a 'good' advert. What was it about this particular advertisement that appealed to you and made you regard is as a 'good' ad? Was it the imagery used, the music, the humorous dialogue, or maybe there was a catchy jingle that just seemed to stick in your head long after the advertisement was over?

Most consumers tend to think the best advertisements are those we remember or which appeal to us. Advertisers would be pleased with this outcome since their message has clearly made an impact on us, but the business will have a different measure of advertising success. They will not be satisfied with merely creating a memorable advert; they need consumers to take some specific action. From the business's point of view, effective advertising is ultimately about increased sales.

Generally speaking, effective advertising succeeds in taking consumers through **four stages: A I D A = Awareness - Interest - Desire - Action**

> The initial aim of an advert is to make consumers **aware** of the product or service. Repeated exposure to advertising usually succeeds in achieving this. Advertisers choose advertising media which are suited to both the product and the target market. The combination of advertising media used to deliver an advertising campaign is called the **media mix**.

> Having created awareness, it is necessary to create an **interest** in the product. This is where the value of market research can be seen, as adverts can be structured to appeal to the target market. Specific features of the product can be emphasised in order to create the highest possible level of interest for this target market. Understanding their needs and motives makes this possible.

> If marketers are successful in developing this interest and appeal, the advert should then increase the customers' **desire** to have that product. It becomes the latest 'must have' item.

> Finally, an effective advert should motivate consumers to take **action** to fulfil that desire. Ultimately this means getting them to go out and purchase the product. This might not be an immediate response and in some cases might not even be a conscious response, but at some point in time the memory of the advert itself, or the awareness it raised, should cause the customer to purchase the product or service.

Advertising media

> **Television:** a visual medium which has mass appeal and is therefore suited to products with very large target markets.

It is expensive, both in terms of the cost of advertising slots and production of adverts. For this reason it is not really suited to smaller businesses, or for those with niche products.

The development of satellite TV networks has increased the advertising power of TV and is used extensively by global companies advertising global products. The combination of audio and visual impact tends to heighten its effectiveness. Advertising can be targeted at a particular viewer group by choosing to show adverts at specific times, also increasing its effectiveness.

> **Radio:** another form of mass medium which is generally less expensive than television advertising. Advertisers can choose from national, local and 'specialist' radio stations, so advertising can be more focused if necessary. Specialist radio stations are those which appeal to specific tastes in music or entertainment, e.g. Newstalk (focus on news and current affairs), Radio na Gaeltachta (Irish language broadcasting) and Lyric FM (classical music). Regional companies can advertise in a more cost-effective way by choosing to advertise to a smaller geographic market. Advertising costs are lower and the message is not being 'wasted' on a wider national audience which may have no interest in the product or service on offer.

The major disadvantage of radio as an advertising medium is the lack of a visual appeal. This makes it unsuitable for some products and generally requires greater creativity to capture the attention of the audience.

> **Newspapers:** provide a choice of both national and local newspapers, giving advertisers a huge range of locations for their adverts. This choice also means that newspaper advertising is accessible for smaller local businesses which have limited budgets or target markets. The major drawbacks with newspaper

unit

5

advertising are the lack of colour and the short life cycle of most newspapers. Daily newspapers may be discarded once read so advertising may have very little opportunity to have an impact.

› **Magazines:** offer the possibility of full colour and can be used to create memorable and effective visual imagery when promoting a product. Colour ads are, however, more expensive to create. Specialist magazines also allow advertisers to target particular consumers, e.g. sports enthusiasts, computer buffs, teenagers.

As magazines are published on a weekly or monthly basis the ads have a longer viewing life, and this is sometimes extended when magazines are passed on to friends or even end up as reading material in doctors' and dentists' surgeries.

› **Cinema:** a popular method of advertising which reflects the relatively high rate of cinema visits by the Irish public. Cinema ads offer many of the advantages of TV advertising but are available at a lower cost. Advertising can be targeted to the age profile or viewing preferences of cinema-goers. For example, products aimed at younger children will be shown during the trailers to 'G' rated movies and so on.

› **Billboards:** still widely used by advertisers to convey messages to consumers as they go about their daily lives. Roadside billboards located on our network of national roads give the opportunity to feature a visual ad campaign in strategic locations and on a large scale. This has the advantage of making them almost 'unmissable'.

› **Internet:** an increasingly popular, powerful and, at times, controversial advertising medium for businesses. Traditional online advertising is usually found on company websites and allows a business to publicise and sell its products 24/7. Marketers can also utilise email to target advertising at new and existing customers.

The growth of **social-networking sites** such as Facebook, Twitter and Myspace has also provided fresh opportunities for advertisers. These sites are used by millions of consumers every day to communicate with friends and share status updates and photos. Many of these sites use sophisticated software to ensure that advertisements are targeted very specifically at those consumers who are most likely to avail of a product or service. This information is gathered by monitoring online usage patterns. This effectively allows marketers to build up profiles of consumers based on the type of web pages they visit or products they purchase online.

Viral advertising/viral marketing has also developed alongside the growth in Internet usage. This type of advertising relies on social-networking sites to spread the advertising message. It differs from the traditional approach since the advert is usually made more appealing by giving it the appearance of being a short film or funny video clip. It relies on the fact that a memorable advert will be willingly passed on from one person to another and effectively becomes self-propagating. This is a big benefit for businesses with small advertising budgets as they can harness an element of creativity and the power of the Internet to spread their message.

Some advertisers have been criticised for deliberately producing provocative or controversial adverts which will create a higher curiosity value and are more likely to be viewed and passed on.

A recent Irish example of a viral ad was the 'I can't wait to grow up' campaign launched by the Irish Society for the Prevention of Cruelty to Children (ISPCC) in June 2011. The fund-raising campaign against physical abuse of children included a viral ad some described as being too graphic. The ISPCC disagreed and hoped that its imagery would move people to action against this type of abuse. Money raised by the campaign was used to fund ISPCC activities including its Childline telephone service.

> **Guerilla marketing/ambush marketing:** Guerilla marketing occurs when a business uses an unusual setting to generate publicity for its product. Because an advert appears in an unexpected setting it often has a more profound impact on the target audience and will succeed in being memorable and raising the level of consumer awareness.

The Piano Gallery used guerilla marketing techniques in this photo depicting a girl playing piano in a cow-field. The image is memorable because of the unusual setting, which also conveys a message about the rural location of this business.

Ambush marketing occurs when a company uses events or occasions organised by some other business to gain publicity for itself. In effect, the event organiser is ambushed or upstaged at their own event. During the FIFA World Cup finals in South Africa, a group of 36 female spectators were removed from a televised game because they were all wearing identical orange dresses bearing the name and logo of a Dutch beer-producer.

Both ambush and guerrilla marketing have the advantages of shock value and can also be successfully undertaken on a relatively small budget.

Factors affecting choice of advertising medium

The media mix chosen by a business will be influenced by some of the following considerations:

> **Cost/budget:** National media, especially TV and radio, can be very costly and would not suit a business with a limited budget. Businesses will always seek to get the best value for money by choosing the most cost-effective media. This means generating the largest possible impact for the smallest possible cost. For this reason a small regional business is unlikely to advertise using national media since expensive advertising is wasted on people who are outside their target market. As outlined previously, a small budget requires an element of creativity on the part of advertisers and their mix may include viral or guerrilla marketing.

unit **5**

> **Target market:** The medium chosen must be one which will be viewed or heard by the target audience. A manufacturer of sports equipment may choose to advertise in specialist sports magazines or during sports programmes on TV or radio. When targeting people in a specific geographic area, it's better to use local media. Global events such as the World Cup or the Olympic Games tend to be sponsored by global companies who have enormous budgets and are targeting a worldwide audience.

> **Type of product:** Some products are more effectively advertised using visual media whereas others lend themselves to radio advertising. Paint manufacturers, like Dulux and Crown, don't make too many radio commercials!

For similar reasons, most food products are advertised on television or in colour magazine ads.

> **Legislation:** Recent changes to the law now make it illegal for certain firms to advertise their products at specific times or via some media. Tobacco, for example, can no longer be advertised on radio and TV. There are also very strict regulations governing the depiction of alcohol in adverts, while health specialists regularly call for advertising controls on adverts for unhealthy food products targeted at children.

Regulating advertising

Advertising can have a powerful effect on consumers, and to ensure it does not abuse this power the government may introduce legislation regulating advertising.

national consumer agency
gníomhaireacht náisiúnta **tomhaltóirí**

putting **consumers** first

The main legislation dealing with advertisements in Ireland is the **Consumer Protection Act, 2007.** As outlined in *Chapter 2: Resolving Consumer Conflict*, this Act sets out the rules that apply to claims made by businesses about goods and services. It seeks to protect consumers from misleading advertisements and ensure that trade is fair. The Act makes it an offence for an advertiser to make false claims about goods, services or prices.

The **National Consumer Agency** is responsible for enforcing the Consumer Protection Act, 2007.

The **Advertising Standards Authority of Ireland (ASAI)** is an independent self-regulatory body for the advertising industry. The following statement which appears on the ASAI website summarises their views on the **essence of good advertising:**

All marketing communications should be legal, decent, honest and truthful.

All marketing communications should be prepared with a sense of responsibility both to the consumer and to society.

All marketing communications should conform to the principles of fair competition as generally accepted in business.

unit 5

The ASAI has updated its Code of Standards for Advertising, Promotional and Direct Marketing in Ireland. These guidelines, effective since 2007, are very extensive and focus on all aspects of marketing and advertising practices. Amongst other things, they deal with distance selling (mail order), children and advertising, food and drinks, health and beauty and financial services.

In addition to direct advertising, which is regarded as **above-the-line marketing,** the promotions mix may also include some or all of the following marketing techniques. These less direct or less obvious forms of marketing are classified as **below-the-line marketing.**

www.asai.ie

Sales promotion

This is the name given to a range of activities (excluding direct advertising) that are used to boost sales. It includes promotions such as free samples, bonus offers, loyalty schemes and prizes. It differs from direct advertising in that sales promotion offers customers an incentive or gimmick to buy a product or service. Customer loyalty may be rewarded with free gifts, money-off coupons or cash-back awards.

Sales promotion is frequently used to help launch new products, or to boost sales of mature or declining goods.

Most sales promotions are temporary and represent an attempt to try to get consumers to switch brands. A small number of sales promotions have become so popular and synonymous with products that they have been retained indefinitely. The 'toy' which accompanies McDonald's Happy Meals is an obvious example and has been so successful that it has been imitated by almost all major rivals. This is one type of **merchandising** which is used by businesses to market their products more effectively.

An alternative definition for merchandising, but also a common marketing tool, involves the use of special point-of-sale displays and promotions. These large eye-catching displays tend to be located at prominent points throughout the retail outlet, particularly close to the entrance and check-out areas or as end-of-aisle displays. They may be accompanied by free samples or special offers. They increase awareness of the brand and promote impulse buying

Personal selling

Some businesses use sales representatives to make direct contact with customers and, using their product knowledge and expertise, sell direct to them. Many sales reps build up close professional relationships with customers over time and this helps build trust and brand loyalty. It is particularly suited to high-value or high-tech items (e.g. farm equipment) or financial services.

unit

5

Because of their close contact with customers, sales reps are in a good position to provide feedback on customer reactions to goods and services. This expert market analysis is invaluable to a business when it attempts to improve its product offering or develop new product ranges.

Many sales staff who operate in this way are paid on a commission basis, which means they get a percentage of the value of those goods which they sell. This provides them with a strong motive to generate sales for the business.

Direct marketing/telemarketing:

Lists of potential customers are contacted personally, usually via email or phone, and offered incentives to choose a particular brand. When such online marketing is unexpected or unwanted it is called **junk mail.**

Public relations (PR)

Public relations will not usually have a direct and measurable impact on sales, but still plays an important part in developing positive customer relationships. The immediate aim of PR is to maintain the good image of a business and its products.

This task is the responsibility of the **public relations officer (PRO)** and is achieved via press releases, press conferences and sponsorships.

Business often gains pre-publicity for major events such as product launches by forwarding event details to the media. This is called a **press release.** It is hoped that some journalists will feature the event in their newspaper or TV coverage, thereby raising the profile of the event and providing the business with 'free' publicity.

A more hands-on approach to using mass media to publicise an event is the **press conference.** In this case the business will arrange a specific meeting with the media at which it will outline its intentions and invite journalists to ask questions. Press conferences are a more proactive approach to PR and are frequently undertaken by political parties and other non-commercial interest groups.

From time to time a business may have to use PR to counter some negative publicity. A recent example was the enormous reputational damage caused to British Petroleum (BP) following the Gulf of Mexico oil spill in 2010.

Sponsorship

Sponsorship allows a company name or brand to be associated with a particular team or event, in return for payment. For example in 2009 the FAI announced details of a ten-year sponsorship deal with Umbro worth €26 million. A sponsorship deal is another example of a co-operative relationship in business. The event or team involved clearly benefits in financial terms while the business hopes that a successful team will make their brand successful by association. From the business's viewpoint the exact return can be hard to measure, but the level of sponsorship undertaken by firms is evidence of its value and success. The major aims of sponsorship for a business are as follows:

> **To create awareness:** The brand now has increased visibility and will benefit from 'free' advertising through its association with a successful team or event.

› **To create brand loyalty:** The business hopes that team loyalty will be transformed into loyalty and support for its brand.

Opel was the official sponsor of the FAI in 1988, when Ireland qualified for its first European Championship finals. This led to a huge upsurge in publicity for the team, but also for the Opel brand. Huge numbers of replica jerseys, each carrying the Opel logo, were sold and the car manufacturer even launched a special edition of its Opel Cadet model to celebrate the event. In a very clever marketing move their TV ad campaign featured Arnold O'Byrne, the MD of Opel Ireland. His presence, coupled with the strong link to a high-profile team, highlighted Opel's connection to Ireland rather than the fact that it was a German car manufacturer. The tactic certainly worked, as Opel sales soared to new heights and they were market leaders by the year-end. Opel's association with the FAI continued through the very successful 1990 World Cup in Italy, after which the cost of sponsorship increased and the agreement wasn't renewed. Despite this, Opel had clearly shown the value of corporate sponsorship and it paved the way for many other sporting organisations and businesses in Ireland to replicate Opel's success.

› **To build relationships with the local community:** Businesses like to be seen to be making a positive contribution to the local community and sponsorship of community events is often used to give something back to loyal customers. It helps the local people to achieve their goals while also creating positive feelings about the business.

SuperValu are the sponsors of both the national Tidy Towns competition and the GAA, and this is seen as a perfect fit for the brand, as the SuperValu chain is made up of many independent local supermarkets trading under the SuperValu identity. The whole ethos of both Tidy Towns and the GAA is about local communities working together to improve their locality and restore an element of pride to it.

unit
5

Chapter Review Diagram – Marketing

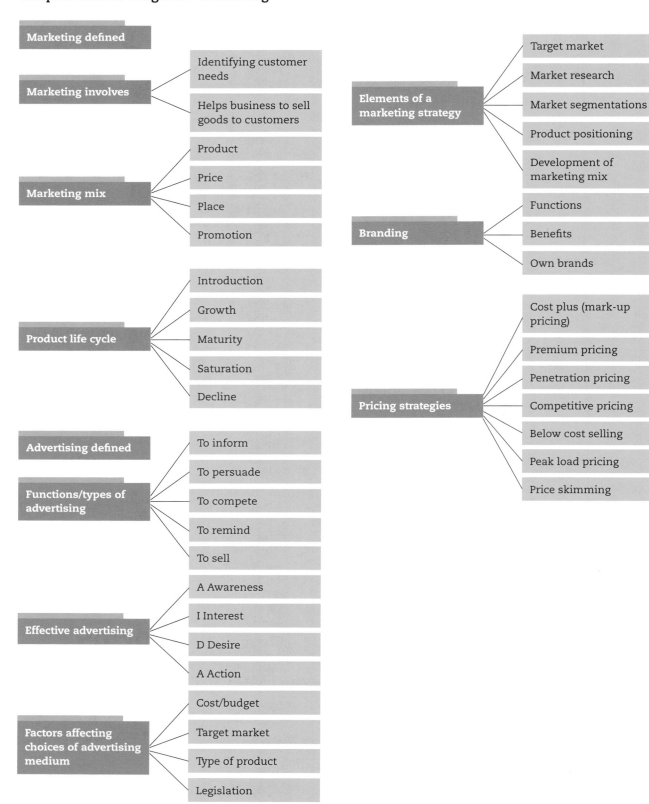

Marketing defined

Marketing involves
- Identifying customer needs
- Helps business to sell goods to customers

Marketing mix
- Product
- Price
- Place
- Promotion

Product life cycle
- Introduction
- Growth
- Maturity
- Saturation
- Decline

Advertising defined

Functions/types of advertising
- To inform
- To persuade
- To compete
- To remind
- To sell

Effective advertising
- A Awareness
- I Interest
- D Desire
- A Action

Factors affecting choices of advertising medium
- Cost/budget
- Target market
- Type of product
- Legislation

Elements of a marketing strategy
- Target market
- Market research
- Market segmentations
- Product positioning
- Development of marketing mix

Branding
- Functions
- Benefits
- Own brands

Pricing strategies
- Cost plus (mark-up pricing)
- Premium pricing
- Penetration pricing
- Competitive pricing
- Below cost selling
- Peak load pricing
- Price skimming

unit 5

Q Chapter Review Questions

1   What is the marketing concept?

2   (a) How does a marketing strategy assist business?

    (b) List five key elements of a marketing strategy for any business.

3   (a) Explain the term 'market segmentation'.

    (b) Name and explain the different types of market segmentation.

4   Use examples to illustrate your understanding of the terms 'product positioning' and 'product portfolio'.

5   In marketing terms what is a USP?

6   List the elements of the marketing mix.

7   Outline the main issues associated with the 'product' element of the marketing mix.

8   Explain the functions of packaging.

9   (a) What is branding?

    (b) List the benefits to a business of having an identifiable brand name.

10   Explain the term 'own brand' and illustrate your answer with two relevant examples.

11   Draft and label a product lifecycle diagram.

12   Explain 'product harvesting'.

13   List six different types of pricing strategies commonly used by businesses.

14   Distinguish between the following pricing strategies:

   › Predatory pricing

   › Price skimming

15   Illustrate three common channels of distribution used by businesses operating in Ireland.

16   Apart from competitive advertising, list and describe four other types of advertising.

17   What is meant by the term 'media mix'?

18   List six advertising media available to Irish businesses wishing to advertise their products and services.

19   What are the factors that a business will consider when deciding on the choice of the advertising medium?

20   Outline how social networking can enhance a business's ability to market its products.

21   Explain viral marketing and distinguish it from ambush marketing.

22   Explain the term 'promotional mix'.

23   Explain the term 'sales promotion'.

24   Describe the main benefits of corporate sponsorship, both to the business which undertakes it and to the organisation or event which receives it.

unit 5

Questions · Ordinary Level

1 Explain the following market research terms and give **one** example of each:

  (i) Field research   (ii) Desk research.   *LCOL 2011 (20 marks)*

2

> **Maria's Design Knitwear Ltd**
>
> Maria has always loved designing and knitting clothes for family and friends. Over the past two years she supplied local boutiques with some of her products and they are proving to be a great success. Maria now wants to turn her hobby into a business. She has received advice from local business consultant Dermot Jones. He advised her to set up a limited company which would give her the advantage of limited liability. He also advised her to conduct market research, to decide on her advertising media, to decide on her target market and to think about a brand name.

  (a) Outline **two** benefits to Maria of having a brand name for her knitwear.   *(10 marks)*

  (b) (i) Explain **one** function of advertising.

      (ii) Describe **three** advertising media that Maria might consider.   *(20 marks)*

  (c) (i) What is meant by the term 'target market'?

      (ii) Name **one** example of a target market.   *LCOL 2011 (15 marks)*

3 (a) State **two** benefits of using a brand name.

  (b) Give **two** examples of global brands.   *LCOL 2010 (15 marks)*

4

> Paula Doherty is the Managing Director of Doherty Ltd which manufactures a range of beauty and skincare products. The products are sold in beauty salons and pharmacies throughout the country. They have developed a new range of skincare products using natural ingredients under the brand name Skin kind. Paula wants to promote Skin kind products on a nationwide basis.   *LCOL 2009*

Describe three methods Doherty Ltd could use to promote the new Skin kind products.

        (20 marks)

5

> Promotion by a business is necessary to bring its products to the market's attention and to encourage consumers to purchase.   *LCOL 2008*

  (a) Promotion is **one** of the four elements of the marketing mix. Name the other three elements and explain one of them.   *(20 marks)*

  (b) List **three** methods (media) of advertising and give an advantage of each one.

        (15 marks)

  (c) Outline **three** functions of advertising.   *(15 marks)*

  (d) Outline two examples of public relations methods used by business.   *(10 marks)*

6 Explain **three** major functions of advertising.

7 Explain what is meant by sponsorship.

unit 5

Q Questions · Higher Level

1 Companies which invest in marketing in downtimes benefit more when markets begin to pick up.

   (a) Discuss the reasons why businesses carry out market research. *(15 marks)*

   (b) Evaluate 'sales promotion' and 'public relations' as forms of promotion. *(20 marks)*

   (c) 'Many businesses spend large sums of money developing a brand name.' Illustrate the benefits of branding for the business and the consumer. *LCHL 2010 (25 marks)*

2

Olympian Ltd is a company that produces a range of high quality branded sportswear. Following a lengthy market research process, the firm is now expanding its business to include a new range of Hoodie Tracksuits, aimed at the teenage market. *LCHL 2009*

   (a) Explain the term 'market segmentation', illustrating your answer with Reference to Olympian Ltd. *(10 marks)*

   (b) Outline **two** benefits to Olympian Ltd of segmenting the market. *(10 marks)*

   (c) Describe the factors that the Marketing Manager of Olympian Ltd should consider when deciding on the selling price of their new range of Hoodie Tracksuits. *(20 marks)*

3 (a) Explain **four** pricing policies that businesses can adopt as part of their marketing strategy and apply **one** of them to a product of your choice. *(30 marks)*

   (b) What is a marketing plan?

   (c) Evaluate the role such a plan can have for a business. *(20 marks)*

   (d) Outline and illustrate the term 'niche market'. *LCHL 2007 (10 marks)*

4 Deirdre Moloney hopes to start up her own cosmetics and personal beauty products business aimed at the consumer market. She has approached you as a marketing consultant for some marketing advice. In one single report, explain to her:

   (a) The significance of 'packaging', 'branding' and 'product life cycle' with reference to this business. *(30 marks)*

   (b) The term 'channel of distribution' and recommend a suitable one for her business. *LCHL 2006 (10 marks)*

5 (a) Describe the important factors that a Marketing Manager would consider when deciding on the price of a new product or service. *(20 marks)*

   (b) In the case of a particular product/service of your choice, evaluate the role of (i) advertising, (ii) public relations, (iii) personal selling in the promotion of the product/service. *(30 marks)*

   (c) Explain the term 'market segmentation'. *LCHL 2005 (10 marks)*

6 Explain the advantages for a business enterprise of adopting the market concept. *LCHL 1999 (10 marks)*

7 Distinguish between the following markets:

   ❯ Niche markets   ❯ Green markets

unit **5**

Chapter 16
Business Expansion

Syllabus Signposts

On completion, the student should be able to:

» 5.5.11 Identify the reasons for and methods of expansion;

» 5.5.12 Identify three main sources of finance for expansion;

» 5.5.13 Analyse the importance of Irish business expansion in the domestic and foreign markets (HL);

» 5.5.14 Compare and contrast equity and loan capital as sources of finance for expansion (HL);

» 5.5.15 Evaluate the elements of the marketing mix (HL);

» 5.5.16 Apply the main sources of finance available for business start-up (HL).

News Flash

Eason plans to invest €20m in expansion

by Ciarán Hancock, Business Affairs Correspondent

Irish-owned retailer Eason is planning to invest €20 million over the next three years to reposition the company within the book trade, which has been hit hard during the recession.

The Irish Times has learned that this will be combined with a restructuring of the business aimed at reducing its cost base by €8 million a year.

Eason's losses halved to €10 million in the 12 months to the end of January 2010, while turnover was down on a like-for-like basis.

Managing director Conor Whelan said that the cost reduction programme would probably involve job cuts.

"It is likely to include both voluntary and compulsory redundancies," he explained.

He said that the savings would address the company's uncompetitive cost base and would be subject to a consul-tation process with staff.

Mr Whelan declined to put a figure on the likely reduction in headcount – Eason employs just under 1,000 staff – but he said that the cost reductions would not involve a "store closure programme" although some of its 60 shops might be deemed to be unviable...

Eason is Ireland's biggest book store and plans to open three franchise stores in the near future at Balbriggan,

Co Dublin; Mullingar in Westmeath and in Carlow.

"We will look at opening more new stores," Mr Whelan added.

He said that the €20 million investment programme would involve the renovation of a number of its shops; new IT systems; changes to its core in-store category offerings, an upgraded online retail presence and a new marketing and brand strategy...

This is an edited extract from **The Irish Times,** WEDNESDAY, 30 MARCH 2011.

For more up-to-date newspaper articles see www.edcodigital.ie

1 Read the newspaper extract opposite and discuss the issues raised.

2 List four stakeholders mentioned in the Eason's newspaper article.

3 Can you explain any of the highlighted terms?

4 Distinguish between voluntary and compulsory redundancies as mentioned in the newspaper article.

Industrial development in recent decades has seen not only the growth in the number of businesses in existence, but also significant growth in the size and scale of many existing businesses. This chapter will consider the reasons for this growth as well as the implications of this growth for the business and its stakeholders. It will also examine the reasons why some small firms are able to survive and compete against larger rivals.

Reasons for Business Expansion

« syllabus signpost
5.5.11

Defensive reasons *'Protecting what we have'*

> **Protecting supplies:** By taking over a supplier of essential raw materials, a business should guarantee its availability and quality. In the past both Coca Cola and Pepsi bought sugar plantations as it helped alleviate their concerns over global prices of sugar. The Ford motor company also owned rubber, steel and glass manufacturers in an attempt to minimise car production costs. This process of buying a supplier of raw materials is called **backward vertical integration.**

> **Protecting a route to market: Forward vertical integration** takes place when a manufacturing business seeks to protect its route to market by taking over or merging with a distributor or retailer.

   Many oil companies have a vertically integrated structure which means they operate along the entire supply chain from exploration, extraction of crude oil, refining, transportation and distribution. Some, including BP and Shell, also own the petrol stations which sell their fuel to consumers.

In the UK many pubs were traditionally owned by local breweries and this not only guaranteed them an outlet for their product, but also provided a barrier to entry for competitors.

> **Cutting costs:** An expanding business should enjoy **economies of scale.** This reflects a lower cost of production per unit due to savings on bulk buying, advertising, etc. Cutting costs will enable a firm to protect market share from low-cost rivals.

> **Bigger is stronger:** A large firm is generally better able to withstand threats from rivals and economic shocks. Although all industries and businesses have suffered during the recent economic downturn, larger companies have generally survived

unit
5

the recession despite having to shed jobs and accept lower profits. This is mainly because of their ability to scale back operations while remaining commercially viable. A strong brand identity, a diversified business and economies of scale all contribute to this resilience.

> **Spreading risk:** By branching out into new areas of business **(diversification),** the risk associated with one product or market is reduced. This is really a case of 'not having all your eggs in one basket'!

Case Study

CRH is an example of a business which has used its size and a strategy of diversification to expand its operations and to withstand the economic downturn.

CRH plc was formed through a merger in 1970 of two leading Irish public companies, Cement Limited and Roadstone Limited. The newly formed group was the sole producer of cement and the principal producer of aggregates, concrete products and asphalt in Ireland. In 1970 CRH had sales of around €26 million, 95 per cent of which were generated in Ireland.

Since that time, CRH has become an international leader in building materials, thereby reducing its dependence on individual markets and achieving a balance in its geographic presence and portfolio of products. CRH now owns operations all over the world, including mainland Europe, the United States, South America, India and China.

Following fifteen consecutive years of growth between 1992 and 2007, 2008 saw major changes in the financial, economic and business climate worldwide. Despite a very challenging backdrop, CRH performed robustly and succeeded in limiting the decline in performance. In 2010 the company generated pre-tax profits of €534 million.

Source: www.crh.ie

Aggressive reasons *'Sometimes attack is the best form of defence!'*

> **Eliminate competition:** A larger company will tend to increase its market share; so many businesses will attempt to dominate a market by growing the size of their operations. This increase in size is often achieved by taking over a rival. The expansion of the Royal Bank of Scotland by means of takeovers is examined on page 326.

> **New products/technology:** One obvious way to gain access to innovative new products or technology is by acquiring the firm that has developed it. This avoids the costs and time involved in developing a copy-cat product and provides an immediate competitive advantage over rivals.

unit
5

This strategy also has the added advantage of adding significantly to the size of a firm's customer base.

Case Study

In May 2011 Microsoft struck an $8.5 billion deal to acquire the online voice and video chat service Skype. The acquisition placed Microsoft in a commanding position in the emerging markets of video content and online telephony. By combining this acquired technology with its existing mobile phone capacity Microsoft has the potential to provide improved videoconferencing and instant messaging services.

> **Synergy:** This is sometimes explained by the sum 2 + 2 = 5 and suggests that in some situations the combination of two or more things produces a result which cannot be achieved by each acting independently. When two firms join together, it is often the case that the new company will be more profitable and productive than when the two firms were operating independently. This might happen because duplicate activities can be eliminated or carried out more efficiently.

e.g. Example

Company A and Company B generated profits of €20m and €15m respectively last year. They have their own in-house marketing departments, each employing twenty staff. Following a merger of the companies a single marketing department employing just thirty staff is responsible for all marketing. In much the same way, sales staff in the merged company may now be required to sell products which were developed by both Company A and Company B. This should increase the revenue generated by each member of the sales team.

The overall result of these savings and efficiencies is a profit of €50m for the merged company. This is a substantial improvement on the combined profit generated by Companies A and B prior to the merger.

Psychological reasons *'It's all in the mind.'*

For some business leaders, the drive to maximise their full potential leads them to continually expand their operations. This reflects their need for self-actualisation, as outlined by Maslow in his theory of motivation.

> **Empire building:** Some entrepreneurs seek to dominate a particular market, either locally, nationally or globally. Rupert Murdoch's media empire is a perfect example.

unit 5

Case Study

In 1952 the then 22-year-old Rupert Murdoch began his business in Australia with just one newspaper. He expanded his business, first across Australia, then into the UK (the Times newspaper group and SKY television), Asia (Star TV network) and the US (Fox news group).

In 2010 the 79-year-old Murdoch was ranked 13th on the Forbes list of the World's Most Powerful People. With a net worth of US$6.3 billion, he was ranked the 117th wealthiest person in the world.

> **Challenge:** Many successful business leaders enjoy the challenge of growing their business, or perhaps diversifying into new areas.

Business Expansion Paths: Organic vs Inorganic

> **Organic growth** is achieved by increasing the size of the existing business. This can be done by adding new products or entering new markets. It is a slow but steady approach, which tends to build on the existing strengths of a business. It may be financed by use of retained earnings or by seeking additional equity capital. This is exemplified by Ryanair, which used the proceeds of a stock market flotation in 1997 to invest heavily in new aircraft.

Case Study

Ryanair was founded in 1985 and began with a single fourteen-seat turboprop aircraft, flying between Waterford and Gatwick Airport.

A year later, the company began competing directly with Aer Lingus and British Airways when it added a second route flying between Dublin and Luton International Airport.

Since that time, deregulation of the European airline industry, the launch of its website and the stewardship of Michael O'Leary have all helped the low-cost airline to expand its operation very rapidly and very successfully. Revenues have risen from €231 million in 1998 to €3,013 million in 2010, with profits increasing from €48 million to €339 during the same period.

unit **5**

> **Inorganic Growth** is achieved through mergers, acquisitions and takeovers. It often involves branching out into new areas of business and is therefore more risky. This approach allows a firm to expand rapidly, but may require increased debt to finance it.

 **Example**

When Malcolm Glazer decided to expand his business interests by buying Manchester United football club he used a **leveraged buyout** to finance the purchase. This meant that the majority of the cash used by Glazer to purchase Manchester United came in the form of loans, much of which were secured against the club's assets, incurring interest payments of over £60 million per annum.

Organic expansion methods

Increased domestic sales

This is a simple strategy in which a business attempts to increase its market share and turnover by widening its geographic presence. For example, a sole trader operating in Dublin may set up a new outlet in Cork. If successful this might be followed by additional branches in Galway and Limerick.

While extra outlets will hopefully increase profitability, they also bring additional risk and a need for extra capital. It may be possible to achieve the same level of expansion by using a franchise model.

New product development

By adding to its product portfolio a business can increase its customer base and so expand into new markets. If the business already has a well-regarded core product it may be possible to develop spin-off products at relatively low cost. The alternative will be to invest heavily in R&D and attempt to diversify its product range.

Exporting

Firms who currently operate only in their domestic markets could consider expanding their business operation into overseas markets. The cheapest strategy would involve producing goods in the existing factory and shipping them abroad for sale to foreign customers. The major benefit is the potential for increased sales and profit, but difficulties may arise with respect to transport, payments, market regulations and cultural issues.

A major decision when embarking on an export strategy is selecting the most effective channel of distribution.

A detailed analysis of the benefits and problems associated with exporting are outlined in *Chapter 22: International Trade*.

Licensing

This is a contractual arrangement in which one company allows another manufacturer to make their product in return for a fee called a **royalty.** Goods must be produced to very precise standards otherwise the brand name will suffer and the licence will be withdrawn.

Guinness, for example, produces and distributes Budweiser in Ireland under licence from Anhauser Busch.

Licensing allows the copyright holder to maximise the profit potential of their creation by renting their intellectual property rights. This type of merchandising is particularly popular in the film and games industries where spin-off products are used to generate additional revenue streams. Characters based on popular movies and television shows are licensed from their inventors and are used to market action figures, board games and video games. Recent examples include *Star Wars*, *Spiderman* and *Toy Story*.

Advantages of licensing

The developer of trademark products avoids the massive costs and risk involved in setting up a manufacturing plant in every target market. They can then focus their efforts on creating new products which may also be licensed out to other manufacturers.

Major benefits to the manufacturer include lower research and development costs, the ability to utilise excess manufacturing capacity, and the potential to introduce more new products in a shorter amount of time.

Case Study

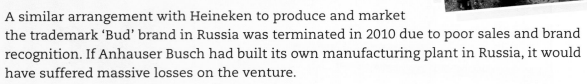

Anhauser Busch uses the world-class manufacturing facility available at the Guinness brewery in Dublin to produce Budweiser under licence. The US brewing giant which owns the Budweiser trademark minimises its capital investment and also has the benefit of Guinness's distribution network.

A similar arrangement with Heineken to produce and market the trademark 'Bud' brand in Russia was terminated in 2010 due to poor sales and brand recognition. If Anhauser Busch had built its own manufacturing plant in Russia, it would have suffered massive losses on the venture.

Disadvantages of licensing

The developer of the product loses some control over production. Great care needs to be taken to monitor quality control as the brand name and reputation might suffer. It also means potential rivals are given access to trade secrets.

The developer of the product loses some of the profit available as they only receive a royalty from the manufacturer rather than all of the sales revenue.

Franchising

This type of operating model has some similarities to licensing, but it takes the process a step further by allowing the franchisee to adopt the products and operating system of the franchisor. The franchisee must operate the business according to very strict and uniform guidelines in order to maintain the brand identity. The franchisee also pays a fee, which is usually a percentage of sales. In return, they get an exclusive right to operate the business in a particular location. They also have the advantage of buying into an already proven and successful business concept. This approach allows the franchisor to expand very rapidly with little risk or capital outlay.

McDonald's has used this model with enormous success to expand its business worldwide.

Glanbia has a long-term and very successful franchise contract with Sodima, the French owners of the Yoplait range of dairy products. In 2009 Yoplait was the second-largest fresh dairy product brand worldwide, with a 10 per cent market share, and the brand achieves global sales in excess of €4 billion.

The franchise agreement is worth €70 million in terms of Irish Yoplait annual retail sales. Glanbia Consumer Foods division employs just under 700 people at ten locations throughout Ireland, with Yoplait being produced at its facility in Inch, Co Wexford.

Franchising is also discussed in *Chapter 14: Getting Started*.

Inorganic expansion methods

Joint venture (strategic alliance)

This is where two or more independent firms agree to work together for the purposes of completing a specific project. Such projects might include developing a new market or a new product. Costs and expertise can be shared. The outcome of the alliance must be mutually beneficial (profitable), and it is important to note that the firms always remain independent.

Star Alliance is an agreement between 27 airlines to pass on customers to one another where passengers need more than one airline to reach a particular destination. While the member airlines compete on some routes they also benefit from passenger referrals and from round-the-world travellers who can avail of a special global ticket valid on all Star Alliance airlines.

Merger

A merger occurs where two or more firms join together, by mutual agreement. Following the merger a new organisation is usually formed. There are plenty of examples of mergers in Irish business history.

unit 5

Example

Glanbia plc was founded following the merger of Avonmore Co-op and Waterford Foods. The newly merged businesses were able to grow the scale of their organisation and compete more effectively with large European competitors in the agribusiness sector.

Takeover (acquisition)

A takeover or acquisition occurs when one company buys a controlling stake in another company. For control of the company a shareholding in excess of 50 per cent is required. The company which has the majority shareholding is called a **holding company,** while the company which has been acquired is called a **subsidiary.** For example CIE is a holding company which was set up by the Irish government. It has three wholly owned subsidiaries, namely Dublin Bus, Bus Éireann and Iarnród Éireann. This means that CIE own 100 per cent of the shares in the three transport companies.

Some companies are accepting of a takeover, either because they would not survive as an independent business, or because shareholders are offered a premium price for their shares.

When the directors of the takeover target resist any attempt to buy out their company, this is called a **hostile takeover.** In such circumstances the board of directors will advise existing shareholders not to sell their shares to the takeover bidder. This may put an end to the takeover bid, or may simply require the bid price to be increased.

The Irish government and the EU monitor all attempts at takeovers and have the power to block takeovers which they deem not to be in the best interests of consumers.

Advantages of a merger/takeover as a method of expansion

> **Economies of scale:** A larger organisation may benefit from lower per-unit production costs as savings arise from bulk buying, mass marketing and less duplication of work.

> **Shared expertise and resources:** The range of skills and resources available as a result of the merger will be greater and this will help address deficiencies in each of the individual companies. This is very similar to the reason why a sole trader might take on a business partner.

> **Access to capital:** The merged organisation may find it easier to access the capital it requires. One of the main reasons why Avonmore Co-op and Waterford Foods merged to form Glanbia plc was to gain access to capital via the stock market. This finance option is only available to public limited companies.

> **Access to technology:** A company can use a merger or takeover to gain control of innovative technology which has been developed by another company. The acquisition may also serve to eliminate a potential rival from the marketplace.

unit
5

> **Diversification:** Some businesses use mergers and acquisitions to expand their business operations into new markets or to add to their range of business activities. If successful this will allow the business to spread the risk associated with one industry or market. CRH is a clear example of this strategy in operation.

Disadvantages of a merger/takeover as a method of expansion

> **Financial cost:** Buying another business is certainly not cheap and unless a company has very substantial cash reserves it will almost certainly need to borrow the money required. This will add to its debt levels and will require annual interest payments. If the takeover is a hostile one there is a danger that the purchase price will be forced upwards and will undermine the value of the acquisition.

Aer Lingus rejects Ryanair's €748m takeover bid

Aer Lingus has rejected Ryanair's €748 million takeover bid for the airline, saying the offer significantly undervalued the carrier.

In a statement this evening, the Aer Lingus board said it had considered Ryanair's renewed €1.40 a share cash bid for the airline but was strongly advising shareholders against the offer.

The Ryanair bid represents a premium of around 28 per cent over the average closing price of Aer Lingus shares for the 30 days to November 28th 2008...

This is an edited extract from **The Irish Times,** MONDAY, 1 DECEMBER 2008.

> **Management issues:** A larger and more diversified business will be more difficult to manage. It may take some time before existing management come to terms with the enlarged organisation and a change in organisational structure may be required.

> **Clash of cultures:** Sometimes there are huge cultural differences between organisations which are impossible to foresee prior to a merger or takeover. Once the takeover has been completed these different approaches to business operations can be difficult to resolve and may result in inefficiencies and industrial relations problems.

> **Redundancies:** The merged business may have less need for staff in some areas of its operations and management. A decision to make some staff redundant may be taken to resolve this issue. Apart from the financial cost to the business, it also heightens the prospect of industrial relations problems.

unit

5

« syllabus signpost
5.5.12

Finance for Expansion

The examples outlined throughout this chapter highlight the enormous costs and potential risks involved in business expansion. For this reason any business pursuing a strategy of expansion will need to consider its financial needs and resources very carefully.

Case Study

The Royal Bank of Scotland (RBS) adopted an aggressive type of expansion strategy aimed at transforming the national bank into a global financial institution. In the space of just seven years it borrowed billions and took over twenty-six other companies. By 2009 it was the fifth largest bank in the world. Unfortunately the strategy backfired as the global credit crunch and massive levels of bad (toxic) debt caused the banking giant to collapse spectacularly in 2009.

The 2007 takeover of Dutch banking group ABN Amro, which coincided with the international financial crisis, highlights the potential risks involved in this strategy. As a result of the takeover, the RBS group suffered severe cash flow problems at a time when banks were struggling to finance their operations.

In late 2007 Royal Bank of Scotland had announced an operating profit of £10.3 billion, the biggest ever for a Scottish company and the equivalent of £1 million per hour. Within eighteen months, the very same bank had set another record, this time by posting a loss of £28 billion, the biggest in British corporate history.

Mirroring the situation in Ireland the UK government had to introduce a £350 billion bank bailout, with RBS receiving in excess of £20 billion.

For an expanding business the main requirement is for long-term finance. This will be used to fund buy-outs, purchase new premises and machinery and invest in R&D.

Its medium-term needs will be for equipment and vehicles, while some short-term finance may be needed for working capital.

Sources of finance

A detailed analysis of all sources of finance is contained in *Chapter 8: Household and Business Finance*. A summary of the major long-term sources suitable for expansion is outlined below:

> **Equity finance**   > **Sale and leaseback**   > **Venture capital**
> **Retained earnings**   > **Grants**   > **Loans**

Equity finance

This involves additional capital being raised from new or existing shareholders. Small businesses may choose to bring in new partners; private limited companies can invite investment from new shareholders while public companies can issues shares through the stock market.

Some large takeovers are funded by swapping shares in the holding company for shares in the subsidiary company. This will allow all shareholders to benefit from the expected increase in future profits and will limit the amount of cash needed to fund the acquisition.

unit 5

All types of equity finance have the potential to impact on control and ownership of the business.

Retained earnings

Shareholders may be willing to forego a dividend and allow business profits to be ploughed back into the expanding company. This is not a long-term strategy and will only receive the support of shareholders if there is a realistic chance of increased future earnings.

Sale and leaseback

A business which owns valuable assets, such as land and buildings, may choose to 'cash in' on their value by selling the asset and simultaneously signing a long-term lease which will allow them continue operating from the same premises. While the building will no longer appear as a fixed asset on the company's balance sheet, the capital raised can be used to purchase additional assets or rival businesses.

Grants

City and county enterprise boards, Enterprise Ireland, the IDA and the EU offer grants to assist business expansion. Enterprise Ireland will assist indigenous firms seeking to export their produce, while small firms can receive funding from their local city or county enterprise board (see also *Chapter 20: Community Enterprise Development*).

The IDA provides finance to help foreign-owned firms operating in Ireland and some EU grant assistance is available for business development projects in some 'green' industries including renewable energy and recycling.

Venture capital

Venture capital companies invest in new or high-risk businesses, often taking an equity stake and a seat on the board of directors. They hope that the business will succeed and value of their investment will grow.

Loans

Some expanding businesses choose to rely heavily on external debt and may use mortgages and debentures to finance their long-term expansion plans.

Mortgages are loans specifically used to purchase property and the deeds of the property provide the lender with security against default. The loan is typically repaid over a twenty- to thirty-year time period.

A debenture is a long-term loan with a fixed interest rate and has a specified maturity date. The €5 million lump sum would be repayable in 2025. While offering immediate access to large amounts of capital it does commit the borrower to fixed annual repayments and the provision of collateral. The expanded business would need to be confident that the expected growth will generate sufficient return to repay the debt.

« *syllabus signpost*
5.5.14

unit
5

327

Debt Capital vs Equity Capital

> **Debt capital** offers the potential to raise large amounts of capital, but is clearly much harder to secure during a credit crunch such as the one which began in 2009. Expansion proposals will need to offer clear potential for growth and sustained earnings if lenders are to be persuaded to provide debt capital.

> **Equity capital** also offers the possibility of raising substantial amounts of capital but the amount available will depend upon the profitability levels and reserves of the business.

> **Debt capital** is expensive and requires the payment of annual interest charges, which may be subject to ongoing increases. This also serves to increase the level of risk associated with this source of finance, as failure to repay debts may lead to the winding up of the company.

> **Equity capital** is a much cheaper source of finance as it does not require ongoing interest payments. This greatly reduces the risk to the business, although shareholders who receive little or no dividends may sell their shares and cause the market capitalisation of the business to fall sharply.

> **Debt capital** does not affect the overall control or ownership of the business but certain fixed assets may need to be offered as security against default.

> Since **equity capital** is raised by issuing additional shares, it has the potential to alter the control and ownership of the business.

Factors affecting choice of finance

While outlined in greater detail in *Chapter 8: Household and Business Finance*, it is worth remembering that the decision on the most suitable source of finance will be influenced by the following key factors:

> **Reasons:** What is the purpose of the loan? It's important to apply the matching principle.
> **Amount:** Long-term sources tend to be more suitable for large amounts.
> **Cost:** Compare the APR of each possible source and lender.
> **Security:** What collateral will be required in case of non-payment/default?
> **Control:** Will finance affect control or ownership? A share issue has the potential to impact on control.

Implications of expansion

The expansion process and its aftermath are likely to have a major impact on an organisation, and the following aspects of the business are likely to be affected:

Organisational structure

The company may need to be restructured to cope with enlarged organisation. As communication and control become more difficult and complex, the business may change from a

traditional functional structure to a more diversified geographic structure. This would allow regional managers to micro-manage operations in a specific location while senior managers can oversee the strategic development of the entire business.

The issue of duplication needs to be resolved in cases of mergers or takeovers. Some restructuring, retraining and redundancy may be required to deal with this problem.

Finance

As previously outlined, extra capital is needed to fund expansion, so financial and budgetary control will also be more difficult in the larger organisation. One solution would be to divide the business into independent profit centres, in line with a revised organisational structure.

Staffing

The larger business will have a clear need for a human resources manager to deal with personnel issues. Staff planning, recruitment and selection as well as training and development will be significant issues for the growing business.

Overall job security will be enhanced in a larger company, but some duplicate jobs may be lost in cases of merger or takeover. Uncertainty as to staffing needs and changes in work practice can cause unrest so the HR manager will need to negotiate these changes. Some staff may need retraining while others may be made redundant.

Product portfolio (product mix)

Some businesses expand by investing in research and development and introducing innovative new products. Others will increase their product range through mergers and acquisitions. In some cases, where competing brands are owned by the same company, it may need to decide which products and brands to retain and which to sell off.

Profitability

Generally speaking, the long-term aim of business expansion is to increase profit levels and this can be achieved via extra sales and lower costs (economies of scale). Extra profit will please investors and make access to capital easier.

Consumers

Reduced competition is generally not beneficial to consumers, either in terms of choice or impact on prices. Very large organisations can often be seen as 'impersonal' and uncaring of customer needs.

It is for some of the above reasons that business expansion needs to be regulated.

Restrictions on expansion

The Irish government and the EU monitor all attempts at takeovers and have the power to block takeovers which they deem not to be in the best interests of consumers. This usually occurs where a takeover would allow one company to gain a dominant market position, thus allowing it to manipulate prices or control the level of supply. The **Competition Authority** is the state body responsible for enforcing Irish and European competition law in Ireland.

www.tca.ie

Irish Law

The Competition Authority was set up to protect consumers from unfair trading practices by market-dominant firms. Any attempt to eliminate competition is monitored and impact on consumer choice and price levels examined. All mergers and takeovers are investigated and can be prohibited by the Authority.

Competition Authority clears the way for Superquinn deal

The Competition Authority has cleared the proposed acquisition of Superquinn by Musgrave. Under the deal Musgrave would take control of Superquinn's supermarket business and some of its properties.

Following an intensive investigation the Competition Authority believes the deal will not substantially lessen competition in markets for goods or services in the State.

During its investigation the Authority looked at four possible problems that might arise as a result of the deal:

› Would the new entity be able to raise prices regardless of the reaction of its competitors and customers?
› Would consumers face higher prices and/or reduced output because of the actions of the new entity and its competitors?
› Could the deal be a strategy for Musgrave to discourage a new competitor from entering the market?
› Could the deal mean that the merged entity could force better terms from suppliers, causing them in turn to price discriminate against smaller retailers, harming consumers in the long term?

Based on a thorough investigation – which included research, a formal request for information from the parties, ongoing contact, obtaining the views of suppliers and competitors and on-site investigations – the Competition Authority takes the view that the transaction will not result in the problems identified.

Source: Competition Authority website, 28 SEPTEMBER 2011.

EU Law

Competition Policy prevents abuse of position by dominant firms. An EU Commissioner investigates large mergers and can restrict or prohibit them. See also *Chapter 23: The European Union.*

Small is beautiful... sometimes!

Despite the recent trend towards business growth and expansion, some businesses choose to remain small and are able to compete successfully and profitably against their larger rivals.

Benefits of remaining small

› A small business is easier to manage. There are fewer products and people involved and this simplifies business management. In the case of sole traders the owner has complete control over the business.

› A small business can forge closer relationships with customers. As the business owner is in a position to deal directly with the customer, there is more opportunity to add a personal touch.

› This focus on customer relations is particularly suited to many sole trader businesses which provide niche products and use job production techniques to meet the specific needs of individual customers.

Drawbacks of remaining small

❯ Operating costs tend to be higher as the small business is not in a position to avail of bulk discount and other economies of scale.

❯ Limited availability of capital and skills mean that a small business might be unable to invest in product development. This obviously makes it more difficult to compete with larger businesses.

❯ Small businesses may find it more difficult to retain key staff who have career ambitions. Opportunities for promotion may be far more limited in a small organisation so some essential staff may leave to pursue their career ambitions elsewhere.

❯ Successful small businesses often become takeover targets for larger rivals, so it may not be possible to retain independence indefinitely.

Chapter Review Diagram – Business Expansion

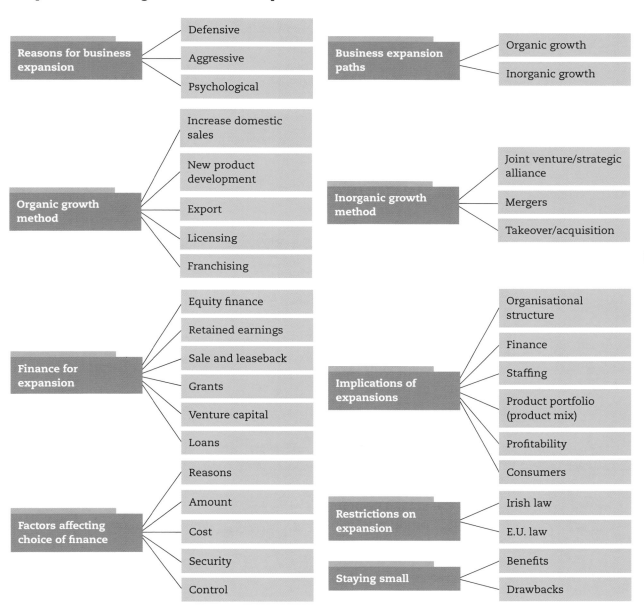

unit 5

Q Chapter Review Questions

1 Outline five reasons for business expansion.

2 Define the term 'synergy'.

3 Distinguish between organic growth and inorganic growth. Illustrate with examples of both.

4 Explain the term 'economies of scale'.

5 Explain one advantage and one disadvantage of licensing for a business which is seeking to expand its operations into overseas markets.

6 Outline two benefits of franchising from the point of view of both the franchisor and the franchisee.

7 Distinguish between a merger and a takeover.

8 List five long-term sources of finance which would be suitable for an expanding business.

9 Outline five implications for a business when it decides to expand its operations.

10 Outline the benefits and drawbacks of businesses deciding to remain small.

Q Questions · Ordinary Level

1

> Repas Ltd is a food manufacturer business in Cork. It supplies and distributes goods to wholesalers and retailers throughout Ireland. Repas Ltd also owns and supplies a chain of supermarkets with outlets in Cork, Waterford and Kerry. Repas Ltd hopes to merge with PricePower2 Ltd. PricePower2 Ltd is a chain of supermarkets with outlets in Dublin and Galway.
>
> *LCOL 2002*

(a) Describe what a merger is and outline the benefits of the merger of Repas Ltd with PricePower2Ltd. *(20 marks)*

(b) Outline **two** sources of long-term finance which may be available to Repas Ltd to finance the merger and explain any one of them. *(20 marks)*

2

> Pratai plc was set up fifty years ago and makes potato crisps for the domestic and export markets. It has expanded through organic growth and now is a major employer in the local area. The demand for its products is growing but the company has limited production capacity. Recent competition from other snack food companies has decreased Pratai's market share.
>
> *LCOL 2000*

(a) Illustrate what is meant by 'organic growth'. *(5 marks)*
(b) Describe **four** reasons why Pratai plc would like to expand their business. *(20 marks)*
(c) Describe **two** methods of expansion that Pratai plc could use. *(10 marks)*
(d) Identify **three** sources of finance that Pratai plc could use for expansion. Explain any one of these sources. *(20 marks)*

3 Explain what is meant by 'channels of distribution'.
LCOL 2009 (5 marks)

4 Explain the term 'franchise'.
LCOL 2007 (10 marks)

5 Outline **three** benefits of expanding the business.
LCOL 2005 (15 marks)

6 Distinguish between the following types of capital:
> Equity capital
> Debt capital

Questions · Higher Level

1 Illustrate your understanding of the term 'synergy'.

2

Marie Nolan is the owner of 'Marie's Pizzas' a successful pizza restaurant with a home-delivery service. Demand for take-aways has increased, as more people are eating at home due to the economic downturn. Marie is planning to expand her business through franchising and her accountant recommends that a business plan should be prepared before going ahead.
LCHL 2010

(a) Evaluate franchising (benefits and risks) as a method of expansion for the pizza business.
(20 marks)

(b) (i) Discuss the factors that should be considered when choosing between different sources of finance.

   (ii) Analyse two appropriate sources of finance for acquiring an additional delivery van at Marie's Pizzas.
(30 marks)

3 (a) (i) Explain the term 'business alliance'.

   (ii) Illustrate the advantages of an alliance as a form of business expansion. *(20 marks)*

(b) Evaluate debt and equity capital as sources of finance for business expansion.
LCHL 2009 (20 marks)

2

Paula and Thomas have recently returned to Ireland having worked with transnational companies for ten years. They wish to set up in business together in Ireland manufacturing a range of new organic breakfast cereals. Paula has particular expertise in production and finance and Thomas is marketing and human resources. In time, Paula and Thomas intend to expand the business into the EU market.
LCHL 2006

(a) Describe the implications for the business of expansion.

(b) Explain **two** methods of expansion you would advise them to consider. *(20 marks)*

5 Describe **three** reasons for business expansion other than to increase profit.
LCHL 2005 (20 marks)

6 Contrast business alliances and franchising as different types of business organisations. Use examples to illustrate your answer.
LCHL 2003 (30 marks)

7 Distinguish between a merger and a takeover.

8 Explain the term 'diversification'.

Applied Business Question

Chocolate Delights Ltd

Colm O'Malley graduated from college with a Master's degree in Agriculture and Food Science before spending several years working in the research and development division of a transnational company. He had a good track record of innovation as well as a natural flair for design and presentation. Earlier this year Colm spotted a gap in the market for handmade chocolates and took the decision to set up his own business, which he named Chocolate Delights Ltd.

Despite Colm's clear enthusiasm and commitment to the project he is acutely aware of the challenges associated with setting up a new business venture. One of his biggest and most immediate problems is where to find the necessary resources and expertise. He has invested €20,000 of his own money as capital and has also secured a small loan from a friend. Most of this money has already been spent on a ten-year lease for business premises and the remainder is earmarked for his marketing budget. He needs machinery and equipment but is concerned he will not have sufficient cash to pay for these items. Colm has also made enquiries with suppliers of raw materials and packaging as he is desperate to get the necessary ingredients required to fulfil his growing order book.

Colm is contemplating carrying out an extensive analysis of the Irish confectionery market but is put off by the costs involved. Nevertheless he realises the importance of producing the right product to satisfy customers' needs and wants. This research, if undertaken, would also provide valuable information on the correct price to be charged and would enable his products to be competitive. He has also heard that selling products directly to the consumer has certain advantages. Colm knows that the confectionery industry is very competitive and understands the importance of developing a unique product offering. At the moment he is unsure about many specific aspects of the industry but feels this can be overcome by appropriate research.

This product will also need to be promoted and Colm is unsure of the exact components of the promotional mix. On balance, Colm is leaning towards the market research idea and the notion that it would be money well spent.

Colm realises that to be successful in this business he must be innovative and offer a product that will be taken up by consumers. His research team consists of experts in the area of confectionery, design and branding. He also relies on consumer feedback. Colm has read about networking and brainstorming in business magazines and has observed some innovative ideas at a number of trade fairs in Europe and the United States. He is very open to new ideas of conducting business and his goal is to ensure that his business will be exemplary and that he will be proud to call it his own.

(a) Analyse **one** short-term, **one** medium-term and **one** long-term source of finance available to Colm's start-up business. Illustrate your answer with reference to the text. *(20 marks)*

(b) Outline the importance of market research in the development of a marketing mix for Chocolate Delights Ltd. Refer to the above text in your answer. *(30 marks)*

(c) Outline **two** internal and **two** external sources of new product ideas that Chocolate Delights Ltd could use to improve its product range. Refer to the above text in your answer. *(30 marks)*

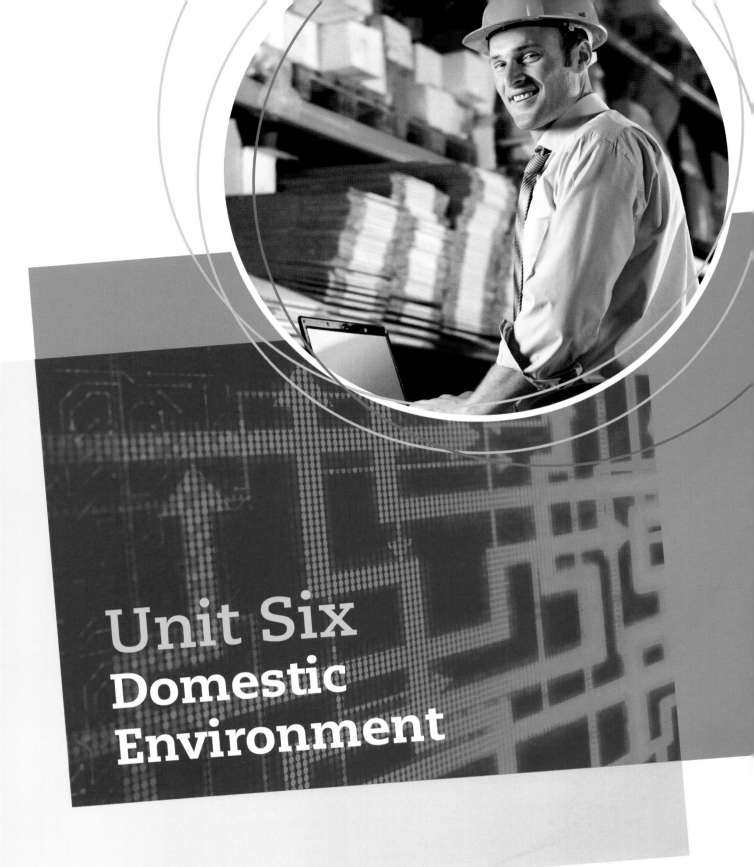

Unit Six
Domestic Environment

Chapter 17
Categories of Industry

Syllabus Outcomes

On completion, the student should be able to:

» 6.7.1 Recognise and illustrate the categories of industries and their contribution to the domestic economy.

News Flash

Are we ready to wean off FDI?

by Barry McCall

The outlook for Ireland in terms of foreign direct investment is not as gloomy as we might imagine – but there are those who would suggest it's time to focus our efforts on our indigenous talent.

Despite the overwhelmingly negative view of Ireland on the international bond markets, and our ongoing banking and fiscal crises, our reputation with multinational investors remains remarkably high.

In fact, Ireland now ranks as the number one global destination for inward investment jobs per capita,

according to IBM's Global Location Trends Report. The report revealed that Ireland remains more attractive than other key global FDI locations, including Singapore, Hungary and the Czech Republic.

This positive view of Ireland on the part of multinational firms is very significant as foreign direct investment (FDI) continues to play a key role in Ireland's manufacturing base. FDI accounts for €110 billion – or over 70 per cent – of total exports in the Irish economy, 240,000 jobs, 55 per cent of corporate tax, €19 billion in direct expenditure, €7 billion

in payroll costs and 73 per cent of business spend on research, development and innovation.

The sentiment of the US multinational sector is also positive says Joanne Richardson, chief executive of the American Chamber of Commerce in Ireland.

"In all, there are some 600 US business operations involving an investment of $165 billion and generating 100,000 jobs. Bilateral trade between the two countries is worth €27 billion. All of this is still in place, and that is a vote of confidence in itself."

On the other hand, former

Intel chairman Craig Barrett argues that Ireland should begin weaning itself off its dependence on FDI.

"Ireland needs to focus on enlarging its indigenous high-tech sector to drive economic recovery," he said on a visit to Ireland earlier this month as chairman of the Irish Technology Leaders Group (ITLG).

"There is significant opportunity for growth driven by these firms. Ireland and the US are in similar circumstances. If we don't take advantage of our skilled workforces and entrepreneurial spirit we will lose out to emerging economies."

This is an edited extract from **The Irish Times,** Friday, 26 November 2010.

For more up-to-date newspaper articles see online www.edcodigital.ie

1 Read the newspaper extract opposite and discuss the issues raised.

2 Can you explain any of the highlighted terms?

A combination of four basic **factors of production** are required by all businesses and economies when attempting to produce goods and services. These factors of production are:

> **Land**　　　 > **Labour**　　　 > **Capital**　　　 > **Enterprise**

Land

In economic terms land refers to resources which occur naturally on our planet. This broad definition includes land used for farming and forestry as well as the oceans, rivers, and mineral deposits. Climate conditions, which allow a region to develop a tourist industry or grow specific crops, can also be included in this economic definition of land.

Land resources are regarded as a fixed factor of production and this reflects the fact that their supply is finite and cannot normally be increased. Any attempt to increase the availability or productivity of land will involve considerable investment of both time and other factors of production. For example, it may be possible to reclaim land from the sea, but this will require enormous expense in terms of manpower and machinery and is likely to take years to achieve.

In recent decades we have come to realise the limited nature of these resources and reserves of oil and some minerals are rapidly diminishing. Extracting the remaining quantities of these commodities will again involve greater costs and risks and its impact on the society is outlined in *Chapter 21: Business Ethics and Social Responsibility*.

The payment or reward associated with the use of land is **rent**.

Labour

As outlined in *Chapter 11: Human Resource Management*, the availability of people is an essential factor for the production of goods, services and wealth. This factor of production is not just about the size of the available workforce, but also about the levels of skill and training associated with it.

In a modern high-tech economy it can be argued that the knowledge and innovation of people is a critical element in developing and delivering unique, high-value goods and services. A country like Ireland, which has a relatively small population, still finds it possible to compete in global markets whereas several more populous countries, especially in the developing world, struggle to do so. While this is partly related to the land resources available, there is no doubt that Ireland's universal education system has been a major factor in our economic growth and development.

The ongoing challenge is to ensure that the Irish labour force continues to have the skills and innovation required to develop a world class knowledge economy.

The payment or reward associated with labour is **wages**.

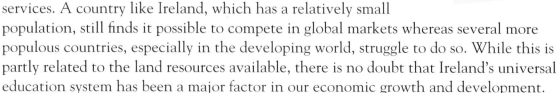

unit

6

Capital

Anything made by people and used to produce other goods and services can be regarded as capital. Examples include machinery, vehicles and factories utilised by individual businesses, as well as national infrastructure such as roads, ports and telecommunications networks.

Capital resources can be combined with labour to make it more efficient and productive. For example, a person may be able to cultivate a small piece of land by hand in order to survive. If we add capital by providing this farmer with basic tools such as a fork and spade, the task will be easier and more productive. Adding extra capital resources such as tractors and specialist equipment enables far greater productivity and allows for the cultivation of a much larger piece of land.

The payment or reward associated with capital is called **interest**.

Enterprise

This factor of production is far less tangible than any of the others and is dependent on the innovation and risk-taking of entrepreneurs. Unlike the other factors of production, enterprise does not have a physical presence. It requires that an enterprising person combines land, labour and capital in order to produce goods and services.

As outlined in Unit 2, enterprise is about initiative and creativity amongst many other skills and characteristics. It can be difficult to define and often difficult to develop. We are all capable of being enterprising, but it often takes time and encouragement to improve our enterprise skills. A major focus of government policy in recent years has been the development of an enterprise culture in Ireland. Various state agencies and government departments have used education and financial supports to encourage and support enterprise and innovation. This is based on the realisation that land, labour and capital resources will continue to be under-utilised unless we have enough entrepreneurs to combine them more productively.

The reward associated with enterprise is **profit**.

Categories of Industry

Industry in Ireland can be classified under three headings:

> Primary sector: extractive industries
> Secondary sector: manufacturing and construction industries
> Tertiary sector: service industries

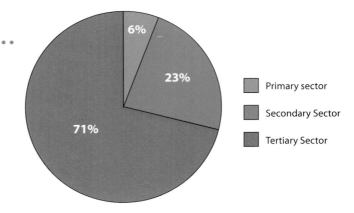

unit 6

Primary Sector: Extractive Industries

« *syllabus signpost* 6.7.1

The primary sector consists of **natural resource based industries** which extract wealth from the land. Farming, fisheries, mining and forestry are all examples of extractive industries in Ireland.

Some extracted material is used in its raw state, but generally the output of these industries is passed on to the secondary and tertiary sectors for use in goods and services. This increases the importance of the primary sector to the Irish economy as it helps minimise imports and also sustains job opportunities in those other sectors.

Despite being an important source of food and fuel, the numbers employed in this sector continue to decline. This has been brought about by the difficult nature of the work and increased mechanisation, as well as quotas placed on output so as to preserve the natural resources.

Some resources are **non-renewable,** which means that once they've been consumed they are gone and cannot be replaced. Examples in this category include peat bogs, coal and natural gas.

Other natural resources are capable of being regenerated or re-used and these are classified as **renewable.** Examples include arable agricultural land, forests and energy generated from wind, wave or solar power.

Agriculture

Economic significance

Agriculture continues to be a major industry in Ireland, though its importance has declined in recent decades. Irish agriculture is primarily a grass-based industry which accounts for over 60 per cent of land use. Agriculture provides valuable raw materials for agribusiness industry and is a significant source of exports.

Ireland has 120,000 farmers, and farming accounts for 4 per cent of total employment in the country. The sector also contributes 6 per cent of all exports leaving the country.

If the food-processing industry is included, then it increases the importance of agriculture to Ireland's economy. This broader agri-food sector accounts for around 10 per cent of employment and around 8.5 per cent of total exports.

Beef and milk production account for around 60 per cent of agricultural output, but the industry also produces sheep, pigs and cereals, along with a range of fresh fruit and vegetables.

Ireland exports almost 90 per cent of its beef output, making it the largest beef exporter in the EU and one of the largest in the world.

unit

6

Problems

> **Irish farms are relatively small** by international standards and this makes it difficult for Irish farmers to compete against larger, more cost-effective rivals. Larger farms are more likely to be capital intensive and benefit from increased mechanisation and economies of scale. Many farmers rely on off-farm employment to maintain their standard of living.

> In common with trends in all EU member states, **farm numbers in Ireland declined continuously over recent decades.** Over half of all farmers are over 55 years old. Demographic and lifestyle changes make it more difficult to attract young people to agricultural careers.

> **Agriculture is a very cyclical industry** and uncertainty over production and income levels only serve to make it a less attractive career choice. Farmers are required to commit large amounts of money when producing crops or rearing livestock. Very often this is funded from personal funds and borrowings. Additional expense will be incurred before the crop or livestock is ready for market and income is received on an annual or semi-annual basis. From a business point of view, this requires very careful cash-flow forecasting and management.

> From its establishment in the 1950s the EU **Common Agricultural Policy (CAP)** offered financial incentives to farmers which included subsidies and guaranteed minimum prices for surplus stock. This helped ensure adequate supplies of food, but eventually led to massive **overproduction.** For this reason, and also on account of budgetary and environmental concerns, this market intervention was ended in the late 1990s. It was replaced with a single farm payment which is no longer linked to annual farm output. This process of separating the payment from farm productivity is called **'decoupling'**. See *Chapter 23: The European Union* for more details on the CAP.

> **Extreme weather conditions** such as drought or flooding can devastate crops, while livestock is vulnerable to illnesses like foot and mouth disease or bird flu. This affects income levels for farmers and damages consumer confidence in their products.

> Consumers are also concerned about the implications of **pollution** and production techniques which involve **genetic modification** (GM crops).

Current and future trends

Based on the importance of the industry to the Irish economy and the issues outlined above the agricultural industry has seen considerable change in recent decades and this trend is likely to continue into the future:

> Fewer people will be employed in traditional agriculture and **farm sizes may increase** as small farms are amalgamated to produce more economically viable units.

unit

6

> These larger farms are also more likely to utilise **mechanisation.**

> We are likely to see more **part-time farming** and the National Farm Survey (2009) estimates that 39 per cent of farm holders had an off-farm occupation.

> An increase in **'alternative' produce and activities** is also likely; examples include deer farming, growing crops for fuel (rape seed, etc.) and the development of agri-tourism, where farmers open their land to the public or develop holiday accommodation and visitor attractions.

> The industry has been attempting to reassure consumers by introducing **traceability** for many food products. The EU has also established standards for organic produce and farmers who comply with these standards can benefit from use of the EU organic logo.

Fishing

Economic significance

Despite being an island nation Ireland has a relatively small fishing industry by European standards. There were just over 2,000 licensed boats in our sea fishing fleet in 2010 and many of these are small craft used for inshore fishing and catching a variety of shellfish.

The Irish seafood industry, which includes fishing, fish farming, processing and marketing employs 11,000 people and contributes about €700 million annually to national income. Irish seafood exports to international markets in Europe, Africa and the Far East are in the region of €375 million each year.

The fishing industry in the EU is governed by an agreed set of rules called the **Common Fisheries Policy (CFP).** This policy brings together a range of measures designed to achieve a viable and sustainable European fishing industry.

Fisheries Facts and Figures

Market value 2010

Home market: €340m

Exports: €375m

Activity

Prepare a bar chart to illustrate 'Key export markets' figures outlined here.

Key Export Markets

France	€100.1m
Spain	€49.7m
Gt Britain	€40m
Germany	€22.2m
Italy	€20.3m
Nigeria	€18.5m

Source: BIM website

unit

6

Problems and trends

> Some fish stocks have been depleted due to **overfishing**.

> The CFP sets out very strict rules and quotas designed to prevent overfishing and preserve fish stocks. A **quota** is a limit on the quantity of fish which can be caught. Since quotas are based on historical fishing trends, Ireland's small fleet means our quota is relatively low.

> The EU has also recently begun issuing quotas for more exotic varieties of fish in an attempt to preserve stocks of more traditional species like cod, mackerel and herring. Many of these newer varieties are fished in deeper waters which are inaccessible for the small boats which make up the majority of the Irish fleet.

Bord Iascaigh Mhara
Irish Sea Fisheries Board

> A **licensing system** operates for all fishing boats and generally speaking new licences are not issued unless existing licence holders decide to exit the industry. This measure is designed to maintain the capacity of the industry and is monitored closely by the EU and government agencies.

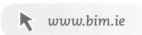

www.bim.ie

> Fishing is seen as a tough way to make a living and requires great dedication and risk taking for uncertain rewards.

> As with agriculture, consumers are concerned about the levels of **pollution and disease** which afflict the seafood industry from time to time. The fact that emissions from the Sellafield nuclear plant are released into the Irish Sea is one source of concern.

> The Commission has started a **review of the Common Fisheries Policy** to ensure the economic viability of the European fleets, conserve fish stocks, integrate with the Maritime Policy and provide good quality food to consumers.

Forestry

Economic significance

Ireland has the third-lowest forest cover in Europe at just 12 per cent of the total land area, compared to the EU average of 40 per cent. Wicklow has the highest percentage of its land under forest at 21 per cent, while Meath is the lowest with just 3 per cent.

Coillte is the commercial state company which owns more than half of all forests in Ireland. It employs 1,100 people and generates income mainly from commercial forestry and renewable energy. The value of Irish forest sector exports is close to €350 million per annum.

Trees also have a role to play in the removal of carbon from the atmosphere and so play an important part in minimising the environmental impact of greenhouse gases.

Problems and trends

> The Irish government is keen to raise the level of **land under forest** in this country and offers grants to farmers and landowners who are prepared to plant forests on their land.

> As trees need to reach a certain level of maturity before yielding a commercial return, these **grants** are necessary to encourage private investors and landowners into the industry.

> **Revenue** is generated from the sale of trees and their derivative products. These include timber for the construction industry and fuel for renewable energy.

> Ireland is nowhere near self-sufficient in timber production and will **continue to rely on imports**, particularly of hardwoods like ash, beech, elm and oak.

www.coillte.ie

Mining

Economic significance

Mining and quarrying continue to be economically significant in Ireland and provide raw materials for manufacturing, construction and energy production.

Tara Mines in Navan, Co. Meath is Europe's biggest zinc mine and the fifth largest in the world. The mine employs 700 people and produces around 200,000 tonnes of zinc and a further 40,000 tonnes of lead every year.

The are over 400 smaller quarries around the country which supply the construction industry with a variety of building materials including stone and sand. Many of these have ceased operations following the collapse of the construction industry in recent years.

Indigenous gas supplies from Kinsale currently provide about 15 per cent of Irish natural gas demand and it is hoped that the development of the Corrib gas field off the Mayo coast will raise this figure to 60 per cent. This will make Ireland more self-sufficient when it comes to our energy needs and will reduce spending on imported gas.

Bord Na Móna extracts peat from Ireland's bog land and sells it as fuel for power stations. Smaller quantities are also sold to households as peat briquettes for fires and peat moss for gardens.

unit

6

343

Problems and trends

> Mining and fuel exploration utilise **non-renewable resources** and there are no guarantees that replacement supplies can be discovered. The working life of mines and gas fields is limited and they are both costly and difficult to replace.

> The **Kinsale gas field** currently only provides a fraction of our energy needs and this will decline in the coming years. Much hope has been placed on the successful exploitation of the Corrib gas field, but the controversy surrounding this development highlights other problems facing the industry.

> Apart from the financial and economic costs, there are strong **environmental and safety concerns** associated with mining and exploration. A strict licensing and planning process needs to be enforced to ensure that the industry acts in the best interests of all the stakeholders.

Activity

Make a list of the key stakeholders in a development like the Corrib gas field and explain the main interest or role that each stakeholder has in the project.

Secondary Sector: Manufacturing and Construction Industries

Manufacturing

« *syllabus signpost* 6.7.1

Economic significance

Industries in this sector add value to the raw materials from primary sector industries in order to make finished goods.

Adding value means processing the raw materials in a way that heightens their appeal to the consumer and increases their economic value. For example, milk can be processed to produce higher-value products like yoghurt and cheese and wood can be manufactured into furniture.

It is more beneficial to individual producers, and to the economy as a whole, if this value is added here in Ireland. This is because it creates additional manufacturing and processing jobs as well as increasing the selling price and profitability of the finished goods.

Trends and problems

> Traditional manufacturing industry in Ireland, which included the clothing and footwear industries, has declined in recent decades. This decline has mainly been due to the level of **competition from low-cost producers** in low-wage economies.

> Some of these lost industries have been replaced by newer **'high-tech' manufacturing** including chemicals, pharmaceuticals, medical supplies, electronics and computer equipment. The majority of these high-tech

unit **6**

producers are foreign-owned multinationals which have set up operations in Ireland and most of the goods they manufacture here are destined for the export market.

> **Indigenous (native Irish) producers** tend to dominate the food and drink sector, but many others produce goods required by the multinational sector. Government policy is clearly focused on developing a strong indigenous sector which is capable of exporting goods. Many **'high potential' companies** have been indentified in the technology and food sectors and these businesses can avail of seed capital, mentoring and marketing advice.

Bruton announces that 24 Irish startups plan to create 445 jobs in coming 3 years

by Finfacts Team

Minister for Jobs, Enterprise and Innovation Richard Bruton TD today announced that 445 jobs will be created in 24 new Irish 'high potential startup companies' which have been supported by Enterprise Ireland in the second quarter of 2011. The jobs will be created over the next 3 years.

Making the announcement, the Minister said: "If we are to rebuild the economy and create the jobs of the future in Ireland, we must not only continue to attract high-end multinational companies, but we must also crucially ensure that more high potential small businesses can establish and expand here. Yesterday I announced that PayPal was adding 200 jobs to our base of employment in world-leading internet companies; but we also need an indigenous engine of economic growth if we are to create the successful future we all want for Ireland."Commenting on the announcement, Greg Treston, Head of High Potential Start Ups and Scaling at Enterprise Ireland, said: "These 24 companies come from a broad range of sectors, confirming that there are significant opportunities for new export-focussed business start ups, particularly in life sciences, bio-tech and medical technology, cleantech, food, telecommunications, internet services and other niche areas. Enterprise Ireland is working closely with these companies in building their business and their international market presence.

These are ambitious companies, with highly innovative products and business development strategies that will enable them to carve out a place in global markets, driving jobs and export sales growth at home."

Source: www.finfacts.ie, 10 AUGUST 2011

The agribusiness sector

Agribusiness is a term used to describe a broad range of agriculture-related activities and includes not only farming but also the processing and marketing of farm produce. By processing raw materials from the primary sector a manufacturer adds value to the goods and creates more jobs in the industry. Glanbia and Kerry Group plc are examples of Irish companies which operate in the agribusiness sector. Since Ireland produces far more food than our population requires, the agribusiness sector exports over 50 per cent of its output and this improves our balance of trade position.

Economic significance of agribusiness

With a turnover approaching €24 billion, food and drink manufacturing is Ireland's most important indigenous industry. The sector directly employs 50,000 people and supports a further 60,000 indirect jobs in all regions of the country. This represents close to 7 per cent of total employment.

The industry also uses 90 per cent of the output produced by Ireland's 120,000 farmers.

unit

6

The food and drink sector accounts for over two-thirds of exports by indigenous manufacturers with 44 per cent of exports going to the UK, 34 per cent to the rest of the European Union and the balance to the rest of the world.

Adding value in the agribusiness sector

It has already been pointed out that the agribusiness sector plays a major role in adding value to the raw materials produced by the primary sector. The example below illustrates the benefits which accrue to individual producers and to the entire economy as a direct result of adding value.

Case Study

Live cattle are exported to France for €10,000 and provide income to the farmer who sold them and also to the haulier who delivered them. Once these cattle are sold they no longer contribute any economic benefit to the Irish economy. This means that any additional revenue or employment which might be created from rendering and processing the beef or from the sale of its by-products will go to the French processor and retailers. It might even be the case that some of these value-added products are imported back into Ireland to be sold by Irish retailers.

If the beef processing is carried out in Ireland, it immediately creates extra employment in our economy and allows for the manufacture of additional products (meat pies, burgers, sausages). These value-added products are likely to be sold at a higher price than the €10,000 achieved for the sale of live cattle and will increase the value of our exports trade.

Similar benefits occur when raw materials from fishing, forestry and mining are processed here in Ireland.

Agribusiness problems and trends

> The Irish agribusiness sector is dominated by indigenous producers which are small by international standards. This **lack of scale** presents them with major challenges when competing with much larger rivals in international markets.

> Many successful indigenous companies are vulnerable to being taken over by larger European rivals.

  To diminish the **threat of takeover** and improve their access to capital, several agribusiness firms have changed their business status from co-operatives to limited companies. Examples include Glanbia and Kerry Group plc.

> Adding value requires a process of product development and this in turn relies on R&D. Indigenous manufacturers in Ireland have one of the lowest rates of **R&D spending** in the EU and this does little to improve their long-term competitiveness.

> Many Irish producers benefit from our **'green' image** and protecting this image and reputation will be a major challenge for the industry in the years ahead.

> The agribusiness industry also suffers reputational damage when **health issues** like bird flu and foot and mouth disease cause consumers to question the safety of the products on offer.

Construction

Economic significance and trends

The construction industry provides Ireland with housing, commercial property and infrastructure. It is a very labour-intensive industry and has the potential to create large amounts of employment for both skilled and semi-skilled workers. The level of activity in the construction industry is often regarded as a barometer from which the health of the rest of the economy can be measured.

As our economy grew, the construction industry mirrored that success. Employment levels increased as demand for property surged ahead in both commercial and residential sectors. Employment in construction rose by 40 per cent between 2002 and 2008. In 2007 employment in the construction sector exceeded 300,000 people and accounted for 13 per cent of Ireland's total employment, compared to an EU average of just 8 per cent.

The value of construction industry output in that same year was €38.5 billion.

Unfortunately, this sector is very susceptible to economic changes, so a combination of a banking crisis, higher interest rates and the inevitable slowdown in consumer spending have had a profoundly negative impact on the construction industry.

By 2011 total employment was just over 100,000, with output valued at €10 billion. By any measure, this is a very spectacular decline and the level of activity in the construction sector is like a magnified version of the economic cycle (see fig. 19.1, p. 384). This huge loss of employment reflects the fact that the industry is very labour-intensive and that unskilled or semi-skilled workers who lose their jobs are less likely to find alternative employment.

As the government's fiscal position gets worse, there is also going to be less spending on infrastructure. This means that more job losses are likely as public sector building projects are abandoned or scaled back.

Tertiary Sector: Service Industries

« *syllabus signpost* 6.7.1

Economic significance and trends

The tertiary or services sector is the **largest and fastest-growing sector** in the Irish economy. As the name suggests, it is not involved in the provision of finished goods but aims to **provide a range of services** to both businesses and consumers. Examples

unit

6

include financial services, medical services, transport services, government services, communication services and leisure services.

Most service industries are **labour intensive** and this has a very positive impact on job creation.

Improvements in ICT have also led to growth in both **technology and internationally traded services.** The IFSC in Dublin was built to attract and support companies who engage in internationally traded services and is home to an array of businesses involved in finance, insurance, consultancy and communications.

Tourism is one of the most significant service sectors in Ireland. The millions of overseas visitors who travel to Ireland generate foreign exchange earnings in excess of €3.5 billion per annum. The sector also creates a huge number of jobs in hotels, restaurants, and transport and leisure services.

Tourism

A large number of the service companies which operate in Ireland are **indigenous businesses** with a great number of them providing services to the multinational sector. These services include transport, catering, communications, insurance and financial services.

Indigenous industry

Economic significance and trends

Indigenous industry means **Irish-owned businesses** irrespective of whether they provide goods and services for the domestic or overseas markets.

As outlined above, the majority of indigenous producers are involved in the **agribusiness** sector.

While the agribusiness sector is one example of success for indigenous Irish manufacturers, there are others who have built their reputations in **electronics, healthcare, ICT and medical sciences**.

Electronics

Most indigenous businesses are **small and medium-sized enterprises (SMEs)** which employ fewer than 250 people. There are currently over 150,000 SMEs in Ireland, of which the vast majority are either small businesses (less than 10 staff) or sole traders.

Despite the relatively small scale of many individual businesses the economic importance of this sector has increased greatly in recent years, particularly since the demise of the construction industry.

Enterprise Ireland is the government agency responsible for the development of indigenous Irish businesses and its client companies account for almost 300,000 jobs (direct and indirect) in the Irish economy.

unit
6

Enterprise Ireland offers a wide range of financial, marketing and mentoring supports to larger indigenous businesses, and in particular those which have the potential to export their products or services

Total **export sales** by Enterprise Ireland client companies in 2010 were almost €14 billion and included new export sales of €1.95 billion. Food sector exports alone grew by 11 per cent.

Indigenous companies also tend to be **very loyal to the Irish economy** and support other indigenous businesses. It is estimated that they spend €19 billion in the economy each year and therefore have a huge economic impact right across the country.

Healthcare

Problems

The issues and problems facing the indigenous sector as a whole are very similar to those outlined in the analysis of the agribusiness sector:

> Small-scale operations which increase running costs

> Intense competition from larger international rivals

> Some traditional industries wiped out by low-wage competitors

> Lack of R&D spending

> Successful companies risk takeover by larger rivals

> Ireland's exports to emerging markets are not significant

Evaluation

Indigenous industry continues to play a very significant part in Ireland's economic wellbeing. Recent years have seen an increase in the number of indigenous start-ups and many of these have been in high-tech areas such as medical sciences and ICT. Though small in size, indigenous companies contribute to both employment and export growth. Indigenous industry also plays a very important role in supporting and supplying the multinational sector.

Transnational companies (TNC)

A transnational company is one which has business operations in several countries at a time. They are also called **multinational companies (MNCs).** The ability of these companies to transcend national borders enables them to locate parts of their business operations in economies which best meet their needs and maximise their profitability.

Examples of transnational companies operating in Ireland include:

> Coca-Cola   > Microsoft   > Bayer   > Facebook

> Intel   > Google   > Pfizer

unit

6

The **Industrial Development Agency (IDA Ireland)** plays a very significant role in attracting TNCs to Ireland and this emphasis on **Foreign Direct Investment (FDI)** has been a cornerstone of Irish industrial policy for several decades.

IDA Investment at Record Levels

by Charlie Taylor

IDA Ireland secured a record number of investments last year, according to new figures released today.

The organisation, which is responsible for attracting companies to the country, said 148 investments were secured in 2011 despite the global economic situation. In addition, there was a 30 per cent increase in the number of companies investing in Ireland for the first time.

Of the 148 investments made last year, 61 were from multinational companies setting up operations here while 87 were made by exisiting client companies. Of existing client investments, 46 were expansions while 41 were in research and development.

IDA Ireland said client companies created over 13,000 new jobs here last year, up 20 per cent on the previous year's 10,897 positions. A total of 6,950 jobs were lost at IDA supported firms last year, leading to a net gain of 6,114 jobs overall.

The number of people directly employed by IDA client companies in Ireland is nearly 146,000.

The ICT, lifesciences, financial services, business services and digital media sectors made up for the majority of newly created jobs in 2011.

Client company investments in the country rose 17 per cent last year, the agency said.

Amongst the most significant investments in Ireland included announcements by Twitter, Intel, IBM, Coca-Cola, Amgen, Pfizer, PayPal, VMware and Analog Devices...

This is an edited extract from The Irish Times, THURSDAY, 5 JANUARY 2012.

An **industrial policy** refers to a government's strategic approach to developing industrial sectors in an economy. Its success often relies on co-operation between the public and private sectors and is achieved through a combination of fiscal policies, capital expenditure, taxation and subsidies. See also *Chapter 19: Business, Government and the Economy.*

Some of these measures apply to the entire economy while others can be targeted to promote desirable or economically significant industries.

Factors which attract FDI to Ireland:

> **Low tax:** Ireland's 12.5 per cent rate of corporation tax is the lowest in Europe and is a major factor in attracting TNCs to set up operations here.

> **Grants:** The IDA offers a number of grants to TNCs which choose to locate in Ireland. These include capital grants for plant and machinery as well as employment and training grants. Since the grants don't have to be repaid they obviously reduce the cost of locating in Ireland.

> **EU access:** Many US and Asian TNCs locate in Ireland because of our EU membership. The EU's single market rules mean that any goods and services produced in Ireland can be sold freely across the EU.

> **Skilled workforce:** Ireland has an enviable reputation for our standard of education and the availability of a large number of college graduates and skilled technicians is a factor in attracting foreign direct investment.

> **Cluster effect:** The presence of some TNCs in Ireland is often enough to draw others to locate here. For example, Ireland is host to thirteen of the top fifteen global pharmaceutical companies and seven of the top ten in ICT.

unit
6

The creation of industry clusters has benefits for both the Irish economy and the businesses which locate here. Clusters tend to promote innovation, increase productivity and encourage new business. For the TNCs involved these can have the same cost-minimising effects as economies of scale.

The Irish economy benefits from the inward investment and job creation while also enhancing its reputation as a business location and centre of excellence. Other examples of this cluster effect worldwide include Silicone Valley (ICT) and Hollywood (film production).

Economic significance

> **Employment:** Over 600 TNCs currently operate in Ireland and can be found in all sectors of the economy.

  These companies make a huge contribution to employment and although the number of direct employees is subject to fluctuation it is certainly well in excess of 100,000 people. The presence of a multinational sector also supports a huge amount of indirect employment, with many of these additional jobs being created by indigenous businesses. Industrial policy has succeeded in creating employment hubs which have a TNC at the centre and several indigenous suppliers being created to provide raw materials and support services.

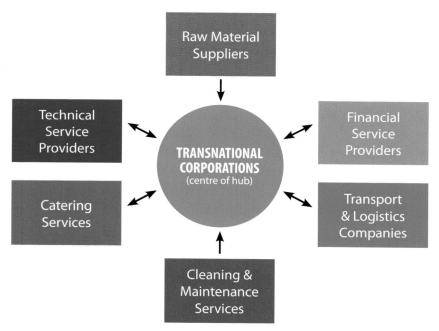

> **Exports:** Multinationals located in Ireland export the vast majority of the goods and services which they produce. FDI accounts for €110 billion – or over 70 per cent – of total exports from Ireland. This has a positive impact on the amount of money flowing into the Irish economy.

> **Taxation:** Although many TNCs locate in Ireland to avail of our relatively low rate of corporation tax, the large profits generated in Ireland mean that they make a significant contribution to the Irish exchequer. FDI accounts for 55 per cent of corporation tax, and TNC operations in Ireland also increase the amount of PAYE received by the government.

unit
6

> **Technology:** Many of the TNCs operating in Ireland are in the growing high-tech industrial sectors, including ICT, pharmaceuticals and medical devices. These are important growth industries and are an ideal replacement for the more traditional manufacturing sectors which have been lost due to low-cost competition. FDI companies also account for 73 per cent of business spending on research, development and innovation.

Pharmaceuticals

> **Irish TNCs:** Just over 10 per cent of TNCs which operate in Ireland are Irish-owned. Examples include Cement Roadstone Holdings (CRH) and Kerry Group. These companies generate both employment and revenue for the Irish economy.

Problems

The following are the main issues and problems associated with FDI in Ireland:

> **Mobility:** By definition, TNCs are very mobile in terms of their operations and are willing to move locations if it benefits their overall profitability. This means they view investment decisions on a global basis and tend to be unsentimental when it comes to local production and employment. If Ireland loses its competitiveness as a business location, we will struggle to sustain current levels of FDI.

> **Over-dependence:** Ireland's over-reliance on the multinational sector has long been identified as a major flaw in our industrial policy. Indigenous businesses find it extremely difficult to compete against these global giants and most of the indigenous employment which has been created in support industries is dependent upon the continued presence of multinationals. In the event that the TNCs decide to relocate their operations abroad, we will lose not only the direct jobs but also those in the indigenous support network. Removing the TNC from the centre of the employment hub will inevitably cause the entire hub to collapse.

> **Competition:** Ireland is not the only country seeking to attract FDI and the level of competition is increasing all the time. Many developing economies are seeking to attract TNCs in order to boost their economic development and provide much-needed employment for growing populations. Ireland needs to maintain its competitive advantage by playing to the strengths outlined above. The importance of issues like taxation, skilled labour and access to EU markets cannot be overstated, since Ireland is a relatively high-cost economy.

> **Profit repatriation:** Most of the profits earned by non-Irish TNCs are returned to their parent country and are not reinvested in the Irish economy. Many would question the wisdom of facilitating these profits through generous grants and tax incentives, when the likelihood is that this money will be sent abroad.

   To counteract this flight of revenue from our economy the Irish government is encouraging TNCs to reinvest some profits in R&D. These types of strategic investment also reduce the likelihood of a TNC leaving Ireland altogether.

Intel is an example of a TNC which has been operating in Ireland for more than twenty years and has committed over €6 billion in its world-class production facility in Leixlip, Co. Kildare.

> **Imports:** While TNCs have very high levels of exports, they also import very large quantities of raw materials. This means that the net effect of their exports is not as beneficial as it might appear.

Evaluation

While there are risks and problems associated with an over-reliance upon FDI, the Irish economy has benefited significantly from the presence of TNCs and is likely to do so for the foreseeable future, albeit subject to greater competition from other countries.

The costs associated with attracting these companies to Ireland are more than justified by the jobs and tax revenue generated by their presence.

Chapter Review Diagram – Categories of Industry

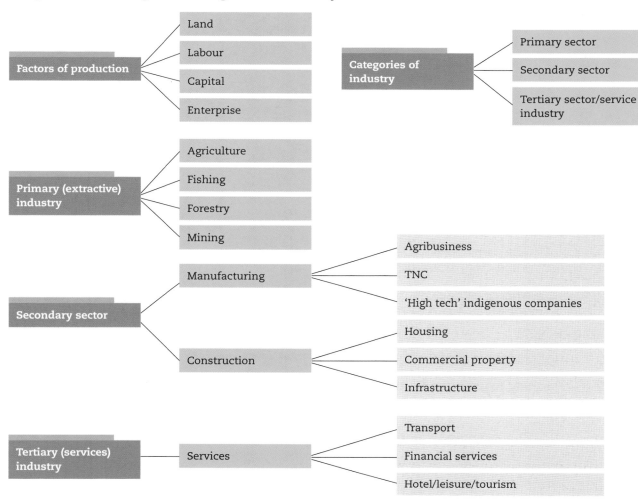

unit 6

Q Chapter Review Questions

1 List the four factors of production and the reward associated with each.

2 Use examples to illustrate the difference between the primary, secondary and tertiary sectors of industry.

3 Outline the contribution of the agricultural sector to the Irish economy.

4 Explain three major problems associated with the Irish agriculture industry.

5 Outline four major problems which may hinder the growth of the fishing industry in Ireland.

6 Explain the term 'agribusiness' and briefly outline its significance to the Irish economy.

7 Outline your understanding of the term 'high tech manufacturing industry'.

8 Explain the benefits to the Irish economy of 'adding value' to goods and services.

9 Explain what is meant by 'indigenous industry'. Support your answer with relevant examples.

10 Outline the role and contribution of the tertiary sector in Ireland's economy.

11 What are transnational companies? List four examples of transnational companies operating in Ireland.

12 What is FDI?

13 Outline four reasons why Ireland is successful in attracting FDI from overseas companies.

14 Outline three major issues or problems associated with FDI in Ireland.

Q Questions · Ordinary Level

1 Transnational companies, Irish-owned firms and the agricultural industry have an important role to play in the recovery of the Irish economy.

(a) Explain **two** benefits of the agricultural industry for the Irish economy.　　(15 marks)

(b) Explain **two** reasons why transnational companies (multinational companies) locate in Ireland.　　*LCOL 2011 (15 marks)*

2 (a) List and explain the **four** factors of production.　　(20 marks)

(b) Outline the importance of the 'primary sector' to the Irish economy.　　(15 marks)

(c) Explain, using **two** examples, what is meant by the 'services sector'.　　(15 marks)

(d) List **two** benefits of a growing 'service sector' for the Irish economy.　　(10 marks)

(e) Name **two** state-owned enterprises which help business to set up in Ireland.

Outline **two** disadvantages of state-owned enterprises.　　*LCOL 2006 (15 marks)*

3 Name the **three** categories (sectors) of industry and give an example of each one.

(i) .... Example...........................

(ii) .... Example...........................

(iii) .... Example........................... LCOL 2005 (10 marks)

4 Explain the term 'transnational company'.

Give one disadvantage of transnational companies to the Irish economy.

5 (a) Explain what is meant by an 'indigenous' firm. *(10 marks)*

(b) Outline **two** reasons for the development of transnational companies.

LCOL 2003 (10 marks)

6

> The Irish economy can be divided into three main sectors: (i) primary, (ii) secondary and (iii) tertiary. The secondary sector in Ireland consists of manufacturing and construction industries. *LCOL 2003*

(a) Explain with examples what is meant by the 'primary sector' of the economy.

(15 marks)

(b) List the challenges facing the primary sector industries in Ireland. *(15 marks)*

(c) Outline the importance of the 'secondary sector' to the Irish economy. *(15 marks)*

7 Draw a bar chart using the following information:

Transnational Companies in Ireland

Country	US	Germany	UK	Sweden	Other
No. of companies	400	180	160	40	150

Q Questions · Higher Level

1 Illustrate how foreign transnationals (i.e. foreign direct investment (FDI) companies) have impacted on the Irish economy. LCHL 2011 (25 marks)

2 Illustrate your understanding of the term 'indigenous firm'. LCHL 2010 (10 marks)

3 Define the 'secondary sector' and outline **two** current trends affecting this sector in Ireland. LCHL 2009 (10 marks)

4 (a) Explain the term 'transnational company' (TNC).

(b) Discuss the reasons for the development of transnational companies in Ireland.

LCHL 2008 (20 marks)

5 Explain the term 'service industry'.

6 Describe the importance of all the categories of industry to the Irish economy.

unit **6**

Chapter 18
Ownership Structures

Syllabus Outcomes

On completion, the student should be able to:

» 6.7.2 Recognise the types of business organisation;

» 6.7.3 Compare and contrast the different types of business organisations;

» 6.7.4 Explain why businesses change their organisational structure over time.

News Flash

1 Read the newspaper extract below and discuss the issues raised.

2 Can you explain any of the highlighted terms?

Dunnes revamps the structure of its ownership

by Richard Curran and David Murphy

The ownership structure behind the billion-euro Dunnes Stores retail empire has been reorganised, documents recently filed with the Companies Registration Office show.

The changes have seen the ordinary shares in the ultimate parent company transferred for the first time from the long-standing ownership trust directly to members of the Dunnes family.

The ultimate ownership of the Dunnes group is held through Dunnes Holding Company, an unlimited liability firm registered in Dublin. Unlimited companies don't have to file accounts.

The trustees of the Dunne family trust have held the ordinary shares in the group since it was set up in the 1960s. Members of the Dunne family, from Margaret Heffernan to Frank Dunne and formerly Ben Dunne, have over the years held 6pc preference shares, which gave them a dividend stream from the profits of the group. But

an EGM in April 2002 approved the change which saw the family shareholders keep their preference shares, while the ordinary shares were transferred from the trustees to a new nominee company run by Dunnes solicitors William Fry.

Documents filed just before Christmas show that these ordinary shares went from the trust directly to members of the family.

The trustees, Noel Fox, Frank Bowen and Bernard Uniacke, still retain an important role through the

creation of a new single "special preference share".

The ownership rights associated with this share are not disclosed, but corporate structure experts have speculated that the reorganisation is aimed at giving the Dunnes more flexibility as to how they are rewarded, the possibility of transferring shares to the next generation, particularly those working as executives, and formalising rules regarding the sale of ordinary shares to each other or outside parties.

Source: Irish Independent, THURSDAY, 22 JANUARY 2004.

For more up-to-date newspaper articles see www.edcodigital.ie

Factors affecting the choice of legal structure

When starting a new business, entrepreneurs will have many important decisions to make. One such decision involves choosing the most suitable legal/ownership structure for operating and managing the business. The choice of 'best' structure will vary from business to business, but the following criteria are often used by entrepreneurs to weigh up the alternatives:

> **Owners' liability:** The extent to which business owners are personally liable for business debts. Sole traders, for example, are totally liable whereas company shareholders are not.

> **Access to capital:** Will the chosen structure allow the business to raise the capital needed for its start-up and possible future expansion?

> **Level of control:** How much control or influence will owners enjoy when it comes to strategic and day-to-day management of the business?

> **Taxation:** The tax liabilities of sole traders and limited companies are different and this can have a major impact on the owner's income.

> **Legal complexity and set-up costs:** Limited companies have a much higher level of legal complexity and this is reflected in the documentation and costs involved in setting them up.

> **Expansion:** Some ownership structures make it easier to expand the business without the need to alter them.

> **Continuity of existence:** If the entrepreneur intends for the business to continue even after their retirement or death, they will need to choose an ownership structure which facilitates this.

Types of Business Organisation

Entrepreneurs need to understand the key features of each structure as well as the relative advantages and disadvantages of each.

It is also possible that the most effective structure for each business may change over time as the business develops and expands.

Types of ownership structure:

> Sole Trader

> Partnership

> Private Limited Company

> Public Limited Company

> Co-operative

> State Ownership

« syllabus signpost
6.7.2

unit 6

Sole Trader

This is a business which is **owned by one person.**
This type of ownership model is suitable for a whole
range of businesses but is particularly common in
the retail and services sectors, which are dominated
by small, independent operators. Examples include
butchers, barbers, hairdressers, plumbers and publicans.

Advantages of being a sole trader

Easy to set up

Where a sole trader is using their own name, there are no legal requirements, so if
Declan Kelly decides to open a butcher's shop, a sign bearing his name and type of
business is all he needs. If a sole trader decides not to use their own name for the
business, they will need to register the business name and ownership details with the
Registrar of Business Names. Declan, for example, would need to register 'Prime Cutz'
if he chooses to use this as a trading name.

In the case of certain types of business a licence may also be needed before trading
can commence. Examples of businesses requiring licences include pharmacies,
bookmakers, pubs and off-licences.

Owner keeps all the profit

Any profits earned by the business belong to the sole trader. While income tax will
need to be paid, there are no shareholders awaiting a dividend.

Privacy

Sole traders are not legally obliged to disclose details of ownership and profitability.
While they do need to comply with the law by preparing annual accounts and tax
returns, these will not be made public.

Independence and control

As the sole owner of the business, the sole trader has complete control and
independence. They make all the decisions and are not accountable to business
partners or shareholders.

Disadvantages of being a sole trader

Unlimited liability

This means that the sole trader's liability for business debts is **not** just limited to the
amount of capital they've invested in the business. In situations where the business
debts are greater than the value of the saleable assets, the sole trader may have to
sell or forfeit personal assets in order to pay business debts. This reflects the legal
situation, which does not distinguish between the sole trader and their business.
In law they are treated as a single entity, so business debts are effectively personal
debts for the sole trader.

unit

6

Lack of capital

Since only one person is financing the business, there is a limit to the amount of capital available from savings and borrowings. This tends to make it difficult for sole traders to expand their businesses and consequently most remain small.

Lack of business skills

Having one person in complete control of decision-making can present difficulties for the business if the sole trader lacks expertise in key areas of business. Sole traders may be forced to make decisions on aspects of business management or marketing which are unfamiliar to them. Bad decisions may be bad for the business and ultimately for the sole trader themselves.

Lacks continuity of existence

There is no legal distinction between the sole trader as a person and as a business. For that reason when a sole trader dies or chooses to retire their business is at an end. While the shop or business premises may continue to operate with a new owner, perhaps even a family member, in legal terms this is a new business.

Historically high failure rate

For all of the reasons outlined above, but in particular due to lack of capital and management skill, sole trader businesses are particularly vulnerable. Once a sole trader's business begins to get into financial difficulty, the owner may be forced to close it rather than run the risk of personal bankruptcy.

Partnership

This business ownership model allows for between two and twenty owners, thereby providing greater access to capital and skills needed by a business. In Ireland, partnerships are common in the accountancy and legal professions, but could operate effectively across a whole range of industries. For example, two builders who have been operating as sole traders might enter into a partnership with an architect. The three of them working together will bring additional expertise, capital and contacts and should allow the newly formed partnership to compete for larger contracts and building projects.

Partners are usually advised to sign a legal agreement called a **deed of partnership** when setting up the business or admitting new partners.

unit
6

The deed of partnership sets out the following:

> Amount of capital each partner will provide
> How profits or losses should be divided
> How many votes each partner has (usually proportionate to the capital provided)
> Rules for admitting new partners
> How the partnership will be brought to an end, or how a partner leaves

Advantages of a partnership

More capital

Each partner may bring money and financial resources to the business. This is a major advantage over a sole trader.

Extra skills and shared workload

A partner may bring other skills and ideas to the business, complementing the work already done by the original trader. The burden of decision-making is removed from one person and each partner can focus on their particular area of expertise and experience. The partnership between the builders and architect outlined above is a perfect example of this.

Less risk

The risk is spread across more people, so if the business gets into difficulty there are more people to share the burden of debt.

Partnerships also enjoy increased credibility with potential customers and suppliers who may see dealing with the business as less risky than trading with just a sole trader.

Disadvantages of a partnership

Profits share

The partnership agreement means that business profits have to be shared amongst the partners.

Less control

Shared decision-making means that each individual partner has less control over the business.

Unlimited liability

General partners have unlimited liability and are 'jointly and severally liable' for business debts. This means they have both a collective and an individual responsibility for all liabilities and this is similar to the position of a sole trader. The deed of partnership may provide for some 'limited partners' but this is relatively uncommon and every partnership must have at least one general partner.

Disputes

Disagreements may arise over workload or areas of shared responsibility. In general, the greater the number of people involved, the greater the potential for conflict. Serious disagreements, particularly over the direction of the business, may undermine the relationships and bring the partnership to an end. It is for this reason that a deed of partnership is needed when setting up the business.

Private Limited Company

A private limited company is a legal form of business organisation which allows for a maximum of 99 owners, called **shareholders**. Where there is a large number of shareholders, they may elect a **board of directors** to run the business on their behalf. Shareholders receive a share of annual profits in the form of a **dividend**. Each share carries voting rights at the Annual General Meeting, so those with the largest shareholding have the greatest say in corporate decision-making.

The names of all private limited companies must end with the word 'Limited' or its abbreviation 'Ltd'. For those companies whose names are in Irish, the word Teoranta (Teo) is used instead.

 **Example**

Arramara Teoranta is a Connemara-based company that harvests seaweed for use in the agriculture, horticulture, and aquaculture industries.

Management of limited companies

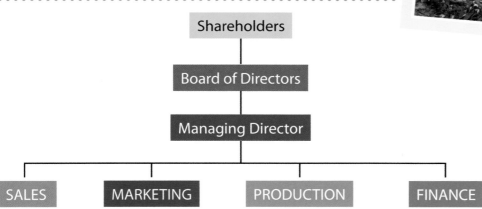

Diagram 18.1

Limited companies are owned by shareholders and the number of shares held by each of these shareholders determines the amount of influence they have over company policy, as well as their share of dividends.

By law, any company which has two or more shareholders must hold a meeting of these shareholders once a year. This **Annual General Meeting (AGM)** provides shareholders with an opportunity to get feedback about the way in which the company has been run and also to influence the future operation of the business. Since each share carries an entitlement to one vote at the AGM, those who have the most shares also have the greatest influence on company management and policy.

When a company has a large number of shareholders, it is impossible for them all to be involved in the day-to-day management of that business and they normally elect a board of directors to carry out this function on their behalf.

The **board of directors** are the senior managers in a limited company and are responsible for devising and implementing its strategic plans. They are elected by the shareholders on the basis of their expertise and they typically retain their positions for a two- to three-year period. The directors hold regular board meetings at which strategic goals are set and plans are made for their implementation.

The **managing director (MD)**, who is also a board member, is the person responsible for the day-to-day implementation of these policy decisions. An alternative title for the managing director is **chief executive officer (CEO)**.

He or she will be assisted in this role by several managers who have responsibility for a particular area of business operations. This area of responsibility may be functional, geographic or product-specific, depending on the type of organisational structure in place. Diagram 18.1 illustrates a typical functional structure.

The **company secretary** plays an important role in making sure that the company fulfils all of its legal requirements under the terms of the Companies Acts. The most important of these functions include:

> Making annual returns to the Companies Registration Office (CRO)
> Maintaining an up-to-date list of shareholders
> Organising important meetings like AGMs and EGMs. This includes preparation of the venue and making sure all shareholders are sent notice and an agenda for the meeting.

Key features of a limited company

Separate legal entity

Unlike a sole trader or partnership, the company has a separate legal existence and is effectively a 'person' in law. This means that it is the company itself, rather than the individual shareholders, which owns property and it is the company which may sue and be sued in respect of its business activity.

This is clearly in contrast to the legal position of a sole trader where the owner and the business are effectively the same and taking legal action against a sole trader's business means suing the owner.

Continuity of existence

The company continues to trade irrespective of director or management changes until it is wound up. Shareholders may come and go, but the company continues as before. This is not the case with sole trader businesses or partnerships.

Limited liability

This means that, should the company fail, the shareholders' liability for business debts is limited to the amount of share capital contributed by them. The personal assets of directors or shareholders cannot be seized to pay off company debts. This is a major advantage for limited companies compared to sole traders and partnerships and has been a major factor in the growth of modern economies.

Limiting a shareholder's liability for debt reduces the risk to their investment and makes them more likely to contribute large amounts of capital. This in turn enables limited companies to grow and expand into much larger organisations.

There are a small number of exceptions to this limited liability protection and these apply to reckless directors who willingly seek to default creditors or are acting '*ultra vires*'.

Ultra vires, a Latin phrase meaning 'beyond powers', refers to a situation where the directors of a company engage in unauthorised business activity.

When a company is being formed a document called the Memorandum of Association sets out the type of activity that business is permitted to engage in. If the directors choose to carry out any other type of business activity, they may become personally liable for any losses which arise. For example, if a company starts to sell insurance but is not registered to do so, it is acting *ultra vires*. Company directors who undertake a merger without consent from shareholders are also acting *ultra vires*.

In Ireland private limited companies must be registered with the **Companies Registration Office (CRO).**

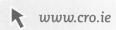
www.cro.ie

Setting up a private limited company

Formation of a private limited company is governed by the provisions of the **Companies Acts, 1963–2009**. The law requires the following steps to be followed when setting up a limited liability company.

> In order to register a company the **Form A1** should be completed and submitted to the Companies Registration Office (CRO) along with a **Memorandum of Association and Articles of Association**.

> The CRO will check all the documents to ensure they have been completed correctly and that all legal requirements have been met. If the CRO is satisfied they will issue a **Certificate of Incorporation**. This is the document which gives effect to the new company and gives it a separate legal identity from its owners. It is sometimes referred to as the 'birth cert of a company'.

unit
6

363

> Before it begins trading the new company must hold its first shareholder meeting, called a **statutory meeting**. The purpose of this statutory meeting is to:

> › Formally present the Memorandum and Articles of Association
> › Issue share certificates to all shareholders
> › Appoint company directors
> › Appoint auditors to examine the company's financial accounts and ensure they comply with all accounting standards and legal requirements
> › Permit a bank account to be opened in the company's name

> Having completed all the necessary formalities and legal requirements, the new company can begin trading.

Company formation – the essential paperwork

Form A1

Form A1 requires the business owners to give details of the company name and its registered office, details of secretary and directors, their consent to acting as such, the subscribers and details of their shares. It also includes a statutory declaration that the requirements of the Companies Acts have been complied with, and sets out the activity which the company is being formed to engage in.

Every company in Ireland must have a written constitution, which is comprised of the following two documents:

> › The Memorandum of Association   › The Articles of Association

Memorandum of Association

This document provides members of the public with important information about the company.

> › The Memorandum of Association states the **company name**. The names of all private limited companies must end with the words Limited or Teoranta. The letters **plc** are used to denote a public limited company.

> › All legal documents relevant to the company should be sent to its **registered office**, so this address must also be included in the memorandum.

> › The main and subsidiary **objectives of a company** are also set out in the Memorandum of Association. As outlined previously, companies which carry out activities not listed in the memorandum are acting *ultra vires*.

> › The Memorandum of Association also establishes the **share structure of the company.** This includes a declaration that the liability of the company is limited and a limit on the number of shares which can be issued. The maximum amount of shares available for issue is called the **authorised share capital**. The amount of capital which has been issued at any given time is called the **issued share capital**.

```
COMPANIES ACTS, 1963 TO 2009
COMPANY LIMITED BY SHARES
MEMORANDUM OF ASSOCIATION
of "The Business Workshop Limited"

1. The name of the company is The Business
   Workshop Limited.

2. The registered address of the company is
   Unit 5, Portlough Business Park, Blackrock,
   Co Dublin.

3. The objectives for which this company has
   been established are:
   • The provision of education and training
     courses for business managers.
   • The provision of management consultancy
     services.
   • The development of online resources
     consistent with education, staff training
     and management consultancy.

4. The liability of the members is limited.

5. The authorised share capital of the Company
   is €300,000 divided into Ordinary Shares of
   €1 each nominal value.
```

```
We, the several persons whose names and
addresses are listed wish to be formed into a
company in pursuance of this memorandum of
association and we agree to take the number of
shares as set out below.
```

Name of Subscriber:	Number of shares taken
John Dillon	5,000
Eoghan Byrne	5,000
Aisling Finn	5,000

Subscriber's signature.	Witness signature
John Dillon	Cathal Smyth
Eoghan Byrne	Anne Byrne
Aisling-Finn	Stephen McCarthy

Articles of Association

This document sets out the rules under which the company proposes to regulate its affairs. It is of greatest significance to shareholders since it deals with the internal rules governing the formation and operation of a company. Each company will set out the articles to suit its own needs but key issues will include procedures for electing directors or for conducting company meetings.

```
COMPANIES ACTS, 1963 TO 2009
COMPANY LIMITED BY SHARES
ARTICLES OF ASSOCIATION
of "The Business Workshop Limited"

1. The name of the company is The Business
   Workshop Limited.

2. The Company is a private company limited
   by shares registered under the Companies
   Acts, 1963–2009.

3. The Regulations contained in Table A* shall
   apply to the Company save in so far as they
   are excluded or modified hereby and such
   Regulations together with the following
   provisions shall constitute the articles of
   association of the Company.

4. The authorised share capital of the Company
   is €300,000 divided into Ordinary Shares of
   €1 each nominal value.

5. The authority to issue all new shares lies
   with the Directors, and shall be issued to
   such persons as the Directors deem suitable.
   New shares shall rank equally with the
   existing shares in issue.
```

```
6. A share certificate must be issued in respect
   of all shares issued.

7. The Company must hold an AGM each year
   within the State.

8. Any shareholder is entitled to be appointed
   as a Director and directors are appointed for
   a 2-year term.

9. Any decision to voluntarily wind up the
   company must be approved by 75% of the
   votes cast at an AGM.

10. The company must submit audited accounts
    on an annual basis,
```

Name of Subscriber:	Number of shares taken
John Dillon	5,000
Eoghan Byrne	5,000
Aisling Finn	5,000

Subscriber's signature.	Witness signature
John Dillon	Cathal Smyth
Eoghan Byrne	Anne Byrne
Aisling-Finn	Stephen McCarthy

unit 6

Advantages of a limited company

Members' liability is limited

The protection given by limited liability is perhaps the most important advantage of incorporation. If things go wrong the shareholders' only liability is for the value of their shares.

Separate legal identity

A limited company has a legal existence separate from management and its members (the shareholders).

Continuity

Once formed, a company can continue indefinitely. It can withstand the replacement, retirement or even the death of directors, management and employees. A company can only be terminated by winding up, liquidation or other order of the courts or Companies Registration Office.

Additional capital

New shareholders and investors can be easily introduced through the issuing of additional shares or the transfer of existing ones.

The process of lending to a company is also easier and less risky than with other business forms and lenders may be able to secure their loans against certain assets of the company.

Taxation

Sole traders and partnerships pay income tax whereas companies pay corporation tax on their taxable profits. There is a wider range of allowances and tax-deductible costs that can be offset against a company's profits. In addition, Ireland's current level of corporation tax at 12.5 per cent is much lower than income tax rates.

Protection of company name

The choice of company names is restricted and where a chosen name complies with the rules, nobody else can use it. The only protection for sole traders and partnerships is trademark legislation.

Disadvantages of a limited company

Set-up procedure and costs

A very clear procedure needs to be followed when setting up a limited liability company and shareholders must comply with all the legal requirements and submit all relevant documents. The costs associated with setting up this type of business are greater than with a sole trader business.

Profits shared

Annual profits are divided amongst all of the shareholders and each receives a share of this profit in the form of a dividend. The amount of this dividend is decided at the company's Annual General Meeting. Dividend payments are in effect attached to each share in the company, so those who hold the most shares will receive the largest dividend payments.

Disclosure

All companies are required to make annual submissions to the CRO and the revenue commissioners. Some of this information is available to the public and to competitors.

Single-member limited company

In keeping with EU regulations it is possible for an individual to set up a limited company which has just one shareholder. A single-member company is required to have a minimum of two directors and a secretary. There is no legal requirement to hold an AGM, but the annual report and a set of financial accounts must still be prepared. The formation procedure for this type of company is the same as for a private limited company.

Public Limited Company

Plcs can raise capital by selling shares

The names of all public limited companies end with the letters plc.

They must have a minimum of seven shareholders and the authorised share capital determines the upper limit on the number of shares available. Shareholders in plcs also enjoy the protection of limited liability.

Public limited companies are incorporated in a similar manner to private companies and a Memorandum and Articles of Association are required. In addition to receiving a certificate of incorporation from the CRO, a plc also receives a **trading certificate**. This document completes the process of establishing the company and permits it to begin trading.

Unlike private limited companies, plcs are allowed to raise capital by **selling their shares** to the general public and/or institutional investors (banks, insurance companies, pension fund managers). This sale of shares takes place through a specialist market called the **stock exchange**.

Advantages of a public limited company

Access to capital markets

The major advantage of this for plcs is that it gives them access to much larger amounts of capital than would be possible under all other ownership options. The vast majority of the capital comes from institutional and corporate investors and there is even the potential to raise capital from overseas investors.

Positive image

Having a stock exchange listing is very prestigious and will certainly improve the image of a company. This is partly because the regulatory authorities enforce very strict criteria for plcs. Only the largest and most trustworthy companies are allowed to receive a stock exchange quotation.

World-class management

This level of prestige associated with a plc and the scale of its operations helps attract the best management available.

unit

6

Improved credit rating

Plcs are generally regarded as less risky from an investor's viewpoint and this lower level of risk often results in an improved credit rating. This will make it easier and cheaper to access additional finance through borrowing.

Disadvantages of a public limited company

Expense

Plcs are very costly to set up and run.

Heavy regulation

In order to protect investors, only very reputable businesses are allowed to receive a stock exchange listing. They must comply with all of the rules set out by the regulatory authorities.

Disclosure of information

To ensure transparency, all plcs are required to publish detailed annual accounts. This information is available to potential investors and rival businesses.

Takeovers

A stock exchange listing allows a company to be valued by the stock market but also by potential takeover bidders. There are many factors which determine share prices, but not all of them are controlled by the company. This may leave a company vulnerable to fluctuations in its share price and overall valuation **(market capitalisation)**. Rival companies can attempt to buy a plc by acquiring its shares.

e.g. Example

> Ryanair bought 29.8 per cent of Aer Lingus after it became a plc.

Co-operatives

As the name suggests, a co-operative involves a group of people working together to achieve shared goals. This type of business is owned by members or shareholders who usually have a common bond and who operate the business for their mutual benefit. The Co-operative Movement has its origins in the struggle for workers' rights which took place in Britain during the Industrial Revolution. The first co-ops were set up by workers as an attempt to improve their living and working conditions.

Setting up a co-op requires at least **seven members** and application details must be approved by the **Registrar of Friendly Societies**.

A number of different types of co-op are common in Ireland:

Producer co-ops

Typically seen in the agri-business sector, they engage in the production and processing of crops and farm produce. Rather than simply selling their raw material to a commercial processor, the farmers who own the co-op set up their own processing facility. As a result, farmers ensure a reliable outlet for their produce and also benefit from the increased profitability which arises when value is added at the processing stage.

The Avonmore and Kerry food brands originated from this type of producer co-op, although both of these businesses have grown to become plcs.

Worker co-ops

In this type of business the workers are also the owners and so their levels of motivation tend to be high. While this is a suitable option for a start-up business many co-ops have resulted from a **worker buy-out** of a business which was threatened with closure. Rather than lose their jobs, the workers may agree to raise the finance needed to save the business and seek to return it to profitability.

Community co-ops

This type of co-op is usually set up to fund and provide some important service for members of the local community. Since it is funded and operated by local people for the benefit of their fellow citizens it is a good example of **community enterprise** in action (see also *Chapter 20: Community Development*).

Financial co-ops

Credit unions are examples of financial co-ops in Ireland. They allow people to pool their financial resources and loan surplus funds to fellow members. The credit union charges interest on loans and any surplus (profit) is reinvested back into the co-op or distributed among members.

The common bond between credit union members tends to be their shared place of employment (ESB Credit Union) or their place of residence (Navan and District Credit Union).

Key features of co-ops

> Members enjoy the protection of **limited liability**. Members only risk losing the amount of money they've invested.

> Decisions at the AGM are on the basis of '**one person, one vote**'. This is seen as being more democratic as each member has an equal say in the running of the co-op.

unit

6

> Members elect a **management committee** which is responsible for managing the day-to-day operations of the co-op. Some large co-ops, including credit unions, also employ professional managers.

> As with limited companies, **profits are shared** amongst the owners. This is usually done on a proportional basis, which reflects the level of business each member had with the co-op during the financial year. In a credit union, those with the largest amounts of savings will receive the largest share of profit.

> All co-ops must submit a set of **audited accounts** to the Registrar of Friendly Societies on an annual basis.

Some producer co-ops have found that the co-operative model limits their ability to raise large amounts of capital needed for expansion. This has resulted in a number of high-profile co-ops changing their ownership structure to plcs. Examples include Kerry co-op, which became Kerry Group plc and the merger of Waterford and Avonmore co-ops to form Glanbia plc.

State Ownership

Often referred to as semi-state, or state-sponsored bodies, these are not government departments, but are companies set up, owned and financed by the state. They tend to operate in areas of key social importance, e.g. transport (CIE), energy (ESB), industrial development (IDA) and communications (RTÉ and An Post).

A government minister is accountable for the overall performance of each state company, with RTÉ, for example, falling under the remit of the Minister for Communications, Energy and Natural Resources.

To ensure government policy is implemented, the minister will appoint senior managers to the board of directors.

Professional managers, with relevant expertise, are employed to run the company on a day-to-day basis.

Some semi-states are run on a **commercial** (profit-making) basis, while others are non-commercial.

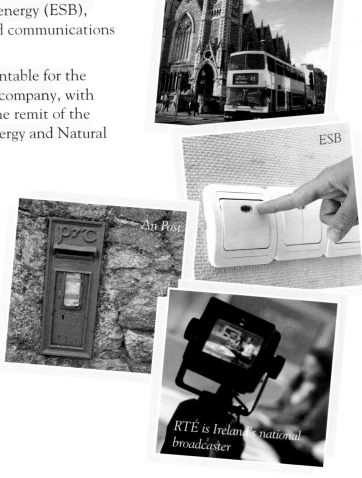

CIE

ESB

An Post

RTÉ is Ireland's national broadcaster

Example

The ESB is a commercial state company and charges customers for the electricity it produces through its account management division, Electric Ireland. In 2010 it reported pre-tax profits of €339 million and in the eight-year period between 2000 and 2008 the ESB paid dividends of €815 million to the Exchequer.

Non-commercial bodies are justified by the provision of essential public services, which private commercial businesses would not be willing to provide at a loss. This is regarded as their **'public service obligation'** (PSO). For example, Bus Éireann loses money on many of its routes and most small rural post offices are not commercially viable. The government continues to fund them by providing both CIE and An Post with an annual payment, called a **subvention**. These loss-making enterprises are supported because the government sees the availability of rural transport and post office networks as being socially desirable. Closing them would have enormous negative consequences, both social and financial, for inhabitants of rural communities.

State companies can be set up by Act of Parliament (so-called **statutory companies,** e.g. An Post), or can be registered in the Companies Registration Office, with the government as its major shareholder, e.g. CIE.

'Privatisation' is the process whereby the government sells off its shareholding to private individuals. For example, Telecom Eireann was a semi-state provider of telephone services until the government decided to sell shares to the public. Once in private ownership, the company became Eircom plc.

Nationalisation is the opposite of privatisation and involves a state takeover of a private business.

For more information on state ownership and intervention, see *Chapter 19: Business, Government and the Economy*.

unit 6

Types of Business Organisations

« *syllabus signpost*
6.7.3

	Sole Trader	Partnership	Private Limited Company (Ltd)
Formation	› Easy to set up › No need to register own name › May need licence (pub etc.) › If not using own name – registrar of business names	› Easy to set up › May need to register name › Usually involves a deed of partnership	› Up to 99 shareholders › Form A1 required › Memorandum of Association › Articles of Association › Must register with CRO › CRO issues certificate of incorporation
Ownership	› 1 owner	› 2 or more partners (max. 20)	› Shareholders (2–50) › 1 share = 1 vote
Owners' Liability	› Unlimited	› Unlimited › Some scope for limited partners	› Limited
Dissolution	› On retirement/ death of owner	› On retirement/ death of owner, or by agreement	› By agreement, bankruptcy or court order › Company can continue even if shareholders change
Management and Decision-Making	› Owner has complete control and makes all decisions › High level of responsibility can be stressful	› More expertise from partners › Shared decision-making	› Shareholders elect board of directors to manage the company › CEO and professional managers co-ordinate day-to-day activities
Finance	› Lack of capital may be a problem › Relies heavily on savings and small loans	› Access to more capital than sole traders › New partners can be admitted if necessary	› Financed by share issues › Easier to borrow money – Overdrafts – Term loans – Debentures
Distribution of Profits	› All profits to owner	› Profits shared by partners	› Dividends paid to shareholders

unit

6

Co-Operative	State-Owned Enterprises (semi-states)	Public Limited Company (plcs)
› Minimum of 7 members › Register with 'Registrar of Friendly Societies'	› Statutory company – set up by Act of law › State-owned company – registered with CRO	› As per private company but trading certificate also required from CRO *(Formation of plc not included in current syllabus)*
› Shareholders (min. 7) › 'One member, one vote'	› State is owner or majority shareholder	› Minimum of 7 shareholders › Max number is determined by authorised share capital
› Limited	› Limited (state guaranteed)	› Limited
› By agreement, bankruptcy or court order › Co-op can continue even if members change	› Wound up by the state › May be sold off (privately)	› By agreement, bankruptcy or court order › Company can continue even if shareholders change
› Democratic and co-operative management style › Members may work in co-op › Board elected by shareholders	› Ministerial responsibility but run on day-to-day basis by professional managers	› Board of directors elected by shareholders › CEO and professional management team run company on day-to-day basis › Shareholders vote at AGM
› Financed by shares, grants and loans	› Financed by exchequer and/or share issues	› Funded by share issue which can be sold to public and institutional investors on stock exchange › Loan capital
› Dividends/profit divided amongst members	› Profits go to exchequer	› Dividends paid to shareholders

unit

6

Changes in business ownership structure

The dynamic nature of the business environment means that businesses must change and evolve if they wish to remain competitive and in some cases this evolution requires a business to alter its ownership structure.

A sole trader, for example, can decide to share ownership of her business with others and form a partnership or a limited company.

Alternatively a co-operative may develop into a limited company or a successful private limited company may decide to seek a stock exchange listing and become a public limited company.

The most common **reasons for changing ownership structure** are:

« *syllabus signpost*
6.7.4

Access to capital

Some forms of business ownership, for example a sole trader or a co-operative, may find that they lack the capital required to develop their businesses. Changing the type of organisational structure may allow the sole trader to acquire business partners who can provide the finance required. The same applies to a co-op which becomes a limited company as it can raise capital by issuing additional shares.

Additional expertise

New business partners bring additional expertise to sole trader businesses. Limited companies may also have the status and finance required to hire experienced managers.

Less risk

Changing from an ownership structure with unlimited liability (sole trader or partnership) to a limited company or co-op reduces the level of risk for business owners and investors. This is an important factor in attracting finance and enabling a business to grow.

Continuity

A limited company has continuity of existence which is not enjoyed by sole traders or partnerships. This means that limited companies continue operating as a business even after the death or retirement of shareholders. A sole trader wishing to ensure the long-term survival of their business may be tempted to change ownership structure.

Privatisation/nationalisation

Changes in government policy or financial necessity may cause the state to either sell off or take control of businesses.

Other changes in business structure

In addition to the major structures outlined throughout this chapter, it is also common for an expanding business to alter its legal structure by engaging in strategic alliances or by franchising its business model. A detailed analysis of both of these options is set out in *Chapter 16: Business Expansion*.

Chapter Review Diagram – Ownership Structures

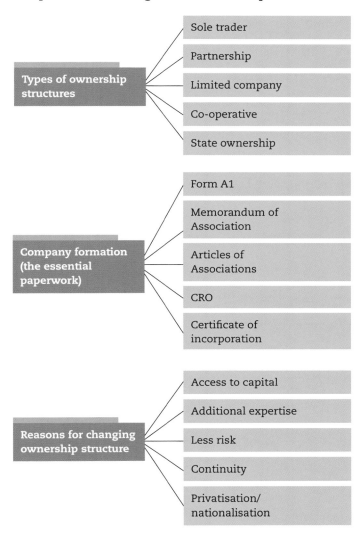

Types of ownership structures
- Sole trader
- Partnership
- Limited company
- Co-operative
- State ownership

Company formation (the essential paperwork)
- Form A1
- Memorandum of Association
- Articles of Associations
- CRO
- Certificate of incorporation

Reasons for changing ownership structure
- Access to capital
- Additional expertise
- Less risk
- Continuity
- Privatisation/ nationalisation

unit
6

Q Chapter Review Questions

1. One important decision facing entrepreneurs involves the choice of a suitable legal/ownership structure for operating and managing the business.

   List five considerations which are likely to influence their decision on choice of legal structure.

2. Explain the term 'sole trader' and list two examples of this type of business.

3. Outline three advantages and three disadvantages associated with operating a business as a sole trader.

4. Explain what is meant by the term 'deed of partnership'.

5. List two advantages and two disadvantages of setting up a business as a partnership.

6. Outline the key functions of a company secretary.

7. List the stages involved in the formation of a limited company.

8. Distinguish between these two documents related to the formation of companies:
   › The Memorandum of Association
   › The Articles of Association

9. Identify three advantages and three disadvantages of setting up a limited company.

10. Define the term 'ultra vires'.

11. Explain the following terms associated with companies:
    › CEO
    › MD
    › CRO
    › LTD
    › Dividends
    › Certificate of Incorporation

12. Outline the key features of a co-operative type business structure.

13. Use examples to illustrate your understanding of the term 'semi-state organisation'.

14. In the context of semi-state enterprises, explain the term 'subvention'.

15. Distinguish between the following:
    › Privatisation
    › Nationalisation

16. Outline three major reasons for changing the ownership structure of a business.

Q Questions · Ordinary Level

1 State two advantages of a private limited company. *LCOL 2010 (10 marks)*

2 (a) Explain the term 'sole trader'.

   (b) Outline two disadvantages of a sole trader business. *LCOL 2009 (15 marks)*

3 (a) Explain what is meant by the term 'partnership'.

   (b) Give three advantages of a partnership as a type of business organisation. *LCOL 2008 (25 marks)*

4 The formation of a private limited company is governed by legislation.

   Outline three reasons why a business would want to become a private limited company.

5 Outline the role of the board of directors in a limited company.

6 Identify some reasons why a sole trader business might change to a partnership.

7 List two reasons why a business might change its legal structure over a period of time.

8 Define the following terms:

   (i) Privatisation

   (ii) Nationalisation

Q Questions · Higher Level

1 Describe the steps involved in the formation of a 'private limited company'.
   LCHL 2011 (20 marks)

2 Outline the reasons why a business may change its organisational structure from a sole trader to a private limited company. *LCHL 2010 (20 marks)*

3 Distinguish between a sole trader and a partnership as a form of business organisation.

   Use an example of each in your answer. *LCHL 2005 (15 marks)*

4 Contrast a private limited company with a public limited company as a form of business organisation. *LCHL 2001 (20 marks)*

unit

6

Syllabus Outcomes

On completion, the student should be able to:

» 6.7.6 Explain the impact of the economy on business;

» 6.7.7 Explain the impact of business in the development of the economy;

» 6.7.9 List the ways in which the Government creates a suitable climate for business;

» 6.7.10 Explain the ways which the Government affects the labour force.

News Flash

Economic crisis is beyond control of any government

by Michael Casey

It is likely that in a year or so the collective memory of how the last government crippled the economy will have become blurred. Anger will have subsided or, more likely, been redirected towards the present Government, which has taken over the poisoned chalice of economic management...

It doesn't really matter how talented or well-meaning the Government may be. The economic problems remain so severe as to be beyond the capacity of any administration, however enlightened. The main reasons for this are as follows: There is no control over interest rates, the exchange rate or the domestic money supply. Fiscal and incomes policies are almost completely being run by the EU troika. It will be virtually impossible to bring about the kind of radical reform needed in the public sector; indeed if industrial relations problems break out we might well see a significant diminution in the quality of public services.

There is very little any government can do to get the banks lending again, or to encourage entrepreneurship or boost consumer spending. The Government on its own will not be able to persuade the ECB to make bank bondholders pay instead of Irish taxpayers. Greece may be allowed a "restricted" default but not Ireland.

In general, the government of a small open economy that is a member of a monetary union and is also in an EU-IMF programme has little or no effect on that economy. (Even in the US, which suffers from none of these constraints, President Obama's stimulus package has not worked very well.) Therefore, as recession continues we should not blame the Government...

This is an edited extract from **The Irish Times**, WEDNESDAY, 27 JULY 2011.

For more up-to-date newspaper articles see www.edcodigital.ie

1 Read the newspaper extract opposite and discuss the issues raised.

2 Can you explain any of the highlighted terms?

Introduction

This chapter will focus on the interdependent relationships involving government, business and the economy. It illustrates the manner in which business activities impact on the economy while economic decisions made by the government can have a profound impact on business. It's vital to understand the key features of an economy and the implications these may have for business.

« *syllabus signpost 6.7.7*

There is also a need to analyse the level of government involvement in the economy and be able to answer questions about **how** and **why** governments intervene.

An **economy** is the collective name used to describe all those involved in the production, distribution and consumption of goods, services and wealth in a country. It includes the contribution of individuals, households, businesses and the government.

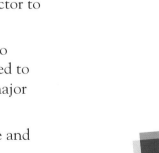

All activity in an economy stems from the four basic **factors of production:**

> **Land**   > **Capital**
> **Labour**   > **Enterprise**

Most individuals and governments do not have sufficient quantities of each factor to enable them to produce all the goods or services they require.

Ireland, for example, has limited land resources and our climate is unsuited to growing certain crops like oranges and grapes. In the past we have also struggled to produce enough entrepreneurs and creating an enterprise culture has been a major challenge facing successive Irish governments.

On the other hand, we have a relatively small but well educated labour force and access to a high level of capital resources.

Ireland's position is similar to any other economy around the world with each having varying amounts of resources at their disposal.

A shortage of resources forces people to make **choices** about the goods and services they can produce. We classify the most essential of these as **needs**. Those things we would like to have but which are less critical to our survival are regarded as **wants**. You may recall that Maslow based his theory of human motivation on a hierarchy of needs and identified basic physical needs for food, clothing and shelter as being the most essential.

Economics is really about the choices people make when utilising these scarce resources. You may never have regarded yourself as an economist, but you are making economic choices and decisions every day, most commonly when you choose how to

unit

6

spend your time and money. Whenever you choose to buy one product over another you have made an economic decision. Whenever your school decides to allocate part of its timetable to a particular subject it is making an economic decision and when a business chooses to become more capital-intensive it too is making an economic choice.

In much the same way governments make choices about how to use the resources and money at their disposal. Each of these decisions involves a **financial cost** and an **opportunity cost.** The financial cost is simply the amount of money spent on particular goods and services, for example €800,000 to build a new school. The opportunity cost is measured in terms of alternatives foregone. This means that a decision to spend €800,000 on a new school removes the chance (or opportunity) of spending that money on a hospital, a school or a homeless shelter. Each of these items, which cannot now be built, represents the opportunity cost of building the school.

When a government prepares its **annual budget** and outlines its spending plans for the year ahead, it is forced to make these kinds of choice. The decisions it makes have implications for every member of society and should reflect the values and priorities of that society. Not all societies and governments will have the same priorities, nor will they use the same selection criteria.

These different approaches to resource allocation have given rise to several **economic models.**

These economic models can be arranged in a spectrum with **free markets** at one end and **centrally planned economies** at the other. In reality, however, most economies are a mixture of these two extreme approaches and are found somewhere in the middle of the spectrum.

No matter which approach is chosen, all economic systems need to answer three important questions.

> **What** is to be produced?
> **How** is it to be produced?
> **Who** will consume what is produced?

Centrally Planned Economy ⇔ Mixed Economy ⇔ Free Market Economy

Free-market economy

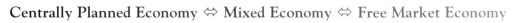

In a free-market system **factors of production are owned by the private sector** and there is no state involvement. Businesses are privately owned and entrepreneurs are motivated by profit. Goods, **services and resources are allocated purely by the forces of supply and demand.** This means that businesses produce goods and services which are demanded by consumers and these goods and services go to those who can afford to pay for them.

The benefits of a free-market approach are that resources go to those who can use them most efficiently and most profitably. Inefficient businesses will be forced out of the market and consumers will have a choice of goods at competitive prices.

Unfortunately some consumers may not be able to afford the market price and will be deprived of even the most basic goods and services. This is a major drawback to a free-market approach and often creates a huge wealth gap between rich and poor. For example, if all education was provided by privately owned, profit-seeking schools, many pupils could not afford to pay the fees and would be deprived of an education. Similar issues would arise in relation to basic food items, housing and healthcare.

Concerns over this type of division and its negative impact on society mean that there is no truly free-market economy in the world today. The USA is probably the closest example we have to a free-market economy, but it too has government regulation of some key areas.

Centrally planned economy

Centrally planned or **command** economies lie at the other end of the economic spectrum and are **totally regulated by government intervention.** They are synonymous with communist governments where **all wealth and factors of production are owned by the state.** As there is no private sector, the government provides all goods, services and employment.

Centrally planned economies generally achieve a more equal distribution of wealth than free-market ones, though average wealth levels are usually lower.

The most common criticisms of command economies relate to their inefficiency, their lack of innovation and restrictions placed on personal and corporate freedom:

> By adopting a top-down structure, a centrally planned economy may be slow to react to consumer demands for goods and services.

> Since the state controls the economy, there is a lack of incentive to innovate and create new technologies.

> The lack of a profit motive can also stifle efficiency and enterprise, which in turn leads to widespread shortages of basic consumer goods. Before 1990 the Soviet Union and most of Eastern Europe had centrally planned economies. Failure to provide citizens with the desired standard of living, as well as suppression of political and economic freedom, led to the collapse of these governments. Just as with the free-market system, it is hard to find a genuine example of a command economy in the world today, but Cuba and North Korea are perhaps closest.

Mixed economy

A mixed economic system combines **some elements of both free-market and centrally planned models** and recognises that there are benefits and flaws in each of those systems.

unit
6

381

In reality, most countries operate using this mixed system and have both a public sector and a private sector. This means that while private industry is encouraged, it is also regulated and supported by government intervention.

Ireland is an obvious example of a mixed economic system. There are large numbers of privately owned businesses which sell goods and services to consumers in the expectation of making a profit. Alongside these private businesses, the state also produces goods and services. State companies like the ESB operate on a commercial basis, while others provide essential services (e.g. transport, healthcare), which may be unprofitable.

The government finances its expenditure mainly through taxation. The level of taxation and overall **government intervention varies from country to country** and reflects a country's position on the economic spectrum.

The USA has relatively little government intervention and has low levels of personal taxation. These policies are designed to encourage and reward innovation and enterprise and have succeeded in creating high levels of wealth.

On the other hand, Sweden has very high personal taxation and excellent state provision of services. Its standard of living is amongst the highest in the world.

This suggests that **the key to economic wellbeing is not so much about the type of system chosen, but rather about how well that system is managed**.

A recipe for success?

There is no universal recipe for economic success and the approach chosen needs to be appropriate for each country and its economic circumstances. The implication here is that policies which have helped to transform a developing economy into a wealthy one may not continue to work as effectively in the future.

Later in the chapter we will consider the impact of several economic variables on businesses. The examples used will highlight the different approaches needed during periods of economic growth and economic decline.

It is also the case that policies which were successful in one economy will not always have the same positive impact in another economy. It is this unpredictable nature of economics which presents governments with their greatest challenges.

Why Governments Intervene

Government intervention in an economy is often justified for some of the following reasons:

1 To develop infrastructure

Governments have traditionally invested in projects which require **large capital expenditure** and may be too expensive for private businesses to set up. Examples include the provision

Tarbert power station

of power plants (e.g. ESB and Bord Gáis) and telecommunications infrastructure (e.g. Telecom Éireann and RTÉ).

When the Irish economy was less developed there certainly was a need for the state to invest heavily in this type of infrastructure, but in recent decades private businesses have greater access to capital. This enables them to compete in the energy, communications and transport industries, with Airtricity, O2 and Ryanair being relevant examples.

As a secondary role the state also helps develop and preserve many of our **natural resources.** Bord Na Móna and Coillte are examples of companies set up for this purpose.

2 To provide services

Commercial businesses will not be willing to provide unprofitable goods and services, even where these are socially or economically desirable. This means that the government will need to step in and provide them at a loss. Rural transport and communications are prime examples of the government meeting its **social obligation**.

The government also spends money providing **advice and support** for private commercial businesses. These services are provided by a variety of non-commercial state agencies including Fáilte Ireland, Bord Bia, Teagasc and Enterprise Ireland.

3 To redistribute wealth

Free-market conditions tend to create poverty traps, and in the interests of economic and social cohesion the government intervenes to redress this imbalance. Taxation and social welfare policies allow wealth to be redistributed to those in need.

Governments also use **taxation and regional policies** to allocate spending and promote development in disadvantaged regions of the country.

4 To regulate and legislate

Unregulated commercial business may be tempted to cut corners in pursuit of profit and this is not in the interests of consumers, workers or the economy. Governments therefore see a need to intervene to **protect** these **stakeholders**.

The **National Consumer Agency** enforces the Consumer Protection Act, 2007.

The **Health and Safety Authority (HSA)** enforces a number of different laws including the Health and Safety at Work Act, 2005.

The Irish government also established the **Competition Authority** to ensure markets are not distorted by cartels and monopolists.

In October 2011 the High Court had to intervene to force the evacuation of Priory Hall apartment complex in Dublin on the grounds that the entire development was a fire safety hazard. The court heard evidence from a fire safety officer that the standard of building work carried out by the developer was completely inadequate and that as a result even a small fire could spread very quickly and devastate the entire complex.

All residents were ordered to leave their homes and the fire service was asked to maintain a twenty-four hour presence at Priory Hall until remedial works could be carried out by the developers.

The current system of building inspection is one of 'self certification' and this example illustrates that the government may need to consider more proactive legislation.

5 To stimulate economic growth

There are times when free markets and private businesses fail to generate the level of economic activity or the type of goods and services needed by an economy. When this happens it falls to the government to take measures to rectify this situation. The main tools available to governments are **fiscal** and **monetary policies.** Both of these approaches are outlined in greater detail below.

The economic cycle

The economic cycle is the term used to describe the way in which **the level of economic activity fluctuates over time** (see figure 19.1). While the pattern of change is ongoing and regular, it is not predictable. This makes economies susceptible to sudden increases or decreases in the level of economic and business activity.

The Economic Cycle

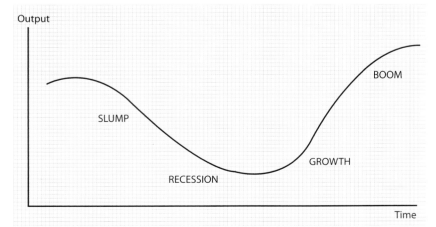

Figure 19.1

unit 6

Economic growth

Economic growth occurs when the amount of goods and services produced in the economy increases from one year to the next. It is measured by comparing the levels of **Gross National Product (GNP)** over a number of years. GNP is calculated by adding the value of all goods and services produced by all Irish businesses in one year.

If a country produced €100m in year 1 and €105m in year 2, then the economic growth rate is 5%.

Ireland's economic growth (2001–2010)

YEAR	2001	2002	2003	2004	2005	2006	2007	2008	2009	2010	2011
GROWTH %	3.9	2.7	5.1	4	5.3	6.5	4.1	-2.8	-10.7	-4.1	-0.3

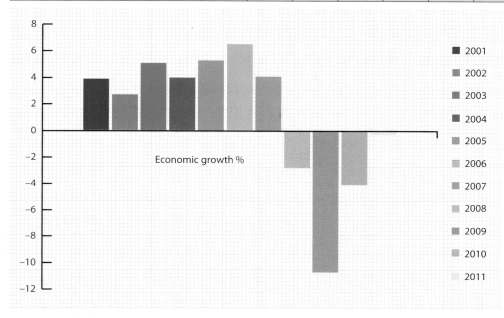

Figure 19.2

Economic boom

This is a term used to describe a **sustained period of rapid economic growth**. During a boom businesses experience very strong demand for goods and services and employment levels should increase. These high levels of demand can, however, cause upward pressure on prices and lead to inflation.

Inflation means an ongoing increase in the price of goods and services. It is measured on an annualised basis by the **Consumer Price Index (CPI)**.

The **'Celtic Tiger'** was the name given to the Irish economy during a period of rapid economic growth (1995–2008). The economy expanded at an average rate of 9.4% between 1995 and 2000 before continuing to grow at an average rate of 5.5% until 2008, when it fell into recession. Average wealth in the economy doubled between 1994 and 2006.

Economic recession

A recession represents a **general slowdown in the level of economic activity**. During a recession GNP, aggregate demand, investment spending, household incomes, business profits and inflation all fall. Bankruptcies and unemployment rates will inevitably rise as the economic cycle contracts.

The Irish economy began to fall into recession in late 2007.

unit
6

Economic depression

When a **recession** is very severe and **continues for a sustained period of time** it is referred to as a depression. Depressions often affect several economies at the same time, and this can be seen in the current economic depression facing the US and many European countries. A depression is characterised by **large increases in unemployment**, and a fall in the availability of credit. As buyers dry up, businesses will cut back on production and many are forced to close.

Some governments may default on sovereign debt during an economic depression.

How Governments Intervene

When a government intervenes in the economy it achieves its aims through the use of **policies,** which are supported by **legislation** and implemented by **state agencies.** For example, the Irish government's consumer protection policy is supported by the Consumer Protection Act, 2007, and implemented by the National Consumer Agency (NCA).

In terms of financial intervention in the economy governments have two broad policy options:

« syllabus signpost 6.7.9

1 **Fiscal policy**   2 **Monetary policy**

Fiscal policy

Fiscal policy deals with **taxation and spending**. Each year the government introduces a national **budget** as this represents its fiscal policy for the year ahead.

The overall national budget can be broken down into **current** and **capital** sections.

Current and capital budgets

The government's **capital budget** takes into account once-off or **long-term income and expenditure.** On the spending side it includes investments in road building and communications infrastructure as well as the construction of schools and hospitals. Capital income is mainly received from the sale of state assets or companies. The capital budget is very important for the longer-term development of an economy as it provides the **infrastructure** needed by households and businesses. Without investment in transport, telecommunications, energy and education Irish businesses would struggle to compete with overseas rivals and Ireland would be a less attractive location for foreign direct investment.

The **National Development Plan (NDP)** sets out the government's capital spending priorities for a five-year period and is an example of a strategic plan. Capital expenditure in 2011 was €4.4 billion.

The **current budget** has a much more short-term focus and deals with **day-to-day income and expenditure**. The vast majority of government income is received from taxation and profits from semi-state companies.

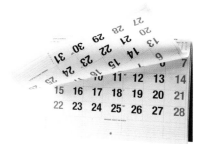

Current expenditure enables the government to utilise the infrastructure it has provided and deliver goods and services to all sections of society. The **payment of public sector wages** and expenditure on **social welfare** make up a very large part of current expenditure. Current expenditure in 2011 was €41.3 billion.

A **balanced budget** is one where **planned income matches planned expenditure** and this balanced position would enable the government to finance all its needs from its own resources.

It is far more likely, however, that there will be a mismatch between planned income and expenditure. Where **income is greater than planned expenditure,** this is called a **budget surplus**.

When a budget is in surplus, the government is taking more money out of the economy than it is putting in and this will tend to reduce the level of economic activity. This is the type of approach which may be required during an economic boom.

A **budget deficit** occurs when the government plans to **spend more money than it will receive in income**. Like households and businesses, a government can fund a short-term deficit from existing reserves or from borrowing. In the longer term a budget deficit will need to be tackled by increasing tax revenue and/or cutting spending.

By running a budget deficit, the government can stimulate economic activity since it is putting more money into the economy than it is taking out. This type of policy might be employed during a recession as an attempt to 'kick start' the economy and increase demand for goods and services.

Exchequer Statement, December 2011

Government Income	€34 billion
Government Expenditure	€45.7 billion
Deficit	**€24.9 billion**

When governments need to borrow money, they sell bonds to investors. **Government bonds** are very similar to debentures in that the money is guaranteed to be repaid at a specific future date and carries a fixed rate of interest. Government bonds are generally sold to institutional investors including banks, investors and pension funds.

The rate of interest which the government is required to pay in order to attract investment in its bonds is determined by the interaction of supply and demand. Recent fears over Ireland's sovereign debt problems and fears of a default have caused Irish bond yields to soar and so have increased borrowing costs for the government.

In July 2011 the yields on Irish two-year money broke through the 20 per cent level. This meant that the government was paying an effective rate of 20 per cent interest on a two-year loan. This was too high a price to pay and the government was forced to seek emergency funding from the European Union (EU) and the International Monetary Fund (IMF) in order to avoid bankruptcy.

In January 2012 the National Treasury Management Agency (NTMA) raised revenue for the Irish government by selling €3.5 billion of government bonds at a rate (yield) of just under six per cent. The bonds will be repaid in 2015 and are intended to ease the government's repayment schedule by replacing similar bonds due to mature in 2014.

unit

6

Demand management

By altering the balance between taxation and government spending the state can influence the level of business activity in an economy. Increased government spending coupled with lower taxes will tend to stimulate a flagging economy by raising demand for goods and services. Conversely, higher taxes and spending cuts will reduce the level of demand in the economy. This is called **demand management.**

In simple terms, demand management tries to keep the level of **economic growth at a gradual and sustainable level.** This is because government and businesses find it easier to plan and expand their operations in a climate which is predictable and sustainable. Severe fluctuations are not helpful and can have long-term impact on economic resources.

The creation of this type of sustainable business climate is one of the most significant ways in which a government can support business development.

During boom periods demand management aims to prevent an economy from growing too quickly (**'overheating'**) by lowering the demand for goods, services and factors of production. By increasing taxation levels the government reduces the amount of money available for people and businesses to spend. If these higher taxes are accompanied by reduced government spending there will be an overall reduction in demand and the level of economic activity will slow down.

Perhaps you are wondering why a government would wish to reduce the level of economic activity. Would it not be better to increase it and create extra jobs and wealth?

The answer is 'yes, it would', but what is at issue here is the rate or pace of that growth.

If demand for resources grows too quickly in an economy, there may be a shortfall in supply, causing prices to rise in the short term and inhibiting longer-term economic growth.

e.g. Example

As the Irish economy grew very rapidly during the Celtic Tiger era, there was a shortage of land and labour. Since the supply of land and natural resources are fixed, the shortage forced prices upwards and this had a knock-on effect right across the economy.

The labour shortage was resolved by a combination of higher wages (wage inflation) and an increase in labour supply. The additional labour was a combination of migrant workers from overseas and Irish adults (mainly women) returning to the workforce.

During a recession demand management represents an attempt to introduce additional investment into the economy. The aim here is to assist businesses by raising the level of aggregate demand. Even a small increase in government investment can permeate through the economy and result in a much greater economic benefit. This is because a portion of the income received by businesses is passed on to their employees and suppliers who in turn spend this money in other businesses. As this spending continues throughout the economy it magnifies the effect of the initial investment. This is known as **the multiplier effect.**

Monetary policy

The **supply of currency** available in an economy can influence the level of economic activity. An **expansionary monetary policy** will increase the available supply of money and result in **lower interest rates** for borrowers. The intention here is to provide businesses with cheap sources of finance which will encourage them to expand. Cheaper loans will also encourage consumers to borrow money and should provide a further boost to spending in the economy.

A **contractionary policy** has the opposite effect and reduces the finance available by increasing interest rates.

Since adopting the euro, responsibility for regulating both the supply and the price of money (interest rates) has moved from the Central Bank of Ireland to the **European Central Bank (ECB).** In effect, our government has no real control over monetary policy.

The Role and Impact of Economic Variables

Irish Central Bank (Dame Street, Dublin)

Economic variables are those elements of the economy which are subject to change. In the case of some of these variables the government has the ability to influence both the direction and degree of change, whereas other economic variables are determined by market forces and the economic cycle.

All of the economic variables discussed in this section have a profound impact on the economy and therefore have implications for all households and businesses in the country.

unit 6

Economic Variables:

> **Inflation**
> **Interest rates**
> **Taxation**
> **Unemployment**
> **Exchange rates**
> **Government spending** (see **Fiscal policy**)

Inflation

Inflation describes a **sustained increase in the price of goods and services** in an economy. It is measured on an annual basis by the **Consumer Price Index (CPI).**

It is better to have a low rate of inflation since this makes it easier for business planning and helps maintain the competitiveness of Irish goods abroad.

Inflation needs to be controlled as it increases the cost of living and erodes the value of money/savings. Below is an example to illustrate the point.

Exam Tip

It's important to note the impact of each economic variable on the economy and the businesses operating within it. Students should also note the impact of economic variables on each other. Attempts by the government to influence one variable may have unintended negative effects on other economic variables. This is particularly true when dealing with inflation.

e.g. Example

Denise has just returned from a holiday and was so pleased with the trip that she is keen to repeat it again next year. The holiday cost €1,000 and Denise decides to set aside a portion of her income each month to fund next year's trip.

Let's assume she chooses not to put the money in a bank, but simply saves it in a drawer at home. In a year's time she will have saved the €1,000 required and will happily set off to purchase her holiday.

Unfortunately for Denise, inflation in the economy is running at 5 per cent, and this pushes the cost of her holiday to €1,050, leaving her €50 short and unable to purchase it.

In this example, inflation has eroded the purchasing power of Denise's money and she is worse off 'in real terms'. This means that, allowing for inflation, her €1,000 will buy fewer goods and services than it did last year.

Recall and Review

A What financial institutions could Denise have used to save her money?

B In what way would this type of institutional saving improve her financial position?

C If Denise chooses to save in one of these institutions, what is the minimum AER/CAR required by Denise to enable her to purchase the holiday?

D As Denise now has just €1,000 for a holiday costing €1,050, can you suggest three possible options available to her?

Answers are on page 403.

When consumers are concerned about increases in the cost of living they will be far more sensitive to price and will shop around for the best value before buying goods and services.

Price increases will mean **higher raw material costs** for businesses. This forces them to accept a lower profit margin or pass on the increase in the selling price of their goods and services. The consequences of these actions are lower levels of profit or reduced turnover and loss of competitiveness.

Businesses will also face **demands for wage increases** from employees during periods of inflation. The purchasing power of wages is reduced by inflation in a similar way to the savings example outlined previously.

Five per cent inflation means a €100 basket of goods will cost €105 next year. An employee who earns €100 will be in a similar financial position next year as the money value of their wages has not changed. However, the quantity of goods which can be purchased with this €100 is smaller and so the employee is worse off in real terms. Employees and the trade unions are likely to seek higher wages to compensate for the reduced purchasing power. This type of increase is called a **cost of living increase**.

One way to limit inflation is to reduce the buying power of consumers. This can be achieved by increased taxation and interest rates. Higher taxes and interest rates will take extra money from households and borrowers and reduce their ability to spend.

As outlined previously, changes to taxation are part of the government's fiscal policy, but interest rate changes are determined by the ECB.

In summary:

> Inflation increases the prices of goods and services and reduces demand for them. Businesses suffer a loss of sales.
> Inflation increases business costs due to more expensive raw materials and wage demands.

Deflation

Deflation occurs when **prices of good and services** in the economy suffer a sustained **decrease.** From a consumer's point of view this might seem ideal, as cheaper goods and services will increase their purchasing power and allow them to satisfy more of their needs and wants.

Unfortunately, for the overall economy and for the businesses which operate in it, continued deflation is a very worrying development. When consumers expect prices to continue falling they are likely to postpone their purchases in order to avail of even better value in the future.

unit 6

Example

Consider an example where a consumer can currently purchase a car for €20,000 and is aware of ongoing price deflation in the economy. This may lead the consumer to assume that the future price of the car will drop, to say €19,000, in a few months' time. As a result the consumer decides to delay the purchase and the car dealer loses business. If other consumers act in the same way, the car dealership may close due to lack of sales. This leads to job losses and lower tax revenue for the government.

There is strong evidence to suggest that this type of effect has occurred in Ireland during the economic downturn (see figure 19.3). It is particularly noticeable in the housing market, where buyers are unwilling to make purchases until the price of property has 'bottomed out'.

Some economists would argue that the negative effects of deflation do more harm to an economy than those caused by inflation. Most would agree, however, that a low level of inflation is ideal for the economy since an expectation of future price increases encourages consumers to buy goods and services.

YEAR	2000	2001	2002	2003	2004	2005	2006	2007	2008	2009	2010	2011
Inflation	2.2	5.6	4.6	4.6	3.5	2.2	2.4	3.9	4.9	4.1	-4.5	-1.6

Figure 19.3: Ireland's inflation rate

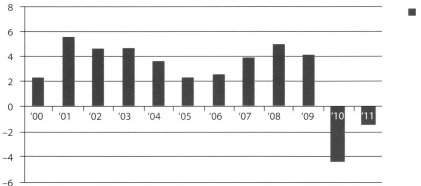

Interest rates

Interest rates represent **the cost of borrowing money** and are used to calculate the amount of money a borrower must pay the lender for the use of their funds. **Low interest rates are good for borrowers** and will tend to stimulate economic growth in the economy. Entrepreneurs can borrow money cheaply when rates are low, and are more likely to invest in new projects which offer reasonable rates of return. This is very important for business development. Equally important is the ability of governments to borrow more cheaply in order to finance their capital budget.

If interest rates increase, the profit margin from these investments is reduced and investment decisions may be deferred or rejected.

Example

A business has an opportunity to expand its operation by building a new manufacturing plant. It will need to borrow most of the money required at a rate of 3 per cent. The extra manufacturing capacity is expected to improve business turnover and yield an overall return of 15 per cent to the business. This effectively provides a 12 per cent net gain for the business and is likely to see the project go ahead.

If interest rates increase to 5 per cent the net gain will fall to 10 per cent and may cast doubts on the viability of the project. If the business is concerned about the future of the economy, they may begin to question whether a 15 per cent return is really achievable.

If the actual return fell by 2–3 per cent, it might not be worth taking the risk to borrow the money needed for the proposed expansion. This combination of higher interest rates and reduced business confidence is likely to see the project postponed. This results in fewer job opportunities being created, less output and less taxation for government.

The European Central Bank sets the base lending rate in the eurozone. In reality, banks borrow money on the financial markets and pay market rates of interest which are always higher than the ECB rate. The ECB rate is still very significant, however, as fluctuations in market rates tend to mirror changes in the ECB base rate.

Before concluding our commentary on interest rates, it is worth emphasising again the inherent conflict between interest rates and inflation. Interest rate cuts usually only provide a short-term boost to an economy since the extra spending and investment which follow will push prices upwards and erode the interest rate benefit.

Governments need to manage this situation very carefully and are sometimes hindered by the ECB's control over monetary policy.

In summary:

> Lower interest rates make borrowing cheaper and encourage governments and businesses to borrow for investment.
> Lower interest rates reduce the cost of existing loans for households and businesses.
> Lower interest rates can lead to inflationary pressure in an economy.
> Higher interest rates have the opposite effects.

unit 6

Taxation

As outlined in the section on fiscal policy, taxation can be used as an **economic tool to help regulate the level of spending in an economy**. To encourage investment and spending the government can lower tax rates.

Lower levels of **income tax** will mean consumers have more **disposable income** to spend on goods and services. This increases business sales and growth.

Reduced **corporation tax** will also help to stimulate **investment and enterprise**. Ireland's relatively low level of corporation tax is seen as a major factor in encouraging TNCs to set up operations here.

Governments can also use more **targeted tax incentives** to benefit specific industries or geographic regions.

Recent examples include the low rate of corporation tax which applies to companies operating in Dublin's International Financial Services Centre (IFSC) and additional tax incentives for R&D spending in the Shannon region.

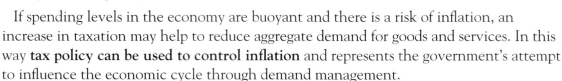

Taxation policies can also be used to discourage some activities and direct the focus of industrial development. The introduction of a **carbon tax** (on fossil fuels) is an example of this policy in action.

If spending levels in the economy are buoyant and there is a risk of inflation, an increase in taxation may help to reduce aggregate demand for goods and services. In this way **tax policy can be used to control inflation** and represents the government's attempt to influence the economic cycle through demand management.

Increases in income tax will reduce the disposable income of consumers and will have a knock-on effect on businesses.

Governments need to be careful about the impact of higher direct taxation. There is a danger that sustained or excessive increases will motivate people to evade taxation. This also encourages the development of the black economy.

The black economy operates on a cash basis

A **black economy** is one which exists alongside the official or legitimate economy but is not regulated, rewarded or taxed in any official way. It usually involves cash transactions and income and profit are not disclosed to the regulatory authorities.

Higher rates of **VAT and excise duties** will increase the price of goods and services in the economy and will usually reduce demand. It will also increase the cost of raw materials for businesses and may lead to less competitive prices for goods produced in Ireland.

unit

6

The Irish government has been under a lot of international pressure to increase our rate of corporation tax. The government's reluctance to do so reflects their fears that additional corporation tax will make Ireland a less attractive location for TNCs.

In summary:

> Lower income taxes and personal taxes will increase disposable income and improve demand for goods and services.
> Lower corporation taxes will encourage investment by businesses and will help attract TNCs to Ireland.
> Tax cuts can be targeted to support specific sectors of the economy.
> Increased taxation reduces spending, investment and economic growth, but can be helpful in controlling inflation.

Unemployment

The unemployment rate measures **the percentage of our workforce which is unable to find a job.** The government will always seek to keep unemployment as low as possible. This goal can be achieved by creating a positive economic climate (low inflation, low taxation and low interest rates), which should encourage consumer spending, investment and job creation.

During the Celtic Tiger era, unemployment rates in Ireland fell to historically low levels, but the recent recession has resulted in much higher levels of joblessness.

There are a number of ways of measuring unemployment, but the most reliable are the **live register** and the **Quarterly National Household Survey** (QNHS).

The **live register** counts the number of people who physically 'sign on' to an unemployment register and claim social welfare payments.

The **QNHS** is a regular survey of 39,000 households in the Republic of Ireland. The survey sets out to establish the number of people who are currently unemployed, but who are actively seeking work. It's regarded as a more accurate measure of unemployment than the live register. This is because not all unemployed people choose to sign on the live register, or in the case of those who were self-employed, they are not entitled to claim unemployment benefit assistance and are unlikely to sign on.

When people lose their jobs they will generally have far **less disposable income** available for buying goods and services and this will obviously impact on many businesses in the economy.

High levels of unemployment will increase government spending in areas like social welfare and training programmes. This type of increase in current expenditure will mean **less money is available for capital projects**.

unit 6

Increases in government current expenditure are likely to be financed through higher levels of taxation. The negative implications of tax increases have been outlined above.

Unemployment tends to have a **deflationary effect on wage levels** and will help reduce business costs in this area. As the available supply of labour has increased relative to the level of demand, the cost of labour (i.e. wages) will be driven downwards. This reflects the intense competition between workers and the fact that those who are desperate for work are willing to accept lower wages in return for employment. This type of situation is often referred to as being an **'employer's market'** and suggests that employers are in a strong position to dictate terms of employment and wage rates.

In summary:

> Higher unemployment reduces disposable income and consequently demand for goods and services.
> High unemployment requires additional current expenditure by governments and may reduce their scope for capital expenditure.
> Taxation may increase as governments seek to replace lost income tax revenue and fund additional social welfare payments.
> Higher unemployment levels will have a deflationary effect on wage rates, thereby reducing business costs.

Exchange rates

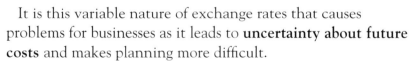

An exchange rate is really just **the price of one currency in terms of another currency.** For example €1 = stg £0.67 means that it will cost €1 to purchase 67p sterling. Exchange rates are not fixed and are subject to the market forces of supply and demand. As with all commodities, high demand tends to mean higher prices while low levels of demand will cause the price to fall.

It is this variable nature of exchange rates that causes problems for businesses as it leads to **uncertainty about future costs** and makes planning more difficult.

Since all countries in the eurozone share a common currency this eliminates the exchange rate risk when they trade with each other. This risk still remains, however, when Irish businesses deal with UK, US and other non-European trading partners.

The UK continues to be our nearest neighbour and most significant trading partner and this exchange rate volatility remains a concern for businesses in both economies.

When the price of the euro increases relative to another currency we say the euro is getting stronger, whereas a lower price indicates less demand for our currency and a weaker euro.

Different sectors of the economy will have different preferences when it comes to the relative strength of the euro, and their views will very much depend on whether they are importing or exporting goods and services.

unit 6

A **strong euro is generally helpful for importers** as it makes foreign goods relatively less expensive.

Here's an example to illustrate the situation.

 **Example**

La Vino Ltd imports wine from California and needs to buy US dollars to pay for $15,000 worth of goods. With the current exchange rate €1 = $1.50, La Vino Ltd will need to pay €10,000 to buy the $15,000 required (i.e. 15,000 ÷ 1.50).

If the euro strengthens in value relative to the dollar, the new rate may mean that €1 = $2.

With this new exchange rate La Vino Ltd will pay just €7,500 to acquire the $15,000 it needs (i.e. 15,000 ÷ 2). This will enable them to make a bigger profit on the imported goods, or perhaps lower the selling price of the imported wine and increase their turnover and market share.

It should be noted that while both of these outcomes are beneficial for La Vino Ltd, cheaper imports are not necessarily beneficial to the Irish economy as a whole. This is because they may be substituted for home-produced goods with a resulting loss for indigenous producers.

The one major exception to this is fuel, and in particular oil. Since oil prices are always denominated in US dollars, a strong euro makes imported oil cheaper and this benefits all households and businesses in the economy.

From an exporter's point of view, a strong euro makes it more expensive for overseas customers to buy their products.

 **Example**

A manufacturer of Irish clothing exports its produce to the US market and their best-selling range of jackets currently sell for €300 each. With an exchange rate of €1 = $1.50, US customers will pay $450 for a jacket (i.e. 300 x 1.50).

If the euro strengthens to a new rate of €1 = $2, the US client must pay $2 for each euro and the price of the jacket rises to $600 (i.e. 300 x 2). This is a significant price increase and may have the effect of making the Irish-produced garment unattractive to US customers.
A strengthening euro or a falling dollar causes this effect right across the export sector and makes Irish exports less competitive.

unit
6

The Role of Government as an Employer

This list of state agencies below illustrates the scale of government involvement in the economy of Ireland and highlights its important role as an employer. The government is in fact the single biggest employer in the economy, with total public sector employment at close to 300,000 people. This figure represents just under 17 per cent of the workforce and includes civil service staff working in government departments, public sector employees (e.g. teachers, nurses, gardaí), as well as those working in state agencies.

« syllabus signpost 6.7.10

The numbers employed by the state increased steadily during the economic boom and this trend has been reversed in recent years as the recession has forced cutbacks in government expenditure. The challenge facing the government is how to achieve these cuts without impacting too severely on important front-line services to the public.

Public Sector Employment (2010)

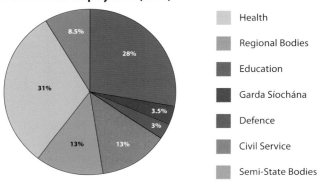

- Health
- Regional Bodies
- Education
- Garda Síochána
- Defence
- Civil Service
- Semi-State Bodies

State agencies

By virtue of its fiscal policy the government invests heavily in the economy and provides a wide range of services to the general public and to the business community. Many of these services are provided by government departments, agencies and state companies. Some of the most significant are set out below.

Role/Support for Business	State Agency
Policy planning and administration	Government departments, e.g. Dept of Education and Skills, Dept of Finance. Local authorities (city and county councils) (p. 399)
Enterprise and business development	IDA Ireland (p. 327) Enterprise Ireland (p. 327, 348) Teagasc (p. 383, 399) County Enterprise Boards (p. 413) Coillte (p. 342) Bord Iascaigh Mhara (p. 341–2)

Marketing	Fáilte Ireland (p. 304)
	Bord Bia (p. 383, 454)
Transport	CIE (p. 370)
	Aer Rianta
Communications	An Post (p. 370)
Training	SOLAS (p. 399)
	CERT (p. 399)
Regional development	Udaras Na Gaeltachta
	Shannon Development Company
Industrial relations	The Labour Relations Commission (p. 44)
	The Labour Court (p. 45)
Taxation	The Revenue Commissioners (p. 168)
Energy	ESB (p. 371)
	Bord Gais (p. 383)
Community development	Area Partnership companies (p. 415)
	Pobal (p. 415)
	LEADER Plus (p. 413)
Regulation	The Competition Authority (p. 329)
	National Consumer Agency (p. 22, 27)

Notes

> **Local authorities:** a nationwide network of city and county councils which provide a variety of local services to businesses in their area, including refuse collection, water and public lighting. Some of these services are provided on a commercial basis and must be paid for by those who avail of the service.

   Businesses pay commercial rates to their local authority and the rateable valuation of each business is linked to the size of the business premises. Local authorities also receive income from motor tax and are responsible for the upkeep and maintenance of the road network in their area.

> **Teagasc** (Agriculture and Food Development Authority): state-funded body that provides research, advice and training services to the agriculture and food industry.

> **CERT:** provides training for the hotel, food and hospitality industries.

> **SOLAS:** In 2011 the Minister for Enterprise and Skills (Ruairí Quinn) announced that the state training agency FÁS was to be disbanded and replaced by a new agency which is to be called SOLAS (Seirbhísí Oideachais Leanunaigh Agus Scileanna). It is expected that SOLAS will take on most of the functions previously carried out by FÁS and the restructuring will also lead to an increased role for the country's VECs, particularly when it comes to the provision of training courses.

Ruairí Quinn

unit
6

Public–private partnerships

The role of state agencies is to provide infrastructure and a range of services which will assist businesses and economic growth. While most of the services are provided by state agencies alone, and often on a non-commercial basis, the government sometimes works in co-operation with the private sector for the provision of infrastructure. These joint ventures are called **public–private partnerships (PPP).**

Under a contractual agreement a private sector firm will design, build and operate an infrastructural project on behalf of the state. Recent examples include motorways, schools and water treatment plants. Most of these projects are financed by the exchequer, though some are part-funded by private investment and user charges. The contract may allow the private operator to collect these user charges for a set number of years (usually twenty or more), after which ownership of the infrastructure reverts to the state. From the government's point of view, PPPs offer a number of advantages:

> This type of project allows the government to avail of private sector innovation and commercial management expertise. Contractors will suffer financial penalties for late delivery of the project.

> Since payment is made over the lifetime of the project, the up-front capital outlay is reduced and the government can get better value from its capital spending programme.

> The nation's stock of infrastructure is built up more quickly as the projects are not entirely reliant on state funding.

e.g. Example

Ireland's first official motorway service areas opened in September 2010 and are located on the M1 at Dundalk and Lusk and the M4 at Enfield. The SuperStop Consortium (of Applegreen, Pierse Contracting and TOP) entered into agreements with the National Roads Authority (NRA) to design, build, finance, operate and maintain three double-sided motorway service areas. These will be run and managed by Applegreen Ltd as part of a tender process that saw the 100% Irish consortium win the PPP Contract from the NRA.

The state-of-the-art service areas provide facilities on a par with those seen in continental Europe, with services for both hauliers and private motorists. This includes 'hotel standard' toilets, showers, children's play areas, plenty of parking and a wide range of food offers.

The overall project represents an investment of more than €70 million with the creation of more than 300 jobs in the six sites.
Source: Applegreen Ltd

The existence of PPP is intended to overcome some of the perceived drawbacks associated with public-sector provision of goods and services; this is part of a wider debate which often questions the level of state involvement in the economy.

The issues of **privatisation** and **nationalisation** are at the heart of this debate.

unit
6

Privatisation

Privatisation involves the sale of state companies or public assets into private ownership. It is usually achieved through the sale of shares. Recent examples of privatisation in Ireland include the sale of Aer Lingus, for which the government received over €240 million for its 75 per cent stake. Other examples include the sale of Eircom and Irish Life.

Nationalisation

Nationalisation occurs when the state takes control of a business or assets which were previously in private ownership. It is in effect the exact opposite of privatisation. Nationalisation usually occurs when the state wishes to gain control over valuable natural resources or when a strategically important private business suffers a financial collapse.

In the 1980s the government stepped in to nationalise the PMPA insurance company when it became insolvent. At the time it was nationalised, PMPA was insuring almost half of all motorists in Ireland. The government could not risk a scenario where so many motorists would lose their insurance cover and so it stepped in to rescue the company. More recently the Irish Government nationalised the ill-fated Anglo Irish Bank in 2009 and currently has a 92 per cent stake in AIB as a result of its recapitalisation with taxpayers' money.

In keeping with the discussion of economic systems earlier in this chapter, it should be pointed out that both nationalisation and privatisation may have political as well as economic motives. Nationalisation clearly increases the level of state control in an economy and is associated with communist or socialist governments, whereas privatisation is supported by those who favour a free-market approach.

Problems with state ownership

Those who oppose state involvement in the economy often cite the following criticisms of state ownership:

> **Lack of competition:** Many state companies are monopolies, which mean they are the only provider of goods and services in the market. This, it is argued, gives them too much control over supply and market prices.

> **Lack of profit motive:** With no competition to challenge them and the absence of a strong profit motive there is a fear that state enterprises will be inefficient. During more difficult trading conditions they may tend to increase prices rather than tackle cost over-runs and overstaffing.

unit

6

401

> **Lack of innovation:** Public accountability and the non-commercial ethos may lead management to adopt a conservative approach to risk-taking. The semi-state sector is traditionally seen as being bureaucratic. This is a management style which entails a very high level of accountability and form-filling (sometimes referred to as 'red tape'). Decision-making is often slow since everything needs to follow a set procedure and be verified with senior managers before action can be taken.

> **Political appointees:** Politicians appoint their nominees to the board of directors of state companies. In some people's eyes this casts doubt on their level of motivation and also leads to wholesale changes at board level following a change of government. In terms of strategic planning, this is not ideal for the business.

> **Lack of capital:** EU rules designed to ensure fair competition between rival businesses restrict the ability of governments to fund some commercial state enterprises. For this reason, some have been forced to seek capital on private financial markets. This seems to have been a consideration when a decision was made to privatise Aer Lingus, as the airline was in need of additional capital to fund the purchase of new aircraft.

Arguments in favour of privatisation

> **Increased revenue for government:** Proceeds from the sale of state companies provide additional revenue to the government. This money can obviously be spent on other areas and is helpful when the government is struggling to balance its annual budget.

> **Greater competition in an industry:** Increased levels of competition tend to be better for consumers as they may have greater choice and at lower prices.

> **Profit motive better for business:** In the longer term the existence of a strong profit motive will make a business more efficient and help ensure its long-term viability.

> **Access to capital:** Private ownership enables a business to access additional capital on international financial markets. This is in keeping with the EU rules restricting government intervention in competitive markets.

> **Share ownership for citizens:** The sale of state companies allows private citizens to enjoy business ownership and also offers these shareholders an opportunity to share in future profits.

Arguments against privatisation

> **Sale of profitable companies:** Since only profitable state companies are likely to be sold, the exchequer will lose the ongoing revenue generated by their profits. At the same time, the government will have to continue funding loss-making operations in order to fulfil its social obligation.

unit 6

> **Loss of control:** Selling state companies may result in a loss of control over some strategically important assets and natural resources (e.g. electricity, gas). This is not always desirable for the country and increases the possibility that these resources may pass into foreign control.

> **Private monopolies:** If a state monopoly is replaced by a private monopoly, the desire for profit may lead to price increases and a reduced level of service. A private monopoly may not act with the same level of social obligation as its semi-state counterpart.

> **High cost of privatisation:** There are very large advertising and underwriting costs associated with privatisation and these will reduce the financial benefit of any sale.

> **Past failures:** Not all previous attempts at privatisation have been successful and this can affect people's attitude to future sell-offs. If investors are reluctant to buy shares the privatisation will generate little revenue and will result in state assets being sold off cheaply.

Cabinet to discuss State asset sale

by *Martin Wall, Industry Correspondent, and Stephen Collins, Political Editor*

The Government will today consider proposals to sell some State assets, including a stake in the ESB.

The ESB proposal is one of the main items set out in a memorandum drawn up by Minister for Public Expenditure and Reform Brendan Howlin on the sale of State assets which will be discussed by the Cabinet today.Under the terms of the EU-IMF deal of last November, which the Government is committed to implementing, there was an agreement to undertake an "independent assessment" of the electricity and gas sectors and to set targets for possible privatisation when the assessment was completed.

Speaking in Dublin this morning, Tánaiste Eamon Gilmore said the Government has committed in the Programme for Government to raise about €2 billion through the sale of State assets. "The Government's economic management council have been looking at the options that are available for some time, there will be a discussion of that at the Cabinet today and that will be based on the memorandum on public expenditure which the Minister is bringing to the Cabinet," said Mr Gilmore.

Yesterday the IMF urged the Government to seek to raise €5 billion from the sale of State assets when delivering its quarterly assessment of the Irish economy… Informed sources said last night the memorandum drawn up by Mr Howlin sets out a range of options for the Cabinet in disposing of State assets. Minister for Transport Leo Varadkar suggested yesterday that the State could sell its remaining 25 per cent stake in Aer Lingus…It is understood that there are no proposals to sell any of the transport companies in the CIÉ group.

This is an edited extract from **The Irish Times,** Thursday, 8 September 2011.

unit 6

Answers to Review and Recall Activity

A Denise could have chosen to save her money in:

> a commercial bank, e.g. AIB, Bank of Ireland
> a building society, e.g. EBS
> a credit union
> the Post Office

B Each of these institutions would provide Denise with a savings account which earns interest. This would offset some or all of the effects of inflation, though the interest earned would be subject to DIRT.

C In order to completely offset the impact of inflation Denise would need to choose a savings account which offers at least 5 per cent AER. Any less will mean she will still face a shortfall on the price of the holiday. Taking DIRT into account will increase the level of interest required by Denise to afford the holiday.

Some lenders offer interest rates which match the annual rate of inflation and are designed to ensure savers do not see their purchasing power completely eroded. Savings schemes of this type are said to be **index-linked,** reflecting the fact that the rate of interest mirrors changes in the consumer price index.

D In her current situation with just €1,000 available to her, Denise has the following options:

> » Borrow the additional €50 required. This may involve additional borrowing and interest charges.

> » Shop around for a cheaper holiday elsewhere. This illustrates the way in which consumers become more price-sensitive in times of high inflation. Businesses which cannot offer value for money are likely to suffer.

> » Postpone the holiday until she has saved the additional money required. This also suggests that consumer demand for some goods and services, particularly luxuries, will be lower during periods of inflation. Not only are prices rising quickly, but it takes longer to save the money required.

Chapter Review Diagram – Business, Government and the Economy

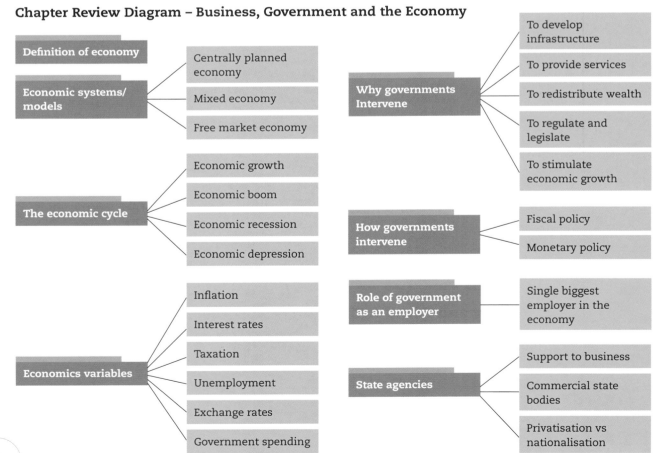

Q Chapter Review Questions

1 What is an economy?

2 Explain the factors of production which are necessary for an economy to succeed and grow.

3 Complete the sentence:

'Economics is the study of……………………………………………………'

4 Use examples to illustrate the difference between financial cost and opportunity cost.

5 Distinguish between a command economy and a free market economy.

6 Explain the statement: 'Ireland is a mixed economy'.

7 Outline the major reasons why governments intervene in an economy.

8 Draw a diagram to illustrate the economic cycle.

9 What is 'economic growth'?

10 Explain the terms 'economic boom' and 'recession'.

11 Distinguish between fiscal policy and monetary policy.

12 In economic terms what is meant by 'demand management'.

13 List five economic variables which have a major impact on the Irish economy.

14 Outline how the following would impact on the Irish economy:

   (i) A reduction in the rate of unemployment

   (ii) A decision by the government to increase taxation levels

   (iii) A surge in inflation

   (iv) An increase in the value of the euro relative to the US dollar

15 Explain:
   › 'black economy'
   › 'live register'

16 State what the following letters stand for:

   (i) GNP   (iii) ECB   (v) PPP   (vii) QNHS

   (ii) CPI   (iv) NDP   (vi) IFSC

17 Outline four reasons why the state intervenes in the markets for goods and services.

18 Outline three arguments in favour of privatisation.

Q Questions · Ordinary Level

1 The following table shows unemployment rates from November 2007 to May 2009.

	November 2007	May 2008	November 2008	May 2009
Total persons on the Live Register	150,000	200,000	250,000	400,000

(a) (i) Draw a bar chart to represent the above information. *(10 marks)*

(ii) Outline **two** effects of increasing unemployment on the government's income and expenditure. *(20 marks)*

(iii) Outline **two** effects of increasing unemployment on business. *(20 marks)*

In recent times there has been a large increase in the number of Irish consumers shopping in Northern Ireland.

(b) (i) State **two** effects of this situation for the Irish economy. *(15 marks)*

(ii) The Irish Government reduced VAT rates in its December 2009 Budget. How can this measure help to reverse the above situation? *LCOL 2010 (10 marks)*

2 The government may consider increasing taxes to help the economy. Using **examples** of taxes, describe **two** effects of increased taxes on the Irish economy. *LCOL 2009 (20 marks)*

3

Unemployment in Ireland is less than 5% but some economists are concerned because interest rates have risen and are forecast to increase. *LCOL 2007*

(a) Outline **three** benefits of low unemployment to the Irish economy. *(15 marks)*

(b) Outline **three** effects of increasing interest rates on Irish business. *(15 marks)*

(c) Describe **two** ways in which the Irish government assists business. *(20 marks)*

4 (a) Explain the term 'inflation'.

(b) Outline **two** benefits of low inflation for Ireland. *LCOL 2006 (20 marks)*

5 Outline **three** ways in which low taxation rates can help business. Use examples to illustrate your answer. *LCOL 2004 (15 marks)*

6 Define the term 'privatisation' and outline **two** benefits of privatising a state enterprise. *LCOL 2003 (20 marks)*

7 What is a centrally planned economy? Outline the benefits of this type of system.

Questions · Higher Level

1

The unemployment rate in the Irish labour market increased from 4.3% in January 2005 to 14.7% in March 2011. *LCHL 2011*

Discuss the effects of increasing unemployment on the Irish economy.

(20 marks)

2 Explain what is meant by the term 'open economy'. *LCHL 2010 (10 marks)*

3 Evaluate, using examples, the arguments in favour **or** against the privatisation of commercial state enterprises in Ireland. *LCHL 2008 (20 marks)*

4

Business activities do not operate in a vacuum. It is important to understand the interaction between the various types of business organisations with the local community and the role of the government and society. *LCHL 2002*

Explain, using an example where appropriate, the impact that business activity has in the development of the Irish economy.

5 Analyse how the economic variables (factors) in the Irish economy have an impact on a local economy. *LCHL 2001 (20 marks)*

6 Analyse the ways in which the government creates a suitable climate for business enterprises in the country. Use examples in your analysis. *LCHL 2000 (15 marks)*

unit

6

Syllabus Outcomes

On completion, the student should be able to:

» 6.7.5 Identify the importance of community initiatives in the development of the local economy.

News Flash

1 Read the newspaper extract below and discuss the issues raised.

2 Can you explain any of the highlighted terms?

Government to slash number of enterprise boards and VECs

by John Walshe

The Government is hoping to save millions in administration costs by cutting the numbers of both County Enterprise Boards (CEBs) and Vocational Education Committees (VECs).

The moves will almost certainly lead to strong political, business and community protests from counties that lose boards and committees.

There are 35 county and city enterprise boards and 33 VECs. The intention is to reduce the numbers to around 20 each.

Separate proposals are being brought before the Cabinet by the Enterprise Minister Batt O'Keeffe and by the Education Minister Mary Coughlan.

The budget for the CEBs, which provide support for the development and growth through capital grants, feasibility studies, information, advice, counselling and mentoring of enterprises with fewer than 10 staff, is €28m.

Since they were set up in 1993, they have been credited with creating 30,726 new jobs.

A spokesman for Mr O'Keeffe said that the minister believed that dedicated state support for the micro-enterprise sector should continue to be provided and such support should be delivered as close to the client as possible.

He confirmed that the minister was evaluating the appropriateness of the current structures of the 35 CEBs...

This is an edited extract from **The Irish Independent**, TUESDAY, 12 OCTOBER 2010.

For more up-to-date newspaper articles see www.edcodigital.ie

Community Development

You may recall from *Unit 2* that we introduced a broad definition of enterprise as *'any attempt to do, or start, something new'* and indicated that this definition can be applied to enterprise on a personal level, a business level, a community level and at national level. Previous chapters have dealt with personal, business and national enterprise and we now wish to turn our attention to the role of enterprise in community development.

Community development is focused on supporting people within the community to work together to develop skills, services and facilities to meet their needs. It is about **empowering local individuals and groups** and helping them take ownership of initiatives that lead to a more equal and active community for all. It emphasises in particular those groups which are socially, economically or geographically isolated.

Community development involves **local people doing something to improve the quality of life in their community**. It requires that they show some **initiative** and **resourcefulness** in order to provide much-needed services or facilities within their locality. To achieve their goals they frequently receive support and assistance from semi-state or other community-based organisations.

National and local governments, supported by EU funding, offer a range of support services designed to assist enterprising communities. This assistance comes in the form of financial and managerial support and is designed to make up for any deficiencies in community resources or skills.

The requirements for a viable community include employment, healthcare, financial services, schools, communications infrastructure and recreational opportunities. It is not always possible for the state or commercial business to provide all of these requirements and this only increases the need for communities to develop a strong enterprise culture.

Community development is really about **self-help** and requires the community to accept that external benefactors including government and 'big business' are not always in a position to provide the services and jobs needed for a viable community.

Poor employment prospects will increase emigration and will lead to the demise of local businesses, clubs and services. This is turn acts as a deterrent to new residents and further undermines the long-term viability of a community.

unit

6

Changing Ireland

Established in 2001, based in a refurbished bungalow in Moyross, Limerick, and managed by volunteers, *Changing Ireland* is the national magazine of the Government's main community-focused, anti-poverty programme, the Local and Community Development Programme (LCDP). It's editorially independent and gives people on the margins a voice.

Mission Statement:

'Changing Ireland' champions Community Development. It enables over 24,000 readers (via print and online) to network more effectively and learn from each other as it promotes Community Development in Ireland. It focuses in each issue on work by the projects in the Local and Community Development Programme. It is intended to be readable and interesting and is written by community workers in various parts of the country – so that it reflects the experience of tackling poverty and exclusion at community level.

Source: www.changingireland.ie

Benefits of community development

« *syllabus signpost* 6.7.5

Increased employment

New enterprises help provide jobs, both directly and indirectly.

Each direct job which is created provides income which is spent in other local shops and businesses. This increases the level of spending within the community and helps sustain additional jobs. This is another example of the multiplier effect in action. In run-down urban areas that are overlooked by 'big business', community initiative may be the only source of employment and in many rural areas it may help curb emigration.

Enterprise culture

The success of community-based enterprises helps establish a 'self-help' culture within a community. This is very important in areas where there is no enterprise tradition. It helps counteract a 'dependency culture' and tries to replace it with an ethos of self-reliance.

Quality of life

The provision of jobs, services and other facilities in a community should enhance the overall quality of life for those who live there. Communities are encouraged to take pride in their locality and tackle antisocial attitudes and behaviour. Many community development programmes focus on members of the community who experience the most disadvantage and are the most vulnerable.

Future success

It is often said that nothing succeeds like success, and one successful community-based initiative can provide the impetus for other projects and may generate spin-off jobs. In this way a community development programme acts as a local enterprise hub and makes it easier to attract funding for additional projects. In areas where community development programmes exist, there is certainly strong evidence to support this view.

Case Study

The Community Development Project in Lifford, Co. Donegal:

> has a childcare facility which allows parents time away from their children to pursue education, training or a return to work. This facility directly increases local employment, facilitates education and employment opportunities for others and offers quality childcare for children.
> has a Community Employment scheme where locals receive training with a view to re-entering the workforce.
> provides community education.
> carries out various youth activities which include after-school groups, homework clubs, breakfast clubs and working with young people not in school.
> supports a range of community groups for lone parents and, older people.

ABC Centre – a success story for Lifford

It's one of Lifford's real success stories – providing childcare and after school facilities for local children in a beautiful, modern building.

The ABC Childcare Centre is a project established under the umbrella of the Lifford Clonleigh Resource Centre and the Lifford Community Development Project. Located in a state of the art premises off the main Letterkenny Road, it caters for preschool children (aged 3–5 years) in the morning while providing an after school service for school going children in the afternoons up until 5pm.

With only five staff employed, the number of children who can be accommodated is understandably quite limited. However, the hope is that with proper funding and support, a full day care facility can open, providing much needed support for local families as well as ensuring anything up to ten new jobs being created in the centre...

Source: Donegal Democrat, FRIDAY, 11 SEPTEMBER 2009.

The community development process

Having identified the need to establish a community development initiative, the following are the **four key steps** involved in the process:

1 People

A meeting of all interested parties needs to be held. This should include a broad representation of people right across the community so that a consensus view can be reached. Community development projects have much more chance of succeeding if they are seen to be inclusive. Not only will this approach provide a wider level of cross-community support, but it will also increase the potential pool of volunteers and skills available.

2 A formal organisation

While cross-community support is vital for the success of the programme, it is not feasible to involve the entire community in its day-to-day operations. In much the same way as a limited company requires a board of directors, a smaller team of key people needs to be appointed to oversee and manage the community project. The setting up of a formal community development association will add legitimacy and status to the project and will be essential when seeking funding.

The current Local and Community Development Programme was introduced in January 2010. This Programme is delivered at a local level by 52 Local Development Companies (LDCs) on behalf of the Department of Arts, Heritage and the Gaeltacht. These local development companies oversee and co-ordinate the activities of over 180 Community Development Projects. These projects are based in disadvantaged communities right across the country.

3 A plan

One of the most important tasks undertaken by the community group is to identify and prioritise its most pressing and immediate needs. This can be achieved by listening to local interest groups or by using brainstorming or SWOT analysis. It may also be

unit

6

411

helpful to conduct an audit of local resources and skills. Not only will this help identify possible projects, but it will allow the management committee to evaluate the skills and resources at their disposal.

The community group will also need to outline its proposals in a detailed and properly structured plan. This will be very similar to a business plan prepared by a start-up business and like all plans it will set out the objectives and timeframe involved. It will also facilitate a co-ordinated approach to the project and help attract funding.

4 Funding

With objectives clearly established and a management structure in place, the final step will involve raising the money needed to undertake the project. Local fundraising events as well as private or corporate sponsorship may provide some of the finance required, but it is likely that state agencies will be the major contributors.

RTÉ Local Heroes in Drogheda

Drogheda like so many towns in Ireland has seen better times. In September 2011 local unemployment stood at over 8,000 people, many of its traditional industries had shut down and its main shopping street was littered with boarded-up premises

Its people decided they'd had enough and traders and townsfolk came together to create a future for themselves.

Working together with the RTÉ TV programme *Local Heroes* experts Feargal Quinn and his team, Drogheda's citizens jumped at the chance to give their economy a boost and create jobs. Their collective efforts were featured in the RTÉ TV series *Local Heroes – A Town Fights Back* (which aired over six episodes during late 2011/early 2012) and this programme illustrates very clearly what's possible when a community comes together with a common purpose.

All of the following were achieved in less than 100 days:

> Drogheda visitor guide and tourism brand created
> More than 200 jobseekers received career advice
> Fifteen internship places created
> Droghedajobs.ie website created with over 120 new jobs posted
> Young Entrepreneur Programme rolled out in two secondary schools
> Drogheda Entrepreneur Network created
> 'Eat local' campaign rolled out across Drogheda
> Time Banking – business people donate their time and expertise
> Foreign Direct Investment mission makes Drogheda gateway to Silicon Valley investment

 www.rte.ie/localheroes

Assisting community development

County Enterprise Boards [CEBs]

A nationwide network of thirty-five City and County Enterprise Boards provide local support for commercial 'micro enterprises'. A **micro enterprise** is a small business with fewer than ten employees. All CEBs offer a similar range of services, but in keeping with their overall goal of promoting local entrepreneurship, they have a county-based focus and seek to meet the needs of their own geographic area. The range of supports they offer to new and existing businesses includes:

> **Advice:** CEBs are a useful starting point for anyone considering opening their own business. They provide entrepreneurs with advice on business formation and registration, company law, market research, patents and intellectual property, as well as guidance on the availability of local and national support schemes.

> **Grants:** A business start-up grant (priming grant) of up to €150,000 is available to assist with capital, payroll, marketing and utility costs.

   CEBs also offer feasibility/innovation grants of up to €20,000.

> **Business mentoring:** The CEBs utilise their extensive network to match experienced business people with new entrepreneurs. The mentor is an independent advisor who agrees to assist the fledgling business for a short period of time. This helps to address the knowledge deficit and avoid costly mistakes which may lead to business failure. The mentor, whose role involves listening, advising and problem solving, does not become involved in the day-to-day management of the client's business.

> **Supports for training and growth:** Small business owners, and sole traders in particular, require a vast range of skills to develop and maintain their businesses. Most CEBs offer courses on areas like management techniques, marketing, budgeting and business planning. Many CEBs also provide support for women in business through dedicated business and networking events. These events deal with specific issues facing women entrepreneurs as well as business-related topics like insurance and taxation.

   In February 2012 the government's 'Action Plan for Jobs' proposed the abolition of individual CEBs and favoured delivery of these services by a central enterprise agency.

LEADER Plus programme

This is an EU-backed initiative which aims to promote and assist enterprise in **rural areas**. LEADER companies are not-for-profit organisations which aim to support small rural business and to strengthen facilities and services for rural communities. They are managed by representatives drawn from community, farming and rural enterprise organisations, as well as state agencies and local politicians.

unit

6

There are currently thirty-six LEADER companies in Ireland, and similar schemes operate in all twenty-seven EU countries.

While co-funding by the EU and the Irish government is a feature of the LEADER programme, each company has autonomy in allocating that funding to projects in its own area. The criteria used to evaluate each proposal are also decided at a local level and will be different for commercial and non-commercial projects. For example, a commercial business seeking cash for business expansion would need to demonstrate a clear ability to create additional revenue or employment. A community-based restoration or conservation project would not need to meet this requirement, but may be approved simply on the basis that it will improve the infrastructure of the local area.

This ability to make decisions at local level, based on local needs and expertise, is a good example of **subsidiarity** in action. The principle of subsidiarity states that a central authority such as the EU should only intervene and make decisions on matters which cannot be effectively dealt with at local level. See also *Chapter 23: The European Union.*

EU criteria governing the current round of LEADER funding require each country to focus its efforts on three major areas, namely:

> improving the competitiveness of the agricultural and forestry sector;

> improving the environment and the countryside;

> improving the quality of life in rural areas and encouraging diversification of the rural economy.

In practical terms this has resulted in funding for a whole range of local initiatives including training, tourism, craft enterprises and environmental conservation projects.

Cavan-Monaghan LEADER is just one of thirty-six similar companies in Ireland. Here are some examples of the types of projects it has funded:

Rally School Ireland

The rally school is a prime example of an innovative rural tourism project which has grown significantly since its inception. In 1999, Rally School Ireland was officially opened with three cars and five staff. Since then the School has trebled its fleet and doubled its workforce. It has attracted over 30,000 visitors who wish to experience the thrill of rally driving, offers winter driver training and has diversified into road safety awareness. The Rally School, which received funding from Cavan-Monaghan LEADER, is estimated to have contributed over €2 million to the local economy.

Self-catering tourist accommodation

The LEADER programme has provided €82,000 for the development and/or refurbishment of self-catering tourist accommodation to three- and four-star standards. The development of self-catering tourism accommodation provides an excellent farm diversification opportunity and Mr Alan Kells, a farmer and self-catering accommodation provider from Castlehamilton, Killeshandra, County Cavan has been proactively marketing his self-catering cottages as a high-standard angling destination to the continental market.

Source: www.cmleader.ie

Area Partnership Companies (APCs)

With aims broadly similar to LEADER companies, Area Partnership Companies were established almost exclusively in disadvantaged **urban areas** and were seen as an attempt to tackle unemployment and social exclusion. Examples include Blanchardstown Area Partnership, Galway City Partnership and South Kerry Development Partnership.

There are now fifty-four APCs in Ireland, addressing the problems of poverty, disadvantage, and marginalisation in their area. This is achieved through the provision of funding, mentoring and training to assist community-based enterprises.

Eighteen of these companies have a predominantly rural focus, and are co-funded by LEADER and Pobal.

government supporting communities

Pobal

Pobal is a government agency which seeks to manage and support a range of community-based programmes. It distributes funding on behalf of the government and seeks to achieve an integrated approach from the various community development organisations.

Community Development: evaluation and future prospects

« *syllabus signpost* 6.7.5

unit 6

While the various community development programmes outlined above have not eliminated unemployment, poverty and social disadvantage they have undoubtedly provided a huge benefit to local communities. They have also achieved this level of success in a very cost-effective manner by building on the strengths of local people and resources.

Notwithstanding these successes, the immediate future is likely to be very challenging for all community development organisations:

> The recent economic downturn has increased the demand for their services at a time when their resources are facing cutbacks.

> Community development programmes are likely to face major restructuring as the government seeks to eliminate duplication and perceived inefficiencies.

> The analysis of Area Partnership and LEADER companies above illustrates not only the growth of these problems but also the elimination of the traditional urban/rural divide.

Chapter Review Diagram – Community Enterprise Development

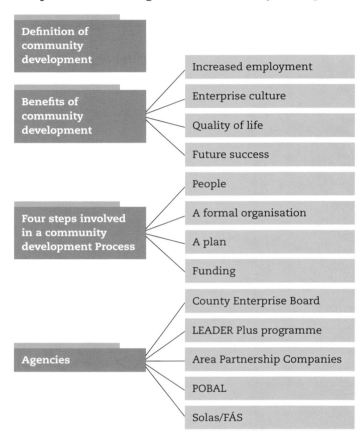

Chapter Review Questions

1 Explain the term 'community development'.

2 Illustrate four benefits of community development for those communities who undertake it.

3 Describe the key steps in the community development process.

4 Outline the role of City and County Enterprise Boards.

5 Describe three ways in which a Leader programme can help develop local enterprise.

6 Explain the role of Area Partnership Companies and give one example.

Q Questions · Ordinary Level

1 Explain **two** services that City/County Enterprise Boards provide for businesses.

LCOL 2011 (15 marks)

2

Local community enterprise is important for the local economy. *LCOL 2003*

Explain **three** benefits of local community enterprise. *(15 marks)*

Q Questions · Higher Level

1 Evaluate the services provided by 'County and City Enterprise Boards' (CEBs).

LCHL 2011 (10 marks)

2 Analyse how local communities and local businesses can benefit from each other's presence in an area. Use an example **in each case** to illustrate your answer.

LCHL 2003 (20 marks)

3 Apart from County Enterprise Boards, outline the role of **two** other organisations which can provide assistance to community development projects.

4 Evaluate how the establishment of a business enterprise in a local community benefits that particular area.

unit

6

Chapter 21
Business Ethics and Social Responsibility

Syllabus Outcomes

On completion, the student should be able to:

» 6.7.8 Identify important environmental issues in business;

» 6.7.11 Define ethical business practice;

» 6.7.12 Describe the characteristics of an environmentally conscious company (HL);

» 6.7.13 Analyse the impact of environmental issues on business (HL);

» 6.7.14 Discuss the social responsibilities of business (HL);

» 6.7.15 Evaluate the effects on a firm's costs of meeting its ethical, social and environmental responsibilities (HL).

News Flash

Ryanair near bottom of 'ethical ranking' list

by Frank McDonald, Environment Editor

Ryanair has appeared in the bottom 10 of an "ethical ranking" of 581 companies, based on environmental performance, corporate social responsibility and information provided to consumers.

The ranking was compiled by Geneva-based Covalence, which measures qualitative data on 45 criteria including labour standards, waste management, social utility and human rights policy.

The company claims that its "reputation index", which is distributed by Thomson Reuters, Bloomberg and Capital IQ, is "a barometer of how multinationals are perceived in the ethical field".

Ryanair is ranked 575 on the latest list, just ahead of Occidental Petroleum, US tobacco company Phillip Morris and oil giant Chevron. At the bottom is Monsanto, chiefly known for genetically modified foods...

The top 10 are headed by IBM, followed by Intel (which has a major plant at Leixlip, Co Kildare), HSBC Holdings, Marks & Spencer, Unilever, Xerox, General Electric, Cisco Systems, Dell and Procter & Gamble.

"Environmental initiatives, eco-innovative products and social sponsorships enabled companies to generate positive coverage in 2009, while issues related to downsizing, CO2 emissions and working conditions caused the most criticisms," Covalence said...

Well-known companies in the top 20 include Alcoa Aluminium, PepsiCo, Nike, Microsoft, Starbucks, DuPont, BASF, Danone and Vodafone, while those in the bottom 20 include Royal Dutch Shell, AIG, British American Tobacco and Halliburton.

This is an edited extract from **The Irish Times,** Monday, 1 February 2010.

For more up-to-date newspaper articles see www.edcodigital.ie

1 Read the newspaper extract opposite and discuss the issues raised.

2 Can you explain any of the highlighted terms?

Ethics

« *syllabus signpost*
6.7.11

Ethics is about **moral rules**. It involves listening to one's conscience and distinguishing between right and wrong. Ethical business practice should involve choosing a course of action which is **legal, decent and honest**.

Ethics and **social responsibility** are closely linked and are based on a belief that business has a responsibility to treat all of its stakeholders in a manner which is morally just and morally fair.

Those who accept that businesses and their managers should be guided by some moral principles would contend that profitability should not be the sole criterion when making decisions. They would argue that a business has a moral responsibility to all of its stakeholders and needs to consider their needs at all times. They would further argue that by taking the best interests of all stakeholders into account, managers are actually acting in the best interests of the business itself. Having a conscience is not only good for society; it may also be good for business.

You may not have thought about business in this way before, but businesses have always exhibited varying degrees of social responsibility and stakeholders are beginning to scrutinise these actions and policies much more carefully.

Unethical business practices

The following are some examples of unethical practice associated with business operations:

> **Bribery and corruption:** illegal payments used to win contracts and influence decision-makers.

> **Child labour:** exploitation of cheap labour and in particular the use of children in the manufacture of goods or extraction of raw materials.

> **Unsafe products:** knowingly selling sub-standard or dangerous goods.

> **Product testing:** controversial testing of cosmetics and pharmaceuticals on animals, etc.

> **Pollution/illegal dumping:** failure to control factory emissions or dispose of waste properly, which can have a hugely negative impact on the environment.

> **Overcharging:** deliberately charging too much for goods or exploiting vulnerable customers by raising prices (e.g. prescription drugs).

Child labour

Illegal dumping

unit

6

In order to avoid these types of behaviour, some businesses and industries have a formal code of ethics in place.

A **code of ethics** is a set of guidelines to assist decision-making and ensure a moral viewpoint is considered.

Case Study

Siemens bribery scandal

In 2008, the German engineering group Siemens agreed a record-breaking settlement following a year of bribery allegations. The agreement, which saw Siemens pay a total of $1.6 billion, followed negotiations and plea bargaining between company lawyers and the US and German authorities after admissions that a €1.3 billion slush fund was used to win overseas contracts between 2001 and 2007.

Siemens and its subsidiaries admitted charges involving the payment of at least $40 million to win a $1 billion contract to produce national identity cards in Argentina. In Israel, the company allegedly provided $20 million to senior government officials to build power plants. In Venezuela, it was $16 million for urban rail lines and in China $14 million for medical equipment.

Siemens avoided penalties of up to $5 billion by co-operating with the US authorities and initiating an amnesty for whistleblowers. Apart from the financial cost, the scandal damaged the German engineering company's reputation and angered competitors and consumers. It was reported that Siemens' actions in rigging deals also meant that citizens in some poorer countries paid inflated prices for infrastructure like power plants and hospitals.

It appears that during the period in question no effort had been made to impose a clear code of ethics on the organisation.

Key Statistics on Child Labour

- 246 million children are child labourers.
- 73 million working children are less than 10 years old.
- No country is immune: there are 2.5 million working children in the developed economies, and another 2.5 million in transition economies (e.g. China, India).
- Every year, 22,000 children die in work-related accidents.
- The largest number of working children – aged fourteen and under – 127 million – are in the Asia-Pacific region.
- Sub-Saharan Africa has the largest proportion of working children: nearly one-third of children age fourteen and under (48 million children).
- Most children work in the informal sector, without legal or regulatory protection:
  - 70% in agriculture, commercial hunting and fishing or forestry;
  - 8% in manufacturing;
  - 8% in wholesale and retail trade, restaurants and hotels;
  - 7% in community, social and personal service, such as domestic work.

Source: International Labour Organisation

Why act unethically?

The following are seen as some the most common reasons for unethical behaviour in business organisations

> **Greed:** Personal or corporate greed are ultimately driven by a desire for wealth and power. Most cases involve an individual or a business putting their own self-interest ahead of the common good. Bribery cases highlight many examples of greed since illicit payments are usually made to individuals for their own personal gain.

> **Profit:** For some businesses a 'profitable' decision is a correct decision, irrespective of moral implications. No account is taken of the impact of a decision on other stakeholders.

> **Fear:** Employees may be fearful that poor performance and profitability will result in job loss or some other form of retribution. This fear may drive them to act unethically. For example, a sales person is under pressure to meet performance targets and feels justified in pressurising an elderly customer into purchasing an expensive product which is of no benefit to them.

> **Lack of regulation:** An environment in which there is inadequate or poorly enforced legislation may facilitate unethical practices. This environment may be localised to a particular business or industry or may even reflect a wider international problem. Following the fallout from the recent banking scandal in Ireland, investigators suggested that regulations in many areas were inadequate. Where regulations did exist some were routinely ignored by both banks and the **financial regulator**. This combination of factors enabled a culture of greed and unethical behaviour to develop in some financial institutions.

> **Lack of leadership:** Since workers tend to follow the example they are given, senior management have an obligation to set the ethos within the company. This is really an example of **corporate culture** in action. A culture of honesty and transparency is preferable to one of secrecy and corruption. The recent banking crises in Ireland have caused many people to question the ethics of certain decisions made by some senior officials in that industry.

> The term **'whistleblower'** is used to describe a stakeholder (usually an employee) who publicly discloses unethical business practice.

Social/Ethical Responsibilities of Business

The following are some of the responsibilities which businesses have towards their stakeholders. Collectively these responsibilities represent the main obligations of business to society.

« *syllabus signpost*
6.7.14

 Companies which adopt a co-operative approach to stakeholder relationships will tend to meet more of these responsibilities.

unit
6

Responsibilities to employees

> To provide **safe and secure employment** for staff.

> **To pay fair wages** for work done.
Employee wages should reflect the employee's qualifications and contribution to the business. Wages should also allow an individual to attain a reasonable standard of living in their country of employment. To safeguard these standards of living and avoid exploitation of workers many EU countries, including Ireland, have a minimum wage threshold.

> **To observe relevant legislation.** Examples include laws on taxation, discrimination and health and safety.

> **To respect human dignity.** This means treating people in a manner which is respectful of their rights and status as human beings.

Responsibilities to customers

> **To provide good-quality produce/service.** In addition to the legal responsibility set out in the Consumer Protection Act, 2007, there is a moral responsibility to ensure that goods are safe and are not likely to harm those who use or consume them.

> **To charge a fair price.** Producers need to balance customers' reliance on a particular product, average income levels and the need to earn a reasonable profit.

The pharmaceutical industry is one which has highlighted a number of complex ethical issues and where the need to earn a commercial return has to be balanced with a need to provide life-saving medication to patients.

Dr Drummond Rennie (Editor, *Journal of the American Medical Association*) had the following to say as part of his contribution to the *Dying for Drugs* documentary, broadcast on Channel 4 on April 27, 2003:

'Pharmaceuticals are a commodity, but they're not just a commodity; there's an ethical side to this, because they're a commodity that you may be forced to take to save your life, and that gives them an altogether deeper significance. They [drug companies] have to remember that they're not just pushing pills, they're pushing life or death and I believe that they don't always remember that. Indeed I believe they often forget it completely.'

> **To ensure that advertising is both truthful and decent** and is therefore not likely to mislead or offend consumers. Businesses also have a responsibility to avoid targeting vulnerable consumers, such as children, with inappropriate advertising.

unit

6

Responsibilities to investors

> **To provide a fair return on investment.** Investors who share the business risk are entitled to a fair share of and rewards that might accrue.

> **To be transparent and honest in all matters.** Investors need to be told clearly about the purpose for which funding will be used and also the level of risk attached to their investment.

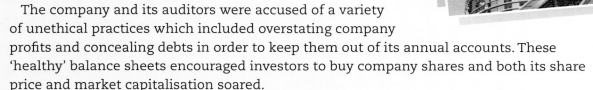

In the space of just fifteen years, Enron developed from a start-up business to become America's seventh-largest company, employing 21,000 staff in more than forty countries. When it was later discovered that the energy company's meteoric rise was based upon fraud it suffered an even more spectacular collapse.

The company and its auditors were accused of a variety of unethical practices which included overstating company profits and concealing debts in order to keep them out of its annual accounts. These 'healthy' balance sheets encouraged investors to buy company shares and both its share price and market capitalisation soared.

Most of these investors lost their money when the truth was uncovered in 2001 and the share price collapsed. In total, investors lost over $11 billion as Enron shares fell in value from $90 to 90 cents in less than eighteen months. Billions were also wiped off the value of pension funds which had invested heavily in the energy company.

Enron filed for bankruptcy in December 2001 and several senior executives received prison sentences following criminal investigations into their role.

As a consequence of the scandal, new regulations and legislation were enacted to expand the accuracy of financial reporting for public companies.

Responsibilities to suppliers

> **To pay them on time.** Firms who delay making payments to suppliers (called 'leaning on the trade') put at risk the survival of other businesses and jobs in those companies.

> **Not to engage in unfair trading practices.** Large companies are in a powerful position when it comes to negotiating contracts with smaller suppliers and may abuse their powerful position to extract unreasonable concessions from vulnerable suppliers who are keen to get a lucrative deal. The payment of so called 'hello money' is an example of the kind of illegal behaviour involved. **Hello money** is a payment made by a small business to a large retailer in return for shelf space in their supermarket.

> **To honour all contracts** which have been entered into. Contracts are legally binding agreements and all businesses should enter into them with the intention of fulfilling their terms and conditions.

unit

6

Responsibilities to government

› **To pay taxes due.** Businesses must pay their fair share of taxation, so that the burden of taxation does not fall more heavily on others.

Tax evasion refers to a deliberate and illegal attempt to escape one's tax obligations. Failing to declare receipts for income tax or VAT purposes or trying to hide money in an offshore bank account are examples of tax evasion.

Tax avoidance is the attempt by a business to minimise its tax liability by availing of provisions set out in tax legislation. Tax avoidance is legal and may involve reinvestment of business profits into a project which attracts lower levels of taxation.

› **To collect and submit taxes as required by law.** Obvious examples which fall into this category are PAYE and VAT.

› **To obey relevant legislation.** This includes general corporate legislation as well as industry-specific rules, regulations and laws. The Consumer Protection Act is an example of a general piece of legislation applying to all businesses, whereas gaming and licensing laws are specific to certain types of business.

Responsibility to the local community

› **To consult and inform on relevant issues.** For example, any plans to expand the business are likely to involve land purchases, planning applications, increased traffic and emissions. All of these issues will impact on the local community and the business should consult with locals in an open and transparent way.

Intel explains its way of working

Intel strives to be a trusted, leading corporate citizen. Corporate responsibility at Intel Ireland reflects our deep respect for people and for the communities around us. This means listening to, learning from, and communicating openly with all the people we work with. It's simply how we do business.

Source: www.intel.com

› **To avoid all types of pollution.** Failure to ensure effective control of emissions and waste disposal is likely to lead to pollution of the local environment and inevitable conflict with the local community.

› **To provide employment.** Businesses should ensure that the communities which support the business and its operations benefit by way of employment.

› **To support local suppliers** where possible. This often makes good commercial sense too as transport costs lower while consumers often show great loyalty to indigenous producers.

Bruton tells Tesco to 'buy Irish' as retail giant creates 500 jobs

by Kevin Keane and Fiach Kelly

A senior minister last night clashed with Tesco over its failure to buy more Irish produce after the supermarket giant announced more than 500 new jobs.

Enterprise Minister Richard Bruton accused the British company of squeezing small Irish producers as it unveiled plans to open a raft of new stores across the country. The minister, who is responsible for job creation, challenged Tesco to stop ignoring domestic producers..Yesterday, the minister told Tesco that Irish producers had driven their costs down. While praising the British retail giant for being a significant employer, he also said it should stock more Irish products.

"I'd like to see more and more of those on the shelves," said Mr. Bruton. "When Tesco first came here, one of the key issues we set in terms of their investment was a need to drive Irish products, to see not only large producers but also small producers finding space on Irish shelves.

"I think perhaps focus was lost on small producers but now there is an opportunity for Tesco and others to recognise that a lot of Irish companies have brought down their costs."

The spokesman for the UK retailer said nine of Tesco's 10 best-selling products were produced in Ireland and that over the last year the retailer had selected a number of small local producers to go in to its stores and had helped them develop their products to the extent that they were now exporting to the UK market.

Source: Irish Independent, SATURDAY, 25 JUNE 2011

Environmental Responsibility

> *We do not inherit the earth from our ancestors; we borrow it from our children.* **Native American Proverb**

« *syllabus signpost* 6.7.8

Closely linked to both ethical and social responsibility is the increasingly important issue of environmental responsibility. The impact of business on our environment is an area of intense concern and scrutiny. Society tends to focus on the following **key issues.**

> Pollution
> Ozone depletion

> Waste disposal
> Natural resources

> Habitat
> Agriculture issues

Pollution

Pollution of the atmosphere from vehicles and factory **emissions** is a major cause of **acid rain** and this has the potential to destroy vast areas of forest and woodland habitats. Destruction of forests is also worrying from the point of view of CO_2 emissions, as trees act as a filter for this potentially harmful gas and help turn it into oxygen.

Pollution of seas and inland waterways also arises from the careless and uncontrolled **disposal of chemicals and effluent.** There are examples of these problems across a whole range of industries, but agriculture and the pharmaceutical industry are most

unit
6

often criticised. Recent government intervention, in the form of capital grants and the REPS scheme, has helped to improve the situation in rural Ireland.

REPS (Rural Environment Protection Scheme) is a programme designed to improve environmental standards on farms. Under this scheme farmers who conduct their farm activities in an environmentally friendly manner are rewarded. The main aims of the scheme are to:

› Promote farming practices and production methods which reflect the increasing concern for conservation, landscape protection and wider environmental problems;

› Protect wildlife habitats and endangered species of flora and fauna;

› Produce quality food in an extensive and environmentally friendly manner.

River pollution levels plummet

A study has found that just 20 rivers in Ireland were severely polluted between 2007 and 2009.

About 52km of Ireland's rivers are seriously polluted, the lowest level in decades.

A study by the Environmental Protection Agency (EPA) has found just 20 rivers were severely affected – half of what it was five years ago – between 2007 and 2009.

Twenty-five lakes were assessed as poor or bad, with 15 of them in Cavan and Monaghan.

The extensive water quality report also looked at tidal areas and found eight areas in a poor state mainly due to waste treatment plants, and it warned that bathing areas Balbriggan in Dublin and Clifden in Galway were consistently the worst.

Micheal O Cinneide, director of the EPA office of environmental assessment, said Ireland is above average in EU terms.

The extensive study found, in total, a third of the river course contains some pollution – some because of wastewater treatment plants and the rest because of farming practices.

Source: Belfast Telegraph, THURSDAY, 24 FEBRUARY 2011.

Ozone depletion

The **ozone layer** is a layer of gas in the Earth's upper atmosphere which protects the planet from the harmful rays of the sun. Damage to the ozone layer has the potential to increase climate change, including global warming and the melting of polar ice caps. It also has the effect of increasing the incidence of skin cancer in humans and can inhibit the effectiveness of some micro-organisms vital to food production.

CFC gases (chlorofluorocarbons) are a major contributor to ozone depletion. These gases are emitted by some aerosols, refrigerators and air-conditioning devices.

International agreements have succeeded to a great extent in reducing CFC emissions. The **Kyoto Protocol** (1997) has set binding targets for thirty-seven industrialised countries and the EU which require them to reduce **greenhouse gas emissions**. These reductions amount to an average of 5 per cent against 1990 levels over the five-year period 2008–2012.

Waste disposal

There are major environmental concerns around the generation and disposal of waste from both households and businesses. In Ireland we have traditionally relied on **landfill** as a means of waste disposal, but this is now becoming environmentally and economically unsustainable. Alternatives include a campaign which encourages people to 'reduce, reuse and recycle' as much waste as possible and Ireland has recently seen the construction of its first municipal **incinerator** at Carranstown in Co. Meath.

The closure of some landfill sites has increased the cost of waste disposal and has led to an increase in the incidence of **illegal dumping**.

The disposal of **toxic waste**, generated in particular by our large pharmaceutical and chemical sector, also remains a topic of controversy.

Natural resources

Most of the energy produced in the world relies on the use of fossil fuels (oil, coal, gas) and other non-renewable resources. Burning these fuels has a negative impact on the environment and is ultimately unsustainable as the quantities available are limited.

The government's 'Better Energy' programme provides subsidies for households who improve the energy efficiency of their homes, thereby creating badly needed jobs in the construction and green energy industries.

A **subsidy** is a payment made by the government to a supplier or consumer of specific goods and services. The intention of the subsidy is to promote the availability of important goods and services by reducing their cost or selling price.

Only when the last tree has died and the last river been poisoned and the last fish been caught will we realise we cannot eat money. **Cree Indian Proverb**

Sustainable development

The idea behind sustainable development is that industrial growth or advancement must not undermine the natural resources of the planet because these resources are necessary for future development.

unit
6

The EU could decide to remove the fish quotas imposed under the Common Fisheries Policy. This would probably lead to an investment in the industry, with extra boats creating extra employment. There would also be investment in processing capabilities and this new value-added sector would mean more jobs for workers and more choice for consumers. Within a few years, however, fish stocks would be decimated from overfishing and some species might be on the verge of extinction. In these circumstances it would be impossible for anyone to make a living from the industry.

This example highlights the fact that whatever gains might be possible from a change in EU policy, they would surely only be short-term. In the long run, this type of development is not viable or sustainable and endangers the very existence of the natural resource upon which we all depend.

Similar issues arise when it comes to industrial development based on fossil fuels, and there are huge concerns over the impact of dwindling supplies and increased demand for these resources.

Many experts contend that oil production is very close to reaching its peak. Once that point is reached a combination of reduced availability and increased demand will lead firstly to price rises and ultimately to a fundamental change in lifestyle and energy usage.

The issue of sustainable development is a major challenge facing our world, as the desire for industrial growth needs to be balanced against the need to preserve limited resources.

Developing economies, like India and China, are reluctant to accept calls for restraint from their more developed neighbours in the US and Europe. This is in part due to their need to support huge population growth but also because they believe much of the blame for overuse of resources lies with the developed world. Negotiations on these issues are ongoing and the inevitable demise of resources will eventually lead to international agreement and compromise.

Peak oil

Peak oil represents the point in time when we are extracting the greatest possible quantity of oil (per day, or per year) that it will ever be possible to extract. Once this day arrives the world will have reached its maximum production capacity and the rate of extraction will enter into a terminal decline.

The model developed by geologist M. King Hubbert suggests a global peak between 2000 and 2020 and there are those who

argue we have already reached this point and that the recent oil price rises are just the beginning of a permanent adjustment.

While this does not mean that we are running out of oil any day soon, it does mean we will struggle to meet existing levels of demand, let alone the increased demand generated by the growth of developing economies.

Peak Oil

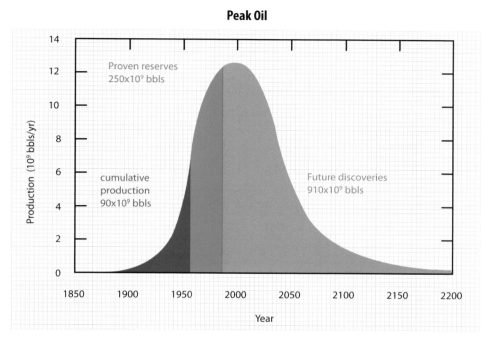

Activity

1 Make a list of items in your classroom whose production depends on the availability of oil.

2 Outline the consequences for your education and lifestyle in the event that these products are no longer available.

3 Draw up a list of opportunities and threats facing businesses as a result of this eventuality.

 www.youtube.com/watch?v=zER6tibeZTI

Habitat

Closely linked to industrial development and to the fossil fuel issue is concern over the destruction of natural habitats. Extinction of species is occurring more frequently and is often brought about by the destruction of rainforests for commercial and agricultural reasons. Unfortunately this excessive depletion impacts on air quality, natural habitats and climate change.

unit

6

Agriculture issues

The world's population now exceeds seven billion people and is greater than at any time in our history. It is also growing faster than it has ever grown before and this is leading to concerns over our ability to feed ourselves. There are already many examples of countries which have been devastated by famine and drought, and most countries are not self-sufficient in food.

In some regions, global warming and the overuse of land have created uninhabitable deserts from once arable farmland.

There are also concerns among consumers about the overuse of chemicals and pesticides in agriculture, while the issue of genetically modified (GM) food continues to be debated.

World population estimates milestones

Population (in billions)	1	2	3	4	5	6	7	8	9
Year	1804	1927	1960	1974	1987	1999	2011	2023	2035
Years elapsed	–	123	33	14	13	12	12	12	12

One of the greatest challenges facing our world in the decades ahead will be the production and equitable distribution of food and water, especially in areas where populations are growing at a faster rate than food supply.

Characteristics of environmentally responsible firms

For businesses to be considered environmentally responsible, they should be expected to:

« syllabus signpost 6.7.12 and 6.7.13

> Conduct **environmental audits**

> Minimise **pollution**

> Promote **recycling**

> Develop a **green culture**

> Use **sustainable raw materials**

Environmental audits

These are detailed independent studies of the impact of business operations on the environment. The audit will examine all aspects of the firm's operations and make recommendations to analyse negative environmental impact. Such audits will examine both current and proposed activities.

> **Environmental Impact Assessment:** a requirement for all new industrial proposals. A detailed examination of its impact on the environment must be submitted in advance of the project being given permission to proceed.

> **The Environmental Protection Agency (EPA)** is an independent state-sponsored body which seeks to ensure that development is sustainable. The Agency has responsibilities for a wide range of licensing, enforcement, monitoring and assessment activities associated with environmental protection. The EPA can prosecute firms who pollute excessively.

The EPA's main responsibilities include:

> Environmental licensing
> Enforcement of environmental law, with powers to prosecute polluters
> Environmental planning, education and guidance
> Monitoring, analysing and reporting on the environment
> Regulating Ireland's greenhouse gas emissions
> Environmental research development
> Strategic environmental assessment
> Waste management

Pollution

A responsible business will attempt to eliminate pollution of the environment caused by any aspect of the firm's activities. This clearly requires a systematic and proactive approach to monitoring emissions, as well as a commitment to implementing 'best practice' when it comes to environmental standards.

Recycling

For many companies recycling is undertaken on a voluntary basis, usually because of cost savings or because of a perceived competitive advantage over rivals.

In a small number of industries, including the automobile industry, the impetus for recycling has a legislative basis. The EU's End-of-Life Vehicle Directive means that new vehicles must demonstrate reusability and/or recyclability of at least 85 per cent by weight. This has led to the removal or reduction of hazardous raw materials, including cadmium, lead and mercury from the manufacturing process.

There are also many examples of companies which have been established to meet the needs of 'green consumers' by producing goods made entirely from recycled materials. One such example of these firms is Tipperary-based Irish Recycled Products.

Irish recycled products are manufactured from waste HPDE, the plastic that is commonly used to make milk and juice bottles. This plastic never naturally biodegrades: a fact that makes it very bad for landfill disposal and very good for outdoor furniture.

Their products will outlast their timber alternatives by several generations and low maintenance means reduced ongoing costs.

Their 100% recycled products demonstrate clearly that financial and social responsibility can go hand in hand, saving you money while helping you to protect the environment.

 www.irishrecycledproducts.ie

 IrishRecycledProducts.ie
Innovative Recycling Technology
One Great Idea - endless applications

Green culture

Environmentally responsible companies ensure that a corporate ethos which promotes environmental responsibility is actively pursued by all employees. To increase motivation and compliance, some form of incentive or reward scheme may be introduced to help with its implementation.

Sustainable raw materials

Environmental responsibility often involves the use of renewable or sustainable sources of raw materials and energy.

> According to the company website, The Body Shop was one of the first major brands to adopt this policy when it launched its Community Fair Trade programme in 1987. The policy continues to be employed today and aims to build co-operative long-term relationships with suppliers of raw materials and ingredients.
>
> In return for high-quality ingredients from sustainable sources, small producers and suppliers receive a predictable source of income at a fair price.
>
> All suppliers must also sign a code of conduct which supports the Body Shop's Ethical Trade Programme, a further initiative designed to improve conditions for all workers in the supply chain. This code of conduct is strictly enforced and sets high standards in relation to employee wages and working conditions, discrimination and child labour.

↖ *www.thebodyshop.com (see Values & Campaigns)*

According to the company website, ice-cream producer Ben and Jerry's is another example of a high-profile brand which is associated with a positive ethical approach to business, and in 2006 the company launched the world's first ever Fairtrade vanilla ice cream. One of the company founders, Jerry Greenfield, had the following to say on the issue.

> *Fairtrade is about making sure people get their fair share of the pie. The whole concept of fairtrade goes to the heart of our values and the sense of right and wrong. Nobody wants to buy something that was made by exploiting somebody else.*

In April 2000, the company founders Ben Cohen and Jerry Greenfield sold the company to multinational food giant Unilever. The brand's new owners have committed themselves to converting the whole range of ice creams to Fairtrade-certified by the end of 2012.

 ↖ *www.fairtrade.ie*

Social and environmental responsibility: cost/benefit analysis

« *syllabus signpost*
6.7.15

A commercial business which wishes to adopt an ethical and socially responsible approach will need to consider both costs and benefits before deciding on the type and extent of its commitment.

Costs

Possible costs include:

> **Capital costs** involved in buying **plant and machinery** that will minimise the environmental impact.

   New technology tends to be more efficient and less likely to pollute the environment, but it often comes at a high financial price.

> **Sourcing environmentally friendly materials** may cost more.

   Paying Fairtrade prices will tend to increase the cost of raw materials. If this is passed on to consumers it will result in a higher price for the finished product, and not all consumers are willing or able to pay this price.

   Any decision not to pass on these increased costs will lead to lower profits for the business.

> **Recycling of waste** may increase costs.

   Additional equipment and staff may be required in order to implement and supervise an effective recycling policy.

> **Safe disposal of hazardous waste** will be expensive.

   As specialist equipment and treatment is required for certain types of hazardous waste (chemical and medical), the costs associated with acting responsibly will increase.

> Providing employees with **improved pay and conditions** will also impact on costs.

   Any effort to improve working conditions and employee wages will again result in lower profits or higher production costs and retail prices.

   During an economic downturn many consumers may feel they cannot afford to shop with their conscience and will simply buy the cheapest goods available.

> **Constant monitoring of environmental impact** will involve greater costs. Yet again there is a human and financial cost associated with a systematic approach to environmental responsibility. For example, policies need to be developed and communicated to stakeholders, while emissions need to be monitored and controlled.

unit
6

Benefits

On the other hand, possible benefits include:

> **State-of-the-art equipment may allow more efficient production.**

The benefits which accrue on an ongoing basis will eventually outweigh the initial capital expenditure involved. This is the same reasoning which applies to issues like the installation of solar panels at home. It is expensive to start with, but within a few years the financial saving from having 'free' hot water on demand will more than compensate for the initial outlay.

> **Recycling and effective waste management may reduce materials costs.**

Waste disposal is expensive and involves both a financial and a labour cost. For this reason any policy which seeks to reduce, reuse or recycle waste will minimise these costs for a business.

> **Improved employee morale can increase productivity** and reduce absenteeism.

This argument suggests that workers who are well paid and enjoy their work will be happier and more productive. In the long run the benefits from increased productivity should exceed the costs associated with higher wages, absenteeism and industrial relations conflict.

> Socially responsible firms may attract **greater customer loyalty.**

There are certainly large numbers of consumers who feel strongly about corporate responsibility and are more willing to support businesses which embrace these values. It is this consumer support which ultimately allows initiatives like the Fairtrade brand to develop.

Consumers can also act as a strong and vocal pressure group when it comes to tackling unethical business practices. Consumer boycotts of Nestlé baby formula and Nike products succeeded not only in highlighting the issues but also forced both manufacturers to take positive action.

Customers also show increased loyalty to businesses which support and sponsor local community-based initiatives, e.g. Tidy Towns competition.

> Social responsibility can be a **marketing tool**, and in some cases provides a unique selling point. The Body Shop is one example of a business which has succeeded in recognising this niche and developing a USP based on positive ethical values.

Activity

Find out what you can about the ethical issues which led to strong direct action by consumers against Nestlé, Nike, Tesco and Union Carbide.

> Responsible businesses are **less likely to face clean-up costs** or the imposition of **'green taxes'**. Green taxes are imposed on firms to offset the social costs associated with industrial pollution (e.g. plastic bag levy).

Types of cost

Social costs are the costs to society of industrial activity; they include pollution, congestion and illness, as well as clean-up costs.

Private costs are the costs to a specific firm of its industrial activity.

unit **6**

Some businesses attempt to increase their profit levels by reducing private costs. This might be achieved by lowering staff wages or cutting corners when it comes to safety issues and pollution control. The actions of these businesses may lead to higher social costs, as the government and society will have to pay a price for these policies.

For example, poor safety measures at a factory could cause an oil or chemical leak into a local lake. The local authority will have to investigate and clean up the problem while the local community will lose a valuable economic and recreational resource.

Unless the business responsible is forced to pay the cost of restoring the lake, it will benefit financially from its actions and is likely to continue with its current approach.

The imposition of green taxes and other penalties compensates society for the loss it has suffered and provides an incentive for businesses to act more responsibly.

Most governments attempt to minimise the social costs of business activities by adopting the 'polluter pays' principle.

Chapter Review Diagram – Business Ethics and Social Responsibility

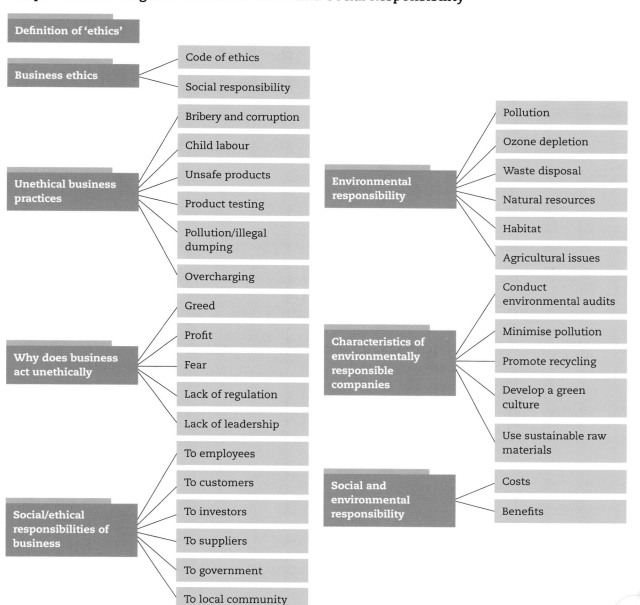

Chapter Review Questions

1 Define the term 'ethics' and explain what a code of ethics is.

2 Briefly outline five unethical practices associated with business operations.

3 List four reasons for unethical behaviour in business organisations.

4 Explain three responsibilities that businesses have to the following stakeholders:

> Employees   > Customers   > Investors   > Suppliers

5 *The impact of business on our environment is an area of intense concern and scrutiny.*

Describe four environmental issues facing modern business organisations.

6 Outline the characteristics of environmentally responsible firms.

7 Explain the term 'Fairtrade'.

8 Distinguish between private costs and social costs.

9 Set out the major costs and benefits for a business of operating in a socially responsible manner.

Questions · Ordinary Level

1

Wholefood Farm Products Ltd

Jim and Martina White own Wholefood Farm Products Ltd, an organic farming and food production business in Cork. They produce a range of fresh and frozen products in a small unit located near their farm. Up until now they have sold on the Irish market only.

They have recently developed a website and have had a lot of enquiries from potential English and other European customers. They are considering expanding their business by exporting to other countries.

Jim and Martina are very conscious of their ethical responsibilities and believe in treating customers and employees in an honest and fair way. They are aware of their environmental responsibilities and of the benefits their business brings to their local community.

LCOL 2010

(a) Outline **two** environmental responsibilities of business.   *(15 marks)*

(b) Explain how Wholefood Farm Products Ltd can behave ethically towards:

    (i) Its customers   (ii) Its employees   *(20 marks)*

2

Goodfoods Ltd is an indigenous company set up by sisters Una and Jane O'Sullivan and it has 14 full-time employees. As a company, it benefits from limited liability.

The company prepares ready-made meals for the home market and is currently considering exporting to foreign markets.

The owners have drafted a code of ethics for the business believing that decisions made should be guided by what is morally right, honest and fair. *LCOL 2007*

(a) Describe **two** environmental responsibilities of Goodfoods Ltd. *(20 marks)*

(b) Using examples, describe how Goodfoods Ltd can behave ethically towards
(i) its employees and (ii) its customers. *(20 marks)*

3 List **three** examples of unethical behaviour by a business.

4 Socially responsible firms may attract greater customer loyalty. Explain what this means.

5 List the responsibilities of the Environmental Protection Agency (EPA).

Questions · Higher Level

1

Customers expect businesses to show regard for the natural environment.

Illustrate the characteristics of an environmentally conscious business.
LCHL 2010 (20 marks)

2

Business is not only about doing things right, it is also about doing the right things.

Discuss the social responsibilities that a business has to its various stakeholders.
LCHL 2009 (20 marks)

3

As global warming becomes a reality for the world, there is an increasing concern for the protection of the environment.

Illustrate how businesses in Ireland today could become more environmentally responsible. *LCHL 2008 (20 marks)*

4 (a) Define 'code of ethics'.
(b) Outline the effects on a firm's costs of meeting its ethical and social responsibilities.
LCHL 2007 (20 marks)

5

All business is important to the economic wellbeing of Ireland.

Evaluate the effect on a firm's revenue **and** costs of meeting its social responsibilities.
LCHL 2005 (25 marks)

unit

6

Q Applied Business Question

Carramore Cheese

Sophie and James Scott are a married couple who run a family farm of 100 hectares. Their farm is located in the townland of Carramore, a rural setting some 40km from Dublin. It's situated near a state-managed forest and in close proximity to a major east–west motorway. Carramore is a very picturesque location and overlooks a large well-stocked fishing lake. The area has obvious tourism potential but it has largely gone untapped and consequently remains relatively unspoilt and underdeveloped.

Having experienced a major decline in sales of livestock the couple considered alternative ways to make a living from the farm. As a result they decided to set up a small cheese-making business and sell their produce as Carramore cheese.

Sophie and James recognise that they have excellent farming land on their doorstep and this is a major factor in producing top-quality milk. This superior raw material can in turn be processed to manufacture a range of value-added dairy products. Many of the local farmers sell their milk directly to a large Dublin-based processor, but a few, like the Scotts, have begun to realise the value of developing a local agribusiness industry. A major challenge in this proposal will involve balancing the economic needs of the local community and the conservation needs of the local environment. Sophie and James are committed environmentalists and are confident that this balance is achievable. A group of local producers have met with officials from An Bord Bia and they are actively seeking support for the development of a Carramore brand. If successful this would act as a regional brand and would be common to all local producers.

Before changing the direction of their farming business, they sought advice from a local community development organisation. This ensured that the couple were guided in the right direction and also provided with valuable advice and access to finance. One of the most important pieces of this advice was the need for the fledgling Carramore cheese brand to build a strong reputation for excellent quality and value for money. The Scotts took this on board and made a clear commitment to customer service and competitive pricing.

The business has grown steadily and now employs fifteen full-time and part-time staff. Staff are well rewarded and highly motivated. The creation of these jobs has increased the amount of disposable income in the Carramore area and has been beneficial to other local businesses. Sophie and James hope that their efforts and success will empower others to be creative and instil a greater sense of entrepreneurship into the community.

The Scotts are keen sports enthusiasts and encourage their own children to engage in several sporting activities. Carramore cheese is also the sponsor the local GAA team and Sophie and James are supportive of its positive impact on young people in the local area.

The last five years have seen an improvement in the general quality of life in Carramore and its hinterland. This has helped to attract more people and businesses into the area and provided a further housing and jobs boost to the area.

(a) Discuss the importance or potential of the different categories of industry to the local economy of Carramore.
(20 marks)

(b) Outline the importance of community initiatives to the industrial and economic development of Carramore and its surrounding area.
(30 marks)

(c) Using appropriate headings to guide your thinking, evaluate how socially responsible the Scotts' cheese-making business is. Refer to the above text in your responses.
(30 marks)

Unit Seven
International Environment

Chapter 22
International Trade

Syllabus Outcomes

On completion, the student should be able to:

» 7.4.4 Discuss the opportunities and challenges facing Irish business in developed and developing markets.

News Flash

Exports soar 11pc during February as imports fall, says CSO, but figures point to emergence of two-speed Irish economy.

by Thomas Molloy

The country's exports surged in February with provisional CSO figures showing a rise of 11pc in goods and services sold abroad. Imports fell by 3pc in the same month.

The Central Statistics Office said preliminary figures for the month showed exports totalled €8.1bn, while imports were almost €4.3bn.

As a result the seasonally adjusted trade surplus rose by 33pc year on year to €3.83bn for the month. This is the highest trade surplus since December 2009. Compared with February last year, exports were up 14pc, while imports rose by 18pc.

The news confirms the emergence of a two-speed economy. The foreign-owned part of the economy has recovered while the rest of the economy lags behind. The export sector is benefiting from a weaker euro. Agriculture, which is experiencing strong milk, beef and grain prices, and the distribution, transport and communication sectors are all seeing strong global demand and exited the recession. But the rest of the private service sector remains flat with construction and the public sector continuing to shrink...

However, more than half of Irish exports go to just two markets – the US and UK. Around 56pc of our imports come from those two countries and Germany.

Enterprise Minister Richard Bruton welcomed the seasonally adjusted rise in exports in February...

Despite the concentration of exports and imports on a few key markets, Mr Bruton hailed efforts to broaden the country's markets.

"Irish companies are widening their market reach, expanding into new international markets, opening up new business.

"This is borne out by the statistics showing Irish exports are at an all-time high, which will be key to our economic recovery," the minister added...

This is an edited extract from the **Irish Independent,** FRIDAY, 22 APRIL 2011.

For more up-to-date newspaper articles see www.edcodigital.ie

1 Read the newspaper extract opposite and discuss the issues raised.

2 Can you explain any of the highlighted terms?

3 Explain the following line from the newspaper article: "The export sector is benefiting from a weaker euro".

International trade involves buying and selling goods and services beyond the boundaries of our domestic economy. Irish businesses buy raw materials from overseas suppliers and Irish consumers like the choice and variety which is available from abroad. On the other hand, Ireland produces a surplus of high quality goods which are sought by overseas buyers, thereby creating a market for Irish goods and services abroad.

Ireland is a small open economy. This means we rely heavily on international trade, but are not large enough to influence world markets. As a consequence we are very vulnerable to changes in the world economy. As recent experiences have shown, a downturn in European or US markets has considerable negative impact in Ireland also.

Imports

Importing involves the purchase of goods and services from other countries. In the case of all imports, money flows out of our economy as we pay for the goods and services purchased abroad.

Visible imports

These are tangible **goods purchased from abroad**, for example Spanish oranges, French wine and Japanese cars. In the case of visible imports these goods arrive into Ireland and money leaves our economy when we pay foreign suppliers. The fact that clearly identifiable goods arrive into our economy makes it easy to see that importing has taken place.

Invisible imports

These are **services purchased from abroad**, e.g. Irish people holidaying in Spain or taking out a policy with a UK insurance company. Since there are no tangible goods entering the country, it can be more difficult to classify invisible trade correctly. For that reason, when dealing with services, it may prove helpful to look at the money flow rather than the 'movement' of services.

unit
7

441

e.g. Example

Irish citizens holidaying in Spain spend money in Spanish hotels, restaurants and shops. This has the same financial effect as when we buy oranges and other goods from Spain and is therefore an import.

Because the Irish citizens are buying a service rather than tangible goods this spending on foreign holidays is classified as an invisible import.

So, to summarise:

> **Visible import:** Irish person buys oranges from Spain.
> **Invisible import:** Irish person holidays in Spain.

In both cases the flow of wealth is from the Irish economy to the Spanish economy.

Exports

Exporting occurs when Irish producers sell goods and services to other countries. In the case of all exports, money flows into our economy as foreign customers pay for the purchase of our goods and services.

Visible exports

These are tangible **goods sold to customers abroad**, for example Irish cheese sold to France or Dublin Bay prawns sold to Spain. In the case of visible exports these goods leave Ireland. This transaction means that money flows into our economy when overseas customers pay us for the goods. The fact that clearly identifiable goods leave our economy makes it easy to see that exporting has taken place.

Invisible exports

These are **services sold by Irish businesses to customers abroad**, for example French people holidaying in Ireland, or a UK client paying consultancy fees to an Irish bank. When dealing with the service sector, there are no tangible goods leaving this country, so it may again prove helpful to look at the money flow rather than the 'movement' of services.

e.g. Example

If we look at the flow of money or wealth involved, we see that French citizens holidaying in Ireland spend money in Irish hotels, restaurants, museums and shops. This has the same financial effect as selling Irish cheese to France and is therefore an export.

Because the French citizens are buying a service rather than tangible goods we classify this spending by foreign tourists as an invisible export.

So, to summarise:

> **Visible export:** French citizen buys agricultural produce from Ireland.
> **Invisible export:** French citizen holidays in Ireland.

In both cases the flow of wealth is from the French economy to the Irish economy.

 Exam Tip

A step by step guide to help you correctly identify and classify imports and exports.

STEP 1

Firstly identify if we are dealing with purchase of goods or services.

If it's goods, it will be visible trade.

If it's services, then it's invisible trade.

STEP 2

When dealing with visible trade (goods): imports are goods in and exports are goods out.

When dealing with invisible trade (services): money leaving Ireland is importing while money into Ireland is exporting.

Ireland's main sources of visible trade 2010

Exports

> machinery
> computer equipment
> chemical/pharmaceutical products
> food
> manufactured materials
> beverages

Imports

> grains
> petroleum products
> machinery
> computer equipment
> chemicals
> textile yarns

Source: Central Statistics Office

unit
7

Why trade internationally? (Benefits of international trade)

The following are some of the major reasons why countries need or choose to engage in international trade:

> **Limited factors of production:** When countries or businesses lack the natural resources or skilled labour to produce certain goods, they may resort to importing them. Land is usually the limiting resource and in Ireland our climate is unsuited to growing certain crops (e.g. grapes, tropical fruits). While we could in theory grow these crops indoors, it would be wasteful of resources and the costs involved would be very high.

The economist David Ricardo first set out the theory of comparative advantage and he argued that the most efficient use of resources resulted from each country specialising in the good where it has a natural (comparative) advantage. It could then use these goods to trade for any other goods it requires but cannot produce efficiently. Since each country will gain economic benefits from this type of trade it is a good illustration of a co-operative relationship in action.

International trade allows countries to specialise in those goods and services which they can provide most efficiently. This leads to the optimum use of resources and will benefit the global economy and the environment.

> **Raw materials:** Certain essential raw materials are not available locally and need to be imported. Fossil fuels such as oil, coal and gas are obvious examples.

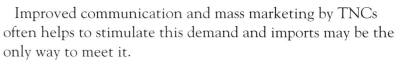

> **Consumer choice:** Consumers demand certain goods and services not produced in the domestic economy, e.g. French wine and cars. This ability to 'shop around' in international markets enables consumers to seek out the best quality and prices available.

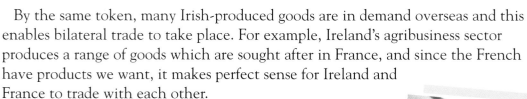

Improved communication and mass marketing by TNCs often helps to stimulate this demand and imports may be the only way to meet it.

By the same token, many Irish-produced goods are in demand overseas and this enables bilateral trade to take place. For example, Ireland's agribusiness sector produces a range of goods which are sought after in France, and since the French have products we want, it makes perfect sense for Ireland and France to trade with each other.

> **Currency:** Ireland needs to export goods and services in order to earn the foreign currency required to pay for essential imports. Oil, for example is priced in US dollars, so selling products and services to America helps generate the currency needed to pay for oil imports.

> **Market size:** Our domestic market is small in size, so in order to benefit from economies of scale producers need to sell additional goods abroad. Larger companies, including TNCs, produce vast quantities of goods in Ireland, far more than a population of 4.5 million people could demand. Most of their production is destined for overseas markets.

Exporting also helps indigenous businesses seeking to diversify. Ireland's domestic economy is relatively small, whereas the EU has a population of over 500 million. This provides opportunities for indigenous businesses to achieve economies of scale.

Who trades internationally?

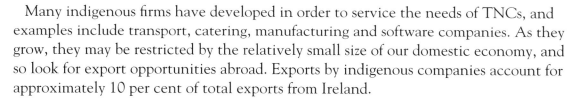

Indigenous firms

These are Irish-owned businesses, which produce goods here in Ireland. The agribusiness sector has many examples of indigenous companies (e.g. Glanbia and Kerry Group) which engage in international trade. Enterprise Ireland is the state agency with responsibility for promoting and developing the indigenous sector and it provides high levels of support to Irish businesses that have the potential to generate exports.

Many indigenous firms have developed in order to service the needs of TNCs, and examples include transport, catering, manufacturing and software companies. As they grow, they may be restricted by the relatively small size of our domestic economy, and so look for export opportunities abroad. Exports by indigenous companies account for approximately 10 per cent of total exports from Ireland.

Transnational corporations

A transnational company (TNC) has its head office in one country, but operates in a several different countries. IDA Ireland has been very successful in attracting TNCs to set up operations here. The vast majority of the goods and services produced by TNCs in Ireland are destined for export markets, with Ireland providing an ideal gateway to the EU for American and Asian transnationals in particular. These companies contribute enormously to employment in Ireland and also account for almost 90 per cent of total exports.

TNCs also import a huge proportion of the raw materials and components they require for their Irish operations. Dell Computers illustrates this process very well as the company utilises a just-in-time stock control system to ensure component parts arrive from overseas suppliers just as they are required for production in Ireland.

Measuring International Trade

The terms 'balance of trade', 'balance of invisible trade' and 'balance of payments' are all used when measuring a country's level of international trade. Each of them takes into account different aspects of trading performance and all have a role to play in highlighting key trends. Generally speaking, the balance of payments is the most economically significant.

unit
7

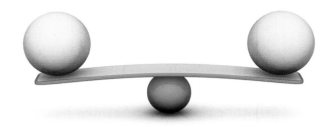

When dealing with all three measures of international trade it should be noted that there is a mathematical possibility that imports will exactly equal exports and the situation will be perfectly balanced. In reality, however, the quantities involved are just too great to expect this balance ever to happen and we inevitably see a surplus or a deficit.

Since a country would ideally like to export more than it imports, we use the term **surplus** to describe a situation where revenue from exports exceeds spending on imports.

When the opposite happens and more is spent on imports than is earned from exports, this will cause a net outflow of money from the economy, and is called a **deficit**.

The examples outlined below use figures to illustrate this more clearly.

Balance of Trade

Balance of trade is the difference between visible exports and visible imports. As outlined previously, visible trade refers to the sale and purchase of goods.

If visible exports > visible imports = Balance of Trade surplus

If visible exports < visible imports = Balance of Trade deficit

Visible Exports	=	€200 billion
Visible Imports	=	€170 billion
Balance of Trade	=	€ 30 billion surplus

This means that the country will experience a net inflow of €30 billion, with overseas customers spending €30 billion more on our goods than we are spending on imported goods.

Balance of Invisible Trade

Balance of invisible trade is the difference between invisible exports and invisible imports. Invisible trade refers to the services sector.

If invisible exports > invisible imports = Balance of Invisible Trade surplus

If invisible exports < invisible imports = Balance of Invisible Trade deficit

Invisible Exports	=	€120 billion
Invisible Imports	=	€140 billion
Balance of Trade	=	(€20 billion) deficit

This means that the country will experience a net outflow of €20 billion.

Balance of Payments

Balance of payments is the difference between total imports and total exports. It therefore accounts for both goods and services.

If total exports > total imports = Balance of Payments surplus

If total exports < total imports = Balance of Payments deficit

Visible Exports	=	€200 billion
Invisible Exports	=	€120 billion
Total Exports	=	€320 billion

Visible Imports	=	€170 billion
Invisible Imports	=	€140 billion
Total Imports	=	€310 billion

Total Exports	=	€320 billion
Total Imports	=	€310 billion
Balance of Payments:		€10 billion surplus

Overall the economy will experience a net inflow of €10 billion as the total value of goods and services exported exceeds the total value of goods and services imported.

Ireland would typically have a large balance of payments surplus each year, and a large part of this is down to the activities of multinational businesses located here.

Ireland's major trading partners, 2010

	Imports (€)	Exports (€)
Great Britain & Northern Ireland	14.7 billion	13.7 billion
Other EU countries	13.1 billion	37.8 billion
USA	6.4 billion	20.7 billion
Rest of the world	11.5 billion	16.8 billion
Total	**45.7 billion**	**89 billion**

Source: CSO

Protectionism: an alternative view

Despite the benefits of international trade outlined previously (p. 444), there are those who argue that engaging in international trade is not always in the best interests of a country and its indigenous industry. Those who adopt a protectionist outlook would prefer to rely on the local economy for the production of goods and services.

unit 7

447

Protectionism requires the government to limit or prohibit free trade and the main arguments in favour of protectionism are as follows:

Job creation

Import substitution will become a necessity and will help generate a huge number of jobs. Import substitution means replacing imported goods and services with indigenous produce.

Industry protection

By restricting the availability of imported produce, indigenous companies will not be subject to such intense competition and will be able to grow and develop. This will also have a positive impact on long-term employment levels.

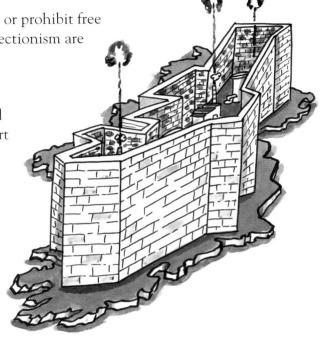

Self-sufficiency

As imported goods become unavailable the domestic economy will have to become self-sufficient in many new areas. This eliminates the risk associated with reliance on other countries for important goods and services.

Balance of payments

By limiting the amounts of imported goods, our balance of payments will improve substantially.

Barriers to trade

National governments seeking to limit the impact of imports on their domestic economy can use some of the following tactics:

Tariffs

A tariff is essentially a tax on imported goods and services. Once imposed it will increase the price of the imports and make them less competitive when compared to indigenous produce. EU trading rules mean that the Irish government cannot impose tariffs on goods produced in other EU countries, but may tax non-EU imports.

Quotas

A quota is a limit on the quantity of goods which can be imported. Quotas are usually applied on an annual basis and once the quota has been reached no additional imports are allowed. This clearly reduces the level of competition for domestic producers.

Subsidies

A subsidy is a payment made to indigenous producers in an effort to improve their competitiveness against imports. EU competition rules again limit a government's ability to subsidise domestic businesses.

Regulations

Governments can attempt to make the process of importation more difficult and complicated by imposing various rules and regulations. These rules usually relate to issues like health and safety or product specifications. By creating a bureaucratic web of 'red tape' the government can increase the cost involved and so discourage importation.

Embargoes

An embargo is a complete ban on imported goods and services. They tend to be used by governments for political or health and safety reasons. Recent examples include an embargo on beef from the UK following an outbreak of BSE ('mad cow disease') and an EU ban on oil imports from Iran in order to pressurise the Iranian government into resuming talks on the nuclear development programme.

Arguments against protectionism

Retaliation

If we impose barriers to imports, other countries are very likely to respond by restricting the sale of Irish goods in their economies. This would cost a lot of jobs in indigenous industry, particularly in the export-focused agribusiness sector. If the restrictions applied to all goods produced in Ireland it would also impact on the transnational sector and would limit our ability to attract FDI.

Limited factors of production

A lack of basic resources would make it very difficult to replace some imports, particularly oil and gas. If exports are also curtailed it may not be possible to earn enough foreign currency to purchase these essential commodities.

Costly and inefficient

The production of some goods (e.g. bananas) by indigenous producers may be very inefficient and wasteful. Inefficient production leads to higher costs and higher prices.

Lack of knowledge and expertise may also mean that import substitution will not be a satisfactory solution to all our needs. This combination of lower quality and higher prices is not likely to keep consumers happy.

Small-scale operations

A small indigenous market limits the scope for economies of scale. Smaller production runs tend to have higher per-unit costs, which in turn lead to higher wholesale and retail prices.

unit

7

449

Opportunities for Irish businesses from international trade

« syllabus signpost 7.4.4

> **Free trade:** Irish firms have access to huge international markets. This should promote growth, diversification and increased profitability. Opportunities in this area are likely to increase as world markets become increasingly deregulated.

Deregulation occurs when barriers to free trade are removed. For example, the USA and the European Union agreed an 'Open Skies' policy in 2008 which deregulated intercontinental flights. The agreement allows any airline of the EU and any airline of the United States to fly between any point in the EU and any point in the United States. As a result of this deregulation Aer Lingus expanded its route network and now flies into several US cities.

> **Economies of scale:** Serving these larger international markets requires indigenous businesses to scale up their operations. This should reduce production costs and improve the competitiveness of Irish industry abroad. Expansion will also generate additional employment.

> **Balance of payments:** An increase in Irish exports will have a positive effect on our balance of payments and boosts the level of economic growth.

> **Public procurement:** EU rules mean that any government contract valued in excess of €130,000 must be subject to a competitive and transparent tendering process. Under this policy companies from all across the EU are invited to tender (bid) for these contracts before the best one is chosen. Several Irish businesses have succeeded in winning very lucrative contracts with foreign governments.

> **Foreign direct investment:** Ireland's location within the EU, the availability of skilled labour and a high level of government investment all help make Ireland an attractive location for TNCs. This is good for employment, and the presence of TNCs creates opportunities for indigenous business development in support industries.

> **Technology/world-class manufacturing:** Most TNCs which locate in Ireland use cutting-edge technology and are world leaders in their industry. Irish workers and management gain valuable exposure to such world-class techniques. Frequently this knowledge can be applied to the benefit of indigenous industry.

> **Irish diaspora:** The large number of Irish emigrants and their descendants living abroad means that the wider international community is full of individuals who are well disposed towards Ireland and its economy. The existence of this diaspora presents Irish business with an opportunity to tap into this economic goodwill and translate it into export and investment opportunities. Trade missions in particular can be targeted at this group.

unit
7

Challenges facing Irish business as a result of international trade

> **Increased competition:** Deregulated global markets also mean Irish firms face increased competition. For example, the Open Skies agreement allows US airlines greater access to European cities. This means that Aer Lingus now competes with Continental and American Airlines on its transatlantic routes.

  Low-cost producers, particularly those from Asia and Eastern Europe also provide very serious competition for Irish businesses and have already decimated some industries, including clothing and textiles.

> **Dominant firms:** Global markets are increasingly dominated by a small number of highly diversified TNCs. These companies have massive advantages over smaller rivals, particularly in terms of operating costs, marketing and brand development. As the number of Irish TNCs is relatively small, very few indigenous businesses are in a position to compete with these industrial giants.

> **Language/culture:** Irish producers who trade internationally will need a good understanding of the marketing and cultural needs of overseas markets. Products may need to be adapted or modified in order to meet customer or legal requirements. Dealing with clients who do not share our language can also prove troublesome.

> **Distribution:** International trade will inevitable involve additional transportation costs. Due to Ireland's geographic location on the periphery of Europe, the impact of these costs may be even greater.

Developments in World Trade

The following factors have either facilitated a growth in world trade or have resulted from that growth. Together they represent a significant set of issues which will impact on global business in the decades ahead.

Growth of transnational companies

In the 1970s there were fewer than 8,000 TNCs worldwide, but today they number almost 85,000. Between them they control two thirds of world trade in goods and services, and in 2008 the combined sales of the hundred largest MNCs amounted to nearly $8.5 trillion.

  These figures clearly show that world trade is dominated by a small number of very large corporations, many of which have more economic power than national governments.

Emergence of trading blocs

A trading bloc is a group of countries who agree to remove trade barriers for goods and services traded among themselves. They also agree to impose a common set of tariffs on imports from countries outside the trading bloc. The EU and NAFTA are well-known trading blocs. NAFTA stands for North American Free Trade Agreement and is made up of the US, Canada and Mexico.

unit

7

Trading blocs allow countries to act collectively in a manner which influences global trade and promotes their own economic development. The removal of restrictions on the movement of goods and services is a major factor in facilitating the growth of cross-border trade.

Improved transport

Huge improvements in the transportation networks and the ability to refrigerate goods during transportation have helped to improve the level of international trade. All methods of transportation have become quicker, but the increased availability of cheap air transport has led to a surge in international trade. This mode of transport allows large quantities of perishable goods to be transported across the globe very quickly.

Deregulation

The removal of trade barriers within specific industries has also encouraged international trade and means that TNCs are now free to trade across national boundaries.

Some would argue that deregulation has allowed TNCs to become too dominant in some industrial sectors and that this is not in the interests of society. For example, the top twenty-three electronics TNCs and their subsidiaries account for an estimated 80 per cent of world sales in electronics.

Emerging markets

Trade figures continue to show that, when it comes to international trade, Ireland relies heavily on traditional trading partners such as the USA, the UK and other EU states. While this pattern of trade clearly reflects geographic, historical and cultural reasons, it carries a risk that opportunities may be lost to develop strong trading links with emerging economies in Asia and Eastern Europe.

In contrast to our traditional trading partners, these emerging economies offer the advantage of growing populations and many of them have seen a spectacular rise in income levels and consumer purchasing power in recent years.

The challenge for Irish business is to get a strong foothold in these fast-growing markets and this will involve successfully negotiating a number of obstacles. These include language and cultural differences as well as the obvious difficulty of serving a market which is so far from Ireland.

While innovation and creativity will be required to overcome these difficulties, there are huge rewards for those who succeed.

Impact of ICT

Improved information and communications technology has helped make the world a smaller place by speeding up the communication process. The Internet allows companies to market and sell their products to overseas customers using electronic fund transfers and credit cards to secure payment.

Advances in communication, including email and videoconferencing, also make it easier to manage a business which has operations worldwide, and is effectively 'open for business' 24/7.

The World Trade Organisation

The World Trade Organisation currently has 140 member countries, which together account for almost 97 per cent of global trade. It aims to deregulate the international trading environment and ensure that international trade operates efficiently, equitably and predictably.

Major Global Markets

> Member countries are bound by WTO rules, which have been agreed during a series of negotiating rounds. The current set of governing rules stems from the Uruguay Round of negotiations, which took place between 1986 and 1994. All member countries must accept these general rules for multilateral trade, including, for example, a ban on the imposition of import and export quotas.

> The WTO has also addressed several specific issues and its actions have led to the removal of barriers to trade and special trading arrangements between nations. Both of these have the effect of providing preferential treatment for some countries and are therefore designed to distort free trade. Their removal helps to create a 'level playing field' for all businesses irrespective of their country of origin.

> The WTO has also addressed the issue of intellectual property rights and has established a set of regulations designed to protect designs and patents. This has not, however, been without controversy and one major issue involves the need to balance the rights of patent holders and the needs of patients for life-saving medicines at affordable prices. If it is possible to provide cheaper generic drugs to these patients many lives may be saved, even though pharmaceutical companies would lose out on profit.

> If a trade dispute occurs between member states, the WTO will seek to resolve it. If, for example, one country imposes a customs duty against a particular country or on a particular good, the WTO may issue trade sanctions against the violating country. The WTO will also try to resolve the conflict through negotiations.

Assisting Irish exports

Irish exporters can receive help from the following:

Public sector

Government departments invite firms to take part in organised trade missions. A **trade mission** occurs when business and/or political representatives travel overseas in order to engage with their counterparts abroad. The purpose of these missions is to increase the level of contact and trade between Ireland and other nations. Irish embassies abroad can also assist with potential export markets.

unit 7

Enterprise Ireland is a state agency which provides market research information, marketing assistance and translation services to Irish exporters. Other state agencies are involved in specific sectors of industry, e.g. Bord Bia and Fáilte Ireland.

Private sector

Irish banks target specific services at exporters. Examples include currency exchange and international fund transfer.

Chapter Review Diagram – International Trade

Chapter Review Questions

1 Distinguish between imports and exports.

2 Distinguish between 'visible' and 'invisible' trade. Illustrate your answer with examples of both imports and exports.

3 Outline five reasons why countries choose to engage in international trade.

4 Explain the term 'balance of trade'.

5 Outline the main benefits of international trade for Ireland.

6 Outline the major arguments for and against protectionism in international trade.

7 Distinguish between the following barriers to international trade:

> A tariff   > A subsidy   > A quota   > An embargo

8 Explain two opportunities and two challenges for Irish business arising from international trade.

9 Explain the term 'deregulation'.

10 Outline four major factors which have facilitated the growth in world trade.

11 What are the main objectives of the World Trade Organisation?

Questions · Ordinary Level

1
> Transnational companies, Irish-owned firms and the agricultural industry have an important role to play in the recovery of the Irish economy. *LCOL 2011*

Explain two reasons why transnational companies (multinational companies) locate in Ireland *(15 marks)*

2 (a) Visible Exports €1,138m, Visible Imports €1,235m.

   (i) From the above information, calculate the Balance of Trade. (Show your workings.)

   (ii) State whether it is a surplus or a deficit. *(15 marks)*

   (b) Explain the term 'Balance of Payments'. *(10 marks)*

   (c) (i) Outline **two** reasons why Irish firms engage in international trade.

   (ii) Identify **two** challenges faced by Irish firms engaged in international trade. *LCOL 2009 (30 marks)*

3 Outline, using examples, two ways in which information technology helps Irish Firms involved in international trade. *LCOL 2008 (20 marks)*

4 Visible Imports €900m and Visible Exports €550m.

From the above information, calculate the Balance of Trade. State whether it is a surplus or deficit.

Questions · Higher Level

1 Illustrate your understanding of the terms 'Balance of Trade' and 'Balance of Payments'. *LCHL 2010 (10 marks)*

2 Using the following data, calculate (i) Balance of Trade, (ii) Balance of Payments. State in each case whether it is a surplus or deficit.

Visible Exports €50 billion, Invisible Imports €40 billion, Visible Imports €30 billion, and Invisible Exports €35 billion. *LCHL 2011 (10 marks)*

3 Discuss how the changing nature of the international economy affects Irish exporters. *LCHL 2011 (20 marks)*

4
> The Irish economy is an open economy and is greatly affected by economic influences from abroad. These influences create both opportunities and challenges for Irish business. *LCHL 2007*

Discuss the opportunities provided by international trade for Irish business. *(25 marks)*

5 Analyse how changes in the international economy are impacting on Irish business. Use relevant examples to illustrate your answer. *LCHL 2006 (15 marks)*

unit
7

Chapter 23
The European Union

Syllabus Outcomes

On completion, the student should be able to:

» 7.4.1 Identify the effects of the single market on Irish business;

» 7.4.4 Discuss the opportunities and challenges facing Irish business in developed and developing markets;

» 7.4.6 Explain the purpose of the main European Union policies and directives (HL).

News Flash

1 Read the newspaper extract below and discuss the issues raised.

2 Can you explain any of the highlighted terms?

State faces €3.2m fine over breach of EU ruling

by Arthur Beesley, European Correspondent

The EU Commission has initiated a second legal action against the Government over its failure to adopt a farming environmental directive and will ask Europe's highest court to fine Ireland at least €3.27 million for breaching a prior ruling of its judges.

A spokesman for environment commissioner Janez Potocnik said Ireland's proposals to meet its obligations "didn't meet the requirements of the directive" on the protection of the countryside heritage. "Two years after the judgment, Ireland has still not adopted legislation to address the issue."

Responding, the Government said the environment and agriculture departments are developing a further response to the judgment and plan to consult with the commission...

In the new case against Ireland the commission will ask the court to impose a fine of €4,000 for each day since the court ruled against Ireland on November 20th 2008 and for each day until the court issues a new infringement ruling. Any failure to comply with a new ruling should be punished by a fine of €33,000 per day.

While a fine of €3.27 million would already be due in respect of the 818 days since the 2008 ruling if the judges found in favour of the commission, the fact that new infringement cases typically take two years to come before the European Court of Justice leaves open the possibility that Ireland could face a fine twice as large as that...

This is an edited extract from **The Irish Times,** THURSDAY, 17 FEBRUARY 2011.

For more up-to-date newspaper articles see www.edcodigital.ie

Origin and Aims

The European Union is a trading bloc which operates as a free trade area for its **twenty-seven member states**, with Croatia due to join in 2013. It began soon after the end of the Second World War and reflects the fact that the continent of Europe had been devastated by hundreds of years of almost continuous warfare. Most of this conflict was over the control of land and resources.

When established by the Treaty of Rome in 1958 it had just six members (France, West Germany, Italy, Belgium, Luxembourg and the Netherlands). The aim of these countries was **to increase economic and political co-operation** as a means of reducing the level of conflict across the continent. It has been largely successful in this aim and has grown to reach its current membership of twenty-seven countries. Ireland joined the EU in 1973.

Just as the EU membership has grown, so too has the range of areas it deals with. The EU is now a **major trading bloc** in the global economy and the income levels of member states have risen steadily.

The EU operates on the principle of **shared sovereignty,** where each of the independent member states concedes some autonomy and control to EU institutions in order to support collective goals. The structure and operation of EU is built around a **series of international treaties** which must be signed into law in all member states. In some countries, such as Ireland, this requires a referendum. A referendum is a public vote which allows citizens to have a decisive say in important matters and enables a change to be made to the constitution. The Lisbon Treaty is the most recently adopted EU treaty and it gave effect to a whole range of changes intended to improve the decision-making process in an enlarged union.

The **EU prepares an annual budget,** which is funded by contributions from member states. While all countries contribute to the budget, the largest contributions come from France and Germany. For many years Ireland was a net recipient of EU funding. This means that although we contributed money to the EU budget, we always received more money from the EU than we actually contributed each year. This money came in the form of grants, subsidies and various other payments, particularly through the Common Agricultural Policy (CAP). Over the decades since joining the EU, the funding has helped to transform the Irish economy from one of the poorest European nations to one of the wealthiest.

In 1973 Irish income levels (as measured by per capita GNP) were 56 per cent of the EU average. By 2010 they were 120 per cent.

unit
7

457

EU Institutions

The following are the major institutions of the EU:

European Council ~ European Commission ~ European Parliament ~ Council of the EU
Court of Justice ~ Court of Auditors

The European Council

This institution was formalised following the ratification of the Lisbon Treaty in 2009.

Membership

The European Council meetings are summit meetings held regularly by **EU heads of state.** The meetings take place at least twice a year and are chaired by the Council's permanent president.

José Manuel Barroso and Herman van Rompuy

Role

Council meetings represent an attempt by heads of state to **set out priorities and a general political direction** for the EU.

These meetings are often used to discuss major issues facing the EU, with recent examples including the budgetary and debt problems experienced by some member states. Most decisions are reached using a consensus approach and, despite the political power and influence of its members, **the Council does not have any powers to pass laws.**

The EU co-decision procedure

Once the overall agenda has been set by the Council, responsibility for day-to-day decision-making in the EU lies with its three main institutions:

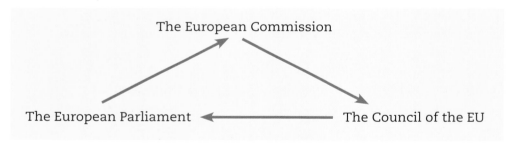

The power to initiate and implement legislation is divided amongst the three institutions and therefore requires a co-operative or consensus approach to policy decisions. This institutional triangle uses a **co-decision procedure** to introduce legislation and policy.

The EU's major institutions are interdependent and must work together to introduce and implement EU policy. This means that no single institution has sufficient power to legislate on its own and each needs to work closely with the other two in order to get their support for its proposals.

Despite this high level of interdependence, each institution draws its membership from a different source and each plays a different role in the legislative process (see also p.463).

The European Commission

Membership

With **one nominee from each member state,** there are currently twenty-seven Commissioners. Nominees are usually **high-profile political or business figures** who have a track record in public or business administration. They are appointed for a five-year term and each is given a specific area of responsibility, for example agriculture, transport or competition policy. The position of EU Commissioner is broadly similar to that of a government minister in our own country and they are **responsible for the day-to-day management of the EU**. They are assisted in their role by the EU civil service.

The headquarters of the European Commission in Brussels

Role

The main functions of the European Commission are:

1 **Proposing new laws:** The commission proposes new legislation and works closely with the Parliament and Council to have them approved. A detailed description of this process is set out on page 413.

2 **Enforcing EU law**: Commissioners are responsible for enforcing existing legislation. They monitor all member states to ensure that governments and businesses are meeting their obligations under EU law. Those found to be in breach of EU policy can be fined or can be sanctioned by the EU's Court of Justice.

3 **Managing the EU's budget**: Each Commissioner has responsibility for spending their budget allocation effectively and impartially. They must ensure EU funding is only allocated to worthwhile projects and are not allowed to show bias towards particular regions or countries. The Court of Auditors assists them in monitoring budgetary spending.

4 **Representing the EU internationally**: As the global economy becomes increasingly deregulated the EU seeks to negotiate agreements with other countries and trading blocs. An example would be the EU Trade Commissioner attending World Trade Organisation (WTO) talks or the Environment Commissioner attending an international conference on climate change.

The European Parliament

Membership

Members of the European Parliament (MEPs) are in the unique position of being **directly elected by EU citizens**.

Each member state has a set number of MEPs, based on its population. The Republic of Ireland currently has twelve seats in the 720-member Parliament, with elections taking place every five years. The European Parliament is located in Strasbourg (France).

unit 7

In order to have a greater influence on EU policy-making, MEPs work collaboratively with like-minded colleagues from other countries. By aligning themselves with established political groupings, it is possible for the relatively small number of Irish MEPs to have a greater say in formulating EU policy.

There is, for example, a large group of Green Party MEPs from right across the continent of Europe. By choosing to vote on the basis of this political affiliation rather than by nationality they succeed in having their views represented in the European Parliament's policy decisions.

European Parliament in Strasbourg

Role

The main functions of the European Parliament are:

1 To represent EU citizens

2 To help introduce legislation

3 To approve and monitor the Commission

4 To approve the EU budget

1 To represent EU citizens

Since MEPs are directly elected by citizens in each member state, they seek to ensure that the EU acts in the best interests of these citizens. Critics would argue that MEPs have limited power and influence in the legislative process and are often disconnected from the public they serve.

2 To help introduce legislation

The European Parliament **does not have the power to introduce legislation on its own,** and works with the Council and the Commission to introduce legislation. The Lisbon Treaty has added to the Parliament's powers by widening the range of issues on which this type of co-decision can be made. Parliament now has legislative involvement in areas like agriculture, energy policy, immigration and the allocation of EU funds.

One of its main functions is to debate and amend proposals put forward by the Commission. Proposals rejected by the Parliament cannot become European law.

In practice, controversial proposals are returned to the Commission with suggested amendments from MEPs. If these amendments are made, it is likely the Parliament will approve the legislation at a later stage.

The fact that the only directly elected body in the EU has limited legislative power leads to criticism of the EU for having a **democratic deficit.** There is a feeling that the real power to influence the direction of EU policy is in the hands of a relatively small group of people (Commissioners and Council members) who are not directly elected by EU citizens.

Contrast this to the role of TDs in Dáil Éireann, who are directly elected public representatives and therefore have a mandate and the power to introduce or amend Irish law.

The Treaty of Lisbon included increased powers for the European Parliament. These powers mean that the Parliament and the Council of the EU work together to introduce legislation (co-decisions) and the Parliament now has power to reject laws which it does not agree with.

3 To approve the Commission

When member states nominate candidates for the Commission, the Parliament must approve the nominees before the Commission is appointed. MEPs who disapprove of even a single nominee have the power to reject the entire list.

4 To approve the EU budget

In keeping with their position as public representatives, the MEPs play a major role in approving the annual EU budget and also monitor the way in which the Commission spends the money.

The Lisbon Treaty

The Lisbon Treaty changed the EU's legislative process. It increased the Parliament's power by extending the co-decision procedure, and it expanded the use of **qualified majority voting** (QMV) in the Council, removing the national **veto** from certain policy areas.

Qualified majority voting means that not all decisions require unanimous support of EU member states. A complex voting system has been devised which allows for majority voting by member states, although the majority is subject to strict population criteria.

This system is designed to ensure that a balance is struck between the need for consensus and the need to make effective decisions. The new voting arrangement prevents larger member states from dominating votes, as some decisions require support from two thirds of member states. The population criteria also mean that several smaller countries cannot force through decisions which impact on the majority of EU citizens.

A veto allows a member state to completely block a proposal and only applies to a very limited number of issues. During the second referendum on the Lisbon Treaty in Ireland, the Irish Farmers Association successfully lobbied the government to ensure Ireland retained its veto on issues relating to the reform of the Common Agricultural Policy.

Council of the European Union (formerly Council of Ministers)

Membership

Council members are **government ministers from EU member states**. The membership of the Council is not fixed and **depends on the topic under discussion**. If it's an agriculture issue, each country will send its agriculture minister, whereas finance ministers will be sent for budget issues and so on.

unit 7

461

Role

The main functions of the Council of the EU are:

1 Goal setting and policy co-ordination.

2 Passing legislation

3 Approving the EU budget

4 Signing international agreements

Council of the EU offices in Brussels

The Council **sets the agenda for future EU policy** and this forms the basis for legislative proposals from the Commission.

EU member states share many common goals and finance ministers work closely to implement an overall economic policy for Europe. The Council plays an important role in co-ordinating national policies to improve economic growth, employment and standards of living across the EU.

Council members may also be required to sign legislation on behalf of member states, or may reject a proposal.

EU Court of Justice

This is an independent court of law with **judges appointed by member states for a term of six years.** The Court of Justice seeks to **ensure that EU laws are enforced and implemented** in a manner which is uniform and fair. It is also involved in the **interpretation of EU law** whenever disputes arise. The court has the power to compel governments and businesses to comply with EU laws and directives and imposes fines against those who fail to meet their obligations.

A 'General Court' also exists and helps alleviate the heavy caseload by dealing with actions brought forward by private individuals and companies, as well as cases relating to competition law.

The Court of Auditors

Its primary role is to **monitor EU budgetary spending**. It aims to ensure the EU budget is spent in a manner which is consistent with implementing EU policy and that money allocated to member states is used for the purpose intended. The auditors carry out investigations and spot checks in EU institutions and member countries as they attempt to verify that European citizens are getting good value for money and that taxpayers' money is not being wasted.

One of the court's most important jobs is to present the European Parliament and the Council with an annual report on the previous financial year.

unit
7

EU Legislative Process

ENACTED   REJECTED

1 Proposals from Commission

Only the Commission has powers to propose new legislation. Before any legislation is drawn up the Commission will engage in a consultation process with interested stakeholders including national governments, industry representatives, community groups, non-governmental organisations (NGOs) and EU citizens.

The consultation process is designed to ensure that the legislation will meet the needs of these stakeholders and will also examine the social, economic and environmental impact of the proposals.

Member state parliaments have the opportunity to object to a legislative proposal if in its view it breaches the principle of subsidiarity.

The principle of **subsidiarity** states that a central authority such as the EU should only intervene and make decisions on matters which cannot be effectively dealt with at local level.

For example, Irish farmers may feel the Irish government is best placed to regulate the industry in Ireland or that decisions on Irish energy consumption should be made at national level.

2 Reviewed by Parliament and Council

Both the Parliament and the Council of the EU will debate the proposed legislation and each may suggest amendments. Interested stakeholders will seek to have their particular viewpoint taken into consideration by lobbying MEPs.

Lobbying is the term used for the activities of pressure groups or interest groups that seek to influence the decision making process in the EU. Representative groups (e.g. IFA) often seek to have their own interests protected or pursued by meeting with members of the Council, Commission or Parliament. During these meetings they will highlight their concerns and try to influence the way in which EU policy is directed. Criticism again arises from the fact that individual citizens have very little power or influence in this process.

3 Redrafting by Commission

The amendments put forward by the Parliament and the Council may require the Commission to redraft the proposal before returning it to both institutions for further consideration.

4 Agreement by Parliament and Council

In the **co-decision procedure** the Council and Parliament must both agree on the wording of the legislation and this can be a very time-consuming process, often lasting more than two years. In practice, the proposals may pass back and forth several times between the Parliament, the Commission and the Council, as they attempt to reach an agreement.

unit 7

463

5 Legislation enacted or proposal rejected

If and when agreement is reached, the legislation is approved and will pass into law. Each member state is then required to implement the new law and EU legislation takes precedence over national laws.

If agreement cannot be reached within the stipulated timeframe, the proposal falls and the legislation is not adopted.

Evaluation and significance of EU legislative process

This process of drafting and passing legislation is quite complex and seeks to balance the needs and wishes of stakeholder groups and EU institutions.

This high level of complexity often leads to criticism that the entire process is too secretive, too bureaucratic and also runs contrary to the principle of subsidiarity.

Many would argue that despite the consultation process, decisions taken at EU level are often far removed from EU citizens and interfere unreasonably in their day-to-day lives.

Despite these concerns, legislation passed at EU level is significant and each member state is responsible for ensuring its effective implementation at national level. Those who fail to comply are likely to face sanctions from the Commission and the European Court of Justice. The court has powers to impose fines for non-compliance and the newspaper extract at the beginning of the chapter provides a clear example of this.

Implementation

EU laws and rules can take a number of different forms, with each having a different type of impact and a different level of importance:

Regulations

Once passed, regulations become **legally binding immediately** and ensure that the same legal position applies **across all twenty-seven member countries.** Since these EU laws automatically apply to all members there is no specific need to introduce national laws, and individuals can rely on regulations in any court cases in their own country. Where a conflict arises, EU regulations take precedence over national laws.

e.g. Example

The EU has a regulation which deals with EU nationals' entitlement to social security benefits when in other member states. This regulation ensures that EU citizens who move between member states are subject to the same obligations and enjoy the same benefits as the nationals of the state they reside in. This means that Irish citizens who relocate to Germany will be entitled to claim social welfare benefits in that country, once they comply with standard qualifying criteria.

In December 2009 the EU also introduced a regulation aimed at phasing out the production and sale of 'traditional' incandescent light bulbs between 2009 and 2012. The regulation applies only to non-directional household lamps and has seen them replaced with more energy-efficient long-life bulbs. The regulation represents an attempt by the EU to reduce energy consumption and help limit carbon emissions.

Directives

Directives provide **guidelines or goals for member states** when implementing EU policy and will **require changes to national laws**. The EU sets out the main aim of each directive as well as the timeframe allowed for countries to comply.

For example, the EU might have a directive requiring that all member states to recycle 75 per cent of their household waste by 2020. It is then up to each individual government to decide how best to achieve this, and to introduce appropriate legislation.

Case Study

The EU introduced a directive on Waste Electrical and Electronic Equipment (WEEE) in 2005. The purpose of this directive was to reduce the generation of electrical and electronic waste and to promote reuse, recycling and other forms of recovery.

The Irish government implemented the WEEE Directive in August 2005 and Irish legislation requires all producers and distributors (retailers) to register with the WEEE Register Society. They are also required to collect and recycle old electrical and electronic equipment from households and consumers.

WEEE Ireland is a not-for-profit organisation, founded by producers of electrical and electronic appliances in order to comply with these legal obligations imposed by the EU directive.

WEEE Ireland arranges for the treatment and recycling of waste electrical and electronic equipment on behalf of its members.

The EU also has directives governing the wearing of seatbelts in passenger vehicles and it too has been implemented by governments in all member states.

unit

7

Decisions

Decisions are very specific rulings and **apply only to named countries or organisations.**
They are legally binding and are usually issued where there has been a breach of EU
law or a dispute has arisen. They may incur a financial penalty for failure to comply.

 **Example**

> The Commission issued a decision against Microsoft for breaching EU
> competition policy and abusing its dominant market position. Fines and
> penalties totalling €1.4 billion were imposed on the software company
> between 2004 and 2007.

Recommendations/Opinions

EU institutions sometimes express their view on certain matters by issuing
recommendations or opinions. These recommendations and opinions enable the EU
to clearly state its position or make suggestions for action, but are not intended to be
legally binding. They are in effect just guidelines or suggestions which can be either
ignored or acted upon.

Major EU Policies

Common Agricultural Policy (CAP)

The Common Agricultural Policy aims to:

« *syllabus signpost* 7.4.6 (HL)

> Develop sustainable agriculture across member states;

> Ensure that the EU is self-sufficient when it comes to agricultural produce;

> Maintain farm incomes and support rural communities.

Implementation

When the CAP was first introduced, the EU used output limits (quotas), export
subsidies, development grants and intervention pricing to ensure an ample
supply of farm produce to meet the needs of the EU. **'Intervention payments'**
were guaranteed minimum prices paid to farmers for surplus stock. These
measures helped meet consumer expectations in terms of quality and
price stability and the intervention payments also allowed farmers
to make a reasonable livelihood from agriculture.

The measures were not entirely successful, however, and
often led to a mismatch between supply and demand,
with the EU having to pay a high price for any unwanted
or unsold farm produce. The cost of implementing the
policies was increasing year on year and accounted for
an ever-increasing portion of the entire EU budget.
Eventually these budget issues, along with global pressure
for deregulation, led to major reform of the CAP.

unit 7

CAP Reform

> Farmers now receive a single payment or **subsidy**, which is not related to production. The process of separating the subsidy from the amount produced is called **decoupling**.

> Intervention purchases have been abolished and farmers are given greater freedom to meet market demands.

> EU farmers are protected from low-cost imports from outside the EU by a series of quotas and tariffs.

> The EU has helped with farm modernisation by providing grants for capital projects.

CAP reform is an ongoing process and is linked to World Trade Organisation agreements (see p. 453). While the ongoing reforms of the CAP have reduced the overall EU spending on agriculture, it is still a major element of the annual EU budget.

Since Ireland has a relatively large agricultural sector and is highly dependent on exports, the importance of the CAP to our economy has not diminished.

Single European Market (SEM)

Aims

The Single European Market is an attempt to create a free-trade area across the entire EU. A major step in achieving this has been the removal of trade barriers between member states.

Implementation

The terms of this policy provide for the **free movement of goods, services, labour and capital across the EU**. In theory, the entire EU becomes one big deregulated marketplace with businesses free to set up or trade in any member state.

'The Four Freedoms'

Free movement of goods

> The removal of border controls and most of the bureaucratic paperwork associated with international trade has greatly simplified the process of importing and exporting goods. It also reduces business costs since less administration is required.

> The EU has also harmonised technical standards across member states which increases the reliability and acceptability of goods produced by all member states. A common European quality standard has been established to reassure consumers and to improve market access for all EU producers.

unit 7

467

> Improvements in transportation and higher levels of competition have also helped reduce costs and increase delivery speeds across the EU.

> Customs officials and police forces continue to carry out random spot checks to prevent crime and the importation of illegal goods.

Free movement of services

> Services tend to be less transferable than goods and often require the presence and intervention of skilled personnel to carry them out. Consequently the liberalisation process has been slower and more limited in the services sector than it has been for goods.

For example, it is most unlikely that an Irish consumer will choose to travel to the UK specifically to avail of hairdressing services. This is because the cost involved is too great and also because an identical service is available locally.

These barriers will only become less relevant as the price of the service increases or the domestic market cannot offer the same level of expertise. It is for these reasons that some Irish citizens choose to travel abroad for medical treatments, including dentistry and plastic surgery.

> The most common types of internationally traded services are in the financial sector (insurance and banking), transport, ICT, retail and consultancy.

> The growth in internationally traded financial services has been greatly assisted by the free movement of capital.

Free movement of people

> The reduced border controls and bureaucracy which allow the free movement of goods have similar benefits for EU passport holders.

> Citizens of one member state no longer need visa or work permits when travelling to another member state.

> Mutual recognition of qualifications has also increased opportunities for citizens to work and study abroad. For example, Irish students can use their leaving certificate results to gain entry to UK and other EU universities.

> The introduction of the EU's Social Charter (see p. 473) helps ensure that EU workers, consumers and citizens will benefit from the same levels of protection no matter where they choose to work, shop or live.

Free movement of capital

> Capital is essential for business start-ups and for business growth, so the relaxation of rules governing the movement of capital within the EU improves the prospects for business development. It effectively means that EU businesses have a much larger pool of money available to them and are also less restricted in moving their own funds from one country to another.

> The introduction of the euro as a single currency in seventeen EU member states represented a major step forward in the free movement of funds.

Not only do these countries share common currency but they also operate under a similar interest rate regime which is controlled by the European Central Bank. Since capital tends to flow to areas where it will receive the greatest reward (interest), the establishment of an identical rate for so many EU countries helps ensure more equal access to funds for all member states and businesses.

It is the combined effect of these four freedoms which creates a climate for business growth and development across the EU.

It intensifies competition and forces business to be more efficient, but it also provides access to much larger markets for those who are successful.

Government contracts must be advertised across the EU and must be given to whichever company tenders the best offer, irrespective of nationality. This is called **public procurement** and means that public contracts are now open to bidders from anywhere in the EU.

In 2009 Irish companies secured 80 overseas public procurement contracts worth over €210 million. A similar number of contracts were won in 2010 and Irish firms secured €200 million worth of contracts with the Olympic Development Authority in the UK.

London's Olympic Stadium

Approximately 1 per cent of Irish public procurement contracts go to overseas companies and the government is taking action to assist Irish SMEs to secure more public procurement contracts. These measures include 'unbundling' large contracts to make it easier for Irish SMEs to compete for them.

« syllabus signpost 7.4.1

Impact of the single market on Ireland

> The introduction of the SEM provided a major jobs boost to Ireland's economy by increasing our attractiveness as a location for **foreign direct investment**. American and Asian companies operating here have unrestricted access to the EU market and so choose Ireland as a manufacturing base.

> The introduction of a single market and common technological standards make it easier for Irish exporters to expand abroad. Irish **exporters** are also forced to increase their levels of efficiency in order to compete in a liberalised market. Access to a single market of over 500 million people also provides the opportunity for **economies of scale**.

> **State subsidies are outlawed** and only the most efficient businesses can survive. Since the mid 1990s the Irish state has been prevented from funding companies like Telecom Éireann, Aer Lingus and Irish Steel. As a result, private sector investment has increased and has brought about the growth of successful businesses like Ryanair.

unit 7

> Irish business has **greater access to capital.** Businesses seeking investment can source capital from anywhere in the EU. The free movement of capital also means that Irish consumers have a greater range of savings and investment opportunities.

> The advent of the Single European Market also enabled Irish businesses to become **less dependent upon the UK market** for both imports and exports. The removal of trade barriers and improved transportation reduced this level of dependence and provided new opportunities for growth in continental markets.

> The free movement of capital has provided a major **boost for the Irish financial services industry.** It enabled the establishment of the Irish Financial Services Centre (IFSC) and encouraged international financial institutions to establish themselves in Ireland, creating thousands of jobs in the process.

> The single market has also brought **increased levels of competition** for indigenous industry as Irish markets are opened up to overseas producers. The clothing industry is among a number of traditional manufacturing industries which have suffered huge job losses as a result of this competition.

> The introduction of the euro as a **single currency** has helped promote international trade between eurozone countries and has therefore facilitated the creation of a single market.

> A **cohesion fund** has been set up to improve infrastructure in underdeveloped areas and prevent a flow of wealth and resources to already affluent regions.

Economic and Monetary Union (EMU)

This policy seeks to create **an economic union,** with member countries sharing a **single monetary policy and a single currency, the euro.** The adoption of this single currency by so many EU member states is also designed to facilitate the operation of the single European market.

Ireland is one of seventeen countries in which the euro is legal tender and these countries are collectively known as the eurozone. Before adopting the single currency, member states must comply with specific criteria, which set limits on inflation, interest rates and national debt. These **convergence criteria** are designed to maintain the stability of the euro.

The five convergence criteria required for eurozone membership are:

> **Price stability:** The rate of inflation cannot be more than 1.5 per cent higher than the average rates of inflation in the three member states with the lowest inflation.

> **Interest rates:** Long-term interest rates should not vary by more than 2 per cent when compared to the average interest rate of the three member states with the lowest interest rates. (This is effectively the same for all due to the ECB role in setting interest rates.)

> **Budget deficits:** National budget deficits must be kept below 3 per cent of GDP.

> **Public debt:** The criteria state that the level of public debt must not exceed 60 per cent of GDP.

> **Exchange rate stability:** Exchange rates (for an applicant country's existing currency) must have been maintained within an agreed margin of fluctuation for the previous two years prior to eurozone membership.

These criteria have been put in place to ensure that the economic conditions prevailing in eurozone member states are broadly similar. The importance of this economic unity has been highlighted in recent years, where concerns over excessive debt levels and large budget deficits in some countries have threatened to undermine the value and long-term viability of the euro. The criteria are set out in the **EU's stability and growth pact (SGP)** and it seems likely that the regulatory authorities will seek far stricter compliance with these criteria in future years.

The administration of this monetary policy and single currency is carried out by the **European Central Bank (ECB)**.

The ECB is located in Frankfurt, Germany and each Eurozone country is represented on its board. Its role is to **protect the integrity of the currency** and ensure **compliance with convergence criteria**, as well as **setting interest rates**.

In 2011 the debt crisis in member states such as Portugal, Ireland, Italy, Greece and Spain (collectively referred to by market analysts as the PIIGS), threatened to undermine the euro and raised serious questions about the long-term viability of the EU. Fears were further heightened in October 2011 when Greece became the first eurozone country to default on some of its sovereign debt.

In order to protect the integrity of the currency the European Central Bank, along with larger member states (mainly France and Germany), was forced to establish a bailout fund in order to reassure market investors that the currency was stable.

In the longer term all EU governments will be forced to adhere far more strictly to the terms of a fiscal compact which sets out the criteria for budget deficits and national debt.

EU 'six pack' on the way

The European Commission has said that the reinforced Stability and Growth Pact (SGP) is to enter into force with a new set of rules for economic and fiscal surveillance, known as the 'six pack'.

The rules are made of five regulations and one directive proposed by the European Commission and approved by all 27 Member States and the European Parliament last October.

The five regulations cover areas like deficit, public debt, government expenditure, macro-economic imbalances and related standards. Member States currently in excessive deficit procedure must comply with the recommendations and deadlines decided by the EU Council to correct their excessive deficit and credit bubbles, such as property booms, will be closely monitored.

Source: Evening Herald, TUESDAY, 13 DECEMBER 2011.

unit 7

Impact of Economic and Monetary Union on Ireland

› The main benefit of monetary union is the **reduction in exchange rate risk** associated with international trade. This risk arises when fluctuations in the exchange rate (or price) of one currency cause it to change value relative to the exchange rate of a trading partner. When this happens, the costs of buying goods from overseas will rise or fall. These fluctuations in the value of currencies make it more difficult for businesses to plan and will increase the level of risk associated with international contracts.

  This risk is eliminated entirely when trading with other eurozone countries as prices are determined in euros and will not fluctuate over the term of a contract.

› Additional benefits of the single currency include cost savings due to the elimination of **currency conversion charges**.

› The fact that goods are priced in euros also allows businesses and consumers in all eurozone countries to **compare prices** more easily.

› Individual member states no longer have the ability to directly control their own **interest rates**. Rates are set at ECB summit meetings, held quarterly. The eurozone also requires strict control of fiscal policy (government spending and borrowing) and inflation. All of this has major implications for government policy and will affect our ability to deal with an economic downturn.

Competition policy

The EU competition policy is designed to regulate the power of large and influential companies which may seek to undermine fair competition. Responsibility for the day to-day implementation of this policy rests with the EU's Competition Commissioner.

EU Competition Commissioner Joaquín Almunia

  The EU will investigate complaints in circumstances where large businesses or governments attempt to break the rules governing free and fair competition. Those found guilty of anti-competitive behaviour may be subject to hefty fines.

  Cartels are illegal while monopolists are not allowed to increase consumer prices or block the entry of new competitors into the market.

  A **monopoly** is a business which is the sole supplier in a particular industry, and so does not face any genuine competition. Where a business dominates a market in this way, there is a danger that it may abuse this power and charge excessive prices for its goods and services. Most examples of monopolies involve state companies and the EU has introduced rules to deregulate many of these markets and increase the level of competition. In Ireland state monopolies like Aer Lingus, Telecom Éireann and the ESB have either been privatised or have been subject to far greater levels of competition from privately-owned rivals such as Ryanair and Airtricity.

A **cartel** is an illegal arrangement by a group of businesses to collude in such a way as to distort the level of free competition in a market. It usually involves a secretive agreement to engage in price-fixing or else to control prices by limiting the available supply. While the market has the appearance of being competitive, the reality is that several firms have agreed to adopt similar pricing policies and not to undercut each other on price. As a result, consumers are forced to pay artificially high prices while business profits increase.

e.g. Example

Despite being prohibited by the World Trade Organisation's international trading rules, OPEC, the best-known example of a cartel, is operated by a group of national governments. These twelve Oil Producing Exporting Countries (OPEC) control more than one third of the world's oil and account for three quarters of known reserves. They exercise a great deal of control over international oil prices by negotiating amongst themselves and setting export quotas for each member country.

The EU competition policy also prevents governments from funding or subsidising indigenous business if this funding is likely to provide the recipient with an unfair competitive advantage over its rivals. Aer Lingus is just one of a large number of European state airlines which have been privatised because the state was no longer in a position to recapitalise them.

Social policy

The EU social policy runs parallel to the economic policies and recognises the need to improve the quality of life for all EU citizens. It has arisen from concerns that the twin goals of economic unity and growth would be pursued relentlessly without any regard for their impact on citizens or the need for equal distribution of wealth. The policy has a number of specific provisions which attempt to **protect the rights of workers and consumers**.

Several social policy directives have been introduced which aim to strengthen the rights of consumers. Recent changes to Irish legislation, including the Consumer Protection Act, 2007, reflect some of these issues.

Health and safety standards for workers, **minimum wage** levels, improved working conditions and holiday entitlements have all resulted from the introduction of the EU's **Social Charter**. These measures are necessary in order to promote the free movement of labour across member states.

Employees are also **protected from discrimination** and the EU has set up a **Social Fund** to help with the retraining of workers in order to provide them with improved skills and job prospects.

Policies aimed at **increasing female participation in the labour market** have led to directives on pregnant workers, and recommendations on sexual harassment in the workplace, as well as equal participation of women and men in decision-making.

unit
7

EU social policy guidelines also encourage national governments to promote **positive integration** and have included a range of measures designed to assist disabled, elderly and migrant citizens. In keeping with this philosophy and an ageing European population, member states have begun to raise the retirement age and are adopting sustainable pension policies.

The Common Fisheries Policy (CFP)

This policy brings together a range of measures designed to achieve a thriving and sustainable European fishing industry, the most important of which include:

> **Establishing rules to ensure Europe's fisheries are sustainable** and do not damage the marine environment. These rules are enforced by national authorities and offenders are punished by fines, confiscation of equipment or in some cases by having their licence revoked.

> **Monitoring the size of the European fishing fleet** and preventing further expansion. This is achieved through very strict control of fishing licences in each member state. Governments cannot issue new licenses unless a current licence holder decides not to have their licence renewed.

> **Providing funding and technical support** for initiatives that can make the industry more sustainable. This includes supporting the development of a broader EU aquaculture sector (fish, seafood and algae farms). The CFP also provides funding for scientific research and data collection, to ensure a sound basis for policy and decision-making.

> **Negotiating on behalf of EU countries** at international fisheries conferences and with non-EU countries around the world. This is part of a realisation that the problems facing the EU fishing industry are also being felt in other parts of the world. In particular it recognises that preservation of fish stocks is a global problem and requires a collective solution.

> **Assisting producers, processors and distributors** to get a fair price for their produce while also ensuring that consumers can trust the seafood they eat.

Impact of EU Membership on Ireland

« *syllabus signpost* 7.4.4

Exam Tip

Higher Level students should be capable of **evaluating** the impact of the EU on Ireland. This involves analysing the positive and negative impacts of EU membership and reaching a balanced conclusion about its value to Ireland.

unit 7

Benefits of EU membership

> **Access to a larger market:** The population of the EU exceeds 500 million people. This is more than 100 times bigger than our domestic market and provides enormous opportunity for Irish business to expand.

> **Foreign direct investment:** As a consequence of this improved market access, Ireland is an attractive location for foreign direct investment (FDI), especially from US multinationals. Many of these MNCs export goods produced in Ireland and this helps our **balance of payments**.

> **Less dependent on UK market:** Although the UK continues to be our main trading partner, Irish business is less dependent upon it than ever before. The percentage of Irish trade taking place with the rest of the EU has grown steadily since we joined the EU in 1973.

> **EU funding and grant aid:** Since joining the EU in 1973, Ireland has been a net beneficiary from EU funding. This means we've received more from the EU budget than we've paid into it. The money has been received via CAP funding, Regional Development Funds and Cohesion Funds.

> **Higher living standards:** Overall standards of living have increased since Ireland joined the EU. At the time we joined, Ireland's per capita income levels were 56% per cent of the EU average. In 2009 per capita income levels in Ireland were 120% per cent of the EU average. This illustrates, in a very quantifiable way, the increase in Ireland's wealth since joining the EU.

> **Infrastructural development:** EU funding has allowed for industrial development in specific areas such as agribusiness, as well as infrastructural advances (e.g. roads, ports, telecommunications) which benefit all Irish businesses.

> **Lower interest rates:** Since adopting the euro, Ireland's interest rates have been set by the ECB and have been significantly reduced. This is in keeping with interest rate policy across the rest of Europe and has helped economic growth and prosperity. Lower interest rates have made it cheaper for households and businesses to borrow money and have encouraged investment and spending in the Irish economy.

> **Social and environmental benefits:** A variety of other EU policies and regulations have had a positive impact on social and environmental standards in Ireland. Examples include increased freedom for EU citizens, better protection for workers and consumers and stricter controls on pollution.

Drawbacks of EU membership

> **Increased competition:** The Single European Market provides Irish firms with increased competition and has resulted in job losses in some industries.

> **Monetary policy:** Since monetary policy in the eurozone is now controlled by the European Central Bank, the Irish government has lost one of its policy tools for regulating our economy.

unit

7

> **Loss of sovereignty:** The concept of shared sovereignty means that decisions taken a long way from Ireland are legally enforceable here. It is sometimes felt that these decisions are not always in Ireland's best interests.

> **Issues with over-regulation:** The principle of subsidiarity states that decisions should be taken at the lowest effective level, and it is therefore not always appropriate to have EU officials make decisions which may impact on individual citizens or businesses. There are those who claim the EU is over-regulated by 'eurocrats' in Brussels.

The Future of the EU

Recent events, including the global recession and the European debt crisis, have highlighted the difficulties of developing a union of sovereign states with close economic ties and a single currency. They have also illustrated that, despite great progress, the goal of economic unity is not yet complete and is likely to remain elusive for some time to come.

The following major issues and challenges are likely to dominate the EU agenda in the months and years ahead:

Economic stability and growth:

The EU has not escaped the global recession or the credit crunch. A major challenge now facing the Union is the restoration of member states to economic growth and prosperity. Success with this goal is likely to require a resolution to the debt crisis in some member states and stricter enforcement of economic convergence criteria in the future. The fiscal compact (see p. 471) makes deficit reduction a legal requirement.

Safeguarding the single currency

The long-term viability of the euro has been called into question recently and the EU is facing a major challenge to restore market confidence in its integrity. If one or more eurozone states were to default on sovereign (government) debt or were to withdraw from the euro, the value and future of the currency would be seriously undermined. The EU needs to resolve the currency crisis and establish a viable plan for dealing with future problems. If financial markets are not convinced about the long-term future of the currency it will continue to lose credibility and value on international money markets.

Enlargement of the EU

There is every likelihood that the EU membership will continue to grow and this will lead to additional budgetary and funding problems. Established members will be required to contribute more and will receive less of the available funding. This may cause political difficulties in some countries.

Croatia is expected to join by July 2013 and Turkey, having already made an application to join, is currently an associate member of the EU. If Turkey were admitted as a full member it would have the second largest population in the EU, and would also be the first Muslim country to join. Negotiations on its membership are currently suspended and reflect the lack of agreement in some areas as well as EU displeasure with Turkey's occupation of northern Cyprus.

EU reform

The Lisbon Treaty introduced major changes for voting and decision-making in the EU and also established a framework for institutional reform. While some reform has been introduced, there are many issues still to be resolved. A major issue is the impact of increased qualified majority voting and the fact that national vetoes may be lost in some areas of EU decision-making.

The role and influence of the EU in deregulated global markets is another area which is likely to cause much controversy and debate in future years.

This excellent website has a huge amount of additional information on every aspect of the EU. 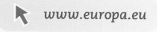 *www.europa.eu*

Chapter Review Diagram – The European Union

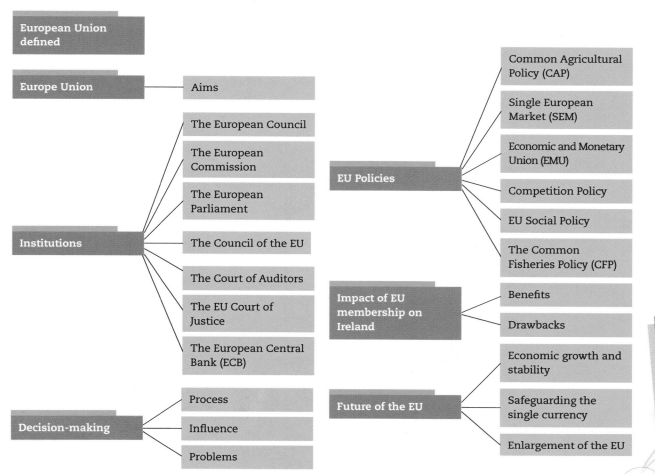

European Union defined

Europe Union
— Aims

Institutions
— The European Council
— The European Commission
— The European Parliament
— The Council of the EU
— The Court of Auditors
— The EU Court of Justice
— The European Central Bank (ECB)

Decision-making
— Process
— Influence
— Problems

EU Policies
— Common Agricultural Policy (CAP)
— Single European Market (SEM)
— Economic and Monetary Union (EMU)
— Competition Policy
— EU Social Policy
— The Common Fisheries Policy (CFP)

Impact of EU membership on Ireland
— Benefits
— Drawbacks

Future of the EU
— Economic growth and stability
— Safeguarding the single currency
— Enlargement of the EU

unit 7

Chapter Review Questions

1 Outline the role of European Council.

2 Explain the interdependent roles of the following major EU institutions:

> Commission   > Parliament   > Council of the EU

3 Outline the main stages in the European Union legislative process.

4 Distinguish between an EU regulation and an EU directive. Illustrate your answer with an example of each.

5 Differentiate between the EU Court of Auditors and the EU Court of Justice.

6 Explain the following terms associated with the EU:

> Democratic deficit   > Subsidiarity

> Lobbying   > Qualified majority voting

7 Outline the main aims of the Common Agricultural Policy and illustrate its impact on the Irish economy.

8 Explain the purpose of the Single European Market and outline its impact on Ireland. Refer to the 'four freedoms' in your answer.

9 In the context of the EU, what is meant by 'economic and monetary union'?

10 List the convergence criteria set out in the growth and stability pact for EMU participants.

11 Write brief notes to outline the aims of each of the following EU policies:

> EU competition policy   > EU social policy

12 Explain the letters:

> EU   > CAP   > ECB

> SEM   > EMU   > EMU

13 Outline three benefits and three drawbacks of EU membership for Ireland.

14 Set out three major issues facing the European Union in the near future.

Q Questions · Ordinary Level

1 Ireland has been a member of the EU since 1973. EU membership has had a significant effect on Irish economic growth and development.

    (a) Outline **three** advantages to Irish business of European Union membership. *(15 marks)*

    (b) (i) Name **two** EU institutions.

        (ii) Explain the role of **one** of them. *LCOL 2008 (20 marks)*

2 Discuss **two** opportunities and **two** challenges for Irish business arising from the enlarged European Union. *LCOL 2007 (25 marks)*

3 Outline **three** effects of the Single European Market on Irish Firms.

4 List **three** EU policies and explain the role of **any two** of them.

Q Questions · Higher Level

1 Discuss the importance for Ireland of any **two** of the following EU policies:

    (i) Competition Policy

    (ii) Common Fisheries Policy (CFP)

    (iii) Common Agricultural Policy (CAP) *LCHL 2010 (20 marks)*

2 Explain the role of the Council of Ministers (Council of the EU) in EU decision-making. Name **two** other EU decision-making institutions.

3

> The EU is less than half the size of the United States, but its population is over 50% larger. In fact the EU population is the world's largest, after China and India.
>
> *LCHL 2009*

Evaluate the opportunities **and** challenges for Irish business in the EU Market. *(30 marks)*

4 Discuss the impact of the Single European Market (SEM) on Irish business. *LCHL 2008 (25 marks)*

5 (a) In the context of the EU, distinguish between a directive and a regulation.

    (b) Choose **one** example of either and describe its purpose. *LCHL 2008 (15 marks)*

6 Outline, using an example, the role of 'interest groups' in EU policy making.

7 Outline the decision-making process of the European Union. *LCHL 2006*

8 Explain the opportunities **and** challenges for Irish business as a result of new member states joining the Single European Market.

9 Illustrate with a relevant example the impact of a European Union policy on economic activity in Ireland. *LCHL 2003 (20 marks)*

Chapter 24
Global Business

News Flash

1 Read the newspaper extract below and discuss the issues raised.

2 Can you explain any of the highlighted terms?

Ireland to top most globalised nations

by Conor Keane, Business Editor

Ireland is on course to become the most globalised nation on Earth next year and will retain the position until at least 2014, according to Ernst & Young and the Economist Intelligence Unit (EIU).

The Ernst & Young Globalisation and the Changing World of Business report, which has been released to coincide with the World Economic Forum in Davos, shows that Ireland has overtaken Singapore to become the world's second most globalised nation, second to Hong Kong in the globalised nation hierarchy.

The index has five measurements to assess a country's global ranking, including its openness to global trade, global capital movements, global exchange of technology and ideas, global labour movements and cultural integration. Each criterion's weighting was validated by 1,000 global business leaders…

Total trade was around 197% of Ireland's GDP in 2010, compared with 166% of GDP for trade in 2009. Exports of chemicals have grown particularly strongly.

CEO of IDA Ireland, Barry O'Leary, said: "This is an excellent recognition of Ireland's strengths and it is particularly encouraging to see that we scored highest globally in exchange of technology and ideas. Ireland's value proposition as a leading location for Foreign Direct Investment (FDI) is based on our reputation as a country that embraces open innovation and the survey result further enhances this reputation."

Speaking about the results, managing partner, Ireland, with Ernst & Young, Mike McKerr, said: "Although domestic economic conditions remain extremely challenging, we must continue to recognise that Ireland retains core strengths which are key to our recovery. Our nation's globalisation ranking demonstrates how well positioned Ireland is to maximise opportunities within international economies."

Mr McKerr said it is also interesting to see the role of tourism helping to further enhance our position…

"With so much of Ireland's economic recovery relying on us maintaining a strong global brand, anything which puts that brand at risk must be tackled quickly or our economic recovery will suffer."

This is an edited extract from the **Irish Examiner**, WEDNESDAY, 26 JANUARY 2011.

unit 7

For more up-to-date newspaper articles see www.edcodigital.ie

Globalisation is a process which has resulted from the deregulation of world markets. By removing barriers to international trade, the world has effectively become one big market and this has led to the growth of global companies. Examples of global companies include Intel, Toyota, Microsoft and Coca Cola.

Growth of Global Firms

Evolution of a global business

Domestic producer

This type of business only serves its home market.

Export business

A domestic producer begins to fulfil some overseas orders. Production continues to be based in the domestic market with only a small level of resources being expended on overseas sales and marketing.

International business

Larger overseas orders eventually require the establishment of a foreign operation which includes an overseas production facility. Each operation serves the needs of its local market and there is little production sharing or co-ordinated marketing.

Transnational company

Production and marketing is organised on a regional basis as the TNC seeks to avail of economies of scale. Elements of the marketing mix may be adjusted to meet regional needs.

Global company

A global company is one which focuses its efforts on serving the entire world market. Its primary goal is to maximise the growth and profitability of the entire organisation and decisions are made on the basis of this objective. This means that the home market is far less significant and when strategic decisions are made, they are made on a global basis.

Additional features of global companies

Global businesses differ from TNCs in that they produce a **standardised product** which is sold worldwide. Global companies will try to avoid making alterations to any element of their marketing mix and will produce and market products which have an appeal to customers all over the world. Global companies seek to use a **global marketing mix**.

The approach taken by global companies allows them to avail of the **economies of scale** which arise from mass production. The fact that products and marketing are standardised enables the global businesses to purchase vast quantities of raw materials, set up very efficient manufacturing facilities and to utilise mass media to promote its goods.

unit

7

481

Production sharing is also common amongst global organisations, with component parts being manufactured in several factories worldwide before final assembly at another location.

Global companies frequently engage in transfer pricing, which enables them to minimise the amount of taxation they pay. **Transfer pricing** involves selling goods or services at a preferential low price to businesses which are part of the same organisation or commercial group.

 **Example**

US food giant PepsiCo owns the Pepsi Cola soft drinks brand as well as a number of fast food restaurants. PepsiCo may decide to set two distinct prices for its soft drink. One is an internal price which applies when selling cola to PepsiCo restaurants and the second is an external price which is used when selling to external restaurants and unrelated businesses.

By altering the internal price level it is possible for PepsiCo to share the profitability between its soft drinks and restaurant divisions. This can be advantageous when seeking to benefit from different international tax regimes. By keeping profits low in high-tax economies and boosting them where taxes are lowest, the overall tax liability of the PepsiCo group can be minimised.

Most economies, including Ireland, have clear rules governing the use of transfer pricing, although global companies still make profitable use of the practice.

Reasons for the growth of global businesses

« *syllabus signpost* 7.4.2

The following factors have facilitated the increased prominence of global businesses in recent decades.

> **International deregulation:** The removal of barriers to international trade has created an environment which is suited to global businesses. The World Trade Organisation (WTO) has played a major role in this area.

> **Technology:** Improved manufacturing technology has made it easier to mass-produce goods and avail of economies of scale. Examples include computer-aided design (CAD) and computer-aided manufacturing (CAM).

« *syllabus signpost* 7.4.3

> **Communications:** Modern telecommunications methods assist the process of managing a global corporation. Information can be transferred very quickly throughout the organisation, making for better planning and control. Videoconferencing is particularly helpful for global businesses as it enables managers in different geographic locations to engage in virtual meetings. This speeds up the decision-making process and minimises the financial and time costs associated with global travel.

unit

7

> **Global media:** Satellite television and the growth of the Internet and social media are vital to companies which rely on mass-marketing. Global companies typically employ a standardised promotional mix.

> **Transport:** Better infrastructure makes it easier to move goods around the world. Advances in air transport and refrigeration are obviously beneficial to global companies.

> **Global product life cycles:** The timing of demand for some products will vary from country to country, with innovative new products tending to be adopted more quickly in developed economies such as the United States or in the EU. When these markets have reached saturation point and demand starts to decline, businesses may seek new markets in emerging or developing economies where standards of living and levels of demand are increasing.

> **Mergers:** As competition has increased, the amalgamation of smaller companies has created large-scale global businesses. Because of their sheer size, these companies need to operate on a global scale in order to sell all of their output.

Global Marketing

The global marketing mix

« *syllabus signpost*
7.4.5

Global product – Global price – Global place – Global promotion

The most successful global businesses are able to utilise the same marketing mix across the entire worldwide market. This is referred to as a **standardised global marketing mix** and reflects the fact that it will not be altered to suit local market needs.

Global companies will only seek to modify some element of the mix if local market conditions make it essential to do so. This might arise in the case of packaging where ingredients and operating instructions must be legible. When a company makes changes to the mix in this way it is called an **adapted global marketing mix**.

For example, car manufacturers may have to adjust for left- and right-hand drive or include air conditioning as standard in countries with hot climates. Companies like Dell and IBM, which manufacture computer hardware, will also have to change the letters and symbols on keyboards. While all of these examples highlight necessary alterations, it's important to point out that global companies will always keep these changes to the absolute minimum. The reason is simple: changes cost money and reduce overall profitability.

unit
7

Global product

This is the element which is least likely to be modified, as doing so will incur the greatest costs. By definition, global business is about **selling the same product to consumers all over the world**. Global products are designed to have universal appeal, with Coca Cola being a perfect example.

Creating a strong and **recognisable brand name** is an important step in generating demand on a global scale. McDonald's is a global foodservice retailer with over 30,000 local restaurants serving its food to nearly 50 million customers in more than 100 countries each day.

The products may be manufactured in several locations worldwide, typically on a regional basis, but unlike their transnational counterparts, global companies will produce identical goods in each location and will use identical production systems to ensure costs are controlled.

Global price

Local market conditions as well as income levels may require prices to be adjusted in some locations. Allowances will also have to be made for transport costs, local taxes and the level of competition. This may alter the positioning of the product, but it will still retain its **competitiveness with rival products**. For example, McDonald's may be seen as a luxury restaurant in countries where incomes are low but it will continue to offer customers the same level of value when compared to its major rivals like Burger King.

Global place

Transport and channels of distribution will be the main issues here. The cost of reaching global markets can be high, especially where several modes of transport may be required. For this reason global businesses may avail of a variety of different channels of distribution. Some may set up manufacturing plants around the world while others, like Nike, produce goods locally under licence. Distribution may be on a regional basis, or via subsidiary companies and agents. Whatever the approach, the aim remains the same: use **the most cost-effective method** to get products to as many customers as possible.

Global promotion

Global media and the use of **Internet advertising** make it easier than ever to reach potential customers.

Global companies do, however, need to be careful to comply with local customs and preferences when developing advertising and publicity campaigns. Audiences in several countries, including Saudi Arabia and Israel, for example, read right to left, so web page templates must be designed in accordance with this cultural trait.

Sponsorship of global events such as the Olympic Games or the FIFA World Cup is also common among global companies. Although the costs involved are extremely high, an association with these events guarantees global media coverage.

Case Study

The Olympic Games represent one of the largest and most effective marketing platforms available to global businesses, and their association with the event enables them to reach billions of people in over 200 countries.

The Olympic movement relies heavily on assistance from the business community for many aspects of its operation, including finance, promotion and technical support.

The Olympic Partner (TOP) programme provides the Olympic movement with an opportunity to secure the commercial sponsorship it needs, while the companies involved benefit from marketing rights which include the exclusive use of designated Olympic images and trademarks. It is therefore a good example of a co-operative relationship in action.

It is impossible to quantify the benefits to the companies involved, but the fact that they are willing to invest so heavily in the programme clearly indicates that they deem it to be worthwhile. It is also significant that the list of companies involved reads like a 'Who's Who' of global giants.

With over 40 per cent of Olympic revenues being generated from these commercial partnerships, they represent a vital element of the Olympic movement's business plan.

TOP Partners for the London 2012 Olympic Games:

Coca-Cola, Acer, Atos, Dow, General Electric, McDonald's, Omega, Panasonic, Samsung, Visa

 www.olympic.org/sponsorship

Marketing campaigns may require some alteration to allow for **cultural and language differences,** and more traditional approaches will be required in countries with little television or Internet coverage.

Getting it wrong: examples of faux pas in international marketing

Orange

The UK telecommunications company Orange had to rethink its campaign slogan when launching its service in Northern Ireland. The brand had successfully used a slogan which declared, 'The future is bright, the future is Orange.' Since the word 'orange' has an overtly sectarian meaning in Northern Ireland it was unlikely to endear the company to nationalist customers.

Binney & Smith, Crayola

Crayola has changed colour names on several occasions due to social pressures. For example, they replaced flesh with peach, in recognition of the wide variety of skin tones. They also changed Indian red to chestnut. The colour was actually named for a special pigment that came from India but people often assumed it was named after Native Americans.

unit **7**

Gerber

Gerber, the name of a famous American baby-food maker, is also a French slang word for vomiting. This unfortunate translation presented a bit of a problem when marketing its products globally and perhaps not surprisingly Gerber doesn't sell its products in France.

Irish Mist liqueur

Irish Mist liqueur had some marketing problems in Germany where its name loosely translates as 'Irish dung'.

Kentucky Fried Chicken, KFC

In Chinese, the Kentucky Fried Chicken slogan 'finger-lickin' good' came out as 'eat your fingers off'.

« syllabus signpost
7.4.4

Opportunities for businesses going global

> **Access to global markets:** Global businesses have the largest possible target market for their goods and services and their pursuit of increased sales and profitability is not restricted by international boundaries. For those companies which develop a product with global appeal, the opportunities are simply enormous.

> **Economies of scale:** Global businesses have several opportunities to avail of the cost reductions associated with economies of scale. Their **raw materials** costs may be heavily discounted because they buy in bulk. A **standardised product** is easy to replicate in different locations and very often the company will use a **standardised production system** which has proven to be efficient and reliable. McDonald's is a global business which illustrates this point.

Economies of scale also arise in the area of marketing since **advertising costs** are spread across a huge number of products.

> **Building a global brand:** The opportunity to develop a global brand that is recognisable the world over is enormously valuable to the future success of the business. It enables global companies like Sony to dominate markets and add to their extensive product portfolio over time.

> **Global business perspective:** With operations management taking place on a global scale rather than a local or regional one, there are further opportunities for increased efficiency and cost savings. It may be possible to engage in **production sharing** and **transfer pricing,** while there are also benefits to be had from shared knowledge and expertise developed across the global organisation.

If financial management also operates on a global basis, it may be possible for divisional funding shortages to be resolved by **internal transfers** between companies in the same group. For example, a need for €5 million by the European division may be met by taking surplus cash from the US operation. This reduces the need for expensive borrowing and has no impact on gearing levels within the organisation.

> **Resilience:** While global companies have few competitors they are susceptible to fluctuations in the global economy. Their sheer scale, however, enables global businesses to withstand most economic and competitive shocks.

Challenges for businesses trading globally

> **Capital costs:** Global businesses evolve over time and a huge amount of capital is needed in order to maintain the necessary level of expansion. Even when the business is operating at a global level it will continue to require enormous levels of working capital.

> **Management difficulties:** Managing a domestic business can be a tough proposition for many entrepreneurs, but it pales in comparison to the challenge presented by global business management.

  The business organisation may be spread over several continents, with dozens of factories and thousands of employees. It may require the co-ordination of multiple divisions and production facilities, with each manufacturing a range of product lines. As the organisation grows in size and complexity, so too does the likelihood of inefficiency, miscommunication and conflict.

> **Cultural differences:** Cultural values and traditions may limit the acceptance of some products or may require products to be modified for sale in particular regions. Food products in particular are likely to be affected by different tastes and cultural norms. For example, in Islam there are certain restrictions on what Muslims can eat or drink, so manufacturers of food products must ensure they conform to Islamic dietary laws.

  Changes to any element of the marketing mix will result in higher costs for global businesses.

> **Intellectual property issues:** Despite international agreements and World Trade Organisation rules it can sometimes be difficult for global businesses to enforce patent protection all over the world. Successful products are always likely to be counterfeited and may also face competition from generic producers. For example, India has a thriving generic pharmaceutical industry which is able to manufacture substitute medicines capable of replacing many well-known brands. Global pharmaceutical companies like GlaxoSmithKline and Pfizer have lobbied policymakers to have these competing products outlawed.

unit
7

Chapter Review Diagram – Global Business

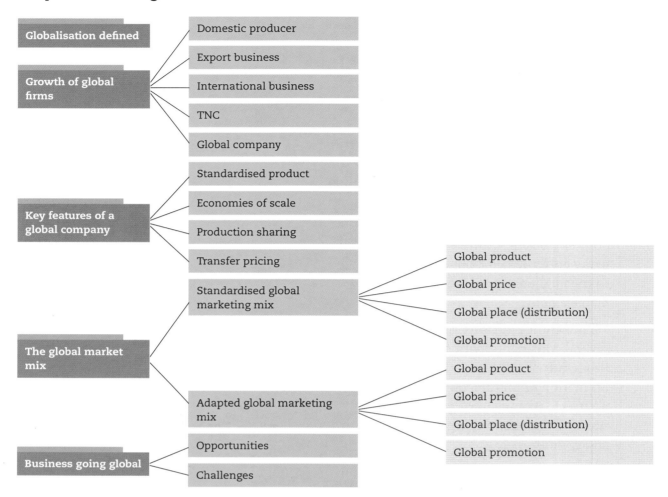

![Chapter Review Diagram]

Globalisation defined

Growth of global firms
- Domestic producer
- Export business
- International business
- TNC
- Global company

Key features of a global company
- Standardised product
- Economies of scale
- Production sharing
- Transfer pricing

The global market mix
- Standardised global marketing mix
  - Global product
  - Global price
  - Global place (distribution)
  - Global promotion
- Adapted global marketing mix
  - Global product
  - Global price
  - Global place (distribution)
  - Global promotion

Business going global
- Opportunities
- Challenges

Chapter Review Questions

1. Define the term 'globalisation'.

2. Name three global companies.

3. Describe the stages in the evolution of a global business.

4. Explain what 'transfer pricing' means.

5. Outline five major reasons for the growth of global businesses.

6. Explain the term 'global marketing' mix.

7. Describe two advantages of global marketing for a business.

8. Analyse four opportunities for businesses that choose to operate globally.

9. Outline four challenges for businesses that choose to operate globally.

Q Questions · Ordinary Level

1 Define global marketing. *LCOL 2002 (10 marks)*

2 Explain how technology has contributed to global trade.

3 Why are different prices charged for identical products in different countries?

4 What are the main opportunities for businesses going global?

Q Questions · Higher Level

1 Explain the term 'global marketing' and name two global businesses. *LCHL 2009 (15 marks)*

2 A business involved in global markets faces additional marking challenges.

Discuss these challenges, using examples to support your answer. *LCHL 2009 (15 marks)*

3 Explain the role of global marketing of products and services in international business. Illustrate your explanation with relevant examples. *LCOL 2002 (20 marks)*

4

Ireland is an open economy. The Irish economy is greatly affected by influences from abroad. The international environment offers Irish business many opportunities and challenges, e.g. the marketing of Irish products abroad and the threat from foreign competitors.

Explain, using examples, the importance of global marketing for a global business.

LCHL 2000 (20 marks)

5 What is a global brand?

6 Describe what is meant by 'adapted global marketing mix'. Illustrate your answer with an example.

7 Identify two characteristics of a global firm.

Q Applied Business Question

Celtic Airlines

Celtic Airlines plc has been in business for almost twenty years and continues to operate profitably on routes between Ireland and the UK. In the past five years it took a successful first step into mainland Europe and now uses its fleet of modern jet aircraft to operate daily flights to and from several capital cities in western Europe. These destinations include Paris, Berlin, Madrid and Rome. Celtic Airlines has managed to find a lucrative niche and markets itself as a 'some frills' airline. Its service offering and pricing strategy have found an audience with the vast majority of European citizens who have neither the income to travel business class nor the patience to tolerate the 'pay as you go' approach of the budget airlines. Celtic Airlines offers its passengers a moderate level of comfort and an exceptional level of customer service. Customers also seem happy with the affordable pricing policy and the fact that it operates a fleet of modern aircraft into a network of major cities. Customer satisfaction is very high and word-of-mouth endorsements create a huge marketing benefit for the company. The airline also spends a large amount of its marketing resources on TV, newspaper and social networking commercials.

The airline industry has undergone a huge upheaval in recent years and as a result of increased competition and a poor economic climate several major airlines have gone out of business. Despite this turmoil and economic uncertainty, Celtic Airlines is contemplating broadening its horizons and is formulating strategic plans to enter the long-haul market. It sees great potential in eastern European markets and is planning to locate a flight hub in Germany from which to serve this region. The citizens of many eastern European states have become increasingly mobile in search of employment and economic prosperity, especially since the enlargement of the European Union and the break-up of the Soviet Union. There are, however, concerns over the dominant market position of low-cost rivals on eastern European routes, which suggests members of the target market are very price-conscious.

Deregulation in the industry has also provided Celtic Airlines with the opportunity to operate on transatlantic routes, and while these routes would bring the threat of major competition the airline sees these transatlantic routes as a more natural 'fit' for its service offering and pricing policy. The major downside to this transatlantic expansion would be the requirement to purchase long-haul aircraft coupled with continued oil price volatility. The need for additional aircraft would require Celtic Airlines to embark on an immediate capital investment programme. Any funds raised would be used to place orders for new aircraft or alternatively to purchase second-hand aircraft from airlines which are closing down. There is also the possibility that Celtic Airlines may be able to increase the scale of its operations by taking over some smaller European carriers.

(a) Describe the impact on or consequences for Celtic Airlines of any major European Union policies. *(20 marks)*

(b) Describe the challenges which may exist for Celtic Airlines in trading internationally. Comment specifically on the increased risks associated with a global strategy. *(30 marks)*

(c) Evaluate the potential for Celtic Airlines to develop into a global business. In your answer make specific reference to the company's marketing mix. *(30 marks)*

A Guide to the Exams

Exam Layout and Structure

Higher Level (Time allowed: 3 hours)

Section 1 (80 marks) – Short questions

Answer (at least) **eight** short questions out of ten. Allow a maximum of 32 minutes.

Section 2 (80 marks) – Applied Business Question

A compulsory question and all parts must be answered. Allow 32 minutes.

Section 3 (240 marks) – Long questions

Four questions must be answered from Section 3 as follows:

> **One** question from Part 1 (Units 1, 6 and 7)
> **Two** questions from Part 2 (Units 2, 3, 4 and 5)
> And **one other** question from either Part 1 or Part 2

Allow 25 minutes per question in Section 3.

This will leave 16 minutes for reading and completing the exam.

Ordinary Level (Time allowed: 2½ hours)

Section 1 (100 marks) – Short questions

Answer (at least) **ten** short questions out of fifteen. Allow a maximum of 35 minutes.

Section 2 (300 marks) – Long questions

Four questions must be answered from Section 2 as follows:

> **One** question from Part 1 (Units 1, 6 and 7
> **Two** questions from Part 2 (Units 2, 3, 4 and 5)
> And **one other** question from either Part 1 or Part 2

Allow 25 minutes per question in Section 3.

This will leave 15 minutes for reading and completing the exam.

Practice makes perfect and perfect practice makes permanent

The idea that it's possible to sit down on the day of the exam and produce brilliant answers without having put in the correct preparation is certainly not one that we accept. In our experience, both as teachers and as examiners, an excellent exam grade is a reward to students who have shown ongoing commitment to consistent hard work and perfect practice.

This commitment to perfect practice requires students to answer every question as if it were an exam question. We want you to make good habits part of your everyday routine and in this way you will start to apply them instinctively. This is important when it comes to the pressurised atmosphere of an examination hall and should enable you to gain confidence and also an improved exam grade.

If you have not engrained these 'steps to success' into your normal routine, it is highly unlikely you'll be able to remember them, let alone reproduce them on the day of the exam. The message here is simple: every single time you sit down to answer an exam revision question you must ensure it is completed in a structure and a time frame which is realistic for an exam situation.

We apologise to those who may have opened this section of the book in the hope of finding some magic formula or short cut to an 'A' grade. While we cannot provide you with this quick-fix solution we do hope to set out a clear and effective approach to achieving the best possible exam grade. We make no apology for the fact that this tried and tested approach involves discipline and hard work.

The best exam answers are:

> relevant to the question asked

> presented in a suitable format or structure

> written within the strict time constraints imposed by the exam

It is our view therefore that producing excellent exam answers requires a combination of **knowledge, structure** and **timing** – and all three require practice!

These recommendations are very much in line with the views expressed in the Chief Examiner's Report, 2010:

'The better answers were from candidates who paid careful attention to the wording of the questions, the mark allocations and planned the use of their time accordingly. Well structured answers which addressed the issues raised were rewarded.'

Things to do Before the Exam

Learn the facts

Learning the content involves taking time to learn the information and practise 'review and recall' of syllabus material.

You may find it helpful to make your own set of revision notes which will enable you to revise all of the important definitions, concepts and issues outlined in each chapter.

To help you in this task we've included syllabus outcomes and chapter review diagrams for each chapter, as well as highlighting many of the key terms in bold print.

Practice written answers

You should hardly need reminding that the Leaving Certificate business exam is a written one and that your grade is therefore totally dependent upon what you actually manage to get down on paper during the exam. For that reason it makes perfect sense for students to develop the skills needed to write excellent exam answers.

If the Leaving Certificate exam is one of the few occasions on which you attempt to formulate a written answer it is highly unlikely that you will achieve your full potential.

Things to do During the Exam

If you provide the examiner with exactly what they're looking for you have a much greater chance of securing high marks. Examiners are instructed to look for certain pieces of information and are also told how many points are required for each answer. As a student you want to make it as easy as possible for the examiner to give you the marks and this is best achieved by following the checklist below:

Our checklist for excellent answers

☑ Answer the question asked.

☑ Pay careful attention to the outcome verb.

☑ Provide the correct number of points required. This involves some understanding of the marking scheme.

☑ Watch your timing.

☑ Provide relevant factual information. This again relies on careful revision of syllabus material

☑ Use examples wherever possible. Exam questions are increasingly likely to require real-world examples to support student answers.

Answer the question asked

---

1. (a) Explain the term 'business ethics'. *(6 marks)*

Student answer:

This means that a business undertakes their actions in an ethical way by doing what is considered the right thing to do for the environment, workers and so on.

(b) State two examples of unethical behaviour in business.   *(4 marks)*

Student answer:

(i) Giving workers reasonable conditions to work in.

(ii) Using recyclable packaging.

Analysis of student answers

This student makes a reasonable attempt to answer part (a) of the question and will score at least 3 of the 6 marks available. It is clear the student has some understanding of the issues involved, but should not have used the word 'ethical' as part of the answer.

Whenever explaining a concept like this **it's important not to rely on that key word as part of your answer**. The student should ideally have used words like 'morals' or 'right and wrong' to explain what ethics is about. The fact that the answer mentions 'doing the right thing' and highlights the impact on the environment and employees helps clarify the situation and will eliminate some of the doubt about the student's level of understanding.

The answer to part (b) of the question is a classic example of a student who failed to read the question carefully and therefore didn't answer the question which was asked. Both of the examples provided are clear illustrations of ethical behaviour in business, but the question asked for examples of unethical behaviour. No marks will be scored for this section of the answer.

The impact of these errors can be highlighted by examining the marks awarded. In this case 3/10 represents just 30 per cent and makes this an 'E' grade answer. If the student hadn't been so careless and had answered the question asked in part (b) the total score would have risen to 7/10, making it a 'B' grade answer.

Understanding the outcome verb

The 2010 chief examiner's report contains the following recommendation:

> "Candidates should pay careful attention to the question cues at the beginning of the sentence…"

The outcome verb is really just the question cue, which tells students the level of detail required in each question. For example the outcome verbs 'name', 'list' and 'state' are very similar and require students to provide a list of relevant headings or key words. None of these particular outcome verbs require students to provide additional detail, analysis or evaluation.

On the other hand outcome verbs such as 'explain', 'outline' or 'describe' all require students to provide more detailed answers.

The word 'illustrate' is becoming increasingly common in exam questions and students need to recognise this clear cue to provide a relevant example.

A full list of all outcome verbs and their interpretation is provided on page 504.

Providing the correct number of points

The exact marking scheme varies from year to year and from question to question, but there are some general guidelines which students can apply to assist them in fulfilling the requirements of the question and improving their exam score.

As a general rule the number of points required for each answer can be worked out by dividing the total marks for that question by five. For example a 20-mark question will typically require four distinct points to answer it fully.

It is often helpful to think of every answer in terms of 'small bite-sized pieces of information'. For example a 10-mark question is likely to be scored on the basis of at least two relevant pieces of information (5 + 5). Each of these can be further broken down to allow 2 marks for a heading (or key point) and an additional 3 marks for explanation or development of that heading. This means that the actual breakdown of the 10 marks = (2+3) + (2+3).

Students who don't realise this tend to write answers which are lacking in detail.

Watch your timing

Poor use of time is one of the biggest reasons why students do worse than expected in exams and your chances of getting this timing right can be greatly improved by 'perfect practice'. This means that all answers must be written in a realistic time frame. Since you will not have the luxury of unlimited time in the exam you need to get used to the discipline imposed by these time constraints. If you fail to get all questions completed in time you will obviously lose marks for the missing answers.

Bearing in mind that every 4 marks contributes 1 per cent to your overall result, a 20-mark question left unanswered will cost you 5 per cent and may change your overall grade. It is very difficult for students who 'throw away' marks in this way to achieve an 'A' grade, so it is really important to stick to the time limits.

Suggested timings for Higher Level students

Section 1 (Short questions): 32 minutes (but aim for 25 minutes if possible)

Section 2 (Applied Business Question): Allow 32 minutes

Section 3 (Long questions): 25 minutes per question (x 4)

This will leave 16 minutes extra for reading the questions and making last-minute changes to answers.

If you can save 5 minutes on Section 1 it will allow you to spend up to 40 minutes on ABQ and many students find this helpful as it takes longer to read the ABQ and compile answers which relate to the case study.

As a general rule, Higher Level students should divide the number of marks per question by 2.5 to work out the time available for each question. For example a 20-mark question should take 8 minutes to complete, and since this usually requires four relevant points, that amounts to 2 minutes per point. In this time students will generally have to provide a **heading**, an **explanation** of that heading and an **example**. Now you see the need for careful revision and the need to write concise, relevant answers!

Section 1 (Short questions): 35 minutes

Section 2 (Long questions): 25 minutes per question (x 4)

This will leave 15 minutes extra for reading the questions and making last-minute changes to answers.

Provide relevant factual information

The importance of providing relevant factual information has already been explained.

For example, an exam question may require students to 'outline the role of the Labour Relations Commission in preventing and resolving industrial relations disputes'.

The LRC has a very specific role to play and students need to show clear understanding of that role. The answer provided must leave the examiner in no doubt that the student knows the correct functions to be attributed to the LRC and there is really no scope for vague or generalised answers. Any suggestion that the student is uncertain or is 'waffling' will be heavily punished through loss of marks.

This type of question also highlights a particular difficulty experienced by students who attempt Question 1 in Section 3 of the HL paper (Section 2 on OL paper).

Many of these questions relate to specific pieces of legislation or the role of certain organisations. Since these provisions are very clearly set out in law, it is absolutely essential that they are listed correctly. For example, the Sale of Goods and Supply of Services Act, 1980, has four provisions relating to the sale of goods to consumers by retailers. The Act states that goods must be:

> ❯ Of merchantable quality
> ❯ Fit for their intended purpose
> ❯ As described
> ❯ As per sample

Any other answers provided by students are clearly incorrect, and will not score any marks.

Use examples wherever possible

In recent years there has been a very noticeable trend towards exam questions which require students to support their answer with specific examples. These examples are always useful for clarifying an answer and they help illustrate that a student understands a particular concept.

Some questions will ask for an example directly, whereas others will use the outcome verb 'illustrate' as a question cue to let students know that an example is necessary.

Both of the following questions require the use of examples:

1. Explain the term 'business ethics'. Outline **two** examples of ethical business behaviour. *(10 marks)*

2. Illustrate your understanding of the term 'business ethics'. *(10 marks)*

The Leaving Certificate Exam: Section by Section

Answering short questions

Many students say they quite like this section of the exam, presumably because they don't have to write very long or detailed answers, but care needs to be taken not to underestimate this part of the exam. It is very easy to lose marks on the short answer section and scoring highly presents a genuine challenge.

Reasons for lost marks

› **Lack of knowledge:** Some students fail to recognise that the short answer questions will test every unit of the syllabus, which again emphasises the importance of studying **all** of the material on the syllabus.

› **Lack of specific knowledge:** 'A' students tend to be excellent at providing **the most relevant** information for the questions asked. The short answer questions do not allow for waffle and students who drift off the point are likely to be heavily penalised. The key to success here is to provide relevant answers using a concise format.

> 'Candidates should practice writing direct, concise and precise answers.'
>
> **Chief Examiner's Report, 2010**

When making revision notes it's helpful to highlight the key points, especially when it comes to defining business terms.

For example, a definition of inflation must comment on the fact that **prices are rising** in an economy and also that this price rise takes place **over a given time period** (usually one year).

› Other reasons for poor scores include a **failure by students to understand the marking scheme and/or outcome verb.** These issues have been discussed previously and in the case of short answer questions often involve a student providing a list of key words rather than the more detailed 'outline' required.

› Students also need to be particularly careful when answering **open-ended questions** of the type which appeared in the 2007 LCHL exam:

> 3. An EU directive is _____
>
> _____
>
> _____
>
> 5. In a legal context, consideration means _____
>
> _____
>
> _____

There is a tendency for students to simply complete the sentence and assume they will receive full marks. This, however, fails to recognise the fact that the 10 marks available will be split (5 + 5) and that a single sentence is only likely to score 5 marks.

For example, consider the following student answer to Q5.

> 5. In a legal context, consideration means *that in a contract* (2) *there must be something of value exchanged between the parties involved.* (+3)

In order to secure the remaining 5 marks it will be necessary to provide additional information, perhaps in the form of an example, such as:

> *Whenever a consumer purchases an item from a retailer a contract exists and the customer receives goods in return for the payment of money.*

Answering long questions

(Higher Level: Section 3; Ordinary Level: Section 2)

When answering questions in this section of the exam it's important to make the right choices.

Students must attempt four questions in all and have a limited amount of choice (see section on exam layout and structure, page 491).

It is quite likely that questions in this section will relate to more than one area of the syllabus and this again illustrates the need to revise all areas of the syllabus.

Take a little time to read each question carefully. Look closely at the marks awarded for **each** part of the question and try to establish which questions you are likely to score highest on.

Each relevant point you provide in your answer will usually be worth 5 marks and should be in the following format:

> **Heading**,
> an **explanation** of that heading, with
> a relevant **example** where possible.

This is sometimes referred to as the S.E.E. format because students should **State**, **Explain** and give an **Example**.

> ### Sample question
> 1. Controlling is a management activity. Outline **four** types of control procedures commonly employed by business.
> (*20 marks*)

Suggested solution

Stock control (2)

Managers need to establish optimum stock levels (minimum, maximum, re-order). There are costs associated with both overstocking (insurance, storage, obsolescence) and under-stocking (lost sales). Just-in-time production may help the situation by ensuring stock is available as required. (+3)

Quality control (2)

A business needs to ensure that all of its products meet legal requirements and customer expectations. In a dynamic and competitive business environment it is no longer just about finished product and there is increased emphasis on Total Quality Management, which stresses the need for quality at every step of the production process. (+3)

Credit control (2)

This involves careful management of both debtors and creditors. It is important to set credit limits for each customer and ensure that debts are collected before payment can be made to creditors. Minimising bad debts is also a priority for businesses and is achieved by careful credit control. (+3)

Financial (budgetary) control (2)

This is about budgeting and careful management of business cash flow. It may involve management accounting, variance and ratio analysis. The bottom line is that a business must have money available to pay bills as they fall due. Managers will need to make use of various sources of finance to meet the needs of their business. These include bank overdrafts, medium-term loans and retained earnings. (+3)

Notice that the suggested solution contains four clear points. Each is relevant to the topic, has an appropriate heading and is developed fully. This is precisely the type of approach which needs to be taken for all exam answers in this section.

The 2010 Chief Examiner's Report states:

> "Candidates are advised to write the heading first and then explain each heading briefly. The question cue 'outline' requires the candidate to give brief detail of the subject matter... The questions set are not invitations for candidates to write all they know about a particular topic."

Answering the Applied Business Question (HL only)

The ABQ is a compulsory question and is really the major difference between ordinary-level and higher-level papers. If you are expecting a good grade on a HL paper then you simply must be able to tackle this question well.

In our experience many students panic and get very flustered when it comes to the ABQ. They sometimes treat this question as if it's entirely unexpected and not at all related to anything they've studied in class.

This could hardly be further from the truth and the fact is that you'll always know in advance which three units the ABQ will be based on (see below, p. 503).

It's also the case that the syllabus material set out in the textbook provides the key to correctly answering the questions posed in the ABQ. What makes this question different is the fact that knowledge alone will not be sufficient to earn full marks. **Students need to be able to link the relevant sections of the syllabus to the specific issues raised in the case study.**

In simple terms each answer requires:

> A relevant heading

> A brief (textbook) explanation of that heading

> A link (usually a quote from the text) which highlights the connection between the syllabus material and the issues raised in the ABQ.

A separate link must be provided for **each point** in your answer, so it is not sufficient to provide just one link for part (a), one link for part (b) and one link for part (c). It is also worth noting that a link should not be used more than once in each part of the question, although if relevant a link can be re-used later in another part of the question.

Links to the text usually take the form of direct quotes, but this is not always necessary or possible and it may be sufficient to make reference to an issue raised in the case rather than quote directly from it.

When quoting from the text be sure to use short quotes since marks may be lost where a student transcribes whole sections of text.

Sample Question: LCHL 2005 (extract)

Circuit Ltd

Tom Ryan is the main shareholder in a busy electrical company...

As the business expanded Tom regularly took on apprentice electricians and all the current employees had trained, or were in training, with the firm. He personally handled the recruitment, selection and development of all staff. He placed emphasis on loyalty, commitment and honesty which he rewarded with regular substantial bonuses. He did not recognise any trade union within the firm but paid the recommended trade union rates to his apprentices and the firm experienced few industrial relations problems or health and safety difficulties...

Tom decided that he would develop a specialised department to concentrate on installing wireless computer networks, using a new and promising technology. This would allow the firm to tender for high margin contracts and would require redeployment of half of the current staff and extensive retraining for them in new skills.

(b) Evaluate Tom's effectiveness as a Human Resource Manager. *(30 marks)*

Headings: the relevant heading should be chosen based on the syllabus material. In this case students would need to know the functions of a human resource manager. These include:

> Human resource planning

> Recruitment and selection

> Training and development

> Performance appraisal

> Employee welfare and rewards

> Industrial relations

Armed with this 'checklist' it will be necessary to choose which of these functions are most relevant or most evident in the case study. It will also be necessary to evaluate Tom's performance. This evaluation can be done under each of the chosen headings or else in a separate point at the end.

In this particular case the most relevant points are set out in the suggested solution below. It is worth noting that there is no clear reference to the 'performance appraisal' function and for this reason it would not be appropriate to use it in this answer. This highlights the challenge facing students when answering the ABQ: taking the knowledge they have learned and illustrating its particular relevance to the topic or business under discussion.

Suggested solution

Human resource planning (2)

This involves looking at the current and future staffing needs of the business and putting in place a plan to recruit or train the necessary staff. If necessary the HR manager may have to devise a redundancy package for surplus staff. (+2) We can see Tom is looking at future staffing needs and 'having decided to set up the new department' Tom has realised this will require the redeployment of half of the current staff and extensive retraining in new skills.' (+2)

Recruitment and selection (2)

This is the process of attracting suitable applicants and then choosing those most suited to the position. There are a number of steps involved in performing this function effectively, including the preparation of job descriptions and person specifications as well as the short-listing and interviewing of candidates. (+2) We are told that Tom 'personally handled the recruitment, selection and development of all staff'. (+2) Based on the staffing needs highlighted during the planning process, the HR department will need to prepare job descriptions and person specifications.

Training and development (2)

HR departments help ensure staff have the necessary skill for their jobs. They organise induction training for new recruits and provide opportunities for upskilling through 'on the job' or 'off the job' training. (+2) Tom has taken a proactive approach by making sure that 'all current employees had trained or were in training with the firm'. (+2)

Employee remuneration (2)

The payment and rewarding of staff is a key element in keeping happy, productive workers. The HR department will devise salary scales and may award monetary bonuses based on performance appraisal. Employee records kept by the HR department can also influence promotion prospects. (+2) Tom 'paid recommended trade union rates to apprentices" and rewarded staff with 'regular substantial bonuses.' (+2)

Industrial relations (2)

This refers to the relationship between employers and their employees. Generally industrial relations are regarded as being positive where a good working relationship exists, whereas bad working conditions and distrust will tend to give rise to a poor industrial relations climate. (+2)

Despite not recognising any trade unions, Tom has a good relationship with staff and we are clearly told 'the firm experienced few industrial relations problems.' (+2)

Evaluation: Based on the information provided it seems that Tom is an effective HR manager. (2) He takes on many of the tasks himself and achieves successful outcomes for his business and his employees. The absence of serious industrial relations conflicts to date seems to illustrate his capacity as a HR manager. (+2)

Analysis of suggested solution

> Each heading clearly relates to the functions of a HR manager. These particular points have been chosen because they are the most relevant and can be supported with reference to the text. One extra point has been included for illustrative purposes.

> There is a short outline of what each function involves.

> The link provided in each case reflects Tom's performance as a HR manager.

'There is a tendency, however, for some candidates to provide purely theoretical answers and not link their theory to the context of the questions. In addition, some candidates find the links in the ABQ but do not provide any theoretical business detail. No marks are awarded for links without relevant business theory.'

Chief Examiner's Report, 2010

In order to avoid making the mistakes pointed out by the Chief Examiner we recommend that students always provide a general (textbook) explanation for each heading and the link to the text is usually best left until last. This general reference should be about businesses in general and should not make any reference to the case study. There is a danger that some students make immediate reference to the case, thereby gaining the marks for a relevant link, but missing out on the marks for explaining the heading.

The units being examined are known in advance and rotate on a five-year cycle:

Units 1, 2 and 3: 2014, 2019, etc.

Units 2, 3 and 4: 2015, 2020, etc.

Units 3, 4 and 5: 2016, 2021, etc.

Units 4, 5 and 6: 2012, 2017, etc.

Units 5, 6 and 7: 2013, 2018, etc.

Business syllabus: outcome verbs

The following verbs are used in the Leaving Certificate Business exam. Students need to be familiar with the requirements of each verb. Some verbs appear in HL exams only.

Students do not need to learn these definitions word for word, but they should understand what the examiner requires when using each outcome verb.

In broad terms it's important to know which verbs require unexplained lists, which require detail, computation, diagrams, etc. Constant practice of past exam papers and analysis of marking schemes will be of great benefit to students in achieving this.

Analyse (HL): Examine an issue in detail by **breaking it down into various parts** and examining possible relationships.

Apply (HL): Use knowledge or information for a **particular purpose**. In the ABQ section of the exam, students must use their textbook knowledge to resolve the issues highlighted a particular business.

Calculate: Work out through use of **numerical data**, ratios, etc.

Compare (HL): Examine two or more things in order to highlight their **similarities or differences**.

Contrast: Examine two items so as to highlight the **differences** between them.

Define: Set out the **exact meaning** of a term or concept. You need to include its **essential qualities**.

Demonstrate: Explain, describe or illustrate **through the use of examples**, charts, diagrams, graphs, experiments, etc.

Describe: Depict or **give a verbal account** of a person, relationship, event, institution, etc.

Differentiate (HL): **Distinguish between** two (or more) things. Highlight separate characteristics.

Discuss (HL): Examine an issue in a **careful and considered** manner. It may be necessary to debate both sides.

Distinguish: Point out the **difference** between things.

Draft: **Draw up an outline**. Generally involves a document or diagram.

Evaluate (HL): Judge or determine the **significance, worth or quality** of something.

Explain: Set out clearly in a **detailed** manner.

Identify: Show you **recognise** something or verify its identity.

Illustrate: Show clearly by means of **diagrams**, graphs or **examples**.

Interpret: **Explain the meaning** of something.

List: Write down the **names of items** which have something in common. Explanation is **not** required.

Outline: Write a **short summary** with general details.

Understand: To grasp the **significance**, implications, or importance of something.

Index

368, 373
public–private partnerships (PPP), 94, 400–401
public relations (PR), 310
public sector, 3
public service obligation (PSO), 371
pyramid schemes, 26

Q

Q-mark symbol, 123, 231
qualified majority voting, 461
quality assurance, 231
quality circles, 76, 122, 226
quality control, 122–123
Quarterly National Household Survey (QNHS), 395
quick ratio, 189–190, 193–194
quorum, 101-102
quotas, 448

R

ratio analysis, 187–192, 273
receivership, 191
recruitment and selection, 202–206
recycling, 431
redress, 22, 27–28
redundancy, 38–39
registrar of business names, 358
regulations, 449
relativity claim, 38
reminder advertising, 304
remuneration, 209
renewable resources, 344, 427
re-order level, 121
reports, 105
REPS (Rural Environment Protection Scheme), 426
research and development, 240
retailers, 19-21, 269, 295, 302
retained earnings/reserves 144–145, 327
return on capital employed (return on investment), 187, 188, 193
Revenue Commissioners, 137, 168-169, 171, 173-174, 177, 183
Rights Commissioner, 45-46
risk assessment, 155
risk management, 155
royalty, 277, 322

S

sale and leaseback, 148, 327
Sale of Goods and Supply of Services Act, 1980, 19–22
sales promotion, 309
savings, 144–145
secondary research, 243
secondary sector, 338, 344–347
secretary (of a limited company), 100–102
seed capital, 55, 145
self actualisation, 81
self-assessment income tax, 169
semi-state bodies, 398
service providers, 5
share capital, 143–144
share option schemes, 212
share ownership schemes, 212
shareholders, 6, 183, 361

shop steward, 36
short-term finance, 134, 135–139, 273
SIMI, 8
Single European Market, 467–470
SIPTU, 36
Skype, 91, 92, 319
small and medium-sized enterprises (SMEs), 348
Small Claims Court, 29
SMART plans, 113–114
social costs, 434
social entrepreneurs, 64
social partnership, 37
social policy, 473–474
social responsibility, 419, 421–424
sole trader, 265–266, 358–359, 372
solvency, 183
span of control, 120
specific performance, 15
spectator leadership, 77
sponsorship, 310–311
spreadsheets, 92
staff development, 207
staff turnover, 35, 213
stakeholders, 4–8
standardised global marketing mix, 483
standard rate cut off point, 169
standing orders (meetings), 102
starting a business, 262–285
state agencies, 240, 398–399
state-sponsored bodies, 3, 370–371, 373
statutory companies, 371
statutory meeting, 364
stock control, 121–122
stock exchange, 367
strategic alliance, 323, 375
strategic plans, 112
strikes, 41, 43
subcontracting, 277–278
subrogation, 160
subsidiary, 414, 463–464, 476
subsidies, 427, 449
subvention, 371
suppliers, 5, 183, 423
surplus, 131, 446
sustainable development, 427–428
SWOT analysis, 110–111
synergy, 319

T

tactical plans, 112
takeover, 324–325
target market, 287, 289
tariffs, 448
tax audit, 169
tax avoidance, 424
tax calculations, 174–176
tax credits, 169
tax evasion, 424
tax forms, 173–174
taxation, 168–177, 394–395
teamwork, 227–230
telemarketing, 310
teleworking, 221
Teoranta, 361
term loan, 139, 272, 327
term life assurance, 163
terms of reference, 104

tertiary sector, 338, 347–353
test marketing, 247
Theory X and Theory Y, 81–82
third-party insurance, 162
time rate, 209
token stoppage, 43
total costs, 250
Total Quality Management (TQM), 122, 230–231
trade associations, 8
trade dispute, 40
trade mark, 294
trade mission, 453
trade reference, 124
trade unions, 35–37
trading account, 184
trading blocs, 451–452
trading certificate, 367
training and development, 206–207, 224–225
transfer pricing, 482
transnational companies (TNCs), 349–353, 445, 451, 481
travel insurance, 164

U

unemployment, 395–396
Unfair Dismissals Acts, 1977 and 2007, 47
unique selling point, 246, 279, 292
universal social charge, 170
unlimited liability, 266, 358, 360
unofficial strike, 43
unsolicited goods, 21, 26
utmost good faith, 103, 159

V

value added tax (VAT), 170–171, 172, 394
variable costs, 250
venture capital, 145, 327
verbal communication, 89
videoconferencing, 92, 221
viral advertising/viral marketing, 306
visible exports, 442, 443
visible imports, 441, 442
visual communication, 89
voluntary redundancy, 39, 201

W

warranty, 14
waste disposal, 427
whistleblower, 420-421
wholesalers, 302
whole life assurance, 163
wildcat strike, 43
word-processing, 91
work to rule, 42
worker co-ops, 269, 369
working capital, 185
working capital ratio (current ratio), 189, 193
World Trade Organisation (WTO), 453
world wide web (www), 92
written communication, 89, 103